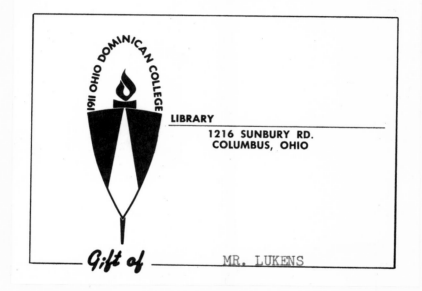

The Forgotten Americans

THE

Forgotten Americans

A SURVEY OF VALUES, BELIEFS, AND
CONCERNS OF THE MAJORITY

by

FRANK E. ARMBRUSTER

with contributions by DORIS YOKELSON

ARLINGTON HOUSE　　　　　NEW ROCHELLE, N.Y.

To Irene, Frank Jr., Ellen Anne and Janet

We gratefully acknowledge the following sources for permission to use their copyrighted material:

American Institute of Public Opinion (the Gallup Poll), for permission to use the Gallup Poll data.

Louis Harris and Associates, for permission to use Harris survey data in the various periodicals and newspapers cited. Copyright: © The Chicago Tribune, © The Washington Post Company.

Purdue Research Foundation, for permission to reprint material from the publication *Reports of Poll, The Purdue Opinion Panel*. Copyright, *Reports of Polls* Nos. 1-71 © H. H. Remmers, Nos. 72-93 © Purdue Research Foundation.

Carnegie Commission on Higher Education, for permission to utilize the material from *Recent Alumni and Higher Education*, by Joe L. Spaeth and Andrew M. Greeley. "Copyright © 1970 by the Carnegie Foundation for the Advancement of Teaching."

Fortune Magazine, for the poll data by Daniel Yankelovich, Inc., in the article "What They Believe," *Fortune*, January 1969. This material is copyright "© 1968 Time Inc." and is being reprinted by special permission of the publisher.

The Public Opinion Quarterly, for permission to reprint excerpts from the poll material which appeared in "The Polls," by Hazel Erskine, in *The Public Opinion Quarterly*. Copyright © Columbia University Press. (This study frequently used material from *Public Opinion, 1935–1946*, by Hadley Cantril and Mildred Strunk [Princeton, N.J.: Princeton University Press, 1951].)

American Institute of Public Opinion (the Gallup Poll), for permission to use the Gallup Poll survey data that appeared in *The Public Opinion Quarterly* in the section entitled "The Polls," by Hazel Erskine.

5

92326

Acknowledgements

I am deeply indebted to Doris Yokelson for her contributions and assistance on the whole project, as well as for the specific sections of the book she wrote. The book could never have been completed without the cheerful cooperation of my wife, who assisted in all phases of the work, and my children, who adjusted their "lifestyle" for a year to a home which lost a father but gained an irritable, sometime author and the permanent litter of this manuscript in production.

I owe a debt of gratitude to Herman Kahn, Max Singer, and Tony Wiener for their patience, encouragement, advice and assistance throughout the long process of developing this document from study outline to published book. Other members of the Hudson Institute staff were also helpful and generous in their advice and assistance, particularly Barry Bruce-Briggs, Raymond D. Gastil, Jane Newitt, Rudy Ruggles, Garrett N. Scalera and William Schneider, Jr. Louise Horton did yeoman's work on production of the manuscript, and Bonnie McRobbie, Josee Laventhol, Carolann Roussel, Maureen Pritchard, Mary McKinney, Gail Kings, and Josephine Mulhall were of great assistance in data gathering and production work.

Except for the signed sections by Doris Yokelson, none of those named is responsible for conclusions and interpretations in this book, which are, of course, entirely my own.

Foreword

This book reflects work begun in 1968 under the Hudson Institute study program. The data and ideas were incorporated into lectures given by the author at the Institute seminars and elsewhere since that time. The manuscript itself is based largely on two studies done at the Hudson Institute. A paper on youth, written by the author, was finished in March 1971 as a Hudson Institute Study, "A Profile of America's Youth" (HI-1461-RR). A second study, "An Outline of a National Profile" (HI-1272/3-IR, containing the youth study unchanged), also by the author, with contributions by Doris Yokelson, was finished in April 1971. This book is largely an updated and considerably expanded version of the latter study, including new public opinion poll data released between March and November 1971. The additional material has not, however, significantly altered the basic thrust of the original study.

Contents

ACKNOWLEDGMENTS

FOREWORD

PREFACE

CHAPTER I
SOME UNDEREXPLORED POPULAR PERCEPTIONS
AND ISSUES   19
A.   Values   21
     1. "Private" Morality
        a. The New Sexual Morality
     2. Religious Practices
B.   Overall Feelings on Morals and Basic Values and Public
     Enforcement of Standards   46
C.   The Availability and Importance of the Majority
     Opinion   67
D.   Issues, Policies and Laws vs. Real Issues, "Code Words"
     and Motivations   69
     1. The 1968 Gun Law
     2. Open Housing Laws
     3. School Busing and Crossbusing, and Other New School
        and Related Neighborhood Programs
     4. Construction Workers Unions
E.   A Message from the 1968 and 1970 Elections?   102
F.   The "Middle American" and His Feelings About His
     Society   146

CHAPTER II
TODAY'S YOUTH   173
A.   Overview of High School Students   174
     1. Pre-1968
     2. Youth: 1968–1971
        a. The Similarity and Dissimilarity Between High School
          Students and Adults
        b. A New Set of Categories
        c. The "Generation Gap" and Anti-Establishmentism
        d. Drugs
        e. Alienation and Decision-Making
B.   Overview of University Students   245
     1. Who Are the Activists?

2. Non-students, Types of Students, Life Styles and Trends

3. Adult Evaluation of the Role of "Youth" in Our Society

4. A New "Elitist" Approach?

5. The Young Workers and the New Life Style

6. Indicators of Youthful Opinion, Political Strength and
   • Awareness

7. A Critical Decision Point and Its Significance to Society

CHAPTER III
AN EXAMINATION OF NEGRO AND WHITE ATTITUDES

	by Doris Yokelson	346
A.	Introduction	346
B.	White and Negro Racial Attitudes	348
C.	Attitudes of Negroes Toward Their Own Lives	372
D.	Negro Feelings about their Economic and Financial Status	381

CHAPTER IV
CONCLUSION

		385
A.	Some Important Factors in the Current Milieu	385
	1. A Return to the Old City Structure?	
	2. Voices from the Past	
B.	The Work Force	396
C.	The Leaders	400
D.	The Majority Opposition	404

APPENDIX
THE CHANGING ATTITUDES OF A COLLEGE CLASS

	By Doris Yokelson	408
A.	Introduction	408
B.	The 1961 College Class	410
	1. Characteristics of the June 1961 College Graduates as of 1968—From the Carnegie Commission Study	
C.	Social and Political Attitudes of the 1961 College Graduates from 1955 to 1968	413
	1. Political Orientation	
	2. Attitudes Toward Current Domestic Issues	
	3. Some Personal Perceptions of High School Students in 1956 and 1970	
	4. Some Feelings of High School Students Toward Change and Democratic Principles	
D.	Alumni Attitudes on Science and Technology	451
E.	Summary	454

8

FIGURES

1.	Availability and Distribution of Birth-Control Information	24
2.	Responses by Catholics to the Distribution of Birth-Control Information	27
3.	Opposition to the Use of Birth-Control Pills	29
4.	Availability of Birth-Control Pills, by Education	30
5.	Sex Education in High Schools	32
6.	Premarital Sex Relations	34
7.	Nudity in Publications	35
8.	Nudity on Stage and in Restaurants	36
9.	Strictness of Laws on the Sale of Pornography	37
10.	Strictness of Laws on the Sale of Pornography, by Education	39
11.	Willingness to Protest the Sale of Pornography	40
12.	Willingness to Protest the Sale of Pornography, by Education	40
13.	Church Attendance—National	42
14.	Influence of Religion—National	42
15.	Is Life Getting Better in Terms of Morals?	47
16.	Is Life Better or Worse in Terms of Morals, Honesty? by Education	48
17.	Adult Attitudes Toward Moral Standards of the Young	50
18.	New Appointments to Supreme Court	52
19.	Do Courts in This Area Deal with Criminals: Too Harshly, Not Harshly Enough, About Right?	53
20.	Courts and Criminals, by Age and Education	54
21.	Death Penalty for Persons Convicted of Murder—National	61
22.	Use of Marijuana in Local High School, by Education	65
23.	Divorce Laws—National	66
24.	Divorce Laws, by Education	67
25.	Wiretapping, by Education	78
26.	Support for Korean and Vietnam Wars	104
27.	Opposition to Korean and Vietnam Wars	105
28.	Preparing Children for the Future	148
29.	Do Colleges Give Students a Balanced View?	148
30.	Feelings Toward College Students, by Education	149
31.	High School Students	177
32.	High School Students and 30-to-49-Year-Old Group	193
33.	Political Party Choice	193
34.	Course Grades by Political Philosophy, High School Students	210
35.	Join the Establishment, High School Students	214
36.	Join the Establishment, High School Students According to Course Grades	215
37.	Negro and White Satisfaction and Dissatisfaction with Family Income	373

9

38.	Negro and White Satisfaction and Dissatisfaction with Housing	374
39.	Negro and White Satisfaction and Dissatisfaction with Work They Do	375
40.	Negro and White Satisfaction and Dissatisfaction with Education of Their Children	378
41.	Trend of Negro Views Since 1949	379
42.	Election Choice—1956, 12th Graders and the 30-49 Year Olds	416
43.	Party Preference—Adults and High School Students	418
44.	Election Choice—1960, 1961 College Seniors, Their Parents (As Reported by the Seniors) and the 30-49 Year Olds	419
45.	Party Preference and Voting Choice—1961 College Graduates, 1956, 1961, 1964, 1968	420

TABLES

1.	Church Attendance: National Trend, 1955-70	41
2.	Church Attendance, Change Between 1958 and 1969 and 1970	43
3.	Church Attendance 1969 and 1970	44
4.	Crime and Its Victims, By Race, 1970	55
5.	A Real Problem in This Neighborhood—Crime	56
6.	Student Disorders	58
7.	Nationwide Poll on Chicago Police Activities During Convention	60
8.	Punishment for Hijacking, Bombing and Starting a Riot	62
9.	Marijuana	63
10.	Firearm Controls	70
11.	Firearm Controls	72
12.	School Integration	83
13.	Busing of School Children	84
14.	Do You Favor?	86
15.	Negro and White Satisfaction and Dissatisfaction with Their Children's Education	88
16.	Discipline in the Local Public Schools	88
17.	Youth Conservation Camps	90
18.	Living Conditions for Blacks	92
19.	Vote for School Taxes	93
20.	National Tests in Local Schools?	94
21.	The Accountability of the School for Students' Progress	95
22.	How Should Teachers be Paid?	95
23.	Power of Teacher Organizations	96
24.	Tenure for Teachers?	96
25.	Most Important Issues—1968	102
26.	Presidential Popularity—Harry S. Truman	106

10

27.	Presidential Popularity—Lyndon B. Johnson	107
28.	President Nixon's Popularity Since January 1970	108
29.	Candidate Who Can Do a Better Job of Dealing with the War, *and* Did We Make a Mistake in Sending Troops to Vietnam	109
30.	Party Which Can Handle Top Problems Best	111
31.	Poll of Democrats (49% of Electorate), *and* Poll of Independents (16% of Electorate)	111
32.	Pre-Convention Trial Heat (All Candidates)	111
33.	Presidential Choice (All Voters)	112
34.	Post-Democratic Convention Poll	112
35.	Gallup Election Analysis Finds Gain by Conservative Forces	118
36.	Liberal-Conservative	120
37.	President Nixon's Popularity	122
38.	Vietnam Peace Plan	124
39.	Withdrawal from Vietnam by the End of 1971?	126
40.	Vietnam Withdrawal Proposal	126
41.	Penalties for Draft Evaders	128
42.	Three-Way Presidential Race—Nixon, Muskie, Wallace—Harris Survey, *and* Two-Way Presidential Race—Nixon, Muskie—Harris Survey	129
43.	Nixon-Muskie-Wallace Test Election	130
44.	Nixon-Kennedy-Wallace Trial Heat	132
45.	Nixon-Humphrey-Wallace Trial Heat	134
46.	Political Philosophy	137
47.	T.V. Impartiality	138
48.	Newspaper Impartiality	140
49.	Congressional Quiz	144
50.	Federal Spending Priorities	147
51.	Cause of Crime	150
52.	Are You Happy?	155
53.	Satisfaction Index—Quality of Life	156
54.	Satisfaction Index—Employment	158
55.	Satisfaction Index—Work	159
56.	Satisfaction Index—Income	161
57.	Satisfaction Index—Income	162
58.	Satisfaction Index—Housing	164
59.	Satisfaction Index—Housing	165
60.	The Future Facing You and Your Family?	166
61.	Confidence in Institutions	168
62.	High School Student Rankings of "Best" Practices: 1954, 1965	174
63.	High School Rankings of "Worst" Practices: 1923, 1954, and 1965	175
64.	Attitude Toward Behavior of Unmarried People, High School Students	176

11

65.	Feelings Toward the American Way of Life, High School Students	179
66.	Feelings Toward Democratic Principles, High School Students	182
67.	Future—Personal Dignity and Love of Fellow Man, High School Students	183
68.	Future—Anxiety and Nervousness, High School Students	184
69.	Future—Effectiveness of Religion, High School Students	185
70.	Church Attendance—1980, High School Students	186
71.	Divorce Rate—1980, High School Students	187
72.	Attitudes Toward Basics of the System, High School Students	188
73.	Influence in Family Decisions, High School Students	190
74.	Relationship with Adults, High School Students	191
75.	Values, High School Students	195
76.	Views on Middle East Dispute, High School Students, *and* Adults	196
77.	Views on Vietnam, High School Students, *and* Adults	198
78.	Vietnam—Humphrey's Position, Adults, *and* Vietnam—Nixon's Position, Adults	199
78A.	Race Relations, High School Students	201
78B.	School Integration, Adults	203
78C.	Busing of School Children, Adults	204
79.	Race Relations, High School Students	206
80.	Political Philosophy of High School Students—April and November 1970	209
81.	The American Way of Life and Need for Discipline	211
82.	Biggest Gripe About Young People Today	212
83.	Self-Report on Use of Drugs, Alcoholic Drinks, and Cigarettes, in Montgomery County Schools	216
84.	Use of Drugs in High School, High School Students	218
85.	Use of Drugs in Own School, High School Students	220
86.	Tolerance Toward Those Using Drugs, High School Students	224
87.	Social Pressure to Use Drugs, High School Students	226
88.	Legalization of Marijuana, High School Students	228
89.	Purdue Poll on Drugs and Narcotics	229
90.	Purdue Poll on Drugs	231
91.	Influence by Parents and Teachers, On High School Students	237
92.	Race and Autonomy in the Family, High School Students	238
93.	Race and Autonomy in School, High School Students	239
94.	Race and Need for Discipline, High School Students	239
95.	Political Party Affiliation, College Students	247
96.	Political ˙ Philosophy, College-Bound High School Students and College Students	249
97.	Political Orientation, College Students—1969	249
98.	Political Orientation, College Students—1970	250
99.	Liberal-Conservative Orientation, All College Students—1970	251

100.	Political Self-Appraisal of the Faculty and 1968 Support for Nixon, by Field of Study	252
101.	Faculty Support of Student Activism, by Field of Study	253
102.	Attitude Toward Vietnam War and Political Self-Appraisal by Field of Study and Relative Academic Status of School	253
103.	Support for Student Activism, by Field Within the Social Sciences	254
104.	Support for Student Activism, Selected Social Science Disciplines, by Age	255
105.	Gripes of Student Demonstrators as Described by All College Students	256
106.	More Say in Running of Colleges	257
107.	More Say on Academic Matters?	257
108.	Number of College Students and Faculty 1940-1969	258
109.	Expel Campus Lawbreakers?	259
110.	Profile of the Student Demonstrator and the Non-Demonstrator	261
111.	Biggest Gripe of College Students About Parents' Generation?	267
112.	Biggest Gripe of Parents About Young People?	267
113.	Legalize Marijuana? Asked of College Students	269
114.	Pre-Marital Sex Relations, Asked of College Students	270
115.	Frequency of Marijuana Use, College Students	273
116.	Frequency of Barbiturate Use, College Students	274
117.	Frequency of Hallucinogen Use, College Students	275
118.	Relevance of Religion, College Students	278
119.	Reason for Success, College Students	279
120.	Importance of Money—Gilbert Youth Survey	280
121.	Preferred Field or Occupation by Age 40, Asked of College Students	281
122.	Distribution of Scholastic Aptitude Scores	284
123.	Current Issues—Fortune Poll	291
124.	Issues of Particular Concern to College Students	292
125.	What's Wrong With America? College Students	293
126.	Current Issues—Fortune Poll	294
126A.	Fortune Poll	296
127.	Criticism of American Society	297
128.	Attitudes Toward Institutions	298
129.	Identification—Fortune Poll	302
130.	Agreement with Parents	303
131.	Admiration and Dislike—Fortune Poll	303
132A.	For President in 1972?	304
132B.	Highly Favorable and Favorable Ratings Among College Students—December 1970	304
133.	Youths' and Parents' Attitudes—Fortune Poll	306
134.	Acceptance of Restraints—Fortune Poll	309
135.	Influence on Career—Fortune Poll	310

13

136.	Gilbert Youth Survey on Life Styles	311
137.	Gilbert Youth Survey on Life Styles	312
138.	Gilbert Youth Survey on Life Styles	313
139.	Gilbert Youth Survey on Life Styles	314
140.	Commitment Issues	316
140A.	Life Style the Respondent Finds . . .	321
141.	Total Population and Persons 15 to 24 Years Old: 1900 to 1970	338
142.	Education, Age and Wallace Vote	340
143.	Interracial Marriages	348
144.	School Integration	349
145.	Vote for a Negro?	350
146.	Busing	351
147.	Speed of Integration	352
148.	Racial Integration of Schools	353
149.	Integration	354
150.	Is There Discrimination Against Negroes?	355
151.	Neighborhood Racial Integration by Class	356
152.	Neighborhood Attitudes	357
153.	Neighborhood Integration	357
154.	Racial Discrimination in Housing	358
155.	Neighborhood Integration—Castlemont	359
156.	Negro Perceptions of White Attitudes	360
157.	Will White Attitudes Toward Negroes Improve?	360
158.	How Negroes Can Attain Goals	361
159.	The Favored Way to Negro Progress	361
160.	Communist Involvement in Civil Rights Demonstrations	363
161.	Negro Feelings Toward Black Panthers	364
162.	Negro Feelings Toward Black Panthers	364
163.	How Do You Rate the Following Organizations?	365
164.	Black Views on Black Panthers	365
165.	What Do Negroes Prefer to be Called?	367
166.	A Real Problem in This Neighborhood	371
167.	A Real Problem in This Neighborhood—Crime	371
168.	Crime and Its Victims, By Race, 1970	372
169.	Negroes Favoring Separatist Response to Each Question	380
170.	Negro and White Economic Status	382
171.	High School Students by Future Plans—March 1955 and June 1970	414
172.	High School Party Preference, 10th, 11th and 12th Grades	415
173.	Party Preference, June 1970—10th, 11th & 12th Grade High School	418
174.	Party Affiliation of 1961 College Class in 1964 and 1968 and Net Change from 1964 to 1968	421

14

175.	Politics of Parents in 1964 (As Described by 1961 Alumni)	421
176.	Liberal Orientation of Alumni and Their Parents (According to Alumni)	422
177.	Political Leanings of Alumni, 1964 and 1968	422
178.	Attitudes on Students and Negro Protests, by Political Leanings	424
179.	Republican Orientation, College Seniors—1961	424
180.	Alumni Retention of Party Affiliation Between 1964 and 1968, by Present Family Income	425
181.	Alumni Attitudes Toward Certain Experiences	427
182.	Most Serious Problems Facing Young People Today, College Seniors—1961	428
183.	All College Students, April-May 1969	429
184.	December, 1970	430
185.	Alumni attitudes on Current Issues	431
186.	Support-for-Militancy Index by Type of College Attended	432
187.	Support-for-Militancy Index by Age and College Quality	432
188.	Support-for-Militancy Index by 1968 Career Field	433
189.	Alumni Attitudes Toward Student Involvement	434
190.	Student-Involvement Indices, by Type of College Attended	436
191.	Student-Involvement Indices by 1968 Career Field	437
192.	Cultural Activities by Sex and College Quality	438
193.	Coefficients of Association Between Indices of Cultural Activities and Background Variables (Gamma)	438
194.	Percent Responding to the Questions . . .	439
195.	What Alumni Would Have Done Differently	440
196.	Any Courses You Wish You Had Taken? College Seniors—1961	441
197.	What Courses Do You Wish You Had Taken? College Seniors—1961	441
198.	Alumni Evaluation of Goals of Faculty and Administration at Their Colleges	442
199.	An Index of Individualism or Willingness to be "Different" from the Group—High School Students	444
200.	Personal Feelings of High School Students, January 1970	446
201.	Things High School Students Worry About, April 1970	447
202.	Willingness to Try New Ideas, High School Students—May 1956	448
203.	Resistance to Changing the American Way of Life, High School Students	448
204.	Obedience and Respect for Authority, High School Students	449
205.	Faith and Trust in a Leader, High School Students	450
206.	Attitudes on Science and Technology for Alumni and for the General Population	452
207.	Coefficients of Association Between Antiexperts Index and Background Variables	453
208.	Antiexperts Index by Type of College Attended	453
209.	Antiexperts Index by 1968 Career Field	453

15

Preface

This study is an attempt to help determine what the national character and attitudes are, and how, or if, they are changing. This is never as simple as it might seem. The task is difficult because in these days issues are sometimes clouded by indiscriminate labeling of certain ideas, persons, and groups.

In my research, I have found that there is greater homogeneity in America than believed, despite the much publicized "polarization," "generation gap," and so on. Furthermore, many ideas about "changes" underway are not "new" at all. They may seem so—perhaps because the "man in the street" has often been stereotyped as a narrow-minded, change-resisting, even intolerant creature. For example, we sometimes think of ourselves as ignorantly puritanical on any public issues dealing with sexual matters. We also sometimes consider ourselves as basically selfish, exploiters of others, even racist. All this may be true to some degree, but, overemphasized, such characteristics distort the image of the personality we are describing. Today some of us have tended to caricature ourselves.

Our "shortcomings" have been greatly emphasized. We shove people into groups with their own sets of ideas—"hard hats," "youth," "conservatives" (often looked on as "bad," if not "evil"), "liberals" (whom conservatives often consider "bad" and "evil"), or "well-informed" persons (that is, those who agree with us). Often these categories were established to implement the analysis of our current situation. Like all simplified "models," however, these have many holes, which frequently appear to go unnoticed and could lead to difficulties, including problems in decision-making. They already have created problems in analysis. A great deal of secondary source material exists on these issues; but with some notable exceptions, much of this knowledge, at least until 1970, appears inadequate. This book, based almost entirely on primary sources, supplies few answers; however, it does introduce some caveats regarding certain widely held assumptions.

The book is divided into three sections. All three cover basic concerns and attitudes, particularly those that, in my judgment, have received in-

17

adequate attention. The main body is based on two very rough and broad categories—the population as a whole and youth. The third section is another look at a minority of the population—the Negroes (11 percent)—because they are the target of so much attention today. We also have an appendix that traces the attitudes of a cohort of college students over a period of time.

In some ways this is an unfair way to view our society. Singling out any group is categorizing people in a way that always results in over-simplification. Negroes are also artisans, white-collar workers, parents, "youth," middle class, poor. Some are rich. And, they certainly are not represented by one point of view or type of spokesman. But as with the singling out of a cohort and youth (and even the subgroup, students), Negroes received special attention in this book in order to follow a familiar format on social problems often used in the media and in many recent studies. Actually, all sections on any category in this book contain information on almost all other categories. There is information on adults, youth, and Negroes in all sections.

Youth—this much-discussed new generation—has been both praised and maligned to a degree unequaled since the 1920s, perhaps not even then. They, too, have recently been classified into groups and subgroups. Much secondary information in this area, in my judgment, has proved less than conclusive; and since this effort was thought of as contributing to the base of understanding of our society, I felt extensive work on this group was needed. I tried to discern what today's youth thinks regarding issues that might change their development from lines analogous to their parents.

One of the main purposes of this book, then, is an attempt to add to what I believe is an incomplete picture of the average American and his problems.

Chapter I

Some Underexplored Popular Perceptions and Issues

By the late 1960s the "average" American had some cause to feel almost like a stranger, not only to many of those who disseminated information in his own country, but apparently even to some elected and nonelected government officials. His beliefs in patriotism, freedom, human dignity, the American dream, did not jibe with the views that some writers, commentators, and academicians had presented the nation and the world. This disparity widened although both groups spoke the same language and often used the same terms.

The "average" American apparently still believes strongly in his system of government and society. He is action- and solution-oriented. At the same time, he is a charitable person. He has concern for his less-fortunate fellow citizens.* Perhaps in the enthusiasm over the "new" social awareness, some forget how deeply he feels about some things. When most citizens reacted hostilely to issues or programs that they felt were inimical to their ideals and to feasible political and economic ac-

---

* "The concepts of Medicare and Medicaid were endorsed by most citizens long before they became law. Likewise, before they were ever federally implemented, such programs as regulation and prohibition of child labor, old age pensions, social security, public works, slum clearance, urban renewal, low-cost housing, federal responsibility for full employment and unemployment compensation, aid to education, veterans' benefits, assistance to depressed areas, anti-poverty legislation have been favored by clear majorities of those venturing opinions." (*Measures of Political Attitudes,* John P. Robinson, Jerrold G. Rusk, and Kendra B. Head, University of Michigan Survey Research Center, Institute for Social Research, Ann Arbor, Michigan, 1969, "Economic and Welfare Issues," p. 34.)

tivity, certain writers, commentators and academicians often seemed to regard them as aliens. Consider, for example, the onrush of articles and TV "specials" on the majority of our own citizens (the "middle" Americans)—a surprising reflection on the authors of the articles and the producers of the programs. The "opinion-makers" spread information through the mass media about the same people who were the audience. These were interesting efforts in many cases because a number of the critics had misconceptions of the average citizen. As late as mid-1970, a TV program was billed in *TV Guide*: "The Silent Majority . . . Housewives, Hardhats, Hardliners who shout, 'Spiro is our hero.' "* Actually, categories such as the "silent majority" and "middle Americans," or those who held opinions in 1969 and 1970 that often coincided with those held by Vice President Spiro Agnew, do not describe economic classes, ethnic groups or levels of education. They describe a state of mind that, as we shall see later, on many key issues, usually cuts across most or all groups. (One should note in passing that more adults in our modern population and in survey samples have some college education —24 percent—than only grade school education—19 percent—and those who graduated from or had attended high school make up 57 percent of the sample. Among voters in 1968, the figures were 26 percent, 22 percent, and 52 percent respectively.)**

In the meantime, the anti-lower-middle-class film *Joe* was produced and it seemed that perhaps there were in print, and now on film, as many caricatures as reasonable likenesses of—of all things—the "silent majority" of our fellow citizens. By 1970, however, the image had come into better focus through a variety of articles and books.*** But, good as these works were, there still seems to be ignorance in some circles of the country about many of the values, thoughts, hopes and aspirations of most of our population.

Since this manuscript was written, a book on television newscasting by Edith Efron, entitled *The News Twisters* (Los Angeles: Nash Publishing Company, 1971) has been published. Although the book's pertinent data cannot, at this date, be added to this book in the appropriate places, its message certainly cannot be ignored.

---

* A description of Channel 5's David Susskind Show, June 14, 1970.
** *Gallup Opinion Index*, April 1968, p. 33. Richard M. Scammon and Ben J. Wattenberg, *The Real Majority* (New York: Coward-McCann, Inc., 1970), p. 59 (U.S. Census Bureau figures).
*** Works by Lipset, Rabb, Ladd, Greeley, Scammon and Wattenberg, Dennis Strong, Eric Hoffer, etc., many of which are referenced in this study.

Miss Efron concentrates on the 1968–70 dissemination of news by television and to some extent by the press. Her analysis primarily covers a seven-week period during the presidential campaign in 1968. She stresses "political issues," but also covers other points. Her evidence is in large part impressive, and much of it is unique. She concludes that television news coverage, at the time of her extensive monitoring of news programs on the three major networks, overemphasized the "liberal" side on many issues. Her monitoring data and statements by those in the media themselves support this conclusion. For example:

CBS's Desmond Smith: "The Left and SDS have been getting a great deal of play. Americans are getting to feel they're not getting the whole story." p. 180

Howard K. Smith of ABC noted "a strong leftward bias" in TV news personnel and stated that the "emphasis" in network coverage is "anti-American." It tends to omit the good about America and focus on the bad. pp. 183, 185, 186

Chet Huntley of NBC, "Our attention has been turned to the cities. . . . We're ignoring the rest of America." p. 178

David Jayne, a longtime reporter and TV producer, said TV newsmen "live in the provincial and parochial confines of Washington and New York City . . . read the same newspapers, bound on one flank by the *Times* and on the other by the *Washington Post*, with perhaps some turning to *Newsweek* and the *New Republic*." p. 182

A. *Values*

Probably one of the most interesting and most worthwhile things to review over a span of years is the basic value system—how has it changed? How does the population as a whole perceive it? The value system, of course, greatly determines how concerned people are about what they see or think they see happening around them; and the degree and kind of concern determines their support of or opposition to events, "movements" and "programs." This is particularly important for "new" programs that demand drastic changes.

In issues regarding fundamental aspects of our society and government, the impact of change on the population can be crucial. We live in an exceedingly complex environment: changes in one area can have

21

drastic, unforeseen effects in others, particularly if those persons initiating the changes are unfamiliar with the multifarious causes of the effects. The population as a whole speaks with a voice that often reflects these potential costs. This does not mean that the "voice of the people" is necessarily right; the "reforms" might have to be carried out anyway. But we must know the costs, for they can be greater than the benefits of the reforms. Often the costs have proved overwhelming: this is surely the case if, in the end, the effort reforms nothing. Many expensive educational programs, for example, seem to fall into this category.

Much difficulty might have been avoided if more attention had been paid to what requisite values were being (or appeared to be) endangered for what benefits. These values are based on a system that, although none of us would agree with it in all details, is the operating mechanism of this country.

1. "PRIVATE" MORALITY

Every value system changes. The gradual change that has occurred in this country over the past decades, generally toward "liberalization" of social and economic attitudes, is obvious. But normally the changes, although often very rapid when compared to other peacefully-evolving societies, have seldom at any point caused the majority suddenly to jettison a part of the value system. Perhaps this is as it should be. Yet, one gets the distinct feeling that, possibly because they lack contact with the "man in the street," influential persons, functioning only from the viewpoint of the immediate present, sometimes think that drastic changes are occurring when they are not. This may be happening for many reasons. Perhaps the most interesting one may stem from a lack of genuine information on the public value system and attitudes. Even persons of influence may be basing their opinions on stereotypes of the public. Often when shown evidence of public opinion, and of the incompatibility of their caricature and reality, they think they see change underway. Sometimes they overlook significant changes in attitudes (for example, regarding mores).

a. THE NEW SEXUAL MORALITY

An area that may have been subject to this stereotyping of the average citizen is that of sexual morality. To understand the present, much light must be shed on what the public has believed on this matter

22

in the past. Today we are inundated with reports of a "new sexual morality" and its impact on adults and adolescents. But let us look at the "history" of attitudes on some issues concerned with sexual morality. We are, of course, limited to the questions that were asked in polls; nonetheless, it is probably a mistake to ignore information that may give at least some indication of past and present adult attitudes in today's general areas of interest. We may even note a trend, instead of a point of reference, for better analyzing changes in public attitudes or predicting future attitudes. The following polls of adults are on a subject that certain segments of our society (besides Catholics, who comprised about a sixth of the population pre-World War II and had the highest number of minors in their parishes) seem to feel is a moral issue.

It is, of course, always difficult to devise a "fever chart" covering many years, particularly when there is such a variation of questions asked about the topic that comparisons are sometimes doubtful. That is why the chart shows double lines where there are changes between the questions asked, and each of the questions is written above the points on the chart. Identical questions were asked over a span of years, however, so there are sections of this graph that, in this respect, are probably valid comparisons. If the changes in the question are taken into account, a general idea of past and present attitudes emerges. The specifics of the question asked, of course, usually makes a difference in the answers. For example, a question in May 1936 was, "Should information on birth control be made legal?" In July of that year, the question was, "Do you believe in the teaching and practice of birth control?"* To assume that "birth control" always meant contraceptives, particularly after the late 1940s when the rhythm method became popular, would be erroneous.

Nevertheless, despite the problems, some feeling for public attitudes over the years may be possible. Variations resulting from statistical error in the polls are approximately four percentage points. Throughout the years, those favoring the legal distribution of information and the teaching and use of birth control, always varied by more than 30 points from those who oppose such activities. To the extent that the

---

* Normally, when there is a question of a law that prevents people from doing something or learning about something that is not considered criminally wrong, there is likely to be less support for the law than there are people who do not believe in the practice in question.

Figure 1

AVAILABILITY AND DISTRIBUTION OF BIRTH-CONTROL INFORMATION*

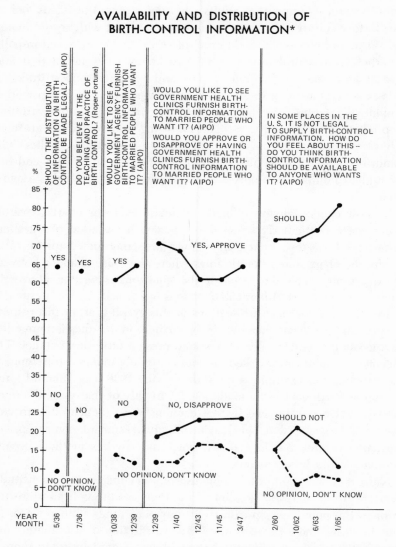

* This graph has been compiled from a series of Gallup and Elmo Roper and Associates–*Fortune* Survey polls found in the article, "The Polls: The Population Explosion, Birth Control, and Sex Education," by Hazel Gaudet Erskine, *Public Opinion Quarterly*, 30 (Fall 1966): 491–493. In all the charts and footnotes, AIPO stands for The American Institute of Public Opinion (The Gallup Poll). Where the designation Roper-*Fortune* is used, it stands for the Elmo Roper and Associates polls done for the *Fortune* Survey. The date of the survey is shown in the chart.

questions are similar, one might assume rough bands of opinion at various levels. Those holding no opinion are much closer to those in opposition. In the lower register we find a band not exceeding 30 percent of those more or less in opposition.

From 1938 to 1947, two questions were asked by two different polling organizations, one in 1938 and 1939, another from 1939 through 1947. Both concerned government distribution of this information to married people who want it, which might even have been interpreted as establishing new units to do this. This, of course, means the use of tax money, which might affect the number of those approving and disapproving of the practice. During World War II, the number of those interested in birth control declined. Perhaps people then were thinking about families and the importance of having the families brought back together again, rather than reducing the probability of having children. Nonetheless, there was always a spread of 35 to 50 points between those in favor and those opposed, and the percentage of those in favor remained within a band of about 10 points, from 60 percent to 70 percent; roughly from 20 percent to 25 percent in opposition; and some 10 percent to 15 percent had no opinion.

The questions during 1960–65 were different again, and involved, as the reader can see, the idea of the justice of laws in certain states preventing people from getting this information when they wanted it. That was a different approach which, as pointed out earlier, is probably less likely to gain support. Moreover, there was nothing involved in the questions that had to do with spending government money and perhaps increasing taxes for such things as new agencies and clinics. This could account for the jump of a few points between 1960 and 1963, when people were asked this new question. Interestingly, support for it remained around 72 percent, and then rose to 74. The jump from 1963 to 1965 was even more noteworthy, because there is a 7-point change during that period; and, of course, there is a similar reduction in the opposition to repealing these laws. The significant change that took place during those years, however, was among Catholics.

Catholic opposition to laws prohibiting the distribution of birth control information jumped 26 percentage points from 1963 to 1965.* Since the Catholics (including minors) now comprise somewhat less than a quarter of the population, a 26-point jump in Catholic adult

* Compiled from Gallup polls appearing in Hazel Erskine, "The Polls," *Public Opinion Quarterly*, 30 (Fall 1966), p. 493.

opposition to such laws would account for a large part of the 7-point jump in overall national adult opinion. This large change in a unique portion of the population is more difficult to assess in relation to a change in American society. We must keep in mind the possible statistical error of 3 to 4 points; but, again, the band of approval versus disapproval continued to have a spread of 40 percent. Once again, the way the question was asked might have made a big difference in the responses of Catholics. A poll in June 1965 showed that, in answer to, "Do you favor or oppose distribution of birth-control information?" 60 percent of Catholics replied affirmatively, but, regarding a *law* to *prevent* other persons from obtaining the information, 78 percent of them registered a resounding no. The same, of course, was true regarding the opposition to distributing the information; in June 1965, 28 percent opposed distribution compared to 12 percent with no opinion. But, as far as wanting a law to prevent people from obtaining birth-control information, in January only 14 percent wanted it, and only 8 percent harbored doubts about how to answer that question.

In 1963, in answer to, "Do you believe in the teaching and practice of birth control?" 45 percent of the Catholics said no; only 42 percent replied yes, and 12 percent had no opinion. It might be interesting to speculate on the amount of "approval" that would have been registered had the question been, "Should laws that prevent people from getting this information be repealed?"

Transcending the rightness and wrongness of the issues, what is interesting in these graphs is that the band of the numbers of persons who favor distribution of birth-control information and who oppose laws prohibiting materials to be distributed, or who favor clinics and agencies, usually hovers around 60 to 75 percent. The switch among Catholics apparently made the difference in shifting the national opinion above that band. Those who *oppose* it, disapprove, do not want agencies, and so forth, are always below 30 percent—roughly around 15 to 25 percent. Thus, the bands of opinion for and against have always had a spread of 30 or 40 points between them, although it might be argued that there is a slight increase in the spread between those favoring distribution of information and those opposing it. Birth-control information is hardly a "new" issue. Although questions concerning it have differed somewhat over the years, opposition to laws prohibiting the dissemination of birth-control information in 1938 was within a few percentage points of such opposition today—with the exception of Catholics. In any event there is some justification for the

26

Figure 2

RESPONSES BY CATHOLICS TO THE DISTRIBUTION OF BIRTH-CONTROL INFORMATION*

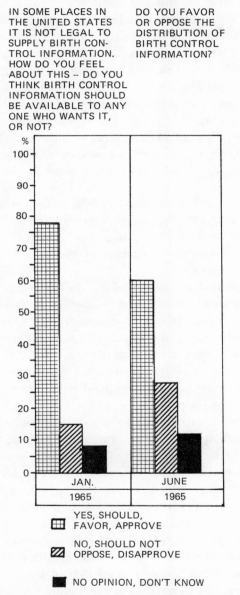

IN SOME PLACES IN THE UNITED STATES IT IS NOT LEGAL TO SUPPLY BIRTH CONTROL INFORMATION. HOW DO YOU FEEL ABOUT THIS -- DO YOU THINK BIRTH CONTROL INFORMATION SHOULD BE AVAILABLE TO ANY ONE WHO WANTS IT, OR NOT?

DO YOU FAVOR OR OPPOSE THE DISTRIBUTION OF BIRTH CONTROL INFORMATION?

YES, SHOULD, FAVOR, APPROVE

NO, SHOULD NOT OPPOSE, DISAPPROVE

NO OPINION, DON'T KNOW

* Compiled from Gallup polls appearing in Erskine, op. cit., p. 493. The June 1965 Gallup Poll was done for *Look* Magazine.

suggestion that the change, if any, has been relatively small, and with the exception of the Catholics, slow. One could argue, therefore, that current attitudes on this subject, among adults, show less effects of a "new morality" than some might think.

What seems clear, however, is that (at least as late as 1967) this attitude probably applied primarily to married persons, and certainly only to adults. This is quite probably still a very important "detail" to the average adult American, which should not be forgotten by those who see a new sexual morality. There has been continued strong opposition to making contraceptives—such as birth-control pills—available to young unmarried girls (see Figure 4). Men were least opposed to making these pills available to college girls through the health officer of the university; but even then, 70 percent of the men disapproved and only 18 approved. Seventy-seven percent of the women disapproved.

In answer to the question, "Should these birth-control pills be made available to teen-agers?," 79 percent registered no and 14 percent yes in 1967. Lest we think we have primarily a "hard-hat" issue, the breakdown of this poll by the education of the (adult) respondents is particularly instructive.

In the case of making pills available to teen-agers, 76 percent of the college-educated objected and 19 approved; 80 percent of those who had attended high school disapproved and 14 approved; 78 percent of those with only grade-school education disapproved, and only 10 approved. A greater number of people who had a grade-school education, however, had no opinion (12 percent). Generally those persons with the least education respond with higher "don't know" or "no opinion" replies in polls.

Any conclusions, even narrow ones, arrived at on some issues described above may be debatable. What is significant, however, is that attitudes on some highly sensitive personal problems, which receive considerable publicity today, probably would not have been regarded with Victorian disdain thirty years ago, either as something to be hypocritically "swept under the rug" or not mentioned in public. Polls from 1936 through 1946 show overwhelming approval for efforts to detect and fight venereal disease. In 1936, 90 percent of those queried favored establishing a "government bureau that would distribute information concerning venereal disease"; only two districts of seven in the country—the West Central (84 percent) and the Pacific Coast (89 percent)—fell below 90 percent in favoring this proposal. Eighty-eight percent

Figure 3

OPPOSITION TO THE USE OF BIRTH-CONTROL PILLS*

THE HEALTH OFFICER OF A UNIVERSITY RECENTLY GAVE PRESCRIPTIONS FOR BIRTH CONTROL PILLS TO TWO UNMARRIED STUDENTS. HOW DO YOU FEEL ABOUT GIVING BIRTH CONTROL PILLS TO GIRLS IN COLLEGE - DO YOU APPROVE OR DISAPPROVE OF THIS?

DO YOU THINK BIRTH CONTROL PILLS SHOULD BE MADE AVAILABLE TO TEENAGERS?

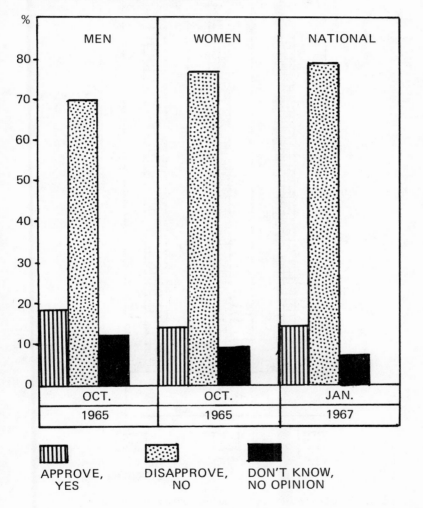

APPROVE, YES   DISAPPROVE, NO   DON'T KNOW, NO OPINION

* Compiled from a Gallup poll of October 1965, appearing in Erskine, op. cit., p. 493; and January 1967 in *Gallup Opinion Index,* No. 20, February 1967, p. 14.

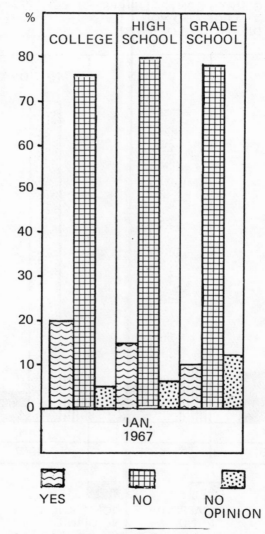

Figure 4

AVAILABILITY OF BIRTH-CONTROL PILLS
BY EDUCATION*

DO YOU THINK THEY SHOULD BE MADE
AVAILABLE TO TEENAGE GIRLS?

YES   NO   NO
OPINION

* Graph drawn from information in the *Gallup Opinion Index,* No. 20, February 1967, p. 14.

favored this bureau setting up clinics to fight the disease. In 1937, 70 percent favored (with only 20 opposed) "providing treatment for all persons afflicted regardless of their circumstances," and 79 percent said yes to a Congressional appropriation of "twenty-five million dollars to help control venereal disease."* In 1938, 87 percent favored Congress appropriating money "to aid states in fighting venereal disease." Sixty-nine percent said they would be "willing to pay higher taxes" to fight venereal disease. In 1937 the public was so "broad-minded" that half of those polled said they favored "legally controlled prostitution" as a means of controlling venereal disease; 31 percent opposed this suggestion, and 18 had no opinion (presumably prostitutes were considered a prime source of venereal disease and government control would mean mandatory medical examinations, licensing, etc.). But 61 percent also favored "fine or imprisonment of all persons afflicted who do not get treated." In the same year, 87 percent were in favor of a confidential blood test for syphilis for all. In 1939, 79 percent believed that newspapers and magazines "should be allowed to describe methods of fighting syphilis," and a year before, 98 percent voted for a law requiring doctors to give every expectant mother a test for syphilis. In 1946, 85 percent favored keeping such laws on the books where they then existed and only 7 percent opposed.**

Despite the overwhelming public support over the years for the dissemination of public information about, and the means to fight, venereal disease, however, today we are told that:

One of the reasons for the continued existence of gonorrhea and syphilis is the widespread belief that decent people don't acquire the disease, decent people don't talk about the disease, and decent people shouldn't do anything about those who do become infected.***

* Gallup polls, December 1936 and May 1937, as cited in Hazel Erskine, "The Polls: More on Morality and Sex," *Public Opinion Quarterly*, 31 (Spring 1967), p. 124.

** Gallup polls, January, May, and August 1937, January and May 1938, February 1946; Roper poll for *Fortune*, August 1939, appearing in Hazel Erskine, "The Polls: More on Morality and Sex," *Public Opinion Quarterly*, 31 (Spring 1967), pp. 123–125. On the radio program "Medicine" (WHN-1050), on January 24, 1971, it was reported that there were an estimated 200,000 cases of gonorrhea in New York City in 1970 compared to 36,000 in the last "peak" year prior to the current epidemic.

*** From a "recent publication" of the Los Angeles Health Department, quoted in "The Venereal Disease Pandemic," by Cokie and Stephen V. Roberts, *New York Times Magazine*, November 7, 1971, p. 67. This same article says that many young persons, including those who are continually reinfected, will not use universally known preventive measures.

Adult approval of sex education in the high schools is high not only because of a recent sexual enlightenment. In fact, considering the 12 percent increase in "disapproval," the public attitude on this question may have been *more liberal* thirty years ago.

Figure 5

SEX EDUCATION IN HIGH SCHOOLS*

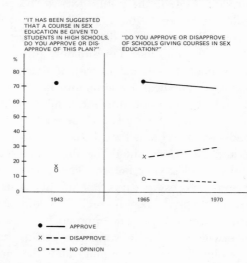

Apparently the general tendency has not been to recoil from the very thought of all sensitive problems, but rather to favor programs directed toward them, provided they are handled by qualified persons who can solve the problems with the least dangers of making new ones, and with the least harm to the family and children. In the case of sex education, there is no solid evidence for the apparent increase in opposition to the program. It could be ascribed to the not unusual sense of less-than-expected value of a program once it is implemented. There is, of course, the possibility that some opposition was linked to disapproval of loose sexual morality. On the other hand, parents of students voted 71 to 72 percent (slightly above the average) in favor of it in 1970. Presumably in 1943 and 1965, the parents also were more in favor of it than persons without schoolchildren, who are normally less likely to vote money for any school program.

* Compiled from Gallup polls of May 1943 and May 1965, appearing in Hazel Erskine, *Public Opinion Quarterly* (Fall 1966), pp. 500 and 501, and of 1970 in the *Gallup Opinion Index*, No. 66, December 1970, p. 20.

There is no implication here that the majority is always right morally and politically, or even that the programs it approves are always feasible. The possible disappointment with the implementation of a sex education program, as may have been evidenced by the increased negative reaction in 1960 and 1970, would likely also have been the reaction in the 1930s had "far-out" programs such as legally controlled prostitution been implemented. Nonetheless, data, such as that shown in Figure 6, suggests that Americans in the 1930s and early 1940s were more "liberal" about some sexual matters than they are today. A factor to consider also is that during the thirties and early forties there may have been less fear of dangers to the morals of children and adolescents, and threats to the family, than there seem to be today. Fears of these dangers may explain why today, in areas in which many feel that the values are becoming more liberal, the change seems to have been in the opposite direction: that is, beliefs in the "old values" have increased. On the matter of premarital sexual relations (an area of vital concern about and to today's youth), to the extent that the questions are similar, the polls for 1937, 1959, 1965 and 1969 indicate such a trend.

The usually strong opposition among adults to premarital sexual relations appears to have increased in the 1960s. The 1969 survey showed 68 percent of the adults queried opposing it. This was so even though the media, the colleges, and even the high schools showed less objection to it than in the past, and although the questions asked in 1965 and 1969 did not deal with promiscuity. The 1965 question even mentioned people "in love" and "engaged to be married" and asked whether they should wait until after the ceremony. Nonetheless, the objection was stronger than in 1959. Here, again, there is a 30-point spread between those believing premarital relations to be wrong and those who don't. The lower bands, showing those persons holding no opinion and those approving, have always remained under 30 percent and opposition has always run 55 points or more. If there were more data, a graph covering these many years could show many peaks and valleys; but, spotty though the data are, they challenge the idea, publicized in the current media, that there has been a significant shift among adults in favor of the new "liberal" sexual morals among the unmarried young.

The following chart shows a similar situation, with different questions, concerning nudity in magazines and newspapers. The question asked in 1939 dealt with paintings, which are quite different from a

Figure 6

PREMARITAL SEX RELATIONS*

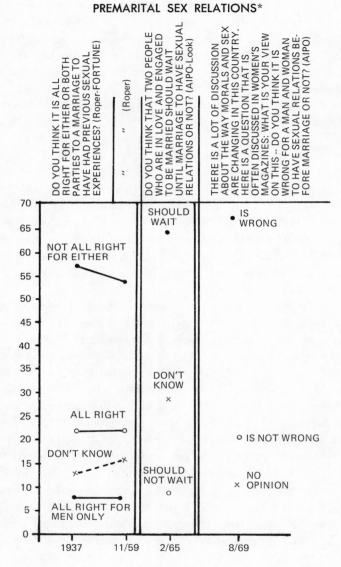

* Compiled from Roper–*Fortune* Survey, Roper and Gallup opinion polls of April 1937, November 1959 and February 1965, appearing in Hazel Erskine, "The Polls: Morality," *Public Opinion Quarterly*, 30 (Winter 1966–1967), p. 673; Hazel Erskine, "The Polls: More on Morality and Sex," 31 (Spring 1967), p. 122; and a Gallup poll of August 1969 in the *Gallup Opinion Index*, No. 52, October 1969, p. 24. The February 1965 poll was done by Gallup for *Look* Magazine.

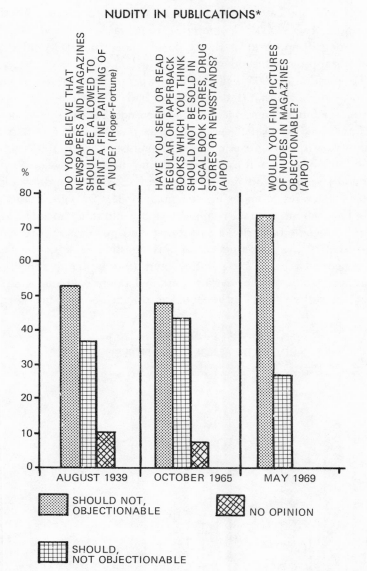

Figure 7

NUDITY IN PUBLICATIONS*

* Compiled from information in Gallup and Roper-*Fortune* Survey polls of August 1939 and October 1965 in Hazel Erskine, "The Polls: Morality," *Public Opinion Quarterly*, 30 (Winter 1966–1967), p. 679, and of May 1969 in the *Gallup Opinion Index*, No. 49, July 1969, p. 22. The May 1969 poll did not offer a "no opinion" choice.

photograph. However, the magazines of that era sold across the counter did not have nude photos in them, at least not (with the exception of *National Geographic*) respectable publications. There was strong disapproval of that type of nudity in 1939, and there is strong disapproval of it today.

The question in 1965 dealt not only with pictures but with the content of paperbacks that the respondents had seen or read, and a larger percentage found them objectionable than not; but the spread between 1935 and 1965 was small and, of course, the different question could account for it. The great jump of 25 points between 1965 and 1969 could have been caused by the change in question between "have you [*actually*] seen or read regular or paperback books" and "would you object to pictures of nudes in a magazine?" The 20-point change from 1939, however, might have resulted from the old reluctance of prohibiting other people from doing something, and people now realizing the full extent of the consequences of this question, besides the obvious difference between a "fine painting" and a nude photograph. By 1969 many magazines on the market contained pictures of nudes and sexually descriptive texts. As recently as fifteen or even ten years ago

Figure 8

NUDITY ON STAGE AND IN RESTAURANTS*

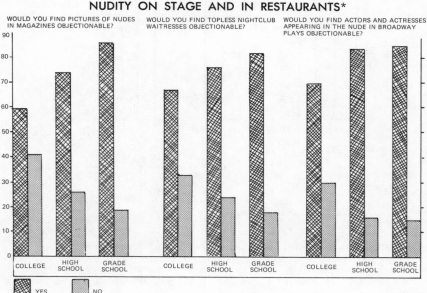

WOULD YOU FIND PICTURES OF NUDES IN MAGAZINES OBJECTIONABLE?   WOULD YOU FIND TOPLESS NIGHTCLUB WAITRESSES OBJECTIONABLE?   WOULD YOU FIND ACTORS AND ACTRESSES APPEARING IN THE NUDE IN BROADWAY PLAYS OBJECTIONABLE?

COLLEGE   HIGH SCHOOL   GRADE SCHOOL   COLLEGE   HIGH SCHOOL   GRADE SCHOOL   COLLEGE   HIGH SCHOOL   GRADE SCHOOL

YES   NO

* *Gallup Opinion Index*, No. 49, July 1969, pp. 22, 23, 24.

36

Figure 9

STRICTNESS OF LAWS ON THE SALE OF PORNOGRAPHY*

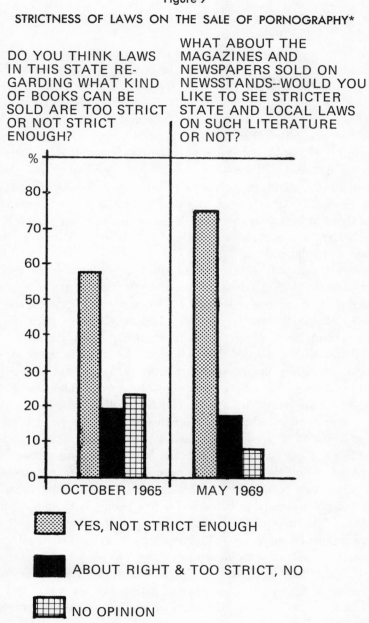

DO YOU THINK LAWS IN THIS STATE REGARDING WHAT KIND OF BOOKS CAN BE SOLD ARE TOO STRICT OR NOT STRICT ENOUGH?

WHAT ABOUT THE MAGAZINES AND NEWSPAPERS SOLD ON NEWSSTANDS--WOULD YOU LIKE TO SEE STRICTER STATE AND LOCAL LAWS ON SUCH LITERATURE OR NOT?

OCTOBER 1965   MAY 1969

YES, NOT STRICT ENOUGH

ABOUT RIGHT & TOO STRICT, NO

NO OPINION

* Compiled from information in Gallup polls in the *Gallup Political Index*, No. 5, October 1965 ,p. 20 and the *Gallup Opinion Index*, No. 49, July 1969, p. 19.

many people had to speculate in answering such questions. In any event, there is no firm evidence that this opposition to nudity, etc. had shrunk in the late 1960s.

The same can be said for the other answers to the questions in Figure 8 regarding nudity on the stage and in restaurants, given according to the education levels of the adult respondents.

Although there is a significant difference of opinion among adults according to education, each group registered strong opposition. This raises the possibility that there is a great concern about the easy accessibility of lewd information (magazines), possibly caused by fear of its availability to minors—a point, at least, that cannot be ignored. Concerned parents know, collectively, very much about children. It is not sufficient to label objection to such literature as "puritanism," when those objecting are parents. Their worry is often primarily for those below "the age of consent"; and this is a timeless and, in my judgment, a valid concern.

Figures 9 and 10 (to the extent that the questions are similar) could indicate that this fear of the dissemination of pornography is increasing. Any increase in support for stricter laws to prevent the sale of such material would be highly significant because normally the public is sensitive to infringements on the First Amendment.

Furthermore, as Figure 10 indicates, the concern over a lack of legal protection against such literature is, again, not just a phenomenon among "hard hats" and vigilante groups. The objection is strongest among those with a high school education, followed by those with a grade-school education. Nonetheless, even 65 percent of the college-educated wanted stricter laws governing magazine content in 1969. The highest satisfaction with the law was among persons with college education, but those who were satisfied were outnumbered better than two to one by the college people who wanted stricter laws. It is noteworthy that in 1969 very few people held no opinion on this issue. The strength of the objection to such material is indicated by the following charts on willingness to join a neighborhood group to protest the sale of such literature.

Willingness to join protest groups is usually a strong indicator of concern for the average adult citizen (it just isn't his way), and it is interesting to note here the closeness of opinion among all categories of education. Those who are college-educated are somewhat more liberal on this issue, as they usually are in most matters that do not involve spending money, but their opinion is closer to that of the less educated

38

Figure 10

STRICTNESS OF LAWS ON THE SALE OF PORNOGRAPHY*
by Education

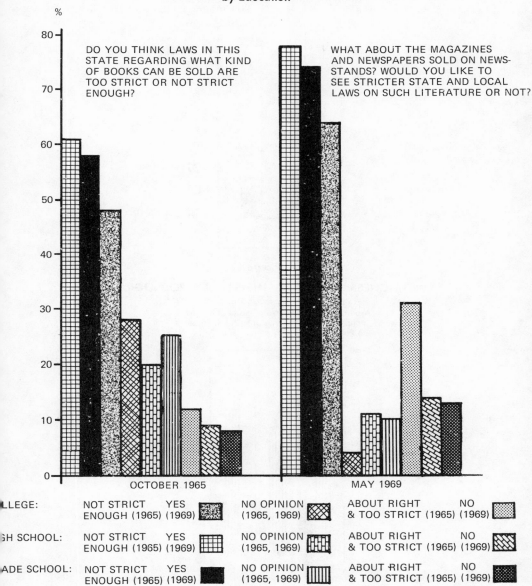

DO YOU THINK LAWS IN THIS STATE REGARDING WHAT KIND OF BOOKS CAN BE SOLD ARE TOO STRICT OR NOT STRICT ENOUGH?

WHAT ABOUT THE MAGAZINES AND NEWSPAPERS SOLD ON NEWSSTANDS? WOULD YOU LIKE TO SEE STRICTER STATE AND LOCAL LAWS ON SUCH LITERATURE OR NOT?

OCTOBER 1965   MAY 1969

LLEGE: NOT STRICT ENOUGH (1965) YES (1969)	NO OPINION (1965, 1969)	ABOUT RIGHT & TOO STRICT (1965) NO (1969)
GH SCHOOL: NOT STRICT ENOUGH (1965) YES (1969)	NO OPINION (1965, 1969)	ABOUT RIGHT & TOO STRICT (1965) NO (1969)
ADE SCHOOL: NOT STRICT ENOUGH (1965) YES (1969)	NO OPINION (1965, 1969)	ABOUT RIGHT & TOO STRICT (1965) NO (1969)

* Compiled from information in Gallup polls in the *Gallup Political Index,* No. 5, October 1965, and the *Gallup Opinion Index,* No. 49, July 1969, p. 19.

Figure 11

WILLINGNESS TO PROTEST THE SALE OF PORNOGRAPHY*

WOULD YOU BE WILLING TO JOIN A NEIGHBORHOOD GROUP
TO PROTEST THE SALE OF SUCH LITERATURE ON NEWSSTANDS?

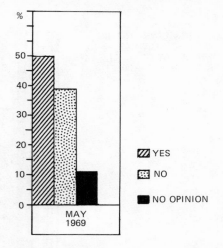

Figure 12

WILLINGNESS TO PROTEST THE SALE OF PORNOGRAPHY**
by Education

Would you be willing to join a neighborhood
group to protest the sale of such literature
on newsstands?

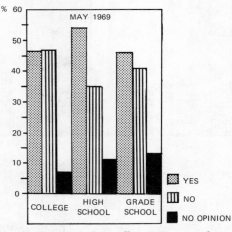

* Compiled from information in the *Gallup Opinion Index*, No. 49, July 1969, p. 21.
** *Ibid.*

than it was on the previous question. In this case the college-educated split just about even on whether they would join a group. Again, this is not a "hard-hat" issue, but one of the general public. This is evidenced by the answers to a question in May 1969 regarding obscene literature sent through the mail: ". . . would you like to see stricter state and local laws dealing with such literature, or not?" Of all adults, 85 percent said yes; 8 answered no; and 7 had no opinion. According to the education of the respondents, 79 percent of those with a college education said yes; 15 said no; and 6 had no opinion. Eighty-seven percent of those who were high-school educated said yes; 7 no; and 6 no opinion. Eighty-four percent of those with a grade-school education answered yes; 7 no; and 9 no opinion.* Most segments of the adult population object to this material. Overall, the data seem to imply that at least on these factors basic values on sexual morality have changed little over the years, and to the extent they have in the past half-decade, they often seem to have grown stronger among the adults.

2. RELIGIOUS PRACTICES

Attitudes on some other fundamental issues might also be worth noting. More people said they believed in God in 1968 (98 percent) than in 1944 (96 percent).** In December 1963, 63 percent said they prayed "frequently."*** Church attendance among adults has declined almost constantly, but gradually, over the past fifteen years from 49

Table 1

CHURCH ATTENDANCE: NATIONAL TREND, 1955–70****

1955	49%	1963	46%
1956	46	1964	45
1957	47	1965	44
1958	49	1966	44
1959	47	1967	45
1960	47	1968	43
1961	47	1969	42
1962	46	1970	42

* Ibid., p. 18.
** Gallup poll of 1968 in the *Gallup Opinion Index*, No. 44, February 1969, p. 15 and of 1944 in Hazel Erskine, "The Polls: Personal Religion," *Public Opinion Quarterly*, Vol. 29, No. 1 (Spring 1965), p. 145.
*** Gallup poll No. 681, December 1963, from Roper Opinion Research Center, Williams College, Williamstown, Massachusetts.
**** *Gallup Opinion Index*, No. 55, January 1970, p. 5, and No. 70, April 1971, p. 44.

Figure 13

CHURCH ATTENDANCE—NATIONAL*

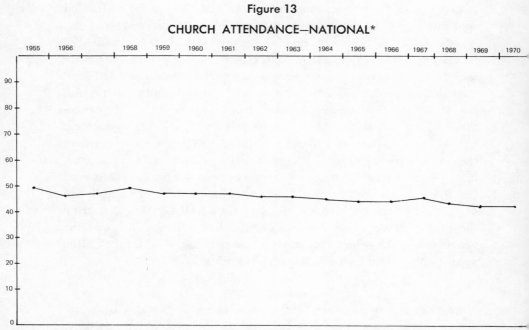

Figure 14

INFLUENCE OF RELIGION—NATIONAL*

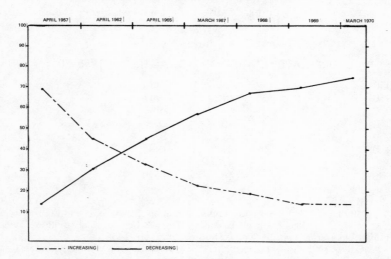

* *Gallup Opinion Index,* No. 44, February 1969, p. 8; No. 55, January 1970, p. 5; and No. 70, April 1971, p. 44.

percent who attended church during the week polled in 1955, to 42 percent in 1969 and 1970.

The feeling about the *influence* of religion, however, obviously showed a much more spectacular change over this time period, which might indicate some feeling on the part of the average citizen about the state of the country.*

Table 2

CHURCH ATTENDANCE
CHANGE BETWEEN 1958 AND 1969 AND 1970**

	1958	1969	1970	Point Change 1958–69	Point Change 1958–70
National	49%	42%	42%	− 7	− 7
Protestant	43	37	38	− 6	− 5
Catholic	74	63	60	−11	−14
Jewish	30	22	19	− 8	−11
21–29 years	48	33	32	−15	−16
30–49 years	51	45	45	− 6	− 6
50 and over	48	44	45	− 4	− 3

Table 3 gives a more detailed picture of those attending church by age, religious preference, education, income, region, etc.:

(A word about the categories listed above, and which will appear in all the Gallup poll results listed throughout this book: they represent only adults—later polls include 18- to 20-year olds. The three education levels mean that the adults listed under each of them have had some college, high-school or grade-school education. Persons with some college education outnumber those with only a grade-school education; those in the 21- to 29-year-old group have almost no members with only grade-school education. The largest percentage of this sample of adults, which is representative of the voting public, have had some high-school education.)

The fall-off in church attendance, particularly in recent years, is interesting to analyze, not only for the amount of the drop but because of who attended church and which religions experienced the greatest

---

* Parents obviously send their children to church; about 60 percent of high school students attend church regularly (see Figure 31), so one might assume they think the influence of religion is valuable, at least for children.

** *Gallup Opinion Index,* No. 55, January 1970, p. 5; *Gallup Opinion Index,* No. 70, April 1971, p. 44.

43

Table 3

CHURCH ATTENDANCE 1969 and 1970
(Emphasis by underlining added)

"Did you, yourself, happen to attend church in the last seven days?"

	1969*	1970**
NATIONAL	42%	42%
RELIGION		
Catholic	63	60
Protestant	37	38
Jewish	22	19
MAJOR PROTESTANT DENOMINATIONS		
Lutheran	38	43
Baptist	37	39
Presbyterian	34	34
Methodist	34	38
Episcopalian	29	29
SEX		
Men	38	38
Women	46	46
RACE		
White	42	42
Nonwhite	41	43
EDUCATION		
College	46	46
High School	42	41
Grade School	41	41
College Students		43***
AGE		
21–29 Years	33	32
30–49 Years	45	45
50 and over	44	45
REGION		
East	45	43
Midwest	46	47
South	40	44
West	35	33
INCOME		
$10,000 and over	43	44
$7,000–$9,999	43	42
$5,000–$6,999	43	40
$3,000–$4,999	42	41
Under $3,000	41	41
COMMUNITY SIZE		
1,000,000 and over	43	39
500,000–999,999	44	42
50,000–499,999	42	41
2,500–49,999	40	44
Under 2,500, Rural	43	44

* *Gallup Opinion Index,* No. 55, January 1970, p. 5.
** *Gallup Opinion Index,* No. 70, April 1971, p. 44.
*** Harris Poll, *Life* Magazine, January 18, 1971, p. 26.

drops. In 1970, more college-educated people were attending than any other education category (46 percent); an equal percentage of high-school educated and grade-school educated people were attending church (41 percent). The West registered the lowest attendance with 33 percent; the Midwest ranked the highest with 47; the East showed 43; the South had 44.

The drop in the adult Catholic church attendance from 1964 through 1970 has been large (from 71 percent to 60 percent) and constant. A 1970 poll indicated that 69 percent of the 15-to-21-year-old group (at least the lower end of which has a high church attendance record) found "liberalized attitudes and new forms of worship make church more interesting to young people."* But during this period of great liberalism in the American Catholic church, according to Gallup polls from 1964 to 1970, "the fall-off among Catholics during this six-year period has come about largely among those in their 20s."** Catholics make up about a quarter of that age bracket of the population, and the drop of 1 percent in that group as a whole from 1969 to 1970 could have been accounted for entirely by Catholics; their average drop-off for all age groups was 3 percent, and the 21 to 29 year olds had the highest dropout rate. Attendance among college students fell off 4 percent from 1968 and high school students showed about a 7 to 8 percent drop from 1965 to 1970.

As can be seen in Table 3, in 1970 the more fundamentalist religions—Baptist, Methodist, Lutheran—registered increases in church attendance; and the South (where the first two religions flourish) showed the greatest regional increase (4 percent). The 1 percent increase in the Midwest no doubt reflects the 5-point jump in church attendance among Lutherans and offsets the decline in Catholic attendance. Lutherans make up only about 7 percent of the population as a whole, but approximately 56 percent of them are in the Midwest.

Presbyterian and Episcopalian attendance remained the same; Judaism and Catholicism suffered all the loss. The 2 percent drop in church attendance in the East no doubt reflects to a large degree the 3-point drop in both Judaism and Catholicism. Catholics constitute about a quarter and Jews 3 percent of the national population; but 84 percent of the Jews and 48 percent of the Catholics live in the East. This be-

* Harris poll, *Life*, January 18, 1971, p. 26.
** *The Philadelphia Inquirer*, report on a Gallup poll, December 25, 1970, p. 14.

45

comes, therefore, a regional phenomenon; trying to decide whether it is basically regional or religious creates a chicken-and-egg problem. Although it might appear to be a religious difference, it could be regional, because the environments differ regardless of the religions that are grouped there. On the other hand, although there may be a great regional difference between the South and the East, for example, how great is that difference and why the sudden change between the two regions in the numbers of persons attending church? All things considered (including the possibility that this change is merely a small irregularity in a trend that will soon revert to "normal"), one must still note that the two religions making the greatest strides toward "sociological" and even somewhat "secularized" churches posted losses between the end of 1968 and the end of 1970. Furthermore, since Catholics and Jews probably accounted for almost all of the losses in the 21-to-29-year-old group, the strength of the fundamentalist religions probably remained about the same in that age bracket, or even increased.

At this point a question must be raised: Is the drop in church attendance among this country's young really due to insufficient speed in developing the liberal, sociological approach in religion? Certainly, if the fundamentalists have held their own, or even increased the numbers of 21 to 29 year olds and minors in their congregations, and the more liberal, sociologically-oriented churches have lost them—and if this trend continues—this question will have to be carefully examined.

To recapitulate: there has been no *drastic* change in the slow rate of decrease of church attendance over the past 15 years, and no change between 1969 and 1970 in the national percentage of churchgoers. From this one year of no change, we cannot, of course, say that this decreasing trend has bottomed out. The most interesting things to look at will probably revolve around the religions that have increased their church attendance despite the decreasing trend.

B. *Overall Feelings on Morals and Basic Values and Public Enforcement of Standards*

There are other factors besides the feeling that organized religion is losing its influence that seem to indicate that the general public may feel that today morals are declining. Figure 15 shows a

Figure 15

IS LIFE GETTING BETTER IN TERMS OF MORALS?*

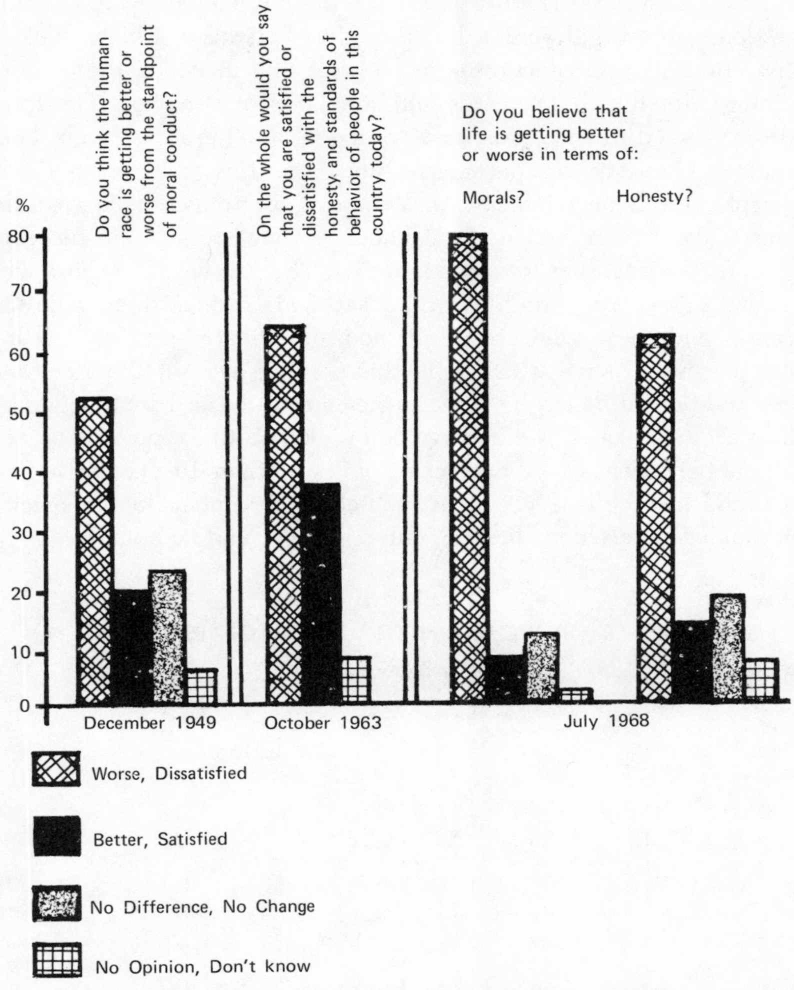

Do you think the human race is getting better or worse from the standpoint of moral conduct?

On the whole would you say that you are satisfied or dissatisfied with the honesty and standards of behavior of people in this country today?

Do you believe that life is getting better or worse in terms of:

Morals?   Honesty?

December 1949   October 1963   July 1968

Worse, Dissatisfied

Better, Satisfied

No Difference, No Change

No Opinion, Don't know

* Compiled from information in Gallup polls of December 1949 and October 1963, appearing in Hazel Erskine, "The Polls: Morality," *Public Opinion Quarterly*, 30 (Winter 1966–1967), pp. 669–670, and of July 1968 in the *Gallup Opinion Index*, No. 44, February 1969, pp. 47 and 48. In the report of the October 1963 poll, the "no opinion" response was assimilated with the satisfied, dissatisfied vote. The "no opinion" response was 8 percent, and we have added it here, making the total vote more than 100 percent. The polls of December 1949 and July 1968 were answered with "better" and "worse," that of October 1963 with "satisfied" and "dissatisfied." The December 1949 poll had "no difference" and "no opinion," July 1968 "no change" and "don't know."

"trend" in opinion, based on very few points; but it may be wrong to ignore what data we have that might indicate a general shift in opinion between 1949 and 1968. The double lines indicate that the questions are quite different, but they deal basically with the idea of satisfaction or dissatisfaction with the direction in which the country is going with regard to morals and standards of behavior. The third question, asked in 1968, was a two-pronged one, inquiring about both morals *and* honesty. It is perhaps fortunate that this particular question was split, for it may indicate that there is a stronger feeling in the country about morals than about honesty. Here morals, one suspects, are more likely to refer to sexual morality. The gap between those who feel that things are getting better, are satisfied, or think there is no difference, and those who are dissatisfied and think things are getting worse, seems to have widened in this period (at least the 1949 and 1968 questions are close enough in meaning to hazard such a guess). There are relatively few who have no opinion on this type of issue and the numbers seem to be decreasing. (Fewer than 10 percent at any time, and as of July 1968, approximately 5 percent.) On the specific question of morals alone in 1968, only 2 percent had no opinion.

Figure 16

IS LIFE BETTER OR WORSE IN TERMS OF MORALS, HONESTY?*

by Education

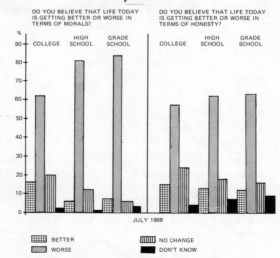

* Graph drawn from information in the *Gallup Opinion Index*, No. 39, September 1968, pp. 27, 28.

On the questions of morals and honesty, this belief of deterioration was strong and cut across all levels of education (see Figure 16).

Figure 17 covers a somewhat longer period with, again, too few points; but, nevertheless, there is some indication of how people have felt about public morals over the years. Again, the questions differ considerably, and the double lines indicate a great change in the type of question. This chart stresses questions about young people and may be important from the point of view of considering whether adults have always considered young persons to be "irresponsible." The total of those believing that standards were the same or better is greater than the percentage of those holding that things were worse. In fact, after World War II, one finds that those who felt that teen-agers behaved better than they (adults) did when they were teen-agers, exceeded by more than 10 percent those who thought they behaved worse. Questions about young people in 1948 and 1949 showed anything but a lack of appreciation for them by the older people. This may have reflected a feeling about the World War II veterans who had come home and were trying to make up for what the years of the war had cost them in education, on jobs, etc.; but, nonetheless, it showed that the older people were far from hostile to them. In fact, in the 1949 poll, those who felt that the youth of that period were better, as far as common sense was concerned, than the young 25 years before, registered 15 points ahead of those who felt they were worse. When those who felt they were the same were added to those who felt they were better, 66 percent of the population felt that these young people were better than, or at least equal to, those of 25 years before; only 28 percent thought they were worse.

There undoubtedly were many peaks and valleys between 1949 and 1965, when the question was asked about the sexual attitudes of teen-agers. The question in 1965 was, "Are their attitudes much different today than yours were?" rather than "Were they better or worse?" Some 62 percent felt they were different and only 29 thought they were the same. The only comparison that one can make here, of course, is between the bars indicating "same." Those who feel that the teen-agers are different could mean different "better" or different "worse." One has a feeling, however, when taking into account previous charts, that "different" is not necessarily "approved of" by most of the people who responded that way.

The value of this chart may lie in its variations of "pro" and "con" responses (as compared to those earlier charts and graphs that had

49

Figure 17

ADULT ATTITUDES TOWARD MORAL STANDARDS OF THE YOUNG*

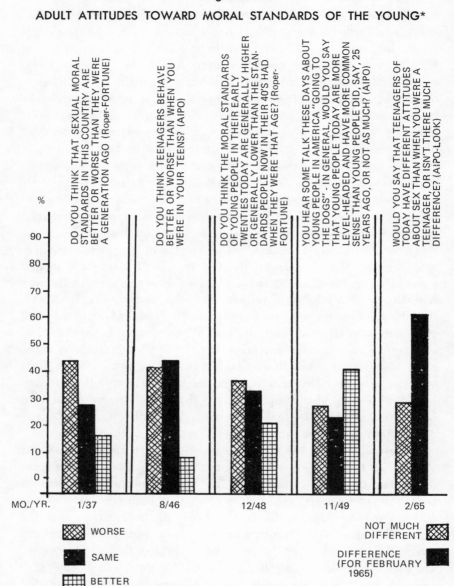

DO YOU THINK THAT SEXUAL MORAL STANDARDS IN THIS COUNTRY ARE BETTER OR WORSE THAN THEY WERE A GENERATION AGO (Roper-FORTUNE)

DO YOU THINK TEENAGERS BEHAVE BETTER OR WORSE THAN WHEN YOU WERE IN YOUR TEENS? (AIPO)

DO YOU THINK THE MORAL STANDARDS OF YOUNG PEOPLE IN THEIR EARLY TWENTIES TODAY ARE GENERALLY HIGHER OR GENERALLY LOWER THAN THE STANDARDS PEOPLE NOW IN THEIR 40'S HAD WHEN THEY WERE THAT AGE? (Roper-FORTUNE)

YOU HEAR SOME TALK THESE DAYS ABOUT YOUNG PEOPLE IN AMERICA "GOING TO THE DOGS" - IN GENERAL, WOULD YOU SAY THAT YOUNG PEOPLE TODAY ARE MORE LEVEL-HEADED AND HAVE MORE COMMON SENSE THAN YOUNG PEOPLE DID, SAY, 25 YEARS AGO, OR NOT AS MUCH? (AIPO)

WOULD YOU SAY THAT TEENAGERS OF TODAY HAVE DIFFERENT ATTITUDES ABOUT SEX THAN WHEN YOU WERE A TEENAGER, OR ISN'T THERE MUCH DIFFERENCE? (AIPO-LOOK)

MO./YR. 1/37   8/46   12/48   11/49   2/65

WORSE
SAME
BETTER

NOT MUCH DIFFERENT
DIFFERENCE (FOR FEBRUARY 1965)

* Compiled from information in Roper-*Fortune* Survey and Gallup opinion polls in Hazel Erskine, "The Polls: Morality," *Public Opinion Quarterly*, 30 (Winter 1966–1967), pp. 671, 675, 676.

distinct and often widely separated bands of pro and con opinion). This might cast some doubt on the idea of traditional disapproval of young persons by adults. It might further point out that today, unlike earlier times, the behavioral patterns of some younger persons alarm adults considerably.

It can be argued that some of the great discrepancies between earlier periods and the 1960s in the polls reflect public reaction to so much exposure given by the media to the behavior of the young (and not-so-young) "swingers" and not to the actual morals of youth. If this were so, the reaction could be to the publicity given to the morals of a small minority of youth rather than to an actual strong difference of opinion between age groups. Other polls seem to indicate that in regard to some of the basic moral issues, the opinions of age groups differ less than some seem to think. This may be a legitimate hypothesis, except perhaps for attitudes on premarital sexual relations, and parents do not depend only on TV or the movies to find out what children think.*

There is some evidence to indicate that the decisions of the Federal and state courts dealing with pornography in recent years have been very unpopular. Decisions, not only in the area of pornography, but in other matters affecting the family and children, have probably made substantial contributions to the opposition to "liberal" judges. Even the lively campaign against the conservative Judge Haynesworth failed to reduce significantly the large number of people who wanted conservative judges on the bench. According to the graph that follows, the percentage of people who wanted conservative judges was 51 in 1968 and 51 in 1969; with all the controversy, it dropped only to 49 in 1970. Conversely, those who wanted a liberal judge dropped from 30 percent in 1968 to 25 in 1969; and again, with all the publicity given to the nomination of Haynesworth, the desire for a liberal judge climbed only to 27 percent, while those with no opinion also rose to 26.

This "First Amendment issue" is interesting, for it is somewhat typical of the type of problem that parents face increasingly, and despite overwhelming opposition, smut apparently cannot be stopped. Interest in the opposite sex among youth, and, for that matter, persons

* There is some indication, however, that some of these movies strike a responsive chord among a minority of young people: 24 percent of persons 15 to 21 said they had seen a movie that reflected their own outlook on life, and of these twice as many named *Easy Rider* as any other; *Getting Straight* and *M*A*S*H* followed. (Harris poll in *Life*, January 8, 1971, p. 30.)

of all ages, has not decreased over the years. It has been, and always will be, a sure-fire source of income for a tiny minority of persons playing on such emotions. The difficulty today is that the restrictions against pornography that have been known heretofore, even in supposedly "loose" countries such as France, have disappeared in the United States in many cases. Clearly, adults of this country are concerned, at least about the difficulties that might arise among the younger set. Pornographic material may not adversely affect adults, but it could have harmful effects on "lifestyles" adopted by minors, primarily because of the typical inability of adolescents to differentiate between fact and fiction in literature, movies, etc.

Apparently the net result is that parents responsible for the morals and mental health of their children naturally react against the license enjoyed by producers of pornographic or erotic material.

Concern over the court system cannot be confined to the legalizing of pornography, however. Crime and disorders have caused much concern among the majority of the public. Most reforms brought about by Supreme Court rulings on the treatment of those apprehended by

Figure 18

NEW APPOINTMENTS TO SUPREME COURT*

National

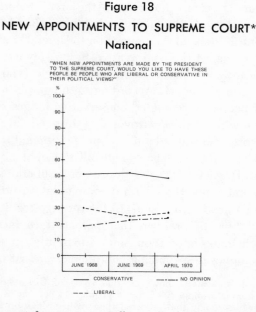

"WHEN NEW APPOINTMENTS ARE MADE BY THE PRESIDENT TO THE SUPREME COURT, WOULD YOU LIKE TO HAVE THESE PEOPLE BE PEOPLE WHO ARE LIBERAL OR CONSERVATIVE IN THEIR POLITICAL VIEWS?"

———— CONSERVATIVE —·—·— NO OPINION

– – – LIBERAL

* Compiled from information in Gallup polls in the *Gallup Opinion Index,* No. 49, July 1969, p. 15 and the *Gallup Opinion Index,* No. 59, May 1970, p. 10.

the police have resulted from the vital democratic principle of protection of individual rights. General public acceptance of these reforms, however, hardly indicates that the majority feels criminals receive "raw deals" or that protection from criminals is adequate. Only a tiny minority (2 percent) feels that our courts deal too harshly with criminals. In fact, during the past five years there seems to have been a significant trend toward the opinion that they are too lenient. Age and education do not significantly affect the percentage of these who feel that the courts are too harsh; it never exceeds 4 percent in any category. There is some variation in the feeling that they are not harsh enough, but opinion is uniformly overwhelming for this premise.

Much of our recent drama and literature, however, is more likely to reflect the point of view that could more easily be associated with the 2 percent who feel the courts are too harsh. These days one seldom sees a TV program or movie based on the idea that our law enforcement agencies and courts are too lenient on the criminal element. On the contrary, particularly if the criminal is of one of several sociological or ethnic groups, the victim is often not the "victim" of the

Figure 19

DO COURTS IN THIS AREA DEAL WITH CRIMINALS: TOO HARSHLY, NOT HARSHLY ENOUGH, ABOUT RIGHT?*

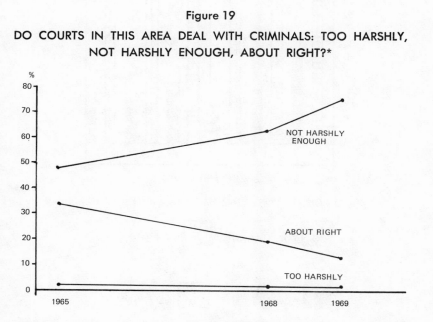

* Compiled from information in Gallup polls in the *Gallup Opinion Index*, No. 1, June 1965, p. 17, and the *Gallup Opinion Index*, No. 45, March 1969, p. 12.

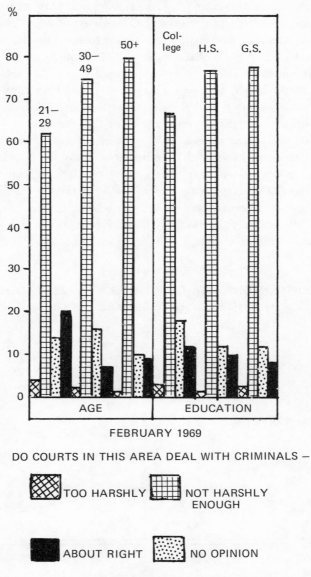

Figure 20

COURTS AND CRIMINALS*

by Age and Education

FEBRUARY 1969

DO COURTS IN THIS AREA DEAL WITH CRIMINALS —

TOO HARSHLY   NOT HARSHLY ENOUGH

ABOUT RIGHT   NO OPINION

* Compiled from information in the *Gallup Opinion Index*, No. 45, March 1969, p. 12.

story—the criminal is; and the police, courts, and "society" are the villains.

To the average citizen, this is not an objective picture. Furthermore, he knows that in real life the victim of the criminal act is often of the same sociological and ethnic group as the criminal, or at least lives in or near a locale of high violence and other crime. He also knows that the connection between poverty and other social problems is not a universal one. He may have come from a "tough" neighborhood himself and have lived when poverty (but not crime) was much more rampant than today, and the difference in living standards between the well-off and poor was, one feels, as much or even more pronounced—e.g., the Great Depression of the 1930s.* He is likely to know about youngsters not being too eager to encounter a policeman, but he

Table 4

CRIME AND ITS VICTIMS, BY RACE, 1970**

Race of Offender and Victim	Criminal Homicide	Aggravated Assault	Forcible Rape	Armed Robbery
Both Same Race	90%	90%	90%	51%
Black vs. Black	66	66	60	38
White vs. White	24	24	30	13
Black vs. White	6	8	10	47
White vs. Black	4	2	—	2

"Urban blacks are arrested eight to twenty times more often than whites for homicide, rape, aggravated assault and robbery."

The same data show that a black woman is six times more likely to be raped than a white woman.

SOURCE: Victim-offender survey made by task force on individual crimes of violence, an agency of the National Commission on the Causes and Prevention of Violence, 1969–70.

* As poverty increased during the Great Depression (after 1932), the combined rate of four major violent crimes (criminal homicide, forcible rape, robbery, and aggravated assault) declined, primarily due to the decline in the rate of the latter two crimes. The combined rate of three major property crimes (burglary, larceny $50 and over, and auto theft) also decreased during the Depression. After World War II the rates began to increase and by the time of the super-affluent sixties, the rates doubled in ten years, with the greatest increase occurring after 1965. *Crimes of Violence*, Vol. 11, A Staff Report Submitted to the National Commission on the Causes and Prevention of Violence by Donald J. Mulvihill and Melvin N. Tumin (December 1969), p. 54.

** *The New York Times*, September 8, 1970, p. 1.

also understands the difference between boyish pranks and viciousness. Furthermore, he recognizes the terror, particularly on the part of women, in these areas today. As Table 4 shows, the truly forgotten citizen is the Negro woman, particularly when one recognizes that many rapes go unreported in the South and in our northern, urban, Negro areas. Her lot is little better, if at all, in the North than in the South. The overwhelming majority of law-abiding Negro men, the husbands, fathers, sons and brothers of the terrified women, are also victims of the high crime rate and probably runners-up for the most-neglected-citizen award.

The high crime rate in Negro neighborhoods in the North probably was a factor in causing the weight of opinion among Negroes (48 percent to 30—22 no opinion) to jibe with the statement, "On a person-to-person, day-to-day basis, the South is a more livable place for blacks than any other place in the nation." (The breakdown of agreement and disagreement and no opinion on this statement among whites was identical with that of Negroes—see Table 18.)

When a society allows violence and lawlessness to increase, the non-affluent usually suffer most. All this is "known" by the "man in the street." He does not take kindly to sympathetic depictions of criminals as victims with little sympathy for the real victims, no matter who they are. Some say the reason for the greater concern about crime really

TABLE 5

A REAL PROBLEM IN THIS NEIGHBORHOOD—CRIME*

	Negroes	Whites
Breaking into houses	59%	48%
Drunkenness	54	21
Gambling	52	3
Drug use among youths	38	14
Purse snatchings	36	13
Prostitution	33	4
Knifings and Shootings	32	4
Muggings	17	4
Loan sharking	6	2
None or don't know	14	34

"Each crime was more troubling to upper-level Negroes than poor whites."

* Roper Research poll, Louisville, Kentucky, early 1970, as reported in Jean Heinig, "A Tale of Two Cities," *The Public Pulse*, April 1970. In a later chapter this study is referred to in greater detail.

comes from the increasing amount of crime spreading into white neighborhoods. This may be true; but in 1970, whites in at least one city, Louisville, Kentucky, rated crime sixth (13 percent voting for it) on the list of neighborhood problems, while three times as many Negroes (39 percent) placed it *third*. Significantly, juvenile delinquency, a quasi-lawlessness behavioral problem, was rated second by Negroes (41 percent) and fifth by whites (14 percent). The lesser degree of concern about crime among whites in Louisville may or may not reflect a nationwide outlook, but a breakdown of the types of crime for Louisville shows a distinctly higher level of risk and violence for Negroes than whites.

Disturbed as he is about crime, the average citizen seems to be aware of the important matter of *degree* of transgression, and apparently realizes that this changes somewhat with circumstances. Public reaction to shoplifting, for instance, by the underprivileged (that accounts for a considerable amount of money, which is made up by higher prices for customers) is nothing like the reaction to violence, lawlessness, and rowdyism by those whom the public apparently considers irresponsible university students. The public apparently has the same reaction to "hippies" (students and nonstudents) from upper-middle-class backgrounds. Too many people have come from real poverty to condone these "imitation-poor." Even today, too many workingmen must "moonlight" and send their wives to work to keep a home for their children and pay ever-increasing taxes. The fact that these taxes directly and indirectly subsidize college students by keeping tuitions down, and even subsidize the "street people" offspring of the affluent through various welfare programs, is a legitimate reason for concern. They also look on education as a vital method of upward mobility that must run smoothly. Persons at all levels of income and education and in every region have been against modern student disorders. At least one conclusion that might be drawn from this last point, however, is apparently contested by some. One group states that before 1970 "dissident students" were regarded favorably by the public. "The year 1970 was different . . . suddenly the climate changed. No longer were dissident students identified by the public as young idealists . . ."[*] This pre-1970 student identity could be true, but insofar as the public before 1970 connected the "dissident students" with

[*] *Youth and the Establishment*, Daniel Yankelovich, Inc., for The JDR 3rd Fund, Inc., New York, N.Y. (1971), p. 71.

campus disorders, this premise may be questionable. In the first half of 1969—incidentally, long before Vice President Agnew made his first speech on the subject—a Gallup survey came up with the following results:

Table 6

STUDENT DISORDERS*

(Emphasis by underlining added)

"In general, would you like to see college administrations take a stronger stand on student disorders, or not?"

	EARLY JUNE		
	Yes	No	No Opinion
NATIONAL	94%	3%	3%
SEX			
Men	94	4	2
Women	93	2	5
RACE			
White	95	2	3
Nonwhite	x	x	x
EDUCATION			
College	91	7	2
High School	95	2	3
Grade School	93	1	6
OCCUPATION			
Professional and Business	94	4	2
White Collar	94	4	2
Farmers	97	2	1
Manual	94	2	4
AGE**			
21–29 Years	89	7	4
30–49 Years	95	1	4
50 and over	94	3	3
RELIGION			
Protestant	96	1	3
Catholic	94	2	4
Jewish	x	x	x
POLITICS			
Republican	96	2	2
Democrat	93	3	4
Independent	93	4	3

* *Gallup Opinion Index,* No. 49, July 1969, p. 26.

** In late 1970 a poll was published in the February issue of *Seventeen Magazine* (p. 127) that covered this subject. Of the 15 to 21 year olds (students and nonstudents) polled 43 percent said the college administrations had not been strict enough, 28 percent felt they had acted about right and 29 percent said they had been too repressive.

Table 6 (continued)

REGION			
East	90	6	4
Midwest	95	1	4
South	96	2	2
West	96	2	2
INCOME			
$10,000 and over	94	5	1
$ 7,000 and over	95	4	1
$ 5,000–$6,999	94	2	4
$ 3,000–$4,999	93	3	4
Under $3,000	90	2	8
COMMUNITY SIZE			
1,000,000 and over	92	3	5
500,000 and over	91	5	4
50,000–499,999	93	4	3
2,500–49,999	96	1	3
Under 2,500, Rural	96	2	2

There is considerable evidence that indicates that the average man is little affected by the publicity accorded the "New Left" activists. The way he felt about the disturbances at the Democratic Convention in Chicago in 1968 might be a good example of this. At the time of the convention almost every national TV network commentator was sympathetic to the "children" who "were being beaten by police," unfriendly to Mayor Daley of Chicago and no booster of either the police or the National Guard. Forty-nine police were hospitalized and 192 "injured"—122 by "thrown objects"; 13 had their "eyes burned by unknown chemicals." One-hundred-and-one demonstrators were hospitalized, and an "unknown number" were injured,* but we can surmise that more demonstrators than police were "injured." There were few reports, if any, of the injured policemen. But there was heavy TV coverage of the fallen, bleeding demonstrators. Yet, the average American apparently did not side with the commentators. Perhaps he saw that many of the violent "children" had to be older than the apprentices and young journeymen "on the job" with him. He also probably looked on the convention as an essential part of the process in electing a president; it had to be done. A poll taken immediately after the event revealed his sentiments:

* *Rights in Conflict,* A report submitted by Daniel Walker to the National Commission on the Causes and Prevention of Violence (New York: Bantam Books, 1968), pp. 351–354.

Table 7

NATIONWIDE POLL ON CHICAGO POLICE ACTIVITIES
DURING CONVENTION*

71.4 percent said security measures were justified.

48.3 percent said that demonstrations were "organized to disrupt the convention and create riot conditions. . . "

"Chicago police and National Guardsmen are using excessive force in suppressing these demonstrations."

Agree	Disagree	No Opinion
21.3%	56.8%	21.9%

"What kind of a job is Mayor Daley of Chicago doing?"

Good Job	Poor Job	No Opinion
61.7%	18.3%	20%

93.5 percent of those polled had seen some Chicago demonstrations on television or had read or heard about them.

There are other indications of a growing concern over lawlessness. Recently the trend toward the abolition of the death penalty, which increased in this country throughout the 1950s and early 1960s, seems to have been reversed. Whether this is a significant reversal remains to be seen; but it is difficult to ignore this indicator in light of the previous ones we have shown in which the public seems to have stiffened in its attitudes toward those things affecting its basic safety and way of life.

Although the seeming about face on the death penalty probably reflects public reaction to the rising crime rate, as mentioned earlier, Americans have maintained the concept of *degrees* of things—or adhere to a gradualist position. This applies to justice and to security. The average citizen tends to believe that absolute justice without mercy can be brutal, while internal security without freedom is death to the spirit.

In general, the "average" American dislikes sudden change in any direction and rejects candidates who espouse "extremist" programs—that is, programs that radically depart from the consensus of the day. On the other hand, some surveys which asked about instituting or maintaining certain practices directly or indirectly guaranteed by the Bill of Rights sometimes showed the public, in general, opposed to instituting

* *New York Times,* August 31, 1968, p. 10. The poll of 1,194 persons was conducted by Sindlinger and Co., Inc., of Norwood, Pa. by long-distance telephone on one day, "using a random sample selected by computer, with a 2.5 percent margin of statistical error."

or maintaining such practices. However, there are other indications that on issues of specific rights of individuals in concrete cases, regardless of how wrong the public thinks these persons (including suspected criminals) may be, and even if the system pays a considerable price, the public tends to favor individuals.

In a Harris survey on the fairness of the "Chicago 7" trial of the defendants arrested in connection with the disturbances of the 1968 Democratic convention, 51 percent of the public said that it had followed the trial. This included higher proportions of the better-educated and more affluent who are usually more tolerant of nonconformist personal behavior than the rank-and-file Americans. These persons were then asked: "Taking everything into consideration, do you think the defendants in the 'Chicago 7' case received a fair trial or not?"

	Informed Public
Received a fair trial	71%
Not a fair trial	19
Not sure	10

Figure 21

DEATH PENALTY FOR PERSONS CONVICTED OF MURDER*
National

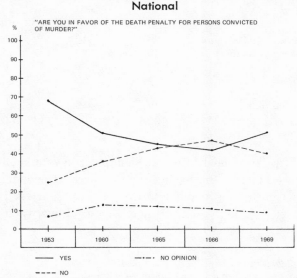

* Compiled from information in Gallup polls in the *Gallup Opinion Index,* No. 45, March 1969, p. 15.

But perhaps more significant: "Although public opinion clearly disfavored the way the 'Chicago 7' defendants and their lawyers conducted themselves in court, a sizable majority, or better than seven in ten, rejected the proposition that 'protesters such as the "Chicago 7" are revolutionaries who want to destroy the system and shouldn't be given the right to a trial.' "* In the public's mind, apparently even revolutionaries dedicated to destroying the system do not forfeit their right to a trial.**

In Table 8, there seems to be evidence that the concept of degrees of justice fitting the crime is more predominant than a blanked "vengeance" approach to those convicted. The respondents, a standard sample of all the population, were given several fixed choices and asked to choose among them. Because of this, even though there is room for "other responses," respondents seemed to pick the standard choices. The *ranking* of the punishment according to the severity of the crime, therefore, seems to be more important than actual penalties.

Table 8

PUNISHMENT FOR HIJACKING, BOMBING AND STARTING A RIOT***

National

	Hijacking	Bombing	Starting Riot
Less than 10 years	26%	12%	43%
10 years or more	39	43	34
Life	16	29	6
Death	4	6	2
Other responses	5	4	5
No opinion	10	6	10
	100%	100%	100%

On issues of laws and law enforcement that have a significant and direct effect on family life, feeling is particularly strong. In late 1970, about 86 percent of the population over 21 opposed legalizing marijuana. In 1969, those opposed (84 percent) were overwhelming in all age and income brackets.

* *Philadelphia Inquirer,* April 27, 1970, p. 10.
** See also Figure 25 and the text prior to it for the lack of approval of wiretapping, apparently even of the telephones of "radicals."
*** *Gallup Opinion Index,* No. 59, May 1970, p. 13.

Table 9

MARIJUANA

"Do you think the use of marijuana should be made legal or not?"

	October 1969* Should	October 1969* Should Not	October 1969* No Opinion	October 1970** Should	October 1970** Should Not
NATIONAL	12%	84%	4%	14%	86%
SEX					
Men	14	81	5		
Women	10	86	4		
RACE					
White	12	84	4		
Nonwhite	15	79	6		
EDUCATION					
College	23	72	5		
High School	10	86	4		
Grade School	6	91	3		
OCCUPATION					
Professional and Business	18	77	5		
White Collar	22	76	2		
Farmers	5	93	2		
Manual	10	85	5		
AGE					
21–29 Years	26	69	5		
30–49 Years	12	83	5		
50 and over	6	91	3		
RELIGION					
Protestant	8	88	4		
Catholic	12	83	5		
Jewish	—	—	—		
POLITICS					
Republican	9	87	4		
Democrat	12	84	4		
Independent	14	82	4		
REGION					
East	16	78	6	17	83
Midwest	9	87	4	8	92
South	7	89	4	13	87
West	17	80	3	17	83
INCOME					
$15,000 and over	17	78	5		
$10,000–$14,999	12	84	4		
$7,000–$9,999	13	82	5		
$5,000–$6,999	13	83	4		
$3,000–$4,999	11	86	3		
Under $3,000	5	89	6		
COMMUNITY SIZE					
1,000,000 and over	19	76	5		
500,000–999,999	17	76	7		
50,000–499,999	12	84	4		
2,500–49,999	7	91	2		
Under 2,500, Rural	7	89	4		

* *Gallup Opinion Index*, No. 53, November 1969, p. 8.

** *Gallup Opinion Index*, No. 65, November 1970, p. 25. This poll results from the new referendum method developed by Gallup, rather than the standard 1,500-sample method.

In the same survey, 9 percent of the college-educated, 3 of the high school-educated and 1 of the grade school-educated had "happened to try" marijuana. Further, in answer to the question, *would* they try a marijuana cigarette, 8 percent of those who had gone to college, 4 of those who were high school-educated, and 2 of those who were grade school-educated said they would.* The greater objection to the use of marijuana by the less well-educated might be construed to be the "fear of the unknown"; but a poll on outlawing liquor in 1966 showed a similar pattern: a law "forbidding the sale of all beer, wine and liquor throughout the nation" was favored by 14 percent and opposed by 83 percent of all college-educated adults; favored by 19 and opposed by 76 of those with a high-school education; favored by 28 and opposed by 69 of those with a grade-school education. The last group had the highest number of "tee-totalers"—almost a half compared to almost a third of the high school-educated people and a quarter of those with some college education.**

The reasons for the last figures are not obvious. Regional differences have an impact here; in the South, where fundamentalist Protestants are more prevalent, there may be a higher percentage of tee-totalers. Coincidentally, there may also be more people with a lower level of education in the South. But this is an inadequate explanation: most people with only a grade-school education are older, even in the South; and there are just not enough old Southerners to account for all the tee-totalers. It is also difficult to argue that the greater abstinence stems from the fear of drunkenness as "the curse of the lower classes." In the same survey the highest number of those who had "trouble in the family" because of liquor were among the college educated—14 percent.

The outlook on the use of marijuana in high schools showed college persons, traditionally the most liberal, having the highest perception of marijuana use.

The better educated might simply be better informed on the extensiveness of marijuana use, but it would be surprising if they had a better feel for this than persons in central-city slums. On the other hand, the college educated are generally more likely to be concentrated in suburbs, near big cities where the problem is severe; those at other education levels are likely to be distributed evenly across the country. This does not explain the slightly more liberal attitude of the

* *Gallup Opinion Index*, No. 53, November 1969, pp. 8–11.
** *Gallup Opinion Index*, No. 9, February 1966, pp. 18–20.

Figure 22

USE OF MARIJUANA IN LOCAL HIGH SCHOOL*
by Education

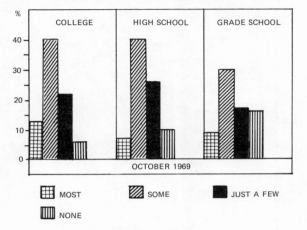

"HERE IS A QUESTION ABOUT THE USE OF MARIJUANA BY
HIGH SCHOOL STUDENTS IN YOUR COMMUNITY: WOULD YOU
SAY IT IS USED BY MOST HIGH SCHOOL STUDENTS IN YOUR
COMMUNITY, SOME, JUST A FEW, OR NONE?"

⊞ MOST   ◪ SOME   ■ JUST A FEW

▥ NONE

better educated on drug and alcohol use. The slightly greater problem they have with alcohol in part probably simply reflects the fact that there are fewer abstainers among this group.

What might be evident here, however, is fear for the family by the less secure groups. Those with a better education usually make more money, live in better neighborhoods, can take more chances and have more to fall back on if something goes wrong. This is perhaps best illustrated by the responses to a question on "law and order" asked in 1965:** "Suppose an innocent person is killed by a criminal—do you think the state should make financial provisions for the victim's family?" Forty percent of the college-educated adults voted yes, compared to an affirmative 61 percent of the high school-educated and 77 of grade school-educated adults. This vote could, of course, be due to the traditional opposition of the affluent college-educated to factors that lead to higher taxes, as well as the less well-educated being more likely to live in areas of higher violence; but one continues to find opinions on adequacy of laws (and other issues) that seem to indicate concern

* *Gallup Opinion Index*, No. 53, November 1969, p. 120.
** *Gallup Political Index*, No. 5, October 1965, p. 21.

Figure 23

DIVORCE LAWS—NATIONAL*

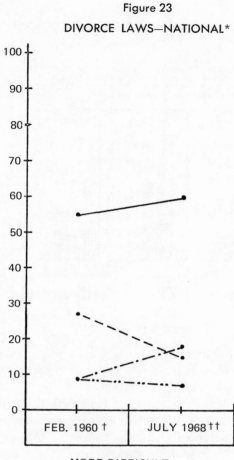

FEB. 1960 †   JULY 1968 ††

——— MORE DIFFICULT

– – – ARE NOW (1960); STAY AS IT IS (1968)

–·–· EASIER

–··– NO OPINION

† 1960: SHOULD DIVORCE BE MADE MORE DIFFICULT TO
GET, EASIER TO GET, OR SHOULD THINGS BE LEFT
AS THEY ARE NOW?

†† 1968: SHOULD DIVORCE IN THIS COUNTRY BE EASIER OR
MORE DIFFICULT TO OBTAIN THAN IT IS NOW?

* Gallup poll No. 624, February 1960, from the Roper Opinion Research Center, Williamstown, Massachusetts, and the *Gallup Opinion Index*, No. 41, November 1968, p. 11.

for the family, particularly among the less well-educated and less affluent groups.

Most people continue to feel that divorce laws make getting a divorce too easy, and the numbers who feel this way are actually increasing. But the size of the minority which thinks that a divorce should be easier to get is also increasing.

Today, the generally held idea is that because of the legal fees involved, divorce laws discriminate against the less affluent (the less well-educated). Recently, there has also been an increase in the number of grade school educated adults who feel a divorce should be easier to get. Nevertheless, in 1968 the less well-educated registered the greatest support for making divorce more difficult.

C. *The Availability and Importance of the Majority Opinion*

One of the major problems in discussing public opinion is how not to give the impression that what the majority wants is automatically right. There are also the questions of what the details of that opinion

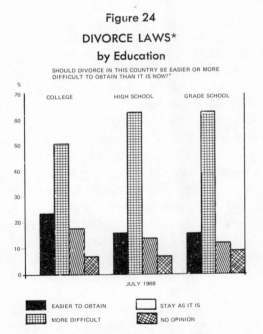

Figure 24

DIVORCE LAWS*

by Education

SHOULD DIVORCE IN THIS COUNTRY BE EASIER OR MORE DIFFICULT TO OBTAIN THAN IT IS NOW?*

COLLEGE   HIGH SCHOOL   GRADE SCHOOL

JULY 1968

EASIER TO OBTAIN   STAY AS IT IS
MORE DIFFICULT   NO OPINION

* *Gallup Opinion Index,* No. 41, November 1968, p. 11.

67

really are and, even then, whose opinion we should heed. If we take only one group's record on being right as a criterion, then, in implementing a program, we must listen to the one that "guessed" correctly most often in the past. If this happens to be a minority of the population, we may have to buck the majority in implementing the program and this can be very difficult; but if this minority were again right (and assuming we have not overlooked side effects that sometimes cause greater damage than the problem we are solving), in retrospect we look good and public support will swing over to the decision. If we choose to ignore the "right" minority opinion and go along with the "wrong" majority opinion, we may be in trouble later; but the "implementation" phase will be much easier.

If, on the other hand, the majority itself has a "track record" not outlandishly inferior to any given minority "advisory" group, it is very unwise to dismiss its desires summarily. One should at least be able to understand its position; for here we not only have all the problems of implementing programs in the face of majority opposition, but we may also be wrong, or at least not demonstrably right.

The possibility of this latter problem is the one that will be addressed. As has been emphasized, a far from paranoid population could reasonably claim that many people in recent years have overlooked the long-held views of most Americans on certain issues and have misinterpreted recent trends because of this oversight. These same people also seem to have ignored—or at least given inadequate attention to—reasonable and appropriate arguments against programs that affect large portions of the population. If true, this is not good for many reasons, not all of them having to do with the merits of the programs in question. Prestigious men should not look bad on public issues. The news media should not look too uninformed, particularly on matters that the average citizen thinks he can check. This leads to a "credibility gap" between the media and the public, and this, in turn, tends to reduce the chances for maintaining a well-informed populace, one of the bases for a working democracy. Proponents of legislation and programs should know arguments (particularly rather logical arguments) that differ from their own and that are held by a majority of the population, or people trusted by the majority. The majority will not be convinced that programs are right or should be supported if its arguments are ignored. Finally, of course, the majority might really *be* right and, if these arguments are listened to, the minority might even change *its* mind.

The problem is not solved by simple lip-service to majority opinions or one-sided presentations of them. Accuracy and the amount of attention given issues and points of view the majority thinks are important, as well as the format of articles and programs in the media, can make a significant difference. Although more of this was done in 1970 and 1971, many dissenting arguments are still not adequately presented. The following sections do not pretend even to scratch the surface of the still largely unpublished story of the "loyal majority opposition." The specific issues and points of view cited (as are the foregoing data) are only examples of factors that can greatly influence policy decisions. Hopefully, these examples will stimulate further research for certain viewpoints when policy decisions come up in the future. Almost no effort has been made in this section to discuss the points of view that differ from those of this "majority opposition." The intent of this effort is to examine the interest of a "majority opposition" that may still feel it is largely ignored when decisions are made.

D. *Issues, Policies and Laws vs. Real Issues, "Code Words" and Motivations*

A major question has been—and to some extent remains—what motivates this majority? For example, there was—and perhaps still is —a fashionable impression, held to varying degrees by some in this country, that many interests of the majority are based on rather undesirable and even indirectly, dangerous habits that probably should be discouraged. Both charges may have some factual basis, at least among a minority of the majority. It could be argued, however, that these charges have been—and perhaps are still—overemphasized in the national press and electronic media, and too little attention has been focused on other responsible points of view that the average citizen considers important.

In the late 1960s, for example, many Americans felt that the emphasis on law enforcement, discussed earlier, was not straightforward. Others asserted that "law and order" were shorthand terms—"code words"—for the suppression of Negroes. Similar statements were made on other equally broad issues. Perhaps the best way to examine this stereotyping is to select and discuss several of the most provocative positions (from the point of view of many in academia, the media, and even the government) on recent issues, proposed legislation, and regulations that affect vast numbers of the population. Some dissenting positions were often attributed to bigotry or inbred violence, even unhealthy sexual drives. Were there other contributing factors, different points of view and/or possible reasonable recommendations in support of even these most provocative positions? If so, let us judge if these points were also adequately considered at the times of the controversies, and even how many of these positions, directly concerned with the desires and sometimes the peace of mind of many people, are generally known today.

1. THE 1968 GUN LAW

Although thousands of articles and editorials were written on the proposed 1968 gun law, many gun owners claimed that most national press, TV and radio coverage of the objections to the proposed legislation was woefully inadequate. In 1967, nearly three-fourths of the public (probably including most of those who live in households where there are guns) favored requiring a police permit to *purchase* a gun.

Table 10

FIREARM CONTROLS*

"Would you favor or oppose a law which would require a person to obtain a police permit before he or she could buy a gun?"

	Favor	August 1967 Oppose	No Opinion
NATIONAL	73%	24%	3%
SEX			
Men	63	33	4
Women	81	16	3
RACE			
White	73	24	3
Nonwhite	x	x	x
EDUCATION			
College	72	26	2
High School	73	24	3
Grade School	73	21	6
OCCUPATION			
Professional and Business	75	24	1
White Collar	74	23	3
Farmers	65	29	6
Manual	72	24	4

70

Table 10 (continued)

AGE

21–29 Years	69	29	2
30–49 Years	73	25	2
50 and over	74	21	5

RELIGION

Protestant	70	26	4
Catholic	82	16	2
Jewish	x	x	x

POLITICS

Republican	73	24	3
Democrat	76	20	4
Independent	68	30	2

REGION

East	82	15	3
Midwest	74	24	2
South	66	28	6
West	66	32	2

INCOME

$10,000 and over	73	25	2
$7,000 and over	72	25	3
$5,000–$6,999	75	23	2
$3,000–$4,999	73	23	4
Under $3,000	73	20	7

COMMUNITY SIZE

1,000,000 and over	81	16	3
500,000 and over	78	19	3
50,000–499,999	75	21	4
2,500–49,999	78	20	2
Under 2,500, Rural	64	32	4

It was clear, however, that a similar majority was against forbidding their use, even by persons under 18 years of age. They did not object to strict restrictions on their use by youngsters, though; perhaps only for certain specific purposes, under regulations such as those applying to hunters under 16 in many states, where these teen-agers may not hunt unless accompanied by a parent or other adult taking the parent's place.

What is clear, of course, is that all citizens are against the criminal use of guns, and apparently in 1967 better than four in five favored registration of pistol owners. Furthermore, most gun owners probably do not strongly oppose a registration process for handguns (and perhaps even rifles and shotguns) if this ownership is looked on as a right of a law-abiding citizen (as is the ownership of an automobile)

° *Gallup Opinion Index*, No. 27, September 1967, p. 17.

Table 11

FIREARM CONTROLS*

"Which of these three plans would you prefer for the use of guns by persons under the age of 18—forbid their use completely, put strict restrictions on their use, or continue as at present with few regulations?"

	Forbid	*Strict Restrictions*	*Continue As Now*	*No Opinion*
NATIONAL	31%	53%	14%	2%
SEX				
Men	27	51	20	2
Women	34	55	9	2
RACE				
White	29	56	14	1
Nonwhite	x	x	x	x
EDUCATION				
College	19	68	12	1
High School	30	52	16	2
Grade School	39	44	14	3
OCCUPATION				
Professional and				
Business	21	66	12	1
White Collar	31	60	9	—
Farmers	13	60	25	2
Manual	36	48	14	2
RELIGION				
Protestant	27	55	16	2
Catholic	37	51	11	1
Jewish	x	x	x	x
POLITICS				
Republican	26	58	15	1
Democrat	36	51	11	2
Independent	25	55	19	1
REGION				
East	43	46	10	1
Midwest	21	62	16	1
South	31	51	15	3
West	25	56	18	1
INCOME				
10,000 and over	23	65	11	1
$7,000 and over	23	62	14	1
$5,000–$6,999	32	54	13	1
$3,000–$4,999	38	46	14	2
Under $3,000	38	42	16	4
COMMUNITY SIZE				
1,000,000 and over	46	43	9	2
500,000 and over	43	46	10	1
50,000–499,999	34	52	11	3
2,500–49,999	29	55	15	1
Under 2,500, Rural	17	61	20	2

* Ibid., p. 18.

that registration does not hamper or endanger.* (Pistol ownership is a somewhat different proposition from long gun ownership, which covers most sporting arms. Many pistols are war souvenirs, target and even hunting weapons, but many are bought and kept for "protection," most are concealable, and they often can be kept handier to scenes of spontaneous violence.)

Regardless of how one feels about the 1968 law, however, the possible opposing arguments to a bill that might affect one or more members of the majority of families in the country (with a much larger percent outside the large cities) may be interesting to examine.**

Hunters (over 20 million of them) and their families may get annoyed when they think someone is implying that they regard their sporting arms as weapons with which to kill people, and may not like to be treated as what might appear to many of them to be odd persons or potential criminals. The millions of other gun owners (target shooters and just plain "plinkers" with 22-caliber rifles) and their families may feel the same. Implementation of the original version of the 1968 gun law would have instituted practices (as we shall see) that might have led to such connotations. Nor was the discussion of the issue in the media reassuring on this point.

One can recall that gun owners were often depicted as members of a "powerful lobby" (by the not-exactly-helpless big TV networks and national newspapers, which saw nothing wrong with citizens petitioning their congressmen on other issues) and were sometimes seen as violent and even fanatical. "Intellectuals" and media people discussed

* A survey by telephone of 442 persons on the day Senator Robert Kennedy was shot showed the two top requirements in answer to the question, "What steps do you think should be taken to prevent such violence in the future?" to be:
  1. Stricter gun laws (laws to keep guns out of the hands of criminals, the mentally disturbed, minors).
  2. Stricter law enforcement (including more police, less leniency on the parts of courts).
This was an emotional period and the survey was smaller and no doubt less scientific than usual, but the continuing mood of the public was probably not that distorted. In 1938, 84 percent of the public favored "a law requiring all owners of pistols and revolvers [as compared to the normal hunting 'long-guns,' rifles and shotguns] to register with the government"; in 1967, 85 percent favored such a law. (Gallup Opinion Index, July 1968, pp. 6–7.) With perhaps a majority of adult males owning guns of some type (see below), in order to have 85 percent of adults favor such a law, a majority of gun owners probably would have to favor registration of handgun owners.
** A Louis Harris survey reported that "the number of homes in which occupants said they owned guns had reached 51 percent." The highest percentage of gun owners were found in rural areas (78 percent). (New York Times, April 23, 1968, p. 30.)

the sexual and psychological aspects of the identification with and the "need" for a gun.* Such TV fare must have sounded strange and unreal to hunters trying to relax before the "tube" with a can of beer, after a hard eight or even twelve hours of work. In reality, hunters seem to put as little stress on guns per se as fishermen put on rods, or as sometime amateur ball players put on bats. For example, they know much about "game cycles," breeds of dogs, the best weather and places in which to hunt, but in general they are usually much less well informed on guns and ballistics. They seem likely to be able to tell you all about their partner's dog, but many apparently cannot even tell you the make of their partner's gun.

As indicated above, most gun owners probably do not object to the simple registration of their firearms with the local police, if for no other reason than to identify them if they are stolen or lost and recovered. Nor, one feels, do most object to giving their name, address, and physical description upon purchase of a firearm. This has long been standard practice for those purchasing hunting licenses, just as with driving licenses. Apparently (from the polls) many have no objection to getting a permit to buy a gun (like a permit to drive an automobile) from the police. These activities are "reasonable" and are done in conjunction with their right to own and (under quite restricted, but generally accepted, circumstances) bear arms. Some, however, feared the eventual loss of their guns and of the right to own them,**

* Nor has this attitude completely disappeared. As late as mid-February 1971, on the "Today Show," Hugh Downs and Roger Caras discussed the "sexual" significance of the gun to gun owners. Hunters as a group apparently do not score well on TV. Another program, "The American Sportsman," which was formerly a show about fishing and hunting, provided some regular entertainment for hunters (and non-hunters) and gave some balance to the picture by depicting hunters as normal men who did not brutally mow down herds, flocks and gaggles of cowering game. Of all the mail the show received, only 8 percent of the people protested against the "slaughter" on the show. However, despite the fact that it was "one of the favorite winter sports shows on television," the anti-hunting people apparently got to the sponsors and it was turned from largely a hunting show into one largely about "ecology." (TV Guide, February 20–26, 1971, pp. 17 and 18.) Although fishing is still consistently seen on it, hunting now is less often depicted. The likes of 92 percent of those who wrote in were inadequate to maintain the program's content.

** These gun owners fear that registration will lead to restrictive taxation (as it has in some countries) or even confiscation. The attitudes of some proponents of the original 1968 legislation, clearly stated on TV (that no guns should be in the hands of private citizens), together with some pro-gun-control written material (even some titles were provocative, e.g., Carl Bakal, No Right to Bear Arms [2nd ed.; New York: Paperback Library, 1968]), did nothing to remove this argument from the discussions.

74

and others disliked the excessive difficulty involved in owning arms under the new law. Some questioned the effectiveness of the law in fighting crime.

Some hunters feared for their sport. Hunters (who are concentrated primarily in rural and suburban areas, away from the TV and radio antennae, the large newspaper offices and many of those who produce and disseminate their material) apparently look on hunting not only as an activity with "the boys," but a *family* sport. Adolescent boys can and do act like men, with all the responsibilities of adult hunters, in the company of their fathers and older brothers. Here is active proof of growing up with real actions (hunters could point out that a boy cannot be "subjective" about an exploding grouse, the whereabouts of his partners or even a valuable hunting dog in the deep woods), under the eyes of experienced, "loving, concerned adults"—family men.

Hunters claim they are great conservationists, pointing out that they alone pay (through license fees) for much of the public land available to all, as well as for the cover and feed for game and non-game birds and animals alike. These fees pay for the restoration of wildlife gone for decades, such as the wild turkey and elk in the East, for the benefit of all. They annually pay for the right to "harvest" the excess animals (supposedly an essential job that, if undertaken by paid government hunters, would cost the taxpayers many millions of dollars); they thus, hunters claim, help maintain healthy animal populations, some of which (such as the deer) match or exceed that of the colonial days, despite the increased human population.* These points may or may not be relevant, but they could be part of the "defense" in the hunting-anti-hunting debate that stems in part from the "gun debate."

Assuming that only part of the above is true and relevant, and assuming that some gun-control measure could be proven essential, any logical objections to a specific bill by a growing percentage of the law-abiding population would seem worth considering. But many hunters claimed very little informed, reasonable coverage of their position was given in the national press and the network TV and radio. This may have lent some credence to that lesser number of hunters who fear for their sport.

* See "Thanks to the Hunter" and "Hunters and Conservationists Share Goals," in *National Wildlife* (magazine of the National Wildlife Federation), October-November 1971, pp. 17–19, for an indication of hunters' attitudes on guns, this family sport and conservation, and the position of the National Audubon Society, etc., on hunting.

What is more surprising, however, is that there *were* respectable arguments the liberal, intellectual non-gunowners could have made that, while recognizing the almost universal desire to reduce accidents, suicides, and the criminal use of guns through legislation, could have indicated caution in supporting this particular legislation. These arguments apparently were largely overlooked or ignored by the national media.

There is some hard-to-ignore evidence that, while and after this legislation was under consideration by Congress and being discussed by the media, mature and intelligent well-informed people had not considered the following argument: the 1968 gun bill in its original form provided opportunities for the abuse of the rights of privacy of tens of millions of Americans.* When the National Crime Information Center had been established, J. Edgar Hoover felt constrained to say:

Most importantly, it will mean no intrusion whatsoever upon the right to privacy.

The NCIC (National Crime Information Center) will have no other purpose than to bring criminals to justice—persons who have violated federal statutes or against whom there is a felony warrant outstanding, and whom the state is willing to extradite. . . .**

Yet,

Under the President's proposal all firearms would have to be registered within 180 days after enactment of the law. . . . The registration records would be maintained in the National Crime Information Center by the Federal Bureau of Investigation. To obtain a federal firearms license, an individual would be required to submit, among other requirements, a statement from a licensed physician attesting to his mental and physical capability for possessing and using a firearm safely and responsibly, a statement from the chief law enforcement officer of his locality attesting to his eligibility for a license; a complete set of his fingerprints certified by a

---

* Besides the virtual absence of such arguments in the national press and media, there were other indications; e.g., I questioned many seminar groups of intelligent, mature and sometimes somewhat influential people on this issue during and after this time and although they knew most pro-gun-legislation arguments and some anti- points, few if any were aware of this problem, but most quickly recognized it as an important one when it was pointed out.

** J. Edgar Hoover, "Now: Instant Crime Control in Your Town," reprinted by courtesy of *Popular Science Monthly*, © 1966 by Popular Science Publishing Co., Inc.

law enforcement officer; and an identification photograph. Licenses would have to be renewed every three years.*

First of all, here was a possible invasion of privacy of the type viewed with suspicion by Americans. A Harvard University study, which used a small, "highly random" sample of 200 persons "representing different ages, social classes and races in the suburban Boston cities of Belmont, Cambridge, and Maynard" (and therefore perhaps less reliable as overall public opinion than the usual nationwide sample of about 1,500 persons) specifically asked about a "computerized data bank on all Americans." The majority (55 percent) opposed it "on the ground that it would threaten privacy."** But there is other evidence of this feeling. About one in five (19 percent) in a large nationwide sample (1,362 people) felt in mid-1970 that his privacy was already being violated by "computers which collect a lot of information about you." And more than one in three (34 percent) felt that "his privacy was being invaded" by people who were trying to find out things about him that "are none of their business." The objections to the invasions of privacy are more likely to come from "those with the most education," men, those who live in small towns and the South.***

Also, despite the desire for stricter enforcement of the laws and the high sensitivity to the recent increase in crime, the weight of opinion is against wiretapping by police. There is some evidence that the public even dislikes wiretapping of specific groups of persons. In an unscientifically designed telephone survey in Philadelphia, the majority (59.7 percent) said the government should not tap the phones of "radicals."****

As the following charts show, although high school- and particularly grade school-educated people were likely to be less familiar with wiretapping, only a small percentage of those who were had no opinion on it. There seems to be an "instinctive" suspicion of it adequate to prevent the weight of opinion from favoring it.

In addition a local invasion of the right of privacy, largely undiscussed, may have resulted from this law. Army files on certain persons, presumably compiled in connection with the military's role in maintaining

* Form letter received upon a request for information from Senator Henry M. Jackson, Chairman of the U.S. Senate Committee on Interior and Insular Affairs, 1968.
** New York Times, December 15, 1970, p. 57.
*** Article by Louis Harris in the Philadelphia Inquirer, August 3, 1970, p. 5, based on one of his surveys.
**** Philadelphia Inquirer, March 19, 1971, p. 39.

domestic order during demonstrations and so forth, were seized upon and exposed by the news media, and a furor ensued over this "invasion of privacy." Despite such feelings among the public, however, major "opinion-molders" made little if any mention of the right of privacy in connection with the 1968 gun law. In fact, these persons largely endorsed this law, which would not only put detailed personal information on many million Americans (including every rabbit hunter) into a computerized system, but, perhaps more important, might cause additional personal information to be put into many local police files. In New York State, under the Sullivan Law covering pistols (of little consequence to hunters and other primarily "long gun" users), a system has resulted that shows what the Federal law, covering all guns, could mean. As a result of the New York law, great amounts of information are on file, not only about the gun owner, but about those who *vouch* for his character.

To give some feel for what might have occurred in some cases, the questions below are taken from a local, downstate New York police department questionnaire concerning the personal history of a *character witness,* demanded by the "chief law enforcement officer" of that district before he would approve a pistol permit applicant. This must be filled out

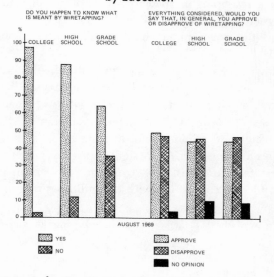

Figure 25

WIRETAPPING*

by Education

* *Gallup Opinion Index,* No. 51, September 1969, pp. 13 and 14.

by the character witnesses (two were required in this town) before they can vouch for a person filling out a pistol permit application (Section 400 of the Penal Law). Under the Sullivan Law, local police departments vary widely in their interpretation of the amount of information they need about applicants and character witnesses. There seems to be little constraint on what they can ask and keep on file about both the applicant for a pistol permit and his character witnesses. Everybody, character witnesses and applicants alike, fills out any and all forms the "chief law enforcement officer" might request, or the gun owner loses what he considers his right—to own a gun. There also seems to be no easy recourse if this officer turns someone down. There is no obvious reason to feel the situation in many local areas (at least for the gun owners themselves) would have to be vastly different under the 1968 bill, which covered *all* guns, including the rifles and shotguns of hunters.

Sample questions from a questionnaire issued by a local police department in New York State, to be filled out by a *character witness* for a pistol permit applicant, are these:

2. Give any variation you have used in spelling your name _____

_____

3. Give any other names you have ever used or been known by and give the reason for using same _____

17. Have you ever received disciplinary action of any type while in the armed forces of the U.S.? _____
If so, give details _____

37. Has applicant ever had or been examined or been treated or confined for a nervous or mental disorder by a private physician or at a clinic, hospital, sanitarium or other institution? _____

These forms are presumably available to anyone in the local police department.* Regardless of one's point of view on gun laws, most thinking men would probably ponder the consequences to personal

---

* Even members of at least one large-city police force are alleged to have illegally released confidential information on people on their files. (See the *New York Times* of February 21, 1971, p. 33, on the alleged sale of confidential information from police files in New York City to private companies.) The information requested of character witnesses about themselves on the long police forms listed above, could be used to affect the reputations of men and women about personal things many care about: veterans do not necessarily mention the few days they spent in the guardhouse due to an offense related to a brawl; and some persons would be delighted to tear down the local "war hero"; a woman with a

privacy of something like the arbitrary and unregulated proliferation of local personal files that might also take place under the proposed federal law on all guns (hunters' shotguns and rifles, as well as pistols) that, as described by Senator Jackson's letter, would require a local law enforcement officer's recommendation to get a permit. Much as all citizens wish to reduce crime and death by firearms, such activities as the filing of the fingerprints, etc., of approximately half the adult males in the country in a central government system, and perhaps additional personal information on them (and in some cases maybe even character witnesses) in many local police stations, should make any prudent man pause.

We know most murders are crimes of rage or passions of the moment, committed by people who are well known to the victims, and that the presence of a gun might lead to a death that otherwise might not have occurred if the gun were not present. This criticism, therefore, in no way invalidates the basic objectives of attempting to reduce crime and lessen the several thousand intentional and accidental gun-shot deaths each year through some form of legislation. Nor does it by any means condemn any and all gun laws as such. It does say, however, that there might have been aspects of the President's proposed 1968 gun law to which many, even its supporters, might have wished to give closer scrutiny.

To make matters worse, gun control law experts freely admitted that, because of the Fifth Amendment to the Constitution, criminals and others prohibited by law from having firearms, who already have them, probably could not be incriminated through licenses, nor would they likely be penalized for not truthfully filling out the forms, and therefore would not be directly affected by them. They even recommended considering exempting them from the licensing requirements. The value of licensing was said to be the restriction of "the flow of guns from legitimate to illegitimate users."* (Of course, the private information, mentioned

---

short, unhappy marriage in her past may prefer not to give that "other name" and the "reason for using same," to local or national police files; a man who has changed his name to have it sound more "American" may also object to such disclosures.

* *Firearms and Violence in American Life,* a Staff Report to the National Commission on the Causes and Prevention of Violence, prepared by George D. Newton and Franklin F. Zimring, pp. 114–118.

"The Fifth Amendment, however, could be invoked against enforcement of such laws. Fifth Amendment problems might be minimized by exempting from licensing, registration, or transfer notice requirements all persons in those categories prohibited by law from possessing firearms."

above, that is not incriminating, would probably have to be put on the local forms by the law-abiding citizen under pain of perjury and possible prosecution). It seems as far as depriving *professional* criminals of guns they already have (or illegally get) is concerned, Federal law making it unlawful for anyone with a felony record to possess a gun would have about the same direct effect on the criminal. The original 1968 law could reduce the guns *added* to the criminal and potential criminal arsenal from *legal* sources, but one should also consider the problems for the non-criminal gun (particularly long gun) owner. (Of course, checking the National Crime Information Center to see if a prospective gun buyer is on record there as a criminal is quite legitimate.)

To repeat, this issue is discussed not because of opposition to the commendable objectives of the gun law per se (reducing crime and loss of life), but because it was a law that so many people of good will apparently thought was a clear-cut case in which one could take a constitutionally and morally incontrovertible, even self-righteous, stand. In fact, however, they may have been failing to detect the possible violation of a liberal principle with respect to the law's effect on this particular large segment of their fellow citizens. Furthermore, these pro-gun-law people managed to push to a high-decibel level their ideas about a subject on which the vast majority of them apparently had no personal experience and very little "in-depth" detailed knowledge. Even though the offensive sections of the law were finally omitted, one gets the feeling that here is a case where one could argue that the rights of a huge group of law-abiding, responsible citizens (in perhaps a majority of our families) were not of concern as much as the rights of some other, much smaller, groups of citizens (e.g., radical students and instructors, rioters, self-proclaimed revolutionaries,) to the "liberal intellectuals," the media, and occasionally even some elected and appointed government officials.

2. OPEN HOUSING LAWS

Another issue on which many took a "moral" stand, but on which they should perhaps have had more first-hand information, was the open housing law. The basic idea behind this law is indisputably correct. But, in hastily pushing the law and in attributing almost all opposition to it as bigotry, many proponents may have overlooked some stipulations that might have helped to achieve the ends the Congress had in mind.

Open housing laws, with no provision for compensation to average income and even to poor, working people for the loss of their down payments on their homes, leaves much to be desired. Furthermore, such action may help to convince many persons that the issue is being decided by "decoupled" elitists, both in and out of government, who don't know, or (worse still) perhaps don't even care enough about details of the problem for the average man. Twenty percent of the population moves every year, many for reasons of employment. They all worry about property values. If, however, those families who must move find that their house has depreciated in a "changed" neighborhood, others in that area may start to sell before values drop further. If a man who must move has no ready cash, other than that in the down payment and paid-up portion of his mortgage, he becomes sensitive to the value of his house. If the price goes down, the bank does not take the loss—the owner does. He is responsible to the bank for the full amount of the mortgage; what is left is his. If less than his original down payment, or even *nothing*, is left, that is what he has for a down payment on the house he must buy for his family at his new location. This may cause "panic"-selling by non-bigots, and at the same time it might reinforce some people's prejudice.

A provision that might at least have reduced the problem (as an example) might be something like the provisions made by corporations when their employees are forced to move at times when their properties draw less than a normal price: a provision in the law guaranteeing (within limits) against a drop in the value of homes because of a "change" in the neighborhood, due to the law, might have calmed the fears of many home owners, reduced opposition to the law, and perhaps even prevented some "panic"-moving.* We cannot be sure how much effect it would have on "panic"-moving or how long this effect would last, because other things cause persons (black and white) to move from neighborhoods: increasd noise, crime, juvenile delinquency, etc.** But such a provision might slow down "panic"-moving and tend to slow or prevent a drop in property values. At the very least, it would have indicated a concern for the father who was one of the 20 percent who would move anyway, but was now faced with

* There is mixed evidence on whether property values drop when Negroes move into a neighborhood; if they do drop, then the fears of the residents are justified and insurance would be helpful; if they do not drop, then insurance would counter "irrational" fears and cost nothing.

** "As the Blacks Move In, the Ethnics Move Out," by Paul Wilkes, *New York Times Magazine,* January 24, 1971. Also see the discussion on Negro sentiments on lower-class Negroes (or whites) moving into their neighborhoods in Chapter III, section B, "White and Negro Racial Attitudes."

the prospect of losing some or all of his down payment because his neighborhood was "changing" due to the open housing law.

Such a provision might cause administrative difficulties (like those the gun control law could make), but it also might not. It might cost the government a fortune and cause the neighborhood to "change" faster if "quick sale" realtors and home owners sell homes to lower-income persons at cheaper rates than usual, because the difference would be made up by the government, and they would get their money anyway. That is what the "within limits" was about; there has to be some incentive to keep up the neighborhood. Also that is what government inspectors would be for.

If, on the other hand, some such law with the necessary safeguards had been successful, it might have decreased the moving (nobody likes to move) and, like a bank without a run on it, it would have cost little. Be that as it may, if some such measures had been taken, somebody would obviously have been concerned that if a man loses his down payment he has no money with which to put a roof over his family when he arrives at his new place of residence.

Misguided actions (e.g., insufficient attention to such problems) are not only ineffective in executing important and necessary programs, but are counterproductive to the very programs they hope to advance. In addition, the average man who tries to shoulder his responsibilities is likely to feel "forgotten" and put upon by the media and the government.

Table 12

SCHOOL INTEGRATION*

Any objection to sending your children to a school where there are a few Negroes, half are Negroes, or more than half are Negroes?

	Northern white parents (% objecting)					Southern white parents (% objecting)				
	1963	1965	1966	1969	1970	1963	1965	1966	1969	1970
Where a few are Negroes	10%	7%	6%	6%	6%	61%	37%	24%	21%	16%
Where half are Negroes	33	28	32	28	24	78	68	49	46	43
Where more than half are Negroes	53	52	60	56	51	86	78	62	54	69

* Gallup polls in the *Gallup Opinion Index*, No. 12, May 1966, p. 16; the *Gallup Opinion Index*, No. 51, September 1969, pp. 5, 6, 7; the *Gallup Opinion Index*, No. 59, May 1970, p. 5.

School busing is another example of such a program. For a long time, anyone against busing was likely to be dismissed, in some circles, as consciously or unconsciously racist, and many no doubt were; but apparently this may have been too simple an analysis of the issues for the average man. As Table 12 shows, the objection to having white children attend schools with Negroes has apparently decreased drastically.

On the question of busing, however, in 1970, the weight of opinion of everyone, including Negroes, opposed it. Nationally, 81 percent opposed and only 14 percent favored it. Over 70 percent of every region in the country opposed busing. By August 1971 this opposition had dropped (73 percent), by October (with schools open) it had increased somewhat (77 percent). Better than three out of four citizens still opposed busing and the weight of Negro opinion still had not shifted to the pro side. There may be a relationship between how much persons are affected and their change in attitude. The opposition of the group most likely to have children in school (30–49 years old) didn't change, the 21-to-29-year-old opposition dropped most, and the 18-to-20-year olds (a new group not polled in 1970) registered the least opposition. If this really reflects parental attitudes, it is quite different from their attitudes on school integration per se: only 14 percent of both public school parents and parochial parents rated it as one of the

Table 13

BUSING OF SCHOOL CHILDREN*

In general, do you favor or oppose the busing of Negro and white school children from one school district to another?

(March, 1970; August, 1971; October, 1971)

	Favor			Oppose			No Opinion		
National	14%	19%	17%	81%	73%	77%	5%	8%	6%
Sex									
Men	13	20	16	83	73	78	4	7	6
Women	15	17	17	79	74	77	6	9	6
Race									
White	11	16	14	85	76	80	4	8	6
Nonwhite	37	43	45	48	46	47	15	11	8

Table 13 (continued)

Education									
College	13	23	22	84	72	75	3	5	3
High School	14	17	15	81	75	79	5	8	6
Grade School	16	17	17	77	70	75	7	13	8
Occupation									
Professional and									
Business	11	21	18	86	74	78	3	5	4
White Collar	13	19	18	81	74	76	6	7	6
Farmers	14	11	15	83	78	75	3	11	10
Manual	16	19	17	78	74	77	6	7	6
Age									
18–20 years**	x	32	28	x	64	63	x	4	
21–29 years	17	25	23	80	69	73	3	6	
30–49 years	16	17	17	79	76	78	5	7	
50 and over	10	15	12	84	74	81	6	11	
Religion									
Protestant	14	15	15	81	78	80	5	7	
Catholic	15	18	19	82	71	74	3	11	
Jewish	x	x		x	x		x	x	
Politics									
Republican	10	11	10	87	81	83	3	8	
Democrat	18	23	12	75	70	74	7	7	
Independent	13	17	17	83	74	77	4	9	
Region									
East	19	22	18	73	68	76	8	10	
Midwest	15	17	17	81	74	75	4	9	
South	8	15	10	87	79	87	5	6	
West	13	22	25	84	69	68	3	9	
Income									
$15,000 and over	8	21	16	88	73	79	4	6	
$10,000–$14,999	10	18	19	88	75	75	2	7	
$ 7,000–$ 9,999	17	21	15	77	72	81	6	7	
$ 5,000–$ 6,999	20	15	17	75	76	76	5	9	
$ 3,000–$ 4,999	17	19	15	76	66	77	7	15	
Under $3,000	14	17	23	76	73	72	10	10	
Community Size									
1,000,000 and over	14	23	25	83	71	69	3	6	
500,000–999,999	16	17	17	75	74	79	5	9	
50,000–499,999	15	21	15	82	71	81	3	8	
2,500–49,999	11	18	15	83	71	78	6	11	
Under 2,500, Rural	14	14	14	81	77	79	5	9	

* *Gallup Opinion Index,* No. 58, April 1970, p. 9.
* *Gallup Opinion Index,* No. 75, September 1971, p. 20.
* *Gallup Opinion Index,* No. 77, November 1971, p. 24.
** This age group was not polled in 1970.

biggest problems (19 percent of adults without children did so).*
Furthermore, as the table shows, objection to schools where half the
students were Negroes was much less among white parents than objection to busing.

Despite the slight lessening of opposition, a very large majority of all
educational, income, and age levels, and of people living in all sizes of
communities, opposed busing in both 1970 and 1971; those favoring it
constituted only 17 percent of the voting population today. Many North-
eastern districts showed opposition in 1970 equal to the national level.

Table 14

DO YOU FAVOR?**

(Write-in Poll to State Senator's Constituents of Nassau County,
Long Island, New York)

The regents-proposed *repeal* of the Lent-Kunzeman Neighborhood
School Law which *prohibits* forced assignment of pupils to schools
out of their neighborhoods on the basis of race, color or creed?

Yes	*No*
(1,216)	(4,798)
20.2%	79.8%

Once more, however, what many "intellectuals" and many in the
media seldom stressed, or were very slow to recognize, was what the
average citizen facing the problem apparently feared: a crisis threatening
a traditional part of the community—the neighborhood school system.
It was not just racism—neighborhood schools were about to be (or were
being) deliberately broken up. This was based on a theory of improvement developed by some well-meaning, but apparently, to the average
man, illogical "educators" and politicians. The results are that, after
many parents have gone into debt to buy a home near a good school,
small children are being bused and "crossbused" miles from home into
strange neighborhoods.

Neighborhood schools were also being broken up as the result of
a program based on the idea that two schools, one kindergarten through
fourth grade, the other of the fifth and sixth grades, are so much better
than a "K through 6" neighborhood school that it is worth all this

* *Gallup Opinion Index,* No. 66, December 1970, p. 16.
** From the *Legislative Report* from State Senator Norman F. Lent, Nassau
County, Long Island, New York, 1970.

trouble. In some areas, crossbusing for racial balance and the new "two-school" (or even "three-school") system were introduced at the same time, compounding the problems. Young children are being sent past their former neighborhood school (now occupied by others) to a distant school, and in these same areas, school taxes are skyrocketing. At the same time, obvious improvements in the educational system as a whole were generally not forthcoming. Reading and math scores had not improved significantly, and in many critical areas they generally continued to fall.

It also appears that even in areas where many new, extremely expensive educational programs have been undertaken, the educational accomplishments continue to decrease. For example, compared to 1965, despite the expanding, progressive, and expensive programs instituted in New York City, the reading ability of students there has decreased. Reading scores of ninth-grade students in this school system, once one of the finest in the country, now lag a year and two months behind the national average.* We may doubt that this phenomenon is unique to New York or even large cities. Similar results can probably be found in suburban, higher SEL (socio-economic-level) areas as well. Where these problems involve minority groups, however, the issues often tend to become clouded by accusations of racism.

This whole educational problem, linked with the spiraling taxes, has caught the average American in a squeeze in the late 1960s. He holds education as the most important means of bettering one's position. He

* *New York Times,* December 20, 1970, p. 1. In 1970, the second grade showed an improvement over 1969, but it was far below 1965. This may be a hopeful sign, but second grade is "easy"; and it remains to be seen whether this is the beginning of a better knowledge of the basics, which will show up in later years, or not. A more disquieting fact is that all the average scores look better as one goes *down* the grades; i.e., third is better than fourth, fourth better than fifth, etc., on a national-average comparison basis. Or, in other words, as one goes up the grade levels, and the demands get *greater*, the students fall farther and farther behind. This is partly due to the fact that the bright students, who might read several years ahead of the others, tend to pull the averages up; as one gets near the twelfth grade (the top of the reading-score grades) it is impossible for any student to have a greater effect on the average score. This is, however, a problem for all schools across the country. In fact, *because* of this, the upper-grade scores may be a *better* measure of what the mass of students is receiving from these expensive programs. Perhaps the most tragic aspect of this problem in New York City is that an ever larger number of the students are from low-income families (many are Negroes and Puerto Ricans) who desperately need this basic education for "upward mobility" in the modern economic and social environment. See also the footnote at the end of Section F, "The Middle American and His Feelings About His Society," in this chapter.

87

is having trouble paying his taxes. He knows something is wrong, but he does not want to give up on this road to success. This is apparently true of both whites and Negroes;* but by 1969 the country as a whole had become less satisfied with its children's education, a reversal of the "trend" of the early sixties. The latest poll shows an increase in Negro satisfaction but it is still below the 1966 level, and white satisfaction continued to fall (14 percent below the 1966 peak and even 10 points below the "low" of 1963).

Table 15

NEGRO AND WHITE SATISFACTION AND DISSATISFACTION WITH THEIR CHILDREN'S EDUCATION**

| | Satisfaction | | Dissatisfaction | |
	Negro	White	Negro	White
1963–1965	43%	73%	45%	21%
1965	44	77	46	19
1966	64	76	23	16
1969	53	65	34	25
1971	57	63	29	26

All income, educational, racial and regional groups feel discipline is inadequate, and Negroes feel this way more than whites.

Table 16

DISCIPLINE IN THE LOCAL PUBLIC SCHOOLS***

(Emphasis by underlining added)

"How do you feel about the discipline in the local public schools—is it too strict, not strict enough, or just about right?"

	Too Strict	Not Strict Enough	Just About Right	Don't Know/ No Answer
NATIONAL				
SEX				
Men	2%	54%	31%	13%
Women	2	52	31	15
RACE				
White	2	52	32	14
Nonwhite	4	62	21	13

* For the importance of education as a means of upward mobility, according to Negroes in one community, see Table 159.
** Compiled from information in Gallup polls in the *Gallup Opinion Index,* No. 4, September 1965, p. 20; *Gallup Opinion Index,* No. 18, November-December 1966, pp. 14 and 17; *Gallup Opinion Index,* No. 47, May, 1969, p. 7; and *Gallup Opinion Index,* No. 76, October, 1971, pp. 16 and 17.
*** *Gallup Opinion Index,* No. 66, December 1970, p. 17.

Table 16 (continued)

EDUCATION

Elementary Grades	1	55	28	16
High School Incomplete	2	56	32	10
High School Complete	2	50	35	13
Technical, Trade or				
Business School	1	62	16	21
College Incomplete	3	55	26	16
College Graduate	2	47	39	12

OCCUPATION

Business and Professional	1	52	32	15
Clerical and Sales	3	52	34	11
Farm	3	42	51	4
Skilled Labor	2	54	31	13
Unskilled Labor	3	57	30	10
Nonlabor Force	*	53	24	23

AGE

21 to 29 Years	4	41	35	20
30 to 49 Years	2	51	38	9
50 Years and over	*	61	24	15

RELIGION

Protestant	2	53	33	12
Roman Catholic	2	56	27	15
Jewish	—	54	25	21
All Others	3	44	31	22

REGION

East	2	54	28	16
Midwest	*	58	31	11
South	3	48	36	13
West	1	52	29	18

INCOME

$15,000 and over	*	47	40	13
$10,000 to $14,999	2	58	27	13
$ 7,000 to $ 9,999	2	52	34	12
$ 5,000 to $ 6,999	1	56	30	13
$ 4,000 to $ 4,999	3	47	36	14
$ 3,000 to $ 3,999	—	54	37	9
Under $2,999	3	51	21	25

COMMUNITY SIZE

500,000 and over	1	61	23	15
50,000 to 499,999	1	58	26	15
25,000 to 49,999	—	70	22	8
Under 25,000	3	44	40	13

* Less than 1 percent.

Table 17

YOUTH CONSERVATION CAMPS

"Some people say that all young men between the ages of 16 and 22 who are out of school and out of work should be required to join a Youth Conservation Corps to carry on their education, learn a trade and earn a little money. Do you approve or disapprove of this plan?"

(Emphasis by underlining added)

	May 1971			August 1964		
	Approve	Dis-approve	No Opinion	Approve	Dis-approve	No Opinion
NATIONAL	66%	27%	7%	73%	21%	6%
SEX						
Male	62	33	5			
Female	71	21	8			
RACE						
White	64	29	7			
Nonwhite	86	10	4			
EDUCATION						
College	47	45	8			
High School	69	26	5			
Grade School	80	11	9			
OCCUPATION						
Professional and						
Business	58	35	7			
White Collar	60	33	7			
Farmers	64	30	6			
Manual	70	26	4			
AGE						
18–20 years	56	42	2			
21–29 years	59	38	3			
30–49 years	66	29	5			
50 and over	72	18	10			
RELIGION						
Protestant	65	28	7			
Catholic	72	22	6			
Jewish	x	x	x			
POLITICS						
Republican	67	25	8			
Democrat	72	22	6			
Independent	59	35	6			
REGION						
East	70	23	7			
Midwest	65	26	9			
South	69	26	5			
West	58	37	5			
INCOME						
$15,000 and over	56	37	7			
$10,000–$14,999	62	31	7			
$ 7,000–$ 9,999	64	32	4			
$ 5,000–$ 6,999	75	21	4			
$ 3,000–$ 4,999	64	26	10			
Under $3,000	81	9	10			
COMMUNITY SIZE						
1,000,000 and over	70	22	8			
500,000–999,999	68	24	8			
50,000–499,999	67	29	4			
2,500–49,999	60	33	7			
Under 2,500, Rural	67	26	7			

There are other indicators that Negroes, perhaps even more so than whites, are concerned for their children (and probably their own safety) in the "permissive" drug- and crime-ridden environment in which so many of them live. They are overwhelmingly in favor of a mandatory Youth Conservation Corps for young men between "16 and 22 who are out of school and out of work."*

An even more striking example of the Negro attitude toward the whole environment in the North, which no doubt is also influenced by the environment for their children, is indicated by Negro support for the proposition that the South is a "more livable place for blacks than any other place in the nation." They have housing problems and other difficulties in the North, as well as in the South. In addition, traditionally they have preferred the way they were treated in the North, so one cannot help but feel that other factors in the North make a difference. One must ask if the drugs, juvenile delinquency, violence, lack of law and order in the vast, impersonal slums of the northern cities do not play a role here. Furthermore, we must wonder if the whole approach to the "solution" of problems of these and other citizens in the North has been appropriate. Despite (or perhaps, at least partly, because of) the many "programs" to "help" them in the North, the Negroes apparently are more likely to feel that the environment for their families in the South is preferable to that in the North.

Perhaps those of us who have rushed to support so many "programs" for the Negroes, and sometimes categorized those who questioned these programs as racist or (if the programs were in the school) racist and "anti-education," should re-examine our positions. Perhaps some of us were concentrating on something other than the key problems. We should also, perhaps, re-examine the credentials of those educators and "involved" people who spoke with such certitude. Apparently some very vocal whites and militant Negroes may have known less than some of us thought they did about the needs or even the desires of Negroes, or such matters as education, family assistance, juvenile delinquency, and housing, in general.

The slum dweller is not the only person to feel the lack of success of expensive new programs in our schools but, in regard to spending

* *Gallup Opinion Index*, No. 73, July 1971, p. 25. Of interest, also, is the apparent coalescence of the inherent liberal attitudes on personal behavior and the conservatism about spending tax money, among college persons—they showed only 47 percent approval.

Table 18

LIVING CONDITIONS FOR BLACKS*

"James Meredith, the first Negro to enter the University of Mississippi, recently said that, 'On a person-to-person, day-to-day, the South is a more livable place for blacks than any other place in the nation.' Do you agree or disagree?"

(Emphasis by underlining added)

| | MID–JULY 1971 | | |
	Agree	Disagree	No Opinion
NATIONAL	49%	30%	21%
SEX			
Male	53	27	20
Female	45	32	23
RACE			
White	49	30	21
Nonwhite	48	30	22
EDUCATION			
College	49	32	19
High School	47	32	21
Grade School	53	22	25
OCCUPATION			
Professional and			
Business	48	31	21
White Collar	51	32	17
Farmers	68	16	16
Manual	45	35	20
AGE			
18–20 years	41	43	16
21–29 years	45	34	21
30–49 years	45	34	21
50 and over	56	22	22
POLITICS			
Republican	55	30	15
Democrat	46	31	23
Independent	61	17	22
REGION			
East	42	34	24
Midwest	50	36	14
South	63	18	19
West	36	33	31
INCOME			
$15,000 and over	47	32	21
$10,000–$14,999	50	32	18
$ 7,000–$ 9,999	50	32	18
$ 5,000–$ 6,999	42	31	27
$ 3,000–$ 4,999	55	24	21
Under $3,000	51	25	24
COMMUNITY SIZE			
1,000,000 and over	39	33	28
500,000–999,999	39	34	27
50,000–499,999	52	30	18
2,500–49,999	50	36	14
Under 2,500, Rural	56	22	22

* *Gallup Opinion Index,* No. 74, August 1971, p. 27.

more money on schools, Negroes indicate as strong or stronger opposition than do whites. All age, racial, regional and educational groups (except college graduates and people earning $15,000 or more per year), now burdened with taxes and apparently less satisfied with the school systems than in the first half of the 1960s, reject more taxes for schools.

Table 19

VOTE FOR SCHOOL TAXES*

"Suppose the local public schools said they needed much more money. As you feel at this time, would you vote to raise taxes for this purpose, or would you vote against raising taxes for this purpose?"

	For	Against	Don't Know/ No Answer
NATIONAL			
SEX			
Men	38%	56%	6%
Women	37	56	7
RACE			
White	38	56	6
Nonwhite	35	58	7
EDUCATION			
Elementary grades	28	63	9
High school incomplete	33	60	7
High school complete	33	61	6
Technical, trade, or business school	48	48	4
College incomplete	47	48	5
College graduate	61	33	6
OCCUPATION			
Business and Professional	54	40	6
Clerical and Sales	38	58	4
Farm	32	65	3
Skilled labor	34	61	5
Unskilled labor	29	63	8
Nonlabor force	32	59	9
AGE			
21–29 years	45	48	7
30–49 years	40	56	4
50 years and over	32	60	8
RELIGION			
Protestant	36	57	7
Roman Catholic	36	59	5
Jewish	59	41	–
All others	45	43	12

Table 19 (continued)

REGION
East	41	54	5
Midwest	34	58	8
South	36	57	7
West	39	55	6

INCOME
$15,000 and over	49	47	4
$10,000–$14,999	41	55	4
$ 7,000–$ 9,999	40	55	5
$ 5,000–$ 6,999	31	59	10
$ 4,000–$ 4,999	33	56	11
$ 3,000–$ 3,999	27	66	7
Under $2,999	27	64	9

COMMUNITY SIZE
500,000 and over	38	56	6
50,000–499,999	36	57	7
25,000– 49,999	49	49	2
Under 25,000	37	57	6

There has been a real money crisis for years, but it was a long time in being recognized; and many educators still object to the questioning of their fundamental premises and programs, which do not always seem valid or feasible. More and more persons are questioning the work and programs of the decision-makers in education. Recent polls seem to indicate that there is a demand for ways to get educators to evaluate and account for their "programs."

Table 20

NATIONAL TESTS IN LOCAL SCHOOLS?*

Would you like to see the students in the local schools be given national tests so that their educational achievement could be compared with students in other communities?

	National Totals	No Children In School	Public School Parents	Parochial School Parents	High School Juniors and Seniors
Yes	75%	74%	75%	80%	76%
No	16	14	19	15	23
No opinion	9	12	6	5	1
	100	100	100	100	100

* Ibid., p. 18.

The public also apparently is in the mood to make the comparative results of such tests mean something.

Table 21
THE ACCOUNTABILITY OF THE SCHOOL FOR STUDENTS' PROGRESS*

Would you favor or oppose a system that would hold teachers and administrators more accountable for the progress of students?

	National Totals	No Children In School	Public School Parents	Parochial School Parents	High School Juniors and Seniors
Favor	67%	66%	68%	71%	65%
Oppose	21	21	21	19	29
No opinion	12	13	11	10	6
	100	100	100	100	100

Furthermore, the public also seems to favor putting teeth in its demand for productivity of teachers.

Table 22
HOW SHOULD TEACHERS BE PAID?**

Should each teacher be paid on the basis of the quality of his work or should all teachers be paid on a standard scale basis?

	National Totals	No Children In School	Public School Parents	Parochial School Parents	High School Juniors and Seniors
Quality of work	58%	57%	61%	52%	59%
Standard scale basis	36	36	35	43	39
No opinion	6	7	4	5	2
	100	100	100	100	100

Parents as well as the adult public as a whole, however, still show a majority (and very close to it, in the case of non-parents) opposing the premise that teachers unions have "gained too much power." But better than one in four feels they have.

* Ibid.
** Ibid.

95

Table 23
POWER OF TEACHER ORGANIZATIONS*

Have teacher organizations gained too much power over their own salaries and working conditions?

	National Totals	No Children In School	Public School Parents	Parochial School Parents	High School Juniors and Seniors
Yes	26%	27%	25%	24%	17%
No	53	49	58	57	72
No opinion	21	24	17	19	11
	100	100	100	100	100

Clearly the mood is not one of blind trust. The growing trend among educators over recent years to downgrade the value of comparative tests (teaching the "whole child" rather than emphasizing testable "subjects") and the increased emphasis on the tenure system, may be in for trouble. On this last issue, the parents and students particularly show opposition.

Table 24
TENURE FOR TEACHERS?**

Many states have "tenure" laws which mean that a teacher cannot be fired except by some sort of court procedure. Are you for giving teachers tenure or are you against tenure?

	National Totals	No Children In School	Public School Parents	Parochial School Parents	High School Juniors and Seniors
For	35%	38%	29%	28%	30%
Against	53	48	60	62	61
No opinion	12	14	11	10	9
	100	100	100	100	100

A 1971 poll showed that the attitudes indicated by the above data had remained generally the same. Finances ranked first, integration second, and discipline third as school problems.*** In 1970 discipline

* Ibid.
** Ibid.
*** "The Third Annual Survey of the Public's Attitude Toward the Public Schools, 1971," by George Gallup, *United Teacher Magazine*, November 21, 1971, pp. M1–M4.

was first and finance and segregation tied for second place, but there was only one percentage point between them so they really were all the same.* Discipline was considered less of a problem in 1971 because of a changed mood in the high schools and tighter discipline enforcement that year.

4. CONSTRUCTION WORKERS UNIONS

An area where "racism" was most likely assumed to be the reason for a lack of integration was in the building trade unions. Here again, there were grounds for some charges of racism. No reasonable man would say that racism does not exist in construction or other trade unions, as it exists, to some degree, in most other sectors of our society. But there were many other factors involved that were, and perhaps still are, misunderstood or ignored by many commentators on this issue. These factors, again, are known to a large portion of the population that is also sensitive to the charges of racism. The results of pushing a purely racist interpretation may have annoyed many of the millions of union men in the country (in some quarters, unions as a whole began to be condemned); and it was perhaps in the end embarrassing to Negroes as a group. This could be excused in the 1950s when Negroes fared so badly economically compared to whites,** and perhaps even in the early 1960s; but it should not have continued to the degree that it did after the tumultuous events of the mid- and late sixties. By then it was not a clear-cut problem. There was, for example, a comprehensive study of the race situation in the apprentice system (as compared to the direct "helper"-journeyman route) in the construction unions. This work was done under contract to the Office of Manpower Automation and Training—OMAT—the Federal predecessor to the Office of Manpower Policy, Evaluation and Research of the U.S. Department of Labor, by the Department of Economics of the University of Texas in 1965–66. The two men who ran the project and published their findings,*** Professors F. Ray Marshall and Vernon M. Briggs, Jr., were known in the field of labor economics and apparently were sympathetic with the Negroes. In their study, they found substantial evidence of racial discrimination in the unions. In fact, almost the entire book is directed at the discriminating practices and other factors that

* *Gallup Opinion Index*, No. 66, December 1970, p. 16.
** They were doing relatively worse in the 1950s than in the 1940s.
*** F. Ray Marshall and Vernon M. Briggs, Jr., *The Negro and Apprenticeship* (Baltimore: The Johns Hopkins Press, 1967).

limited Negro membership in construction unions, and recommends public and private policies to change them. But the book also unearthed much data that shed some new light on the problem.

Detailed surveys of ten cities—New York, Philadelphia, Cleveland, Detroit, Washington, Cincinnati, Houston, Atlanta, Pittsburgh, and San Francisco-Oakland—besides pointing out that the situation varied from construction union to construction union and from city to city, clearly indicated the following points:

1) There were not that many Negroes who wanted such jobs, particularly by means of initially low-paying, apprenticeship programs.*

2) There were signs of real problems (in New York, for instance) that had nothing to do with the unions except that incidentally these problems made it difficult for minority youths to meet the requirements of the employers' and unions' apprenticeship systems. The biracial Rogers Committee reported in 1964:

One of the greatest eye openers to this Committee was the apparent abandoning of many youths in our school system. Most of the Committee was shocked that boys who were graduates of our vocational high schools. . . . could not spell such words as "brick," "carpenter," "building," etc., or could not add inches and feet. . . . It is quite apparent that they are a product of a social system that pushed them through the earlier grades of school without insuring that they had the basic tools necessary for a minimal academic education. . . . We call attention to this problem because the apprentice in any trade must come equipped with these tools.

Summing up its work, the Committee stated:

We had been led to believe that there were thousands who couldn't gain admittance into the building trades unions. As a committee we felt that the numbers who came forward were small and those qualified were even smaller in number.

---

* "Civil rights and union leaders have been surprised at the apathy shown by Negro youngsters toward apprenticeship programs even when they had a chance to get in." Most wanted white-collar jobs, professional or quasi-professional. Only 3.2 percent of the seniors in fourteen Negro and two all-white high schools aspired to skilled trades.

In the great "drive" to get Negroes and Puerto Ricans into unions in 1963, 1,624 apprenticeship and 494 journeyman applications were submitted; of the potential apprentices, 528 were disqualified (129 were nonresidents, 202 were either too old or too young, 197 lacked minimal education); of the 1,096 remaining, 426 (39 percent) did not show up for an interview. Of those who were interviewed, passed the next screening, and were "referred" and accepted by the unions, many "decided not to avail themselves of the opportunity once it was offered to them." Marshall and Briggs, op. cit., pp. 39, 55–57.

When an intensive pre-examination "boning up" program—similar to bar review school for lawyers—was made available exclusively for Negroes, their numbers passing the apprenticeship exams rose spectacularly. In fact, they scored higher than many whites.

3) Factors, such as nepotism in the unions, were not directed at minorities, but at non-relatives of craftsmen. (The arguments for skilled workers of one craft following in the same family, father to son, are too well known to outline here.) Seasonal layoffs among construction workers (white construction workers work less days per year than nonwhite workers in other fields) make them sensitive to their numbers, so they tend to keep them down.

4) It isn't necessarily because the life on the job is always hard for the Negro, either.

Although racial prejudice continues to be an important factor in apprenticeships, little overt racial hostility seems to be expressed against Negro apprentices once they get in the programs. Indeed, there are many cases in which employers or union leaders have gone out of their way to see that Negroes "made it."°

The report concludes:

Since it was assumed that the absence of Negroes from these programs was due mainly to discrimination, much of the early public policy sought to combat discrimination, especially by unions. However, as time went by and apprenticeship sponsors adjusted their policies to comply with these civil rights regulations, and as surprisingly few Negroes either filed charges . . . or applied for apprenticeship openings when they became available, it became increasingly clear that anti-discrimination policies would have to be supplemented with other policies to recruit, counsel, and sometimes supply remedial tutoring programs, if progress was to be made in this area.°°

° Ibid., pp. 35–36, 58–59.
°° Ibid., p. 191. Another study, of the aerospace industry in the Los Angeles area, where 60 percent of all nonwhite applicants and only 6 percent of white applicants were hired recently, also has an interesting appraisal of some of the Negro's "problems" in this area, which aren't generally discussed in the media. Herbert K. Northrup, "The Negro in the Aerospace Industry," Herbert K. Northrup and Richard L. Rowan, et al., *Negro Employment in Basic Industry: Studies of Negro Employment* (Philadelphia: University of Pennsylvania Industrial Research Unit, Wharton School of Finance and Commerce, 1970), 1:169.
The few Negroes in foreman positions, for example, may stem from the fact that many don't *want* to be foremen, for the same reasons that many whites don't want to be. The pay differential (if any, because overtime for the craftsman can easily put him over the foreman's rate) isn't worth the headaches. Some Negroes in nonconstruction industry jobs apparently also have a fear of being looked on as an "Uncle Tom" who has "sold out" to the whites if they take supervisory positions. Northrup and Rowan, et al., op. cit., p. 184.

This is a somewhat different picture from that presented and held by many influential persons who write, comment, and even make decisions on such matters.

To repeat, this is by no means an attempt to *prove* that the problem of racism is nonexistent in construction unions. Quite the contrary. If men are denied any opportunities solely because of their race, creed or color, such barriers must be eliminated, in unions as elsewhere. It must be remembered, however, that increasing the numbers of any specific group (ethnic or otherwise) into any new area may be a more complex undertaking than some may think, and often for reasons that are not simply racist.

Nor is it a dead issue in the building trades. Negro membership in building trades unions actually declined from 7.4 percent in 1968 to 6.8 percent in 1969, and new apprenticeship rules published in the *Federal Register* in 1971 call for "affirmative action plans" by all federally registered apprenticeship programs to hire more nonwhites. The unions say the rules would "substitute quotas for quality" and the programs would be "inundated . . . with unqualified short-term dropouts at the expense of dedicated future craftsmen."* Hopefully, this new Federal effort will be successful. As more and more white-collar jobs and college educations are offered to Negro students from our urban slum schools, however, the number of Negro youths who can qualify (without lowering standards), *and* who want to go through the grueling low-paying apprenticeship years, may in itself cause problems in meeting "quotas." Similarly, since any new group is always low on "seniority," if larger numbers of Negroes are in any starting group when layoffs come, more Negroes are likely to be laid off, though Negroes apparently did not fare that much worse than whites in the 1970 recession. In fact, in the case of one construction union working on the World Trade Center in New York City, when layoffs came in the fall of 1971, white, full-scale A-card journeymen, normally with more seniority, were laid off, while nonwhite, temporary B-card employees, normally with less seniority, were kept on. This was a complete reversal of traditional construction work practices throughout the country, regardless of the ethnic makeup of the crews. Apparently, this was an attempt to achieve "racial balance" quickly on a job based not on the number of nonwhites in each seniority, and perhaps even

* *New York Times,* February 14, 1971, p. E-3.

skill category, but somewhat on the basis of the demographic makeup of the summertime crews and/or perhaps the geographical area. Here again, this may be a very short-sighted approach to solving a social and economic problem. If an admissions committee of a union once thinks that if it accepts Negroes in the traditional process, that come layoff time, its white journeymen will be laid off and the Negroes, regardless of where they are on the seniority (and perhaps even skill) level, will be kept on, then it may be difficult to get such committees to accept them in the first place.

This issue is far from settled. There are other indicators, perhaps including army training programs for soldiers about to be discharged, which may eventually show that certain ethnic groups tend to favor certain types of work which may not include that performed in the building trades. This phenomena may be at work here to the extent that the ratio of Negroes to whites in these unions will normally not equal that ratio among the population as a whole (particularly in the lower age brackets). We cannot overlook the fact that despite the vigilance of such organizations as the American Civil Liberties Union, brewers in St. Louis traditionally have included a high percentage of Germans, stone masons in the Northeast have a high percentage of Italians, and 80 percent of the entrepreneurs in the New York City area are Jewish. There may be a reason, other than prejudice, why a New York man of Jewish descent has traditionally apparently preferred to struggle along with his own business (even though it be just a tiny, far-from-the-most-lucrative enterprise, e.g., a candy store) rather than take a high-paying job in a construction union. There may be valid reasons besides prejudice why certain ethnic groups in our free society choose certain types of work. If we ignore them when we establish "programs" we may not only harm the economy and even society, but even harm those we try to "help," by, in effect, downgrading their chosen fields.

Overlooking such issues as those just mentioned can be counter-productive for everyone and, in many cases, particularly for those groups they are designed to help. Being wrong in this case, again, can be very bad, and not only because the "man in the street" may feel his "side of the argument" is being ignored.*

* A summary discussion of some of the complexities of this issue industry-wide was compiled by Jane Newitt, *"Race Relations and Prejudice,"* a background paper, HI-1535-D, Croton-on-Hudson, N.Y.: Hudson Institute, November 1, 1971.

E. A Message from the 1968 and 1970 Elections?

In the past two elections (1968 and 1970), the "average" man heard some odd interpretations of what the key issues were, what solutions were acceptable, what motivated him and what, if anything, the elections showed. In 1968, for example, because Vietnam headed the list of issues bothering an increasing number of people, many concluded that anti-Vietnam candidates would garner a large vote:

Table 25

MOST IMPORTANT ISSUES—1968*

	July	May
Vietnam war	52%	42%
Crime and lawlessness (including riots, looting, juvenile delinquency)	29	15
Race relations	13	25
High cost of living, taxes	9	8
Poverty	3	4
General unrest in nation	2	3

This apparently was an oversimplification of the functioning of the electorate; however, a look at the public's attitude about wars may be in order. The one issue that dominated and so often over-rode all others, domestic and foreign, was the threat of or actual involvement in war. In nearly 60 Gallup polls taken from 1935 through February 1970, "keeping out of war," "danger of war," and "possibility of war" was rated 40 times as one of the three most important issues of the day, and 32 times as *the* most important issue. Not surprisingly, in polls taken in 1935 and 1937, "keeping out of war" and "neutrality" were in the top three, and in two polls in 1939, "keeping out of war" was listed as the most important issue. By 1947 it was again one of the top three. It was number one in 1948 (Berlin Blockade?), October 1949, and May 1950. The Korean War started in June 1950, and it remained one of the three most important issues (mostly number one) until the truce in the summer of 1953. "Keeping out of war" was the

* *Gallup Opinion Index*, No. 38, August 1968, p. 15. A few percent had no opinion or gave other categories, and some gave more than one answer, so totals exceed 100 percent.

number one public concern in April 1954, July 1955, October 1956, September 1957, February 1958, November 1958 (Taiwan Straits crisis?), February 1959, October 1959, March 1961, and March 1964. The Vietnam War became number one in November 1964, and again in August 1965, and stayed there, with the exception of a poll in October 1967, throughout 13 polls up through February 1970. In May 1970, the war ranked second place, behind campus unrest, and in September or October 1971 it was again second, with the state of the economy first.*

Support for wars since 1945 seems to be at least as closely related to the casualties, duration, and degree of "progress" of the war as to the cause and who the enemy is. This is not a recent phenomenon—the length of a war and the number of casualties always make some difference. During the Civil War, fought by the North to end human bondage and preserve the Union (certainly laudable causes), support dwindled as the war dragged on and armies and casualties increased. By 1863 New York City was so torn by anti-draft riots that Federal regiments had to intervene to restore order. If wars are short and casualties light, as in the Spanish-American War, support is probably less likely to drop. International affairs are complicated and people normally tend to trust the President's judgment in them, but nobody wants a war before it starts.

The idea of going to war before Pearl Harbor was very unpopular. In 1940, during the Battle of Britain, Americans were opposed to sending war materials to Britain in U.S. ships for fear of becoming involved in the war with the Nazis (even though 70 percent felt that aiding Britain was the best way to stay out of war).** In June 1941 the draft extension passed the House of Representatives by one vote, even though it had a proviso that no U.S. draftees could be sent overseas. In 1941, although 85 percent of the public wanted to stay out of the war, 62 percent said they would rather enter the war than see Britain lose.*** Nevertheless, once we were involved, World War II had much higher support than the Korean or Vietnam involvements. In early 1944, 73 percent answered "no" to the question of whether people would eventually come to feel it was a "mistake" to enter the war. Even in

---

* *Gallup Opinion Index*, No. 76, October 1971, p. 3.
** *Gallup Poll Reports 1935–1968, American Institute of Public Opinion* (The Gallup Poll), Princeton, N.J., 1969, p. 119.
*** Ibid., pp. 119 and 123.

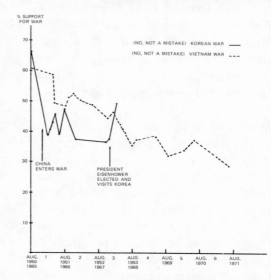

Figure 26

SUPPORT FOR KOREAN AND VIETNAM WARS*

Korea and Vietnam, the President had public support, once he committed himself; but casualties, time and perhaps inconclusiveness seem to have decreased this support.

A comparison of the support and opposition to the Korean and Vietnam wars over the years of involvement, based on responses to almost identical questions, might be worth examining.** In answer to the questions asked by the Gallup organization,

1. "Do you think the United States made a mistake in going into the war in Korea, or not?"
2. "In view of the developments since we entered the fighting in Vietnam, do you think the U.S. made a mistake sending troops to fight in Vietnam?"

the results were as follows. "Yes" was considered an opposition vote, "no" a support vote.

The foregoing graphs are interesting when one considers that the

* AIPO (Gallup) data from Mueller, op. cit., pp. 360, 363, and the *Gallup Opinion Index*, No. 73, July 1971, p. 3.
** For a definitive assessment of the issue of U.S. public support for overseas military involvements from World War II to the present, see John E. Mueller, "Trends in Popular Support for Wars in Korea and Vietnam," *American Political Science Review*, 65 (June 1971) pp. 358–875.

Figure 27

OPPOSITION TO KOREAN AND VIETNAM WARS*

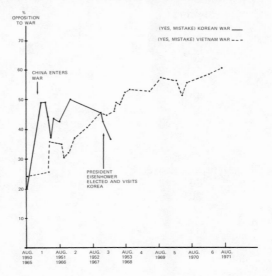

Vietnam involvement was conducted under the drumfire of antiwar opinion in the media, antiwar demonstrations, etc., and in the face of widely and constantly publicized combat deaths and casualties (by early 1969 the deaths had exceeded those of the entire Korean War, while the casualties had reached that point by early 1968).**

Of course, wars are only one factor in determining a President's popularity; but while their effect can be, and particularly in the case of small wars often is, overshadowed by other issues, they apparently adversely affect his popularity. Yet during the Vietnam War the President's popularity has never sunk to levels it did during the Korean "police action."

President Nixon's popularity seemed to hold up somewhat better (rising from 53 percent to 59 percent, right through the Cambodian operation and students' "strike" in the spring of 1970). He is "disengaging" us "honorably" from Vietnam; but one feels that, despite the relatively low casualties (compared to participants and length of involvement) in this war, the inconclusiveness, length and perhaps the manner of prosecuting this war, were beginning to discourage people to the extent

---

° *AIPO* (Gallup) data from Mueller, op. cit., pp. 360–363; and the *Gallup Opinion Index*, No. 73, July 1971, p. 3.
°° Mueller, op. cit., p. 365.

Table 26

PRESIDENTIAL POPULARITY—HARRY S. TRUMAN*

1950	Approve	Disapprove	No Opinion
February	45%	40%	15%
April	37	44	19
May	40	45	15
June	37	45	18
Korean invasion			
July	40	37	17
August	40	40	20
September	43	32	25
October	39	42	19
1951			
Communist Chinese invade Korea			
January	36	49	15
March	26	57	17
April	28	57	15
General MacArthur recalled			
June	24	61	15
July (mid)	25	59	16
Truce talks begin			
July (late)	29	54	17
September	31	57	12
Communists terminate truce talks			
October	32	54	14
November (early)	29	55	16
November (late)	23	58	19
December	23	58	19
1952			
February	25	62	13
May	28	59	13
June	32	58	10
November	32	55	13

that in 1971 it might be affecting the President's popularity. Of course, the continuing recession is probably a bigger factor.

To repeat, at least since World War II it seems to make little difference who the enemy is, or what the cause is, the Americans, like most people in the world, dislike wars. This doesn't mean that Americans won't or can't fight wars. Quite the contrary. Over the last hundred years our citizen soldier armies, as in the Civil War and World Wars I and II, proved in time to be second to none in the world. Traditionally we are a warrior nation—but only reluctantly, and it is not

° *Gallup Opinion Index*, No. 12, May 1966, p. 24.

counted among our assets. We are particularly non-bellicose when there are, or are likely to be, American casualties. That was true fifty years ago. It is true today.

Those who thought, however, that because the American voter disliked the Vietnam War, he would back a "dove" candidate in 1968 misjudged him again. In general, Americans know a bad situation when they see it, but they also know that the world is full of bad deals,

Table 27

PRESIDENTIAL POPULARITY—LYNDON B. JOHNSON*

1967	Approve	Disapprove	No Opinion
January	47%	37%	16%
February	46	37	17
March	45	42	13
April (early)	45	41	14
April (late)	46	38	16
May (early)	48	37	15
May (late)	45	39	16
June (early)	44	40	16
Glassboro Summit talks			
June (late)	52	35	13
August	39	47	14
September	39	47	14
October	38	50	12
November	41	49	10
December	46	41	13
1968			
January	48	39	13
February	48	39	13
TET offensive			
March (early)	41	48	11
March (late)	36	52	12
LBJ announces plan not to seek reelection			
April	49	40	11
May (early)	46	43	11
May (late)	41	45	14
June	42	45	13
July	40	48	12
August	35	52	13
October	42	51	7
November	43	44	13
1968 Presidential election			
December	44	43	13
1969			
January	49	34	14

* Gallup Opinion Index, No. 56, February 1970, pp. 15–16.

many of which cannot be avoided, and they will endure difficult situations for a surprising length of time. (Here is perhaps one of the "average man's" greatest points of difference with some of the young New Leftists who probably appeared to him to believe that doing unpleasant things isn't considered sensible under almost any circumstances regardless of the consequences.) "Dove" candidates may have appeared to the common man to be recommending that we act just as if the Communists weren't there; or "negotiate"; or leave the Vietnamese to settle their own affairs; or that the Communists really wouldn't be so bad if they took over. In 1968, the war was still young enough and the public morale remained high enough (see Figures 26 and 27) that

Table 28
PRESIDENT NIXON'S POPULARITY SINCE JANUARY 1970*

	Approve	Disapprove	No Opinion
Oct. 29–Nov. 1	49%	37%	14%
Oct. 8–11	54	35	11
Aug. 27–30	49	38	13
Aug. 20–23	51	37	12
June 25–28	48	39	13
Pentagon Papers			
June 4–7	48	37	15
May 14–16	50	35	15
April 23–25	50	38	12
April 3–5	49	38	13
March 12–14	50	37	13
February 19–21	51	36	13
Laos Invasion			
January 9–10, 1971	56	33	11
Dec. 5–7, 1970	52	34	14
Nov. 14–16	57	30	13
Oct. 9–13	58	27	15
Aug. 28–Sept. 1	56	30	14
July 31–Aug. 2	55	32	13
July 10–12	61	28	11
June 19–21	55	31	14
May 22–25	59	29	12
May 2–5	57	31	12
Cambodian Operation			
April 17–19	56	31	13
March 20–22	53	30	17
Feb. 28–Mar. 2	56	27	17
Jan. 30–Feb. 2	66	23	11
Jan. 16–19	63	23	24
Jan. 2–5, 1970	61	22	17

* From the *Gallup Opinion Index,* No. 67, January 1971, p. 1 and the *Gallup Opinion Index,* No. 77, November 1971, p. 1.

such "solutions" as yet made no sense to the "average man," who knew that in "the real world" people with armed might subjugated others, and that freedom perished when a totalitarian power conquered a people. He therefore rejected the "doves" and leaned toward the more "hawkish" (but far-from-bellicose) candidates. Eugene McCarthy did not win the New Hampshire Democratic primary in 1968, President Johnson did—and as a write-in candidate, without campaigning. Furthermore, many who voted for McCarthy did not know he was a "dove," so it is difficult to determine whether this position helped or hurt him. In any event, without a charismatic leader on either side (and Robert Kennedy's death eliminated the one candidate who might have played such a role), the issues made a difference. Clearly, the "dove" candidates lacked the wherewithal to make Vietnam a viable campaign issue.

Because few reacted favorably to outright "dovish" alternatives to the Vietnam War, other issues, some considered less important than Vietnam, weighed heavily. Perhaps coincidentally, those holding "dovish" attitudes toward the Vietnam War were likely to hold less popular attitudes on domestic issues such as law and order (including the quelling of student rioters) and education—this was critical.

The average voter probably felt he knew more (and had a better

Table 29

CANDIDATE WHO CAN DO A BETTER JOB OF DEALING WITH THE WAR*

Nixon	52%
McCarthy	29
No Opinion	19

Nixon	54
Humphrey	27
No Opinion	19

DID WE MAKE A MISTAKE IN SENDING TROOPS TO VIETNAM?**

Yes	No	No Opinion
53%	35%	12%

"The public, as many public opinion studies show, seeks an honorable way out of the Vietnam war." McCarthy's "problem has been to find a solution to the war that is favored by a substantial majority of voters."**

* *Gallup Opinion Index,* No. 39, September 1968, pp. 3, 6, 7.
** From the *New York Times,* August 25, 1968, p. 74, report on a Gallup poll.

idea of what needed to be done) regarding domestic issues than about Vietnam. For example, New Jersey's statewide election in 1967 revealed a vast hostility to busing. A statement by the state's Director of Education, a Democrat, endorsing the urban-suburban mix of school children by busing, cost his party dearly. Further, across the country voters rejected school budgets at the highest rate ever known by persons vitally concerned with education. A money crisis was developing, and the new and expensive programs, pushed by the educators, were not yielding the promised results. The lack of discipline in high schools and colleges also had a bad effect. But "dove" candidates were hardly likely to oppose the new and expensive school programs, the lack of discipline, or busing, or to strike a strong law-and-order posture. According to many ultraliberals, "law and order" were code words for anti-Negro sentiments.

In the spring of 1968, those who pointed out that the data did not support an expected swing to the Left were denounced by many in the party structures. Apparently many local Democratic committees split and some even "purged" themselves of those who ardently believed that the nation was going toward the "middle of the road." One cannot be too hard on local politicians during this period, however. National Democratic leaders and almost everyone in politics (except George Wallace) shunned the "centrist" domestic issues.* These issues, rather than Vietnam, formed the crux of the election. Had they been understood, the Democratic party's fate might have been different. McCarthy's victory over Robert Kennedy in the Oregon primary received very much attention—more attention, in fact, than Nixon's equally significant victory over Ronald Reagan. The Republican vote in this primary election had highlighted the "center" position of the electorate; the real Right and Left couldn't make it in November. Further, it seemed the Democratic candidate didn't appear close enough to the center. With Robert Kennedy dead, no matter who headed its ticket, the Democratic party faced a tough fight, and matters worsened as the summer wore on (see Table 30).

It was also clear that if the Democratic Convention followed the mood of the party's voters, McCarthy didn't have a chance. (Neither, for that matter, did the party's right wing. The right-wing Mississippi

* In a TV interview in February 1969, philosopher/longshoreman Eric Hoffer said what had probably occurred to many: that the clash is between the intimidated—the "silent majority"—and the arrogant—the New Left. In such cases the intimidated always lose—it is a shame that we have to wait for that "cracker" (Wallace) to say what everybody is thinking and no one has the courage to say.

Table 30

PARTY WHICH CAN HANDLE TOP PROBLEMS BEST*
1968

	July	May
Republicans	31%	30%
Democrats	27	28
No opinion	42	42

Table 31

POLL OF DEMOCRATS (49% OF ELECTORATE)**

	Humphrey	McCarthy	Not Sure
August 24	56%	38%	6%
July 26–29	46	40	14
June 11–15	48	40	12

POLL OF INDEPENDENTS (16% OF ELECTORATE)

	Humphrey	McCarthy	Not Sure
August 24	29%	56%	15%
July 26–29	32	48	20
June 11–15	30	54	16

Table 32

PRE-CONVENTION TRIAL HEAT (ALL CANDIDATES)***

	Total Democrats	Total Independents
Humphrey	54%	25%
McCarthy	30	50
Maddox	6	8
McGovern	3	3
Not sure	7	14

delegation was not seated; neither was the right wing of the Georgia delegation.) He had continued to lose ground until only 30 percent of the Democrats wanted him—approximately the percentage of delegates he drew. More independents, given a choice of Democratic candidates, favored McCarthy, but most independents have usually voted Republican (see Tables 31 and 32).

The above survey is noteworthy because of the claim of the militants at Chicago that they did not get their fair share of representation in

° *Gallup Opinion Index*, No. 39, September 1968, p. 15.
°° Louis Harris survey reported in the *Washington Post*, August 29, 1968, p. 10.
°°° Ibid.

111

the convention. Actually, they were represented to the degree the polls showed they would be. True, they did not get a majority of the delegates, but there was no reason they should have.

But, more important, polls after the end of August indicated that the trend was away from any Democratic candidate and that hopes of reversing the situation appeared dim:

TABLE 33

PRESIDENTIAL CHOICE (ALL VOTERS)*

	August 24	July 26–29	July 8–14
Nixon	40%	36%	35%
Humphrey	34	41	37
Wallace	17	16	17
Not sure	9	7	11
Nixon	41	35	34
McCarthy	35	43	42
Wallace	8	7	8
Not sure	8	7	8
Nixon	42	x	35
Johnson	36	x	41
Wallace	16	x	17
Not sure	6	x	7

Table 34

POST-DEMOCRATIC CONVENTION POLL**

"Whom would you vote for today?"

Nixon	Humphrey	Wallace	No opinion	None of the three
33.7%	28.5%	15.7%	12.6%	9.5%

"Who do you think will win November 5th?"

Nixon	Humphrey	Wallace	No opinion
45.3%	33.6%	3.9%	17.2%

It is unlikely, after the violence at Chicago—which, as we have seen, did not sit well with the voters***—that a candidate with a closer

---

* Louis Harris poll, The Washington Post Company, August 28, 1968, p. 1.

** Survey in a UPI report in the *Washington Evening Star*, September 4, 1968, p. 10. This was a nationwide telephone survey of 1,844 registered voters conducted by Albert E. Sindlinger.

*** See Table 7.

identification with the rioters would have done better than Vice President Humphrey, who was not that closely identified with them. Perhaps Humphrey could have made more headway with the average voter if he had condemned the rioters in no uncertain terms. But the fact that after the Democratic convention, he never passed the Republican candidate or pulled up even with him in the polls—a usual occurrence following the publicity of a convention—was an ominous sign for the Democrats.

Perhaps we should pause here to examine just how deep the electorate's annoyance might have been, with circumstances that resulted in disturbances such as those at the 1968 Democratic Convention. The fundamental issue at the convention may have been that of "participatory democracy" by a vocal minority versus "representative democracy" by majority opinion. No one suggests that a majority opinion has an inherent wisdom that always makes it more reliable than the views of any minority. But on some issues, this popular opinion is based on very strong feelings. These, in turn, might be based on presumed danger to something important to them (such as choosing a major party presidential candidate), or on long and serious consideration, or on much personal experience in a very complex and sensitive society.

Nonetheless, it appeared to many—in the late 1960s (and perhaps during most of 1970)—that more and more attention was being paid to the opinions of some very young, inexperienced, "decoupled" and quite atypical people—activist college students and teachers.* The data seem to indicate that it is probably highly misleading to attribute the absence of crowds representing the majority opposition to public apathy or tacit approval of the activists. A verbal minority talks about "participatory democracy," but to the average man that may really mean mobs in the street and minority influence by pressure and even blackmail.

The very busy adult population feels its duty is to *vote*—and on the average it does so to a much greater degree than the "student electorate." Working Americans do not like to or feel they should spend their overcommitted time countermarching or battling in the streets. This doesn't mean they cannot do it. Many do and are quite good at it, at any level of violence. The greatest mistake some young, intellectual, "pseudo-revolutionaries" might make is confusing the general public's reluctance to take to the streets with an inability to do so. Their

---

* By 1970 their audience included a special Presidential Commission on Campus Unrest.

113

ability was demonstrated on Wall Street in 1970, when under a shower of tickertape from cheering white-collar workers, a small band of blue-collar (and even some white-collar) workers scattered, in a matter of a few minutes, about 1,500 antiwar demonstrators.

After the "hard-hat" actions in New York in 1970, some observers feared a wave of violence; but they did not know average citizens. It is a heady experience to take temporary control by action; it is a different matter to get feelings of power from the experience. Besides, it is hard to give "power to the people" when they feel they already have it legally. The "average man," usually a practical-minded sort, knows how much is involved in *really* "taking over," even if he wants to, but he is not interested. Further, average citizens know about violence, and they reject it overwhelmingly.*

The probability of "participatory democracy" becoming a pattern for the average man—even as a way to draw attention to his woes—is practically nonexistent. Although his "track record" of "hunches" on such current topics as education, poverty, crime—or even the negotiations in Paris with the Vietnamese Communists (polls showed he expected no results from them)—is no worse than that of the "involved" who get the publicity, he is basically a "dull" sort, seldom making "news."

It may be reasonable to assume, then, that the widespread resentment in recent years over the students and over "participatory democracy" probably moved many rank-and-file voters toward the tougher-sounding Nixon; and that Vice President Humphrey's failure to condemn the Chicago rioters strongly cost him votes. Nevertheless, the organizations usually supporting the Democratic standard-bearer turned out for Humphrey; this might not have been possible if McCarthy had been the party's nominee. The unions are an excellent example of this support:

There were hundreds of radio and television broadcasts. Mr. Labor himself, George Meany, hit a network of 330 stations five straight times. . . . Thousands of locals hit the airwaves with their own appeals.**

Almost two-thirds (64 percent) of northern trade union members who had

* Only 11 percent of Negroes said they would join a riot, and only 5 percent of whites felt a counter-riot is justified if Negroes riot. The results are apparently somewhat age-sensitive. Twelve percent of white adolescents between the ages of 16 and 19 said they felt a counter-riot was in order. (Angus Campbell and Howard Schuman, *Racial Attitudes in Fifteen American Cities* [Ann Arbor: University of Michigan, Survey Research Center, 1968].)
** *New York Daily Column,* November 8, 1968.

backed Wallace initially *did not* vote for him . . . Wallace retained more backing among the better-educated and more affluent of his northern supporters, while in the South these groups were much more likely to have defected by Election Day than those less educated and less privileged.*

The final tally was 43 percent for Humphrey and Nixon, 13 for Wallace.**

The closeness of the election is somewhat deceiving, however, for there was a much stronger swing toward the center than may seem apparent from the down-to-the-wire finish. For example, the *Wall Street Journal* reported:

In balloting reported yesterday on issues totaling $7.8 billion, voters rejected proposals for $3.8 billion, or about half of the reported dollar total. It was the largest dollar amount on bonds ever defeated on an election day.***

The Federal Reserve Bank of San Francisco reported $4 billion of $9 billion in bond issues were rejected.**** Eleven out of 17 school bonds (about 65 percent) were defeated; this was a reversal of a three-year trend. (From 1964 through 1967, 73 to 77 percent of bond issue dollars were approved.) A Los Angeles secretary may have voiced the opinion of many voters when she said, "Until they clean up those damn colleges I'm not going to vote them any more money." A draftsman reflected the feeling of lack of results: "I'm sick and tired of shoveling money out to politicians who never get anything good done with it."†

According to the polls, dissatisfaction with the schools had begun to increase about this time (this was so among both Negroes and whites).‡ But there were other indications that the swing was away from the Left. For one, the people who voted for Wallace were hardly likely to be liberals. The overwhelming number of them were

---

* According to Gallup poll data, the number of Wallace voters among non-southern "skilled laborers" was the same (7 percent) as among non-southern "white-collar workers" (6 percent of "business," 3 of "professionals" and 13 of "unskilled labor" from the same regions voted for him). (Seymour Martin Lipset and Earl Raab. *The Politics of Unreason: Right-Wing Extremism in America, 1790–1970* [New York: Harper and Row, 1970], pp. 384, 385 and 395.)

** Except, reportedly, among the faculty of one of our "better" universities: "Faculty preference at Princeton in the 1968 elections were: Humphrey, 80 percent, Nixon and Dick Gregory [the Negro comedian-politician] 10 percent each." (*National Review*, February 25, 1969, 156.)

*** *Wall Street Journal*, November 7, 1968, p. 3.

**** *Newsweek*, February 24, 1969, p. 66.

† *Wall Street Journal*, November 7, 1968, p. 3.

‡ See Table 15.

from the South, which is normally Democratic, it is true; but not many of them were likely to vote for the 1968 Democratic platform. They might, of course, have abstained from voting; but it is hard to conceive of a majority of those who voted not choosing the more "hawkish," conservative Nixon over the more "dovish," liberal Humphrey. The normally Democratic Wallace voters in the North who had not been wooed back by George Meany and others, were hardly likely to vote for Humphrey if Wallace had not run. It seems, therefore, that the popular vote for Nixon would have been somewhat greater if Wallace had not run. In any event, one might have felt that the voters had issued a mandate for a more conservative course.

This was by no means the unanimous conclusion of the press. Numerous editorial writers and reporters on the first-rate papers interpreted the election results differently:

Since many potential Wallace supporters shifted to Mr. Nixon to enable him to carry Kentucky, Tennessee, and the Carolinas, while others shifted to Mr. Humphrey and helped him win Pennsylvania and Michigan, it is impossible to calculate how the election would have gone if Mr. Wallace had not been a candidate . . .°

The election gave him [Nixon] no clear sense of direction. He won with only 43.4 percent of the vote—some 300,000 more votes than Hubert Humphrey —and one must reach back to 1912 and Woodrow Wilson, who won with 41.9 percent, to find a more obscure and less convincing mandate.°°

The periodic between-campaign polls . . . have shown that no more than about 10 percent of Americans could be counted as bigots.

Wallace got the bigot vote and only a bit more by working hard to paper over and make respectable the appeals to segregationists that were really his only stock in trade.°°°

There were even some confusing headlines which did not accurately capsulize the respective dispatches.

NEW HOUSE SHOWS
A LIBERAL LEANING
ON DOMESTIC BILLS

° *New York Times*, Sunday, November 10, 1968, p. 12E.
°° *New York Times*, Sunday, November 17, 1968, Sec. IV, p. 1.
°°° *New York Times*, November 10, 1968, p. 2E.

G.O.P. GAIN OF 4 SEATS IS
OFFSET BY THE DECLINE IN
BEDROCK CONSERVATIVES*

The House is expected to remain predominantly conservative in fiscal and social policies. It has been following public opinion in a swing to the right for some time. But some of its members believe the measure of its performance rests largely on the kind of legislation forthcoming from the White House.**

All the above quotes were taken from two Sunday editions of the *New York Times*. The Sunday *Times* is more widely read than the daily edition and the average citizen was probably more likely, therefore, to see these remarks, particularly those articles containing them which appeared on page 1. On the other hand, the Sunday *Times*, about three weeks later, carried an article headed, "Gallup Election Analysis Finds Gain by Conservative Forces," giving comprehensive tables of data on presidential elections from 1952 through 1968. (A minor point, but perhaps still unfortunate–this item appeared on page 84; a month after the election it may no longer have been "newsworthy" enough to have at least begun on a rather dull page 1.)

It is interesting to note the fall-off of Democratic votes, in comparison to the 1960 election, among "manual" workers, people under 30 and the college-educated—in fact, among all categories (including registered Democrats) except for the "nonwhites." Those with a grade school education defected the least; but this group contained a relatively high percentage of Negroes who went 85 percent Democratic compared to 68 in 1960. Both Democrats and Republicans lost independent voters to Wallace.

Was the man in the street trying to register a protest or give a "centrist" mandate to the new administration? The results of a postelection analysis done by the Survey Research Center of the University of Michigan, which has been studying the American voter for decades, were described by the director of the study as follows:

. . . the survey data make it clear that Nixon would have won the election if Wallace had not become a national candidate. For after the election most of the Wallace voters rated Nixon considerably higher than Humphrey on a 0-100 scale and presumably would have given Nixon a considerably greater

* *New York Times*, November 17, 1968, p. 1.
** Ibid., p. 47. Same article.

117

Table 35

GALLUP ELECTION ANALYSIS FINDS GAIN BY CONSERVATIVE FORCES*

(Emphasis by underlining added)

	1952		1956		1960		1964		1968		
	Dem.	Rep.	Dem.	Rep.	Dem.	Rep.	Dem.	Rep.	Dem.	Rep.	Wallace
NATIONAL	44.6%	55.4%	42.2%	57.8%	50.1%	49.9%	61.3%	38.7%	43.0%	43.4%	13.6%
Men	47	53	45	55	52	48	60	40	41	43	16
Women	42	53	39	61	49	51	62	38	45	43	12
White	43	57	41	59	49	51	49	41	38	47	15
Nonwhite	79	21	61	39	68	32	94	6	85	12	3
College	34	66	31	69	39	61	52	48	37	54	9
High School	45	55	42	58	52	48	62	38	42	43	15
Grade School	52	48	50	50	55	45	66	34	52	33	15
Professional and Business	36	64	32	68	42	58	54	46	34	56	10
White Collar	40	60	37	63	48	52	57	43	41	47	12
Manual	55	45	50	50	60	40	71	29	50	35	15
Farmers	33	67	46	54	48	52	53	47	29	51	20
Under 30	51	49	43	57	54	46	64	36	47	38	15
30–49 years	47	53	45	55	54	46	63	37	44	41	15
50 years and older	39	61	39	61	46	54	59	41	41	47	12
Protestant	37	63	37	63	38	62	55	45	35	49	16
Catholics	56	44	51	49	78	22	76	24	59	33	8
Republicans	8	92	4	96	5	95	20	80	9	86	5
Democrats	77	23	85	15	84	16	87	13	74	12	14
Independents	35	65	30	70	43	57	56	44	31	44	25

* As reported in the *New York Times*, December 8, 1968, page 84.

118

margin of victory if Wallace had not been on the ballot. For example, Nixon's median rating among Wallace voters was 60 compared to only 46 for Humphrey (Wallace's own median rating was 87 among his voters). Apparently most of those Democratic identifiers who chose Wallace because they were dissatisfied with the Democratic candidate would have defected to Nixon instead if Wallace had not been a candidate.*

Oddly, as the following headline shows, not everyone drew the same conclusions, even from the same analysis:**

WALLACE RACE DIDN'T CHANGE A THING IN 1968 THE EVIDENCE IS IN

This article reported on the same Survey Research Center's postelection study, and, as in the article memtioned earlier, the headline writer did not reflect the body of the article. For example, the article included the following statements:

There is strong evidence that their [the voters'] choice, had Wallace not been on the ballot, would have been Mr. Nixon.

Fully half of the Wallace voters said they felt cold toward Humphrey, but only 26 percent were cold toward Mr. Nixon.

In other words . . . Nixon was more palatable than Humphrey was to them.

Certainly Nixon would have won anyway (which might be what the headline writer had in mind); but the change that would have occurred, had Wallace not run, would have been significant. The mandate would have been clearer—at least it is likely we would not have had "to reach back to 1912 and Woodrow Wilson," or perhaps even past 1960, "to find a man with a more obscure and less convincing mandate."***

In 1969 and 1970 the average man seemed to indicate that he was

* Arthur C. Wolfe, "Challenge from the Right: The Basis of Voter Support for Wallace in 1968," prepared for delivery at the Annual Meeting of the American Psychological Association, Washington, D.C., September 1, 1969. Arthur C. Wolfe ran the 1968 national election study for the Survey Research Center of the University of Michigan.

** Reported by Philip Meyer in the *Chicago Daily News*, May 7, 1969.

*** Elections, particularly presidential elections, are of great interest to those using public opinion polls, for, with all their "unknowns," they are about the only litmus paper against which to test reported national public opinion. The 1968 election appeared to support the indications in the pre-election polls.

still basically in the position he was in 1968. How "conservative" did he feel? Terms mean different things to different people. But it is important to note certain points about who felt that way, or at least who was reluctant to say that he was a "liberal." Conservative was "fast becoming a dirty word on the college campus," for example.[*] Not so for the average person: in April, 1970, he felt much more conservative than liberal. Farmers and white-collar workers considered themselves conservative, and so did professional and business people—even more so. The manual worker, "hard hats," posted the lowest number describing themselves as conservative. The college-educated constituted the greatest percentage feeling conservative, the grade school-educated the lowest. People in large cities, as well as in the non-metropolitan areas, and of all income levels, felt that way quite strongly. Even the weight of Democratic opinion no longer fell on the liberal side.

Table 36

LIBERAL-CONSERVATIVE[**]

Suppose you had to classify yourself as either a liberal or a conservative, which would you say you are?

	Liberal	April 1970 Conservative	No Opinion
NATIONAL	27%	45%	28%
SEX			
Men	29	48	23
Women	26	43	31
RACE			
White	27	48	25
Nonwhite	30	29	41
EDUCATION			
College	39	49	12
High School	26	48	26
Grade School	20	36	44
OCCUPATION			
Professional and Business	32	52	16
White Collar	30	46	24
Farmers	19	46	35
Manual	27	42	31
AGE			
21–29 years	41	43	16
30–49 years	27	47	26
50 and over	23	45	32

[*] Gallup Opinion Index, No. 60, June 1970, p. 14.
[**] Gallup Opinion Index, No. 59, May 1970, p. 8.

Table 36 (continued)

RELIGION			
Protestant	24	24	48
Catholic	33	39	28
Jewish	x	x	x
POLITICS			
Republican	18	62	20
Democrat	33	35	32
Independent	30	45	25
REGION			
East	30	43	27
Midwest	33	44	23
South	18	48	34
West	27	50	23
INCOME			
$15,000 and over	39	47	14
$10,000–$14,999	29	50	21
$ 7,000–$ 9,999	29	47	24
$ 5,000–$ 6,999	25	45	30
$ 3,000–$ 4,999	27	39	34
Under $3,000	14	37	49
COMMUNITY SIZE			
1,000,000 and over	32	44	24
500,000–999,999	34	40	26
50,000–499,999	32	43	25
2,500–49,999	22	50	28
Under 2,500, Rural	20	49	31

Furthermore, the President's popularity had continued to maintain its general level in 1969 and 1970 (see Table 28). In 1970 his support, too, came from all areas, levels of education, ages and income brackets. By mid-1971, his support among the college-educated, white-collar workers, and farmers had slipped to the point where they no longer towered over the other categories as his supporters, but by October 29-November 1, these categories had returned to their dominant places in the support column. A majority of Negroes and 50 percent of Democrats opposed the President, and his support among Negroes and the 18-to-21-year-olds continued to fall. Although his support among manual laborers recovered enough so that he broke even, this category, along with big city dwellers, generally continues to show low levels of support.

Despite the fact that the country was going through the worst recession in nine years in 1970, Americans were still conerned with the

Table 37

PRESIDENT NIXON'S POPULARITY

Do you approve or disapprove of the way Nixon is handling his job as president?

	Approve				Disapprove				No Opinion			
	Oct.[a] 1970	Feb.[b] 1971	June[c] 1971	Oct.[a] 1971	Oct.[a] 1970	Feb. 1971	June 1971	Oct. 1971	Oct. 1970	Feb. 1971	June 1971	Oct. 1971
NATIONAL	58%	50%	48%	49%	27%	36%	39%	37%	15%	14%	13%	14%
SEX												
Men	61	53	48	51	27	38	43	38	12	9	9	11
Women	55	47	48	48	28	35	35	35	17	18	17	17
RACE												
White	61	52	50	52	25	35	37	35	14	13	13	13
Nonwhite	25	33	25	20	56	48	52	60	19	19	23	20
EDUCATION												
College	59	59	46	59	31	34	45	31	10	7	9	10
High School	60	48	48	48	27	37	39	38	13	15	18	14
Grade School	53	43	47	41	26	39	32	40	21	18	21	19
OCCUPATION												
Professional and Business	64	56	51	59	27	37	39	33	9	7	10	8
White Collar	64	41	45	53	22	38	45	33	14	21	10	14
Farmers	64	53	47	45	19	35	38	35	17	12	15	20
Manual	53	50	42	42	31	35	48	42	16	15	15	16
AGE												
18–21 years*	x	x	46	41	x	x	43	44	x	x	11	15
21–29 years	52	49	45	59	35	40	43	42	13	11	12	9
30–49 years	60	50	45	51	28	36	41	32	12	14	14	17
50 and over	59	48	52	49	24	36	33	37	17	16	15	14
RELIGION												
Protestant	59	54	51	52	35	40	35	34	13	11	14	14
Catholic	59	46	45	47	27	40	41	39	14	14	14	14
Jewish	x	x	x	x	x	x	x	x	x	x	x	x

Table 37 (continued)
PRESIDENT NIXON'S POPULARITY

	Oct.ᵃ 1970	Feb.ᵇ 1971	Juneᶜ 1971	Oct.ᵈ 1971	Oct. 1970	Feb. 1971	June 1971	Oct. 1971	Oct. 1970	Feb. 1971	June 1971	Oct. 1971
POLITICS												
Republican	82	76	73	75	10	15	16	16	8	9	11	9
Democrat	44	36	34	35	39	50	51	51	17	14	15	14
Independent	57	50	46	48	27	35	42	33	16	15	12	19
REGION												
East	59	50	46	50	29	35	38	36	12	15	16	14
Midwest	53	48	47	50	33	38	39	36	14	14	14	14
South	64	52	51	52	20	33	35	35	16	15	14	13
West	54	47	45	41	29	43	47	43	17	10	8	16
INCOME												
$15,000 and over	71	54	49	59	23	39	42	33	6	7	9	8
$10,000–$14,999	60	55	45	46	26	32	45	39	14	13	10	15
$ 7,000–$ 9,999	57	50	48	53	31	36	39	34	12	14	13	13
$ 5,000–$ 6,999	54	48	47	48	26	38	37	37	20	14	16	15
$ 3,000–$ 4,999	49	45	48	46	31	38	38	38	20	17	14	16
Under $3,000	52	38	50	43	27	44	29	39	21	18	21	18
COMMUNITY SIZE												
1,000,000 and over	50	47	42	41	39	37	46	41	11	16	12	18
500,000–999,999	52	43	44	43	30	44	42	44	18	13	14	13
50,000–499,999	58	46	44	50	31	40	42	37	11	14	14	13
2,500–49,999	67	50	53	60	17	40	34	28	16	10	13	12
Under 2,500, Rural	61	57	50	50	22	29	33	36	17	14	17	14

ᵃ *Gallup Opinion Index*, No. 64, October 1970, p. 7.
ᵇ *Gallup Opinion Index*, No. 69, March 1971, p. 1.
ᶜ *Gallup Opinion Index*, No. 74, August 1971, p. 4.
ᵈ *Gallup Opinion Index*, No. 77, November, 1971, p. 1. These figures are from a poll of October 29–November 1, 1971.
* Not included in 1970 polls.

issues that had concerned them in 1968. They didn't like the Vietnam War, but still felt that just "bringing the boys home now" was no viable alternative to the President's policy. In late May, after Cambodia became a theater of battle, the largest minority voted for the more difficult choice in Vietnamization (except to escalate); i.e., not to dump the Vietnamese government, even if it took years for them to get ready to take over the war. Only 23 percent favored immediate withdrawal.

Table 38

VIETNAM PEACE PLAN*
(Emphasis by underlining added)

"Here are four different plans the U.S. could follow in dealing with the war in Vietnam. Which do you prefer?"
  A. Withdraw all troops from Vietnam immediately
  B. Withdraw all troops by July 1971—that is, a year from this coming July
  C. Withdraw troops but take as many years to do this as are needed to turn the war over to the South Vietnamese
  D. Send more troops to Vietnam and step up the fighting

| | May 22–24, 1970 | | | | |
	A	B	C	D	No Opinion
NATIONAL	23%	25%	31%	13%	8%
SEX					
Men	21	26	32	14	7
Women	27	26	26	13	8
RACE					
White	20	26	32	14	8
Nonwhite	48	20	18	7	7
EDUCATION					
College	18	30	34	12	6
High School	21	26	31	15	7
Grade School	31	19	25	11	14
OCCUPATION					
Professional and					
Business	21	27	34	12	6
White Collar	22	23	32	18	5
Farmers	22	22	32	11	13
Manual	26	25	30	13	6
AGE					
21–29 years	23	29	32	11	5
30–49 years	22	25	31	16	6
50 and over	25	23	30	11	11

* *Gallup Opinion Index*, No. 61, July 1970, p. 5.

Table 38 (continued)

RELIGION					
Protestant	20	25	33	13	9
Catholic	29	26	26	13	6
Jewish	x	x	x	x	x
POLITICS					
Republican	17	27	37	14	5
Democrat	27	23	29	12	9
Independent	23	28	26	13	10
REGION					
East	27	26	28	12	7
Midwest	24	28	32	10	6
South	22	21	30	14	13
West	15	26	32	20	7
COMMUNITY SIZE					
1,000,000 and over	35	21	22	17	5
500,000–999,999	32	24	24	15	5
50,000–499,999	16	28	36	11	9
2,500–49,999	24	23	32	10	11
Under 2,500, Rural	19	26	33	13	9

When faced in the same time period with an either/or question on withdrawal within 18 months, the weight of opinion came out for withdrawal in that time period.

Several months later, in a Louis Harris "real-time" polling show produced by ABC-TV on January 13, 1971, the part of the question about "tying the President's hands" was left out. The percentage of those in favor of the Hatfield-McGovern proposal to withdraw all troops by the end of 1971 then was 61 percent. Furthermore, a Gallup poll showed 55 percent in favor of such a bill in late 1970 and approval had greatly increased by January 1971. At about this time, as indicated in Figure 27, opposition to the war had reached the 60 percent mark. As in the May poll on "Vietnamization," listed just prior to the one above, those with more education, greater affluence and more professional employment tended to be less "dovish" than the rest of the population.

In answer to the question, asked in mid-June 1971,

Suppose one candidate for congress from your district said that he favors getting *all* U.S. armed forces out of Vietnam by July of next year. He is

125

Table 39

WITHDRAWAL FROM VIETNAM BY THE END OF 1971?*

"It has been proposed that Congress pass a resolution that all U.S. troops be withdrawn from Vietnam by the end of 1971. Opponents say such a resolution would tie the hands of the President. Would you favor or oppose a resolution in Congress which would require all U.S. troops to be withdrawn from Vietnam by the end of 1971?"

	Favor	Oppose	Not sure
NATIONWIDE	44%	35%	21%
REGION			
East	54	26	20
Midwest	45	37	18
South	38	39	23
West	36	40	24
Border states	41	39	20
POLITICS			
Republicans	37	42	21
Democrats	46	32	22
Independents	51	38	11
SEX			
Men	39	45	16
Women	49	26	25
AGE			
Under 30	43	38	19
30–49	55	31	14
50 and over	36	36	28

Table 40

VIETNAM WITHDRAWAL PROPOSAL**

"A proposal has been made in Congress to require the U.S. government to bring home all U.S. troops from Vietnam before the end of this year. Would you like to have your congressman vote for or against this proposal?"

(Emphasis by underlining added)

	January 9–10, 1971		
	Vote For	Vote Against	No Opinion
NATIONAL	72%	20%	8%
SEX			
Male	72	20	8
Female	78	14	8
RACE			
White	71	21	8
Nonwhite	81	12	7

* Louis Harris survey as reported in the *Philadelphia Inquirer*, August 17, 1970, p. 3.
** *Gallup Opinion Index*, No. 69, March 1971, p. 11.

Table 40 (continued)

EDUCATION

College	60	34	6
High School	75	18	7
Grade School	80	10	10

OCCUPATION

Professional and Business	62	32	6
White Collar	71	21	8
Farmers	74	16	10
Manual	77	16	7

AGE

21–29 years	76	20	4
30–49 years	75	21	4
50 and over	68	20	12

RELIGION

Protestant	68	23	9
Catholics	80	16	4
Jewish	x	x	x

POLITICS

Republican	64	28	8
Democrat	78	15	7
Independent	71	21	8

REGION

East	77	18	5
Midwest	75	17	8
South	65	24	11
West	69	23	8

INCOME

$15,000 and over	62	31	7
$10,000–$14,999	75	21	4
$ 7,000–$ 9,999	74	22	4
$ 5,000–$ 6,999	67	20	13
$ 3,000–$ 4,999	69	17	14
Under $3,000	87	5	8

COMMUNITY SIZE

1,000,000 and over	77	15	8
500,000–999,999	72	23	5
50,000–499,999	67	24	9
2,500–49,999	74	21	5

opposed by a candidate who says we must leave about 50,000 troops there to help the South Vietnamese. Other things being equal, which candidate would you prefer? (*Gallup Opinion Index*, No. 74, August 1971, p. 23.)

61 percent endorsed the candidate for withdrawal and 28 percent for one favoring leaving 50,000 troops there (compared to 72 percent for total withdrawal and 20 percent against in the January poll listed above.) But, in this poll there was not the appreciable spread between the categories of people polled mentioned above. In any event, the average person

Table 41

PENALTIES FOR DRAFT EVADERS*

If a young man refuses to be drafted, which one of these things do you think should be done?
  A. Make him serve in the army in a non-combat unit
  B. Make him serve on special civilian projects here at home
  C. Send him to jail for a term
  D. No penalty—let him go back to his usual work

| | *April 1970* | | | | |
	A	B	C	D	No Opinion
NATIONAL	39%	27%	16%	8%	10%
SEX					
Men	40	21	22	8	9
Women	38	32	11	9	10
RACE					
White	40	27	17	7	9
Nonwhite	23	34	10	24	9
EDUCATION					
College	35	35	14	7	9
High School	42	25	19	6	8
Grade School	35	25	14	14	12
OCCUPATION					
Professional and					
Business	39	29	17	6	9
White Collar	40	29	16	6	9
Farmers	44	25	13	6	12
Manual	37	28	18	9	8
AGE					
21–29 years	30	30	22	11	7
30–49 years	42	28	16	6	8
50 and over	41	25	16	9	12
RELIGION					
Protestant	38	26	17	9	10
Catholic	43	28	16	6	7
Jewish	x	x	x	x	x
POLITICS					
Republican	47	27	13	5	8
Democrat	37	28	16	9	10
Independent	35	27	19	11	8
REGION					
East	41	26	15	9	9
Midwest	39	30	14	9	8
South	36	22	19	9	14
West	36	33	17	5	9
COMMUNITY SIZE					
1,000,000 and over	38	27	19	10	6
500,000–999,999	42	26	16	10	6
50,000–499,999	38	28	20	6	8
2,500–49,999	38	23	18	9	12
Under 2,500, Rural	37	30	13	8	12

* *Gallup Opinion Index,* No. 59, May 1970, p. 9.

is no more happy about this war than about the other wars of this century, and he apparently is tiring of the long years of engagement and lack of success, as well he might.

Interestingly, support for the war and the President remained as high as it did for as long as it did (July 1970—44 percent for, 35 against withdrawal of troops in 1971) in the face of a majority opinion that it was a mistake to have sent troops (reached in August 1968). This may reflect the "dirty-job-that-must-be-done" syndrome (mentioned earlier) and/or trust in the President on complicated matters of foreign and defense policy. The attitude toward those who dodge the draft was also interesting, particularly regarding which groups of people felt strongest about different proposed sanctions.

Table 42
THREE-WAY PRESIDENTIAL RACE—NIXON, MUSKIE, WALLACE—HARRIS SURVEY*

	Nixon	Muskie	Wallace	Not Sure
Latest	39%	44%	12%	5%
January 1971	40	43	11	6
November 1970	40	46	10	4
September	43	43	10	4
May	42	38	12	8
April	47	36	10	7
February	49	35	11	5
November 1969	49	35	11	5
October	51	35	9	5
May	51	33	11	5

TWO-WAY PRESIDENTIAL RACE—NIXON, MUSKIE—HARRIS SURVEY

	Nixon	Muskie	Sure Not
Latest	42%	48%	10%
January 1970	46	49	5

But, back in 1970, at the beginning of the Congressional election campaign, Nixon was outdistancing all comers, despite the recession, the action in Cambodia and the Kent State tragedy. The Cambodia

* Louis Harris survey reported in the *Philadelphia Inquirer*, March 19, 1971, p. 12.

Table 43

NIXON–MUSKIE–WALLACE TEST ELECTON

"To get some idea of the national political situation at this early stage, suppose the presidential election were to be held today. If Richard Nixon were the Republican candidate and Edmund Muskie were the Democratic candidate and George Wallace ran again as a third-party candidate, which would you like to see win?"

Based on Registered Voters

	Nixon			Muskie			Wallace			Other			Undecided No Opinion		
	July* 1970	May† 1971	Oct.‡ 1971	July 1970	May 1971	Oct. 1971	July 1970	May 1971	Oct. 1971	July 1970	May 1971	Oct. 1971	July 1970	May 1971	Oct. 1971
NATIONAL	43%	39%	43%	36%	41%	35%	13%	12%	13%	2%	NA	2%	6%	8%	7%
SEX															
Men	43	40	44	34	39	33	15	15	14	2	NA	2	6	6	7
Women	43	39	42	37	42	38	11	9	11	2	NA	1	7	10	8
RACE															
White	45	42	45	34	38	32	14	12	14	1	NA	2	6	8	7
Nonwhite	22	16	21	58	64	69	2	9	1	8	NA	3	10	11	6
EDUCATION															
College	53	44	49	36	46	39	6	5	6	2	NA	1	3	5	5
High School	41	35	42	29	41	35	14	13	14	1	NA	2	5	8	7
Grade School	39	37	39	27	35	32	20	17	17	2	NA	1	12	11	11
OCCUPATION															
Professional and Business	52	44	55	35	41	33	6	9	7	1	NA	1	6	6	4
White Collar	51	48	43	30	41	36	9	5	16	1	NA	1	9	6	4
Farmers	46	48	56	29	31	17	17	16	16	3	NA	10	5	5	1
Manual	36	32	31	39	45	42	17	15	15	2	NA	2	6	8	10
AGE															
18–20 years	NA	NA	34	NA	NA	48	NA	NA	7	NA	NA	4	NA	NA	7
21–29 years	38	32	38	44	44	40	5	17	14	4	NA	3	9	7	5
30–49 years	42	36	41	37	45	39	15	13	11	1	NA	2	5	6	7
50 and over	45	44	48	32	37	29	14	10	14	2	NA	1	7	9	8

130

Table 43 (continued)

RELIGION															
Protestant	47	46	47	31	34	30	15	13	15	2	NA	2	5	7	6
Catholic	40	32	36	42	50	43	10	8	10	1	NA	1	7	10	11
Jewish	x	x	x	x	x	x	x	x	x	x	x	x	x	x	x
POLITICS															
Republican	82	75	81	7	12	6	7	8	7	–	NA	1	4	5	5
Democrat	19	16	20	56	63	56	15	13	13	2	NA	2	8	8	9
Independent	36	38	35	38	36	34	17	15	20	3	NA	3	6	11	9
REGION															
East	45	42	43	41	41	38	6	9	5	1	NA	1	7	8	10
Midwest	44	43	45	39	42	34	9	9	11	2	NA	1	7	9	8
South	39	34	42	24	38	28	28	20	23	–	NA	3	6	8	7
West	43	43	40	40	44	43	10	8	13	1	NA	2	5	5	3
INCOME															
$15,000 and over	50	45	49	38	45	35	5	6	11	2	NA	2	5	4	5
$10,000–$14,999	48	40	45	33	45	38	14	8	7	2	NA	2	3	7	8
$ 7,000–$ 9,999	41	34	38	41	41	33	12	16	19	1	NA	1	5	9	8
$ 5,000–$ 6,999	44	44	44	31	35	35	15	15	12	1	NA	1	9	6	6
$ 3,000–$ 4,999	36	34	35	35	39	36	15	16	17	2	NA	2	12	11	11
Under $3,000	35	37	39	34	30	34	22	16	16	1	NA	2	7	15	10
COMMUNITY SIZE															
1,000,000 and over	42	32	41	41	49	41	7	9	7	2	NA	2	8	10	9
500,000–999,999	40	33	32	49	53	43	7	8	17	1	NA	–	4	6	6
50,000–499,999	43	40	43	39	43	36	12	9	11	1	NA	1	5	8	9
2,500–49,999	41	42	47	32	36	36	17	15	11	2	NA	3	7	7	4
Under 2,500, Rural	47	44	46	26	33	26	18	16	18	3	NA	3	6	7	7

* *Gallup Opinion Index*, No. 62, August 1970, p. 6.
† *Gallup Opinion Index*, No. 72, June 1971, p. 10.
‡ *Gallup Opinion Index*, No. 77, November 1971, p. 10.

131

Table 44

NIXON–KENNEDY–WALLACE TRIAL HEAT*

Question: "If Richard Nixon were the Republican candidate and Edward Kennedy were the Democratic candidate and George Wallace ran again as a third-party candidate, which would you like to see win?"

| | May 1971 | | | | March 13–14, 1971 | | | |
	Nixon	Kennedy	Wallace	Undecided	Nixon	Kennedy	Wallace	Undecided
NATIONAL	42%	41%	10%	7%	46%	38%	11%	5%
SEX								
Male	42	40	13	5				
Female	42	41	7	10				
RACE								
White	45	36	11	8				
Nonwhite	10	84	2	4				
EDUCATION								
College	53	36	5	6				
High School	41	42	10	7				
Grade School	35	40	14	11				
OCCUPATION								
Professional and Business	50	36	8	6				
White Collar	53	36	6	5				
Farmers	40	41	6	13				
Manual	34	47	13	6				
AGE								
21–29 years	29	50	14	7				
30–49 years	41	42	11	6				
50 and over	47	36	8	9				
RELIGION								
Protestant	49	33	12	6				
Catholic	32	51	7	10				
Jewish	x	x	x	x				

Table 44 (continued)

POLITICS				
Republican	77	12	6	5
Democrat	17	63	12	8
Independent	44	36	11	9
REGION				
East	44	42	7	7
Midwest	42	41	7	10
South	35	40	19	6
West	49	38	5	8
INCOME				
$15,000 and over	50	36	7	7
$10,000–$14,999	46	39	8	7
$ 7,000–$ 9,999	37	42	12	9
$ 5,000–$ 6,999	41	47	9	3
$ 3,000–$ 4,999	37	40	14	9
Under $3,000	37	39	11	13
COMMUNITY SIZE				
1,000,000 and over	38	48	6	8
500,000–999,999	34	46	8	12
50,000–499,999	45	44	6	5
2,500–49,999	42	38	14	6
Under 2,500, Rural	45	33	14	8

* *Gallup Opinion Index*, No. 72, June 1971, p. 11.

133

Table 45

NIXON–HUMPHREY–WALLACE TRIAL HEAT*

Question: "If Richard Nixon were the Republican candidate and Hubert Humphrey were the Democratic candidate and George Wallace ran again as a third-party candidate, which would you like to see win?"

| | May 1971 | | | | March 13–14, 1971 | | | |
	Nixon	Humphrey	Wallace	Undecided	Nixon	Humphrey	Wallace	Undecided
NATIONAL	42%	39%	12%	7%	46%	36%	12%	6%
SEX								
Male	44	37	15	4				
Female	40	41	10	9				
RACE								
White	45	35	13	7				
Nonwhite	10	79	5	6				
EDUCATION								
College	49	40	6	5				
High School	42	39	13	6				
Grade School	38	37	17	8				
OCCUPATION								
Professional and Business	48	36	10	6				
White Collar	52	37	7	4				
Farmers	45	29	14	12				
Manual	34	45	16	5				
AGE								
21–29 years	33	41	19	7				
30–49 years	41	41	13	5				
50 and over	46	36	10	8				
RELIGION								
Protestant	48	32	14	6				
Catholic	38	44	10	8				
Jewish	x	x	x	x				

Table 45 (continued)

POLITICS				
Republican	79	8	7	6
Democrat	17	60	15	8
Independent	42	37	15	6
REGION				
East	44	38	11	7
Midwest	44	39	9	8
South	35	38	21	6
West	47	40	8	5
INCOME				
$15,000 and over	47	39	8	6
$10,000–$14,999	48	38	8	6
$ 7,000–$ 9,999	37	37	18	8
$ 5,000–$ 6,999	43	40	13	4
$ 3,000–$ 4,999	34	45	15	6
Under $3,000	35	36	17	12
COMMUNITY SIZE				
1,000,000 and over	36	46	9	9
500,000–999,999	35	51	7	7
50,000–499,999	42	46	8	4
2,500–49,999	49	30	15	6
Under 2,500, Rural	45	29	19	7

* Ibid., p. 12.

135

offensive had begun to look like a success, so criticism of it began to lose much of its "tragic blunder" tone; this was not true of Kent State. It appeared once more that, as of mid-1970, there were no easy alternatives to the President's foreign policies that appealed to the public, and his harder stance on such domestic issues as crime and campus disorders apparently offset his image on economic issues. President Nixon's lead over his potential opponents was dwindling, however, according to the Harris polls. By the November 1970 election, he trailed Senator Edmund Muskie. As of March 1971, Louis Harris reported that Nixon was even further behind the Senator from Maine.

A Gallup poll taken about the same time differs from the Harris survey shown above; Gallup shows Nixon again leading Muskie 43 percent to 39.* The May poll gave Muskie an edge, 41 percent to 39 over Nixon, with 12 for Wallace; but by October the President's percentage had climbed back to 43 percent and Senator Muskie's had fallen to 35. Despite the lack of clarity on this issue at present, it is interesting to note with which groups the greatest support for the President lay in July 1970, and how they had switched by May 1971 and to some extent returned by October 1971.

One thing shown by these polls which is quite interesting is the significant change in some aspects of the Wallace column between July 1970 and May and October 1971; e.g., the young 21-to-29-year-old voters' support for him seems to have tripled (from 5 percent to 17 and 14).

As of the May 1971 Gallup poll the President ran neck and neck with Senator Kennedy; Senator Humphrey was close behind and both Senators had gained on him since the last poll in March. But their constituencies were slightly different from Senator Muskie's (e.g., more youth, less college-educated, business and professional, etc.).

A poll taken October 29-November 1, 1971, on the President's popularity showed the June 1971 "defectors" from his usual support groups (college-educated persons, those with higher incomes, from smaller communities, etc.) had returned, and his popularity overall was holding up, so "trial heats" taken in the same period might look different, but one feels they wouldn't show "landslide" tendencies either way. (See Table 37.)

The May 1971 poll asked the "liberal-conservative" question again, but gave a wider choice than the poll in Table 36, so it is impossible to compare them. There is a 13-point edge on the side of identified "con-

---

* *Gallup Opinion Index,* No. 71, May 1971, p. 9.

Table 46

POLITICAL PHILOSOPHY*

Question: "How would you describe yourself—as very conservative, fairly conservative, middle-of-the-road, fairly liberal, or very liberal?"

	Very Conservative	Fairly Conservative	Middle-of-the-Road	Fairly Liberal	Very Liberal	No Opinion
			Early May 1971			
NATIONAL	11%	28%	29%	19%	7%	6%
SEX						
Male	12	26	28	20	8	6
Female	11	29	29	19	6	6
RACE						
White	12	29	30	18	6	5
Nonwhite	8	21	23	27	14	7
EDUCATION						
College	9	28	27	26	8	2
High School	11	29	32	18	6	4
Grade School	15	23	25	14	10	13
OCCUPATION						
Professional and Business	9	31	24	26	6	4
White Collar	11	29	28	21	8	3
Farmers	19	13	46	7	6	9
Manual	10	28	30	19	7	6
AGE						
21–29 years	9	25	28	26	9	3
30–49 years	12	31	29	17	6	5
50 and over	13	26	30	17	7	7
RELIGION						
Protestant	13	31	28	17	6	5
Catholic	8	24	35	20	6	7
Jewish	x	x	x	x	x	x
POLITICS						
Republican	17	36	28	13	3	3
Democrat	8	25	28	24	9	6
Independent	12	25	30	19	8	6
REGION						
East	11	24	30	22	7	6
Midwest	13	26	31	18	7	5
South	12	31	25	17	7	8
West	8	30	30	20	9	3
INCOME						
$15,000 and over	10	28	29	23	9	1
$10,000–$14,999	11	30	29	22	4	4
$ 7,000–$ 9,999	11	28	30	20	6	5
$ 5,000–$ 6,999	9	28	31	18	6	8
$ 3,000–$ 4,999	18	25	26	13	11	7
Under $3,000	10	25	26	18	11	10
COMMUNITY SIZE						
1,000,000 and over	10	24	30	24	7	5
500,000–999,999	9	25	24	23	11	8
50,000–499,999	14	27	29	23	5	2
2,500–49,999	12	32	28	18	8	2
Under 2,500, Rural	11	29	30	13	8	9

* *Gallup Opinion Index*, No. 72, June 1971, p. 15.

servatism" versus identified "liberalism" (fairly and very), but one cannot tell whether this is a gain or a loss for either position. One still gets the feeling, however, of an asymmetrical Gaussian ("bell-curve") distribution—heavy in the center, but skewed somewhat to the right.

Perhaps such a poll may better reflect a "value system" in this day and age; "liberal" and "conservative" positions may have recently hinged on such issues as law and order, school busing, pornography, drug abuse, and permissiveness in schools, which can cut across the spectrum of standard "political" positions based on classical economic and social issues.

Something, noted by many commentators earlier, had finally become obvious by 1970. Whether the delay was due to inadequate coverage of issues, such as those mentioned previously, is not important here. What

Table 47

T.V. IMPARTIALITY*

(Emphasis by underlining added)

There has been much talk about whether the TV networks deal fairly with all sides in presenting the news dealing with political and social issues. How do you feel about this . . . do they deal fairly with all sides or do they tend to favor one side?

| | December 1969 | | |
	Deal Fairly	Favor One Side	No Opinion
NATIONAL	40%	42%	18%
SEX			
Men	39	46	15
Women	41	38	21
RACE			
White	40	43	17
Nonwhite	40	38	22
EDUCATION			
College	38	53	9
High School	44	41	15
Grade School	34	34	32
OCCUPATION			
Professional and			
Business	43	46	11
White Collar	41	48	11
Farmers	33	40	27
Manual	38	42	20

* *Gallup Opinion Index*, No. 55, January 1970, p. 9.

Table 47 (continued)

AGE

21–29 years	46	43	11
30–49 years	38	44	18
50 and over	38	40	22

RELIGION

Protestant	39	43	18
Catholic	42	41	17
Jewish	x	x	x

POLITICS

Republican	37	48	15
Democrat	46	38	16
Independent	36	44	20

REGION

East	43	39	18
Midwest	39	42	19
South	35	44	21
West	45	44	11

INCOME

$15,000 and over	37	50	13
$10,000–$14,999	40	51	9
$ 7,000–$ 9,999	42	44	14
$ 5,000–$ 6,999	38	45	17
$ 3,000–$ 4,999	43	38	19
Under $3,000	39	24	37

COMMUNITY SIZE

1,000,000 and over	41	44	15
500,000–999,999	37	50	13
50,000–499,999	43	42	15
2,500–49,999	46	37	17
Under 2,500, Rural	34	41	25

is important is that in December 1969 the weight of public opinion was that the media was biased. A "credibility gap" of sorts existed between the media and the people. One must wonder how long this "gap" had existed, and if it had continued throughout 1970.

Again, of great interest in these polls, is who felt the media was biased, and what this might indicate. The feeling was generally strongest among college-educated people. The weight of opinion in all occupational categories came out on the side of thinking the media biased. Republicans and independents (who today are more conservative than liberal) felt the bias more strongly than Democrats; so one can assume

Table 48
NEWSPAPER IMPARTIALITY*
(Emphasis by underlining added)

What about the newspapers—in presenting the news dealing with political and social issues—do they deal fairly with all sides or do they tend to favor one side?

| | December 1969 | | |
	Deal Fairly	Favor One Side	No Opinion
NATIONAL	37%	45%	18%
SEX			
Men	37	49	14
Women	36	42	22
RACE			
White	36	46	18
Nonwhite	39	41	20
EDUCATION			
College	32	60	8
High School	41	42	17
Grade School	30	40	30
OCCUPATION			
Professional and			
Business	37	52	11
White Collar	41	51	8
Farmers	28	48	24
Manual	36	42	22
AGE			
21–29 years	37	48	15
30–49 years	38	45	17
50 and over	35	44	21
RELIGION			
Protestant	37	45	18
Catholic	35	47	18
Jewish	x	x	x
POLITICS			
Republican	34	50	16
Democrat	40	43	17
Independent	35	48	17
REGION			
East	39	46	15
Midwest	36	47	17
South	34	42	24
West	38	46	16
INCOME			
$15,000 and over	35	53	12
$10,000–$14,999	44	48	8
$ 7,000–$ 9,999	34	50	16
$ 5,000–$ 6,999	42	41	17

* *Gallup Opinion Index,* No. 55, January 1970, p. 9.

Table 48 (continued)

INCOME (continued)

$ 3,000–$ 4,999	31	46	23
Under $3,000	34	32	34
COMMUNITY SIZE			
1,000,000 and over	40	45	15
500,000–999,999	35	52	13
50,000–499,999	35	48	17
2,500–49,999	39	46	15
Under 2,500, Rural	35	40	25

that those who thought there was a bias felt it was generally toward the Left.

This feeling may have existed during the 1968 campaign, but in 1970 events had brought about changes. By the second half of 1970 and into January 1971, the media had taken notice of the great "silent majority" and reporters tried to find out what it thought. Also, by late 1969, instead of having to wait for "that cracker" to say what everyone was thinking but no one had "the courage to say," a surprise spokesman was on the scene. Spiro Agnew was a hard man to ignore, not only because he was Vice President of the United States, but because he was a "sleeper." People seem to have misjudged him, for before long he was easily holding his own with (and often bettering) newsmen, TV showmen, and others. Here was a counterattack based on some of the majority's positions that was apparently at least as logical as many of those held by the heretofore more publicized minority. Agnew was no Harry Truman, but his point of view struck a responsive chord with millions of Americans.

Evidence at the time indicated that the public did not reject him. In late 1969, for the first time in recent history, a vice president was third on the "most admired man" list (behind the perennial number one and two men, the President of the United States and Billy Graham).* In a nationwide Gallup survey, taken in May 1970, 49 percent of the public had a favorable impression of Spiro Agnew. In the same poll, however, only 19 percent considered him presidential material.**

* *Gallup Opinion Index,* No. 55, January 1970, p. 6. A year later (1970) he was fourth behind President Nixon, Billy Graham and Senator Edward Kennedy. (*Gallup Opinion Index,* No. 67, January 1971, p. 8.)
** *Gallup Opinion Index,* No. 61, July 1970, pp. 8 and 9.

As the 1970 congressional campaign progressed, the Vice President came under varying degrees of attack from some members of the national media and became anathema to much of the academic world. Many university students condemned him and were cited by some commentators as evidence that he was dividing the country.[*] There is no question that the Vice President was perhaps a rough and even uncouth campaigner, and his tactics at this time may have tarnished his image. Furthermore, statements attributed to him since would be very likely to "turn off" the average man; but he was taking punches in the infighting as well as giving them. Even the *New York Times* threw a few. In the three-way race among Senator Charles Goodell (liberal Republican), Congressman Richard Ottinger (liberal Democrat) and James Buckley (Conservative), Agnew campaigned for Buckley and against Senator Goodell. And in an editorial on October 26, 1970, the *Times* commented on the decision of the candidate of its choice, Goodell, to remain a candidate:

A nation starved for political leadership heard last night the moving voice of a public official [Goodell] determined to keep freedom from being assassinated by the ruthless nightriders of the political right.

The average person saw a rough, tough, even dirty campaign; but there were some indications that many felt that when certain "liberals" —cried "foul" when Vice President Agnew became rough on anti-war protesters, they were hoisting a double standard of behavior—and at least one liberal columnist said as much at the time.[**] Recently the Vice President has received some recognition of the part he plays. James Reston wrote (in the *New York Times*, November 3, 1971) that Agnew "did not choose the role he has played as Vice President. He has been the battering ram of the Republican party, assigned by the President . . ." and that "it is easy to argue against his philosophy and his pugnacious tactics, but at least he says in private what he says in public; and since very few politicians in Washington risk such candor, he is not a man to be lightly dismissed in the coming struggle of the Presidential campaign."

[*] Actually 94 percent of the population opposed college demonstrators before he made his first speech about them (see Table 6) and only 80 percent opposed them after he made his speeches (*New York Times*, June 7, 1970, p. 49). Obviously something other than the Vice President's speeches was affecting public opinion on these issues.

[**] John Roche, syndicated column, Nyack, N.Y.: *The Journal News*, August 7, 1970, p. 20.

Despite the expensive, hard campaigning in 1970, however, real "political awareness" of many "details" about Congressional races apparently did not change during the campaign. The number of people who even knew the name of their incumbent candidate for the House of Representatives did not break the majority mark among the young (21–29), women, Negroes, those with only grade-school education and residents of large cities. Apparently there was going to be the usual high percentage of straight party-line voting (or perhaps what they felt the national party stood for) and/or lack of interest in the House races among these groups in this off-year election.

No doubt the individual senatorial candidates, for many of whom the "national" figures from both sides did most of their campaigning, were much more likely to be known, and perhaps even their positions on issues understood, by many who did not know their congressman.

It will probably be a while yet before the significance of the 1970 election will be adequately understood; but, as in 1968 (and as correctly noted in 1970 by political analysts Scammon and Wattenberg[*]), there was a Left-Right problem and the candidate who stressed some issues so dear to the New Left would be in trouble. Some "new politics" liberals running for the Senate (such as Ralph Yarborough of Texas) were washed out in primaries; others burned the midnight oil perhaps reading Scammon's statistics and definitely talking to hard-nosed politicians like Mayor Daley, and emerged in the morning with either a new attitude or mum on New Left issues. Slogans some name candidates had employed a year earlier were not used in this campaign. Police were no longer "storm troopers in blue," but the good guys; "revolutionaries" were no longer described as merely "misguided," but as bad—period. There were changes in attitudes on gun control laws. Pennsylvania's Senator Hugh Scott stated that he was wrong in backing President Johnson's 1968 gun law and now opposed such laws. Hubert Humphrey, on November 2, 1969, had sent a four-line reply to a group that queried him on his views on gun laws, stating that, "I think it is sufficient to say that I supported the firearm legislation that was submitted to Congress by President Johnson"; on August 10, 1970, and apparently now aware of the importance of the question to many citizens, he replied to the same group with a two-page letter stating, among other things, that he had now "come to other con-

[*] Richard M. Scammon and Ben J. Wattenberg. *The Real Majority* (New York: Coward-McCann, 1970).

143

Table 49

CONGRESSIONAL QUIZ*

Do you happen to know the name of the present Representative in Congress from your district?

	March 1970		September 1970	
	Yes	No	Yes	No
NATIONAL	53%	47%	53%	47%
SEX				
Men	59	41	60	40
Women	47	53	46	54
RACE				
White	56	44	54	46
Nonwhite	27	73	38	62
EDUCATION				
College	64	36	65	35
High School	54	46	54	46
Grade School	40	60	38	62
OCCUPATION				
Professional and				
Business	61	39	61	39
White Collar	59	41	57	43
Farmers	66	34	62	38
Manual	44	56	43	57
AGE				
21–29 years	42	58	44	56
30–49 years	54	46	55	45
50 and over	56	44	54	46
RELIGION				
Protestant	53	47	53	47
Catholic	52	48	56	44
Jewish	x	x	x	x
POLITICS				
Republican	60	40	56	44
Democrat	47	53	51	49
Independent	55	45	52	48
INCOME				
$15,000 and over	64	36	68	32
$10,000–$14,999	60	40	59	41
$ 7,000–$ 9,999	55	45	54	45
$ 5,000–$ 6,999	46	54	43	57
$ 3,000–$ 4,999	46	54	47	53
Under $3,000	36	64	36	64
COMMUNITY SIZE				
1,000,000 and over	46	54	44	56
500,000–999,999	51	49	57	43
50,000–499,999	56	44	55	45
2,500–49,000	61	39	60	40
Under 2,500, Rural	50	50	51	49

* *Gallup Opinion Index*, No. 58, April 1970, p. 20, and No. 64, October 1970, p. 10.

clusions" on this issue; that he was an avid sportsman, a hunter from way back; his wife was a hunter; his three sons were hunters, etc.* Senator with "charisma" and/or of states with small hunter populations, who approved of the original 1968 gun law, could afford to hold their ground,** but most of the others soft-pedaled or changed their positions. Senator Joseph Tydings of Maryland did not and lost in an upset.*** There was little talk of the blame for crime resting on all of us for our failure to do enough to root out the alleged causes of it—poverty, injustice, bad housing, and so forth—and hardly a mention of Vietnam.

Some television commentators stated that liberal candidates had managed to defuse the "law and order" issue. What they seem to have meant was that they had altered their position or had turned around entirely on it. They were clearly on the defensive, and this in a time when a Republican administration was experiencing the worst recession in nine years. Furthermore, this administration had admitted it had been trying to "cool" the economy, as well as shift from a wartime to a peacetime economy, and that some unemployment was to result. The opposition tried to use the recession issue, but at this time of high and rising unemployment *and* a continually spiraling inflation, they could not seem to cash in as much as they might have nationally. Liberals lost ground in the Senate; their gains in the House were minimal. The fact that more Democratic Senate seats were at stake than Republican ones does not tell the whole story (besides, Southern Democrats don't fit the normal "Left" pattern). Nor does the fact that Nixon (like John Kennedy) took so few House members in with him that he was bound to lose less entirely explain the minimal loss in this off-year election. People out of work or with their jobs in jeopardy, without overtime work, facing increasing inflation and increasing debts, were voting in the national elections *for* the administration that "caused it." And this among an electorate which was 44 percent registered Democrats compared to 29 percent Republicans (27 percent Independents) in July 1970.****

How much of this can be attributed to the Vice President's discussion of issues which the average citizen considered important, and

* *American Rifleman*, November 1970, pp. 44 and 45.
** Ibid., p. 45. See Edward Kennedy's letter in this issue.
*** He had other troubles, particularly in Montgomery County, but few feel that these alone, without the hunters' objection to his promises to work for much stricter gun laws, would have been sufficient to unseat him.
**** *Gallup Opinion Index*, No. 62, August 1970, p. 3.

145

how much was built-in, regardless of whether these problems were discussed or not, is difficult to determine. It may be even more difficult, however, to argue that in 1970 he was ineffective or even counter-productive to the Republican cause, as many now claim. Even if Agnew's personal influence slipped in late 1970, he helped to keep the issues which would help the Republicans before the public. People did not blindly hold their opinions solely because he held them; he was, in the main, simply articulating publicly opinions already held privately. One point is very hard to disprove: the Vice President may have done much to attract normally Democratic votes in a time when the economic policies of the administration looked bad. Perhaps many of the average voters in 1970 cared for something besides materialistic well-being, and perhaps they were willing to take some risk with such well-being for what they considered the good of their children, the country, the society. In any event, despite the growing recession, in this congressional election the voters failed to decisively "throw the rascals out."

F. The "Middle American" and His Feelings About His Society

This aspect of the average man is often well disguised, but polls show that he is concerned with the welfare of others.* He continually prefers to have his taxes spent on education and domestic "helping"-type programs rather than on space, defense, or even things that might benefit him personally more, such as a highway program.

The adult citizens of average age (age 47 in 1970) belong to that large group which was the product of post-World War I "baby boom." They grew up in the Great Depression, and, after leaving their jobs to fight in the biggest of all our wars, they returned as young adults to take responsibilities again as workers, employers, parents and taxpayers, and even students (the G.I. Bill college people were one of the most serious and talented, large groups of students in modern times**). They helped to further expand our economy, reduce poverty and il-

* Harris poll in *Life*, August 15, 1969, p. 23.
** One author, stressing the value of experience in college students, says the following about the G. I. Bill students who "flooded" American campuses: "Every educator then 'knew' that these large masses of students would inevitably 'debase' academic standards. Instead, every teacher found out that the real problem was that these students were so incredibly superior that they made demands the faculty could not satisfy." (Peter F. Drucker, *The Age of Discontinuity* [New York: Harper and Row, 1969], p. 324.)

literacy, save Europe economically through the Marshall Plan, eradicate disease, and put men on the moon. In fact, the crew that went to the moon in January 1971 was led by the 47-year-old Alan B. Shepard, Jr.

The vast majority of their children are much like their parents and the one thing the parents want is that life for their children not be as hard as they had it. In most cases, almost any effort or sacrifice is not considered too great for this goal. Ironically, this last desire might be counterproductive in some instances, and many an average citizen is concerned about perhaps having fallen down in this most important of all jobs—giving their children the guidance and training they need.

By May 1970, there was concern about bias in our colleges, to which half of our high school graduates were headed. Again, the parents of college background had the greatest fears; but in this case the difference between categories could vary in relation to how much each was likely to know about college. There was less "instinctive" feeling on this issue—as the large percentage of "no opinions" shows—among those of less education.

Table 50
FEDERAL SPENDING PRIORITIES*
(After the moon landing)

Which 3 or 4 (of 1-11 areas) would you *least* like to see cut in federal spending?

Aid to education	60%
Pollution control	38
Federal poverty program	34
Federal aid to cities	26
Federal highway financing	24

Which 3 or 4 on this list (1-11) would you like to see *cut first* in federal spending?

Foreign aid	69%
Vietnam	64
Space program	51
Federal welfare	37
Other defense spending	26
Farm subsidies	24
Poverty program	19
Aid to cities	12
Highways	11
Antipollution	5
Aid to education	4

* See the footnote on the first page of the section, "Some Unexplored Popular Perceptions and Issues," earlier, for a reference to a discussion of thirty years of survey data on the issue.

147

Figure 28

PREPARING CHILDREN FOR THE FUTURE*

Do you think parents generally do a good job or a poor job of preparing their children for their future?

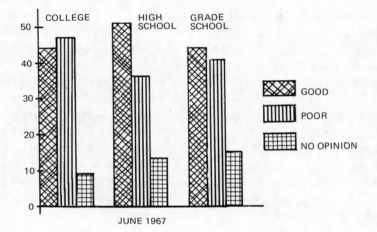

JUNE 1967

Figure 29

DO COLLEGES GIVE STUDENTS A BALANCED VIEW**
By Education

"SOME PEOPLE SAY THAT COLLEGES DO NOT GIVE
STUDENTS A BALANCED VIEW OF THE NATION'S
PROBLEMS —— THAT IS, THEY DON'T GIVE THE SAME
IMPORTANCE TO THE VIEWS OF RIGHT WING OR
CONSERVATIVE LEADERS AS THEY DO TO LEFT WING
OR LIBERAL LEADERS. DO YOU AGREES WITH THIS
STATEMENT?

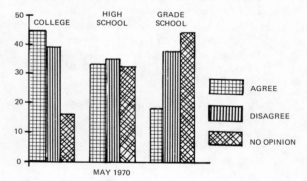

MAY 1970

* Compiled from *Gallup Opinion Index,* No. 26, August 1967, p. 24.
** Compiled from *Gallup Opinion Index,* No. 61, July 1970, p. 23.

148

If there was any instinct it was with the less educated and it was against this premise—and this is logical if one considers the degree of respect which, according to earlier polls, education and the educated commanded among the population as a whole.

According to the following chart, however, there has also been an "instinctive" feeling against greater student control of our campuses. This was evident despite the "instinctive" respect. College-educated persons who better understood the situation came out on the same side.

Figure 30
FEELINGS TOWARD COLLEGE STUDENTS
By Education

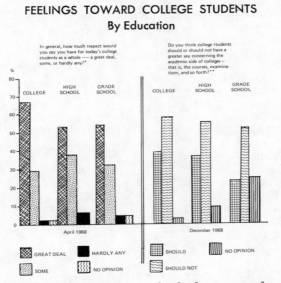

Many parents—particularly those who had come up from the lower socio-economic levels by dint of much effort and hard work—had sought a better life for their children through education. Now, apparently, such a future was uncertain. Both Negroes and whites were less satisfied with the education of their children in 1969 and 1971 than they were in 1966, and perhaps with good reason (see Table 15). The high school curriculum in New York State, for example, has downgraded such basics as standard Ancient History. Even American History no longer seems to provide the fundamentals as well as it used to. Teaching of these subjects has been largely replaced by "relevant," current-events-type instruction. But the funda-

* Compiled from *Gallup Opinion Index*, No. 35, May 1968, p. 24.
** Compiled from *Gallup Opinion Index*, No. 43, January 1969, p. 10.

149

Table 51

CAUSE OF CRIME*

Which in your opinion is more to blame for crime and lawlessness in this country—the individual or society?

October 9–13, 1970

	Individual	Society	No Opinion
NATIONAL	35%	58%	7%
SEX			
Men	35	58	7
Women	36	58	6
RACE			
White	35	58	7
Nonwhite	37	53	10
EDUCATION			
College	30	63	7
High School	36	58	6
Grade School	39	51	10
OCCUPATION			
Professional and			
Business	29	63	8
White Collar	37	59	4
Farmers	35	58	7
Manual	36	56	8
AGE			
21–29 years	29	66	5
30–49 years	35	57	8
50 and over	38	55	7
RELIGION			
Protestant	36	57	7
Catholic	36	58	6
Jewish	x	x	x
POLITICS			
Republican	37	57	6
Democrat	42	49	9
Independent	32	60	8
REGION			
East	32	61	7
Midwest	32	63	5
South	42	50	8
West	37	55	8
INCOME			
$15,000 and over	28	67	5
$10,000–$14,999	34	60	6
$ 7,000–$ 9,999	35	59	6
$ 5,000–$ 6,999	38	54	8
$ 3,000–$ 4,999	39	51	10
Under $3,000	40	50	10

* *Gallup Opinion Index*, No. 65, November 1970, p. 15.

Table 51 (continued)

COMMUNITY SIZE

1,000,000 and over	33	61	6
500,000–999,999	37	57	6
50,000–499,999	37	55	8
2,500–49,999	33	60	7
Under 2,500, Rural	35	57	8

mentals of history, the chronicle of mankind, so vital if people are to make judgments about the version of the current events they hear in high school, college and elsewhere, were (and remain) downgraded in some states. The colleges were directly and indirectly costing more and more tax money but seemed to be dropping in stature, and they were becoming less accessible to any but the very rich or the poor.*

Despite the somewhat-better recent coverage in the media, the average man's basically good qualities and efforts to eliminate his admitted faults had not eliminated the flack from his many critics. He was still attacked for being a bigot and was bombarded with "messages" on TV, despite his record of increasing support for school integration, and on-the-job training and poverty programs. At the same time, derogatory "Polish jokes" (incidentally, taken in great good humor by the overwhelming majority of Polish-Americans) continued to circulate among the very groups of "intellectuals" who accused the average man of bigotry.

Offensive advertising on television accused the "average man" of training his children to be racists or of insensibility to the plight of the Negro. One, sponsored by the New York City Human Rights Commission, speaks of bigotry being poured into the "dear little ears" of very small children, who have to be "carefully taught" to hate "those their relatives hate." Another program gives a tour of a neighborhood, showing a vacant lot as a "playground" and the street as a stickball "diamond." The viewers are then supposed to be shocked and feel guilty about these conditions. The fact that many of the audience played ball

---

* The new "programs" were said to be harmful to both white and nonwhite qualified students. See Thomas Sowell, "A Black Professor Says Collegs are Skipping Over Competent Blacks to Admit 'Authentic' Ghetto Types," *New York Times Magazine,* December 13, 1970, p. 36, for a description of the alleged effects of the new admissions programs on many well-qualified Negroes.

in the streets and roamed vacant lots in their youth (and felt lucky if someone didn't complain to the police) seems to have escaped the programmers. The average man cannot see as shocking his not unhappy boyhood spent in similar areas in a much harder economic period.

"All in the Family," a very well-acted and (aside from the sometimes labored "racism" injected into it) an often very funny series on a "blue-collar" family where the father (who clashes with a "swinging" son-in-law) is a bigot, was introduced on TV. There appeared no counterpart series on "limousine liberals," however, based (for example) on a theme something like that found in Tom Wolfe's hilarious exposé of "Radical Chic."

Nevertheless, the average American indicated that he understood the responsibility of society for some of our critical domestic problems. Even in the area of law and order, of such high priority from his point of view, the average American felt that the crime rate was more society's fault than the individual's. This, of course, can cut both ways. Some can think that society is too permissive; others can feel that its lack of opportunity and its oppressiveness drive people to extremes. Consequently, both show up as blaming society rather than the individual. Unfortunately, the following chart does not distinguish between the two viewpoints, but the numbers are close for all educational and income levels, with no great variation in the "no opinion" column.

But, as indicated earlier, it was very hard to shake the "middle" majority's faith in the system and in the society. In the same poll, despite their grave qualms, 58 percent refused to describe the society as "sick," although 36 felt that it was (again, probably from both the "left" and "right" point of view) and 6 had no opinion. This, by no means, indicates that they are not concerned by what they feel is happening in the country. In a survey taken about six months later, a large majority felt the country was "on the wrong track."

"Do you feel that things in this country are generally going in the right direction today, or do you feel that things have pretty seriously gotten off on the wrong track?"*

Right track	23%
Wrong track	64
No Opinion	13

* Jean Heinig, "Is America Off the Track?" *The Roper Report,* July 1971, p. 1.

152

Their specific concerns were less easily evaluated, however, as the responses to the two questions on specifics, taken in the same time period, indicate.

Which one or more of the things on this list do you feel is a major cause of the problems in this country today?*		What do you think is the *most* important problem facing this nation today?**	
Use of drugs	47%	Vietnam	33%
War in Vietnam	40	Economic	22
Racial tensions	33	Drug addiction	12
People forgetting the Golden		Race relations	7
Rule	31	Crime and lawlessness	7
Lack of strong leadership	30	Other international problems	7
The economic situation	27		
Too much emphasis on money		Youth protests, unrest	6
and materialism	26	Division in America	4
Permissiveness	23	Pollution, ecology	4
Radical attempts to force		Lack of religion, moral decay	2
change	20		
Communism	18	Education and related needs	1
Youth and its values	13		
Growing conservatism	4	Other responses	9
Too much technology	4	No opinion	1
	316%		121%

Perhaps the most interesting "discrepancy" is the ranking of "drug problem" and the size of the groups choosing "race problem." The feelings by specific segments of our society, according to the Roper poll, are interesting. Thirty-eight percent of the college-educated and only 10 percent of those with a grade school education considered "permissiveness" a major factor. Sixty percent of Negroes compared to 45 percent of whites chose the use of drugs. Forty-one percent of Negroes compared to 32 percent of whites chose racial tensions as major factors.

An interesting, and—if we forget his ability to "take it"—surprising insight into the feelings of the average man, however, may be the results of a poll taken in early December 1970—at the end of a year of

* Ibid., p. 1.
** *Gallup Opinion Index,* No. 73, July 1971, p. 5.

153

recession and (according to much of the media) turmoil, a "general students' strike," and "campus" "revolution." In answer to the simple "summary" question, "In general, how happy would you say you are?" the results were as shown in Table 52.

A comparison with a poll taken in 1947 asking the same questions as 1970 and 1971 polls brings out some interesting points. In 1947, only 49 percent were satisfied with their family income, and in 1971, 65 percent were; 69 percent were satisfied with their housing in 1947, 73 percent in 1971. In answer to the same "summary" question, 38 percent said they were "very happy" in 1947 and 43 percent felt that way in 1970. Not surprisingly, the person with the highest income is more likely to be "very happy" than a man in the income bracket below his—and so on, down the line, to the poorest interviewed. Negroes, divorced or widowed people and those with the least education rated low on the "happiness" scale. What is interesting, however, is that in 1947, only 23 percent of the 21-to-29 year olds (including World War II veterans) were "very happy;" but no one pointed to a crisis among youth—and rightly so. Today, 55 *percent* of 21-to-29-year-olds declare themselves "very happy," 39 percent "fairly happy," and only 5 *percent* "not happy."* In a Harris poll covering a "national cross-section of the 26 million Americans who are between the ages of 15 and 21," taken at the same time and appearing in *Life* magazine on January 8, 1971, the results were as follows:

Has your life been happy so far?   Yes—90%
    (no percentages given for "no" and "no comment")
Why do you say that?
    1) I've had a good home and good family.
    2) I've had and done about everything I wanted.
Do you expect your future to be as happy or even happier?
    Yes—93%
    (no percentages given for "no" and "on comment")

Yet, we have been told that we have a "grave crisis" among youth. Furthermore, at the very times these polls were taken, some seemed to feel that youth (or at least a large segment of it) was so disenchanted

* Ibid. Also, the *Gallup Opinion Index*, No. 76, October 1971, pp. 11 and 13, and a report on a Gallup poll in the *Philadelphia Inquirer*, January 14, 1971, p. 1. There were some "Sunday Supplement"-type articles in 1946 on the problems of the readjustment of veterans, which made good copy, but turned out to be far from applicable to the vast majority of veterans.

Table 52
ARE YOU HAPPY?*

In general, how happy would you say you are—very happy fairly happy, or not happy?

	Very Happy	Fairly Happy	Not Happy	Don't Know
		1947		
NATIONAL	38%	57%	4%	1%
		December 5–7, 1970		
NATIONAL	43	48	6	3
SEX				
Men	42	49	6	3
Women	44	46	7	3
RACE				
White	46	46	5	3
Nonwhite	20	63	12	5
EDUCATION				
College	51	42	4	3
High School	44	49	4	3
Grade School	35	50	11	4
OCCUPATION				
Professional and Business	53	40	4	3
White Collar	48	43	8	1
Farmers	41	47	5	7
Manual	43	50	4	3
AGE				
21-29	55	39	5	1
30-49	42	51	4	3
50 and over	38	50	8	4
POLITICS				
Republican	45	47	4	4
Democrat	38	50	8	4
Independent	47	46	6	1
INCOME				
$15,000 and over	56	37	4	3
$10,000–$14,999	49	47	3	1
$ 7,000–$ 9,999	47	46	5	2
$ 5,000–$ 6,999	38	52	7	3
$ 3,000–$ 4,999	33	54	7	6
Under $3,000	29	55	13	3
COMMUNITY SIZE				
1,000,000 and over	38	51	10	1
500,000–999,999	34	54	7	5
50,000–499,999	46	46	5	3
2,500–49,999	48	43	6	3
Under 2,500, rural	45	47	4	4

* *Gallup Opinion Index*, No. 67, January 1971, p. 21.

and unhappy, and so certain to remain that way as they grew into their thirties and forties, that we should particularly harken to those "unhappy" youth who wanted to change and jettison parts of this sensitive, free, democratic system. This point will be examined in detail in the following section on youth.

The latest poll (September 1971) shows that the public's satisfaction with "the quality of life" in their communities continues to be high (75 percent). But clearly the biggest cities are the trouble spots (only 61 percent of their residents are satisfied) and nonwhites (who make up an ever-increasing percentage of the residents of these cities) show the smallest majority (51 percent) who are satisfied. The young (18 to 20) were five points below the national average at 70 percent and the 21-to-29 year olds, where the lower-paid, "beginner" workers, parents and

Table 53

SATISFACTION INDEX—QUALITY OF LIFE*

Question: "Would you say you are satisfied or dissatisfied with the quality of life in your community?"

| | September 1971 | | |
	Satisfied	Dissatisfied	Don't Know
NATIONAL	75%	21%	4%
SEX			
Male	76	21	3
Female	74	22	4
RACE			
White	78	18	4
Nonwhite	51	44	5
EDUCATION			
College	73	23	4
High School	75	21	4
Grade School	77	20	3
OCCUPATION			
Professional and			
Business	75	23	2
White Collar	75	23	2
Farmers	80	15	5
Manual	73	22	5
AGE			
18–20 years	70	28	2
21–29 years	65	30	5
30–49 years	76	21	3
50 and over	81	16	3

* *Gallup Opinion Index*, No. 76, October 1971, p. 18.

156

Table 53 (continued)

RELIGION
Protestant	77	19	4
Catholic	73	24	3
Jewish	x	x	x

POLITICS
Republican	83	14	3
Democrat	73	23	4
Independent	73	23	4

REGION
East	73	23	4
Midwest	80	17	3
South	73	22	5
West	72	24	4

INCOME
$15,000 and over	79	18	3
$10,000–$14,999	77	19	4
$ 7,000–$ 9,999	73	24	3
$ 5,000–$ 6,999	75	22	3
$ 3,000–$ 4,999	71	25	4
Under $3,000	73	20	7

COMMUNITY SIZE
1,000,000 and over	61	35	4
500,000–999,999	77	20	3
50,000–499,999	69	25	6
2,500–49,999	81	17	2
Under 2,500, Rural	84	13	3

homemakers are clustered, showed only 65 percent satisfaction. But each age bracket showed increasing satisfaction thereafter.

No doubt this attitude toward their communities reflects everything from the problems of crime and violence in some communities to higher taxes, decreased services and permissiveness, to oppressiveness, and "penny-pinching." But the effects of the current recession may also be reflected here. We have no 1970 responses to the identical questions, but the following Gallup analysis of twenty years of such data, published in the *Public Opinion Index* of October 1971 shows definite changes in trends in some indicators since 1969, and, one feels, had these questions been asked in December 1970 (when the preceding "Happiness" survey was taken) the downward trend would also have been evident.

It is interesting to note that, although satisfaction with the type of work one does is down somewhat, about four out of five workers like

Table 54

SATISFACTION INDEX—EMPLOYMENT*
22-Year Trend

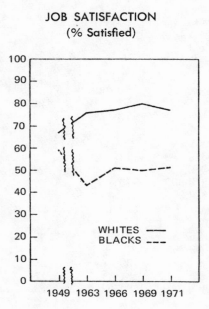

JOB SATISFACTION
(% Satisfied)

THE WORK YOU DO?

Whites

	Satisfied	Dissatisfied	Don't Know
1949	69%	19%	12%
1963	90	7	3
1966	87	8	5
1969	88	6	6
1971	83	9	8

Blacks

	Satisfied	Dissatisfied	Don't Know
1949	55	33	12
1963	54	33	13
1966	69	18	13
1969	76	18	6
1971	63	25	12

* Ibid., p. 14.

Table 55
SATISFACTION INDEX—WORK*
Question: "Would you say you are satisfied or dissatisfied with the work you do?"

| | September 1971 | | |
	Satisfied	Dissatisfied	Don't Know
NATIONAL	81%	11%	8%
SEX			
Male	80	12	8
Female	82	10	8
RACE			
White	84	9	7
Nonwhite	63	25	12
EDUCATION			
College	87	9	4
High School	81	12	7
Grade School	77	10	13
OCCUPATION			
Professional and			
Business	91	7	2
White Collar	84	10	6
Farmers	86	9	5
Manual	83	12	5
AGE			
18–20 years	66	18	16
21–29 years	82	15	3
30–49 years	85	11	4
50 and over	81	8	11
RELIGION			
Protestant	83	10	7
Catholic	83	11	6
Jewish	x	x	x
POLITICS			
Republican	84	9	7
Democrat	80	11	9
Independent	82	13	5
REGION			
East	79	13	8
Midwest	84	10	6
South	84	10	6
West	77	12	11
INCOME			
$15,000 and over	91	8	1
$10,000–$14,999	86	11	3
$ 7,000–$ 9,999	82	11	7
$ 5,000–$ 6,999	82	10	8
$ 3,000–$ 4,999	73	14	13
Under $3,000	70	24	6

* *Gallup Opinion Index*, No. 76, October 1971, p. 15.

Table 55 (continued)

COMMUNITY SIZE

1,000,000 and over	75	16	9
500,000–999,999	78	11	11
50,000–499,999	80	13	7
2,500–49,999	83	7	10
Under 2,500, Rural	87	9	4

their jobs, while only about one out of ten registered dissatisfaction. What is no doubt largely reflected by the recent drop in satisfaction is a lack of ability during the recession to change jobs, compared to 1969, when the percent of those satisfied with their jobs was in the high eighties and those dissatisfied were well below one in ten.

As one would suspect, the satisfaction with the job one holds generally correlates with age (better and higher-paying jobs usually go along with more experience and seniority), degree of education and salary; but it also correlates directly with size of the community and there is a noticeable downturn in satisfaction of those 50 years of age and older (as there was in "happiness" in 1970—see Table 52), and also a downturn in dissatisfaction.

A study of 270 white, male, union, industrial workers in an industrialized area of the Northeast (probably performed in late 1970 or early 1971) found that 19 percent felt their "current job is not very much like the kind I wanted," which seems to equate somewhat with the slightly higher rate of dissatisfaction among manual workers found in the larger poll. Furthermore, 81 percent apparently chose the other two options: their job was either "very much" or "somewhat like the job" they wanted when they "first took it,"* which may equate with the 80 percent male satisfied group in the larger poll.

A significantly higher number of industrial workers than the 19 percent listed above were rated as "discontented," however, because of other complaints about their positions. Those 50 years of age and older contained the highest number who were "discontented."** Overall, however, only a small minority of all categories are dissatisfied with their jobs.

* "Discontented Blue-Collar Workers—A Case Study," by Harold L. Shepard, *Monthly Labor Review* (April 1971), pp. 25 and 26.
** Ibid., p. 26.

Table 56

SATISFACTION INDEX—INCOME*
22-year trend

INCOME SATISFACTION
(% Satisfied)

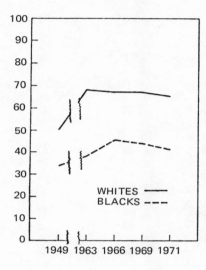

YOUR FAMILY INCOME?

Whites

	Satisfied	Dissatisfied	Don't Know
1949	50%	38%	12%
1963	68	30	2
1966	67	29	4
1969	67	30	3
1971	65	33	2

Blacks

1949	34	56	10
1963	38	62	—
1966	45	49	6
1969	44	54	2
1971	41	57	2

* *Gallup Opinion Index*, No. 76, October 1971, p. 12.

161

Table 57

SATISFACTION INDEX—INCOME*

Question: "Would you say you are satisfied or dissatisfied with your family income?"

| | September 1971 | | |
	Satisfied	Dissatisfied	Don't Know
NATIONAL	62%	35%	3%
SEX			
Male	62	35	3
Female	63	34	3
RACE			
White	65	32	3
Nonwhite	41	57	2
EDUCATION			
College	70	27	3
High School	59	38	3
Grade School	63	34	3
OCCUPATION			
Professional and Business	76	21	3
Farmers	60	38	1
White Collar	60	39	2
Manual	58	38	4
AGE			
18–20 years	64	33	3
21–29 years	54	42	4
30–49 years	60	38	2
50 and over	69	29	2
RELIGION			
Protestant	65	32	3
Catholic	59	38	3
Jewish	x	x	x
POLITICS			
Republican	71	26	3
Democrat	60	37	3
Independent	60	38	2
REGION			
East	63	34	3
Midwest	63	33	4
South	61	36	3
West	63	35	2
INCOME			
$15,000 and over	79	19	2
$10,000–$14,999	65	31	4
$ 7,000–$ 9,999	60	39	1
$ 5,000–$ 6,999	57	40	3
$ 3,000–$ 4,999	56	42	2
Under $3,000	54	41	5

* Ibid., p. 13.

Table 57 (continued)

COMMUNITY SIZE

1,000,000 and over	52	44	4
500,000–999,999	64	34	2
50,000–499,999	63	33	4
2,500–49,999	66	31	3
Under 2,500, Rural	66	32	2

Not surprisingly, satisfaction with income has also decreased some-what during the recession; but, as one would also suspect, not dras-tically. Lack of overtime is probably a big factor here, and, bad as the recession is on those who have lost or cannot find jobs, they fortunately still make up only a small fraction of the work force. Other factors, such as the effects of inflation and perhaps rising expectations in the second half of the 1960s, seem to account for a longer-term slightly downward trend. Presumably such discontent would show up in "em-ployment dissatisfaction" but more of it may show up in income satis-faction survey results.

A detailed analysis of who is more satisfied may not be surprising. Youth (18 to 20) and people over 50, both with less family responsibility, are more satisfied than 21-to-39-year olds (21-to-29-year olds, with less experience on the job and lower pay, are again least satisfied)*; people with higher incomes and those with college educations are more satis-fied than those with lower incomes, and nonwhites (with the highest percentage of low-income families) are the least satisfied.

Satisfaction with housing has not shown the same trend as that of satisfaction with income. It has generally held steady since 1966 for Negroes, while the steady increase in satisfaction with housing ex-pressed by whites between 1949 and 1969 seems to have been halted and at least temporarily reversed.

Still, the overall satisfaction level remains high (73 percent) and con-stant across the country. The big cities, with their high costs, high crime rates, and large number of slum-dwellers, again show the greatest level of dissatisfaction. As on the other issues, the better educated and better paid, etc., show more satisfaction with their housing. There is almost no variation with age, however, until the over-50 group is reached.

* "Discontented" industrial workers over 50 seem to resent the need for their wives to work to raise family living standards. See Shepard, op. cit., p. 30.

163

Table 58

SATISFACTION INDEX—HOUSING*
22-year trend

HOUSING SATISFACTION
(% Satisfied)

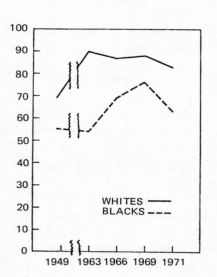

YOUR HOUSING SITUATION?

Whites

	Satisfied	Dissatisfied	No Opinion
1949	67%	28%	5%
1963	76	21	3
1966	77	19	4
1969	80	18	2
1971	77	19	4

Blacks

1949	59	32	9
1963	43	54	3
1966	51	44	5
1969	50	48	2
1971	51	46	3

* Ibid., p. 10.

Table 59
SATISFACTION INDEX—HOUSING*

Question: "Would you say you are satisfied or dissatisfied with your housing situation?"

September 1971

	Satisfied	Dissatisfied	Don't Know
NATIONAL	73%	23%	4%
SEX			
Male	78	19	3
Female	70	26	4
RACE			
White	77	19	4
Nonwhite	51	46	3
EDUCATION			
College	83	15	2
High School	72	25	3
Grade School	67	26	7
OCCUPATION			
Professional and			
Business	83	15	2
White Collar	77	21	2
Farmers	73	21	6
Manual	67	30	3
AGE			
18–20 years	72	27	1
21–29 years	72	25	3
30–49 years	72	25	3
50 and over	77	18	5
RELIGION			
Protestant	75	21	4
Catholic	73	25	2
Jewish	x	x	x
POLITICS			
Republican	81	14	5
Democrat	69	28	3
Independent	75	22	3
REGION			
East	73	25	2
Midwest	73	20	7
South	73	24	3
West	75	21	4
INCOME			
$15,000 and over	86	12	2
$10,000–$14,999	77	21	2
$ 7,000–$ 9,999	69	27	4
$ 5,000–$ 6,999	74	22	4
$ 3,000–$ 4,999	67	29	4
Under $3,000	69	26	5
COMMUNITY SIZE			
1,000,000 and over	63	33	4
500,000–999,999	79	19	2
50,000–499,999	74	23	3
2,500–49,999	77	20	3
Under 2,500, Rural	76	19	5

* Ibid., p. 11.

Americans seem less satisfied with the future facing their families, as they see it. Events since the early 1960s, and perhaps rising expectations, have tended to diminish this satisfaction. Perhaps most significant is the failure of nonwhites to feel more satisfied with the future of their families (actually, the figures show a tendency for satisfaction to decrease). Perhaps our many well-intentioned "programs" are not solving the Negroes' foremost problems.

There are some recent indications, however, that the average man is not as satisfied today with the "leadership" situation in the country as he was previously. A recent survey showed the following changes from 1966 through 1971:

Table 60
THE FUTURE FACING
YOU AND YOUR FAMILY?*

Whites			
	Satisfied	*Dissatisfied*	*Don't Know*
1963	67%	22%	11%
1971	56	29	15

Blacks			
1963	45	42	13
1971	43	45	12

SATISFACTION INDEX—THE FUTURE*

Question: "Would you say you are satisfied or dissatisfied with the future facing you and your family?"

	September 1971		
	Satisfied	*Dissatisfied*	*Don't Know*
NATIONAL	55%	31%	14%
SEX			
Male	59	28	13
Female	51	34	15
RACE			
White	56	29	15
Nonwhite	43	45	12
EDUCATION			
College	63	26	11
High School	50	35	15
Grade School	58	28	14
OCCUPATION			
Professional and			
Business	64	25	11
White Collar	59	30	11
Farmers	47	33	20
Manual	49	37	14

* Ibid., pp. 19 and 20.

166

Table 60 (continued)

AGE
18–20 years	56	34	10
21–29 years	50	39	11
30–49 years	51	35	14
50 and over	61	24	15

RELIGION
Protestant	56	30	14
Catholic	56	32	12
Jewish	x	x	x

POLITICS
Republican	62	23	15
Democrat	54	33	13
Independent	50	36	14

REGION
East	56	28	16
Midwest	55	33	12
South	57	29	14
West	52	36	12

INCOME
$15,000 and over	65	25	10
$10,000–$14,999	52	31	17
$ 7,000–$ 9,999	54	35	11
$ 5,000–$ 6,999	51	36	13
$ 3,000–$ 4,999	53	32	15
Under $3,000	58	27	15

COMMUNITY SIZE
1,000,000 and over	49	40	11
500,000–999,999	60	27	13
50,000–499,999	58	30	12
2,500–49,999	57	26	17
Under 2,500, Rural	53	32	15

Most Americans well understand that artisans and even supervisors can be and frequently are incompetent; but one of this society's traditional weaknesses may be that many Americans still have trouble believing that it is possible to have many "professional," "educated" people who are incompetent; to have many military, foreign and domestic policy "professionals" and decision-makers with less insight and shrewdness than many men in the street possess; and to have many top administrators without the skill of some lowly entrepreneurs or foremen. Average citizens are often in a quandary, therefore, since they want problems solved rather than just discussed. They want situations "corrected" when wrong. This may be somewhat naïve as some problems simply may not be "solvable," but on the other hand, Americans,

Table 61*

"As far as the people running these institutions are concerned, would you say you have a great deal of confidence, only some confidence, or hardly any confidence at all in them?"

	Great Deal	Only Some	Hardly Any	Not Sure
Major Companies				
1971	27%	50%	15%	8%
1966	55	35	5	5
Organized Religion				
1971	27	40	25	8
1966	41	32	17	10
Education				
1971	37	46	15	2
1966	61	32	5	2
Executive Branch of Federal Government				
1971	23	50	18	9
1966	41	42	11	6
Organized Labor				
1971	14	42	35	9
1966	22	42	28	8
The Press				
1971	18	51	26	5
1966	29	50	17	4
Medicine				
1971	61	29	6	4
1966	72	22	2	4
Television				
1971	22	48	25	5
1966	25	44	26	5
Banks and Financial Institutions				
1971	36	46	13	5
1966	67	26	3	4
Mental Health and Psychiatry				
1971	35	40	15	10
1966	51	32	6	11
The U.S. Supreme Court				
1971	23	41	27	9
1966	51	29	12	8

° Harris survey, the *New York Post*, October 25, 1971.

Table 61 (continued)

The Scientific Community				
1971	32	47	10	11
1966	56	25	4	15
Congress				
1971	19	54	19	8
1966	42	46	7	5
Advertising				
1971	13	42	40	5
1966	21	43	30	6
The Military				
1971	27	47	20	6
1966	62	28	5	5
Local Retail Stores				
1971	24	56	15	5
1966	48	42	7	3

through good fortune or skill or both, have made great progress in many areas. Furthermore, they really don't expect *everything* to be righted, and are used to putting up with troubles.

Besides inflation and the recession, the causes for the average citizen's loss of "confidence" in the "people running these institutions" are difficult to fathom. Barring some recent, otherwise unrecorded, significant shift of opinion, however, his general "conservative" leaning over these same years seems to indicate that, aside from such issues as opposition to the Vietnam War and pollution, his lack of confidence comes from causes often different from (and perhaps opposite to) those of the recent left-leaning "protest movement" (e.g., he is hardly likely to be critical of the people running our educational systems for being too "repressive," or of the Supreme Court for not being "liberal" enough). Of course, the above table also records the protest movement's loss of confidence in leadership, so we have a combined effect in these numbers.

Nevertheless, Americans continue to pour out their taxes, their support, to solve problems; and apparently few of those important to them get solved, even though they are told the "finest minds" are at work on them. Instead, they are often given excuses, or conclusions that nothing can be done about anything in the foreign policy or military areas, and that if we try to solve such problems they will just get worse; or conclusions that fashionable, "ultra-liberal" theories about solutions of domestic problems really are apropos and what we need are even larger, more expensive programs based on these same theories, when it is apparent that, compared to the "old" systems they replaced, many of the new "systems" and "programs" are everything from relatively ineffective to potentially disastrous when applied to actual social problems.

Indeed, the full story of the ineffectiveness (or ill effects) of many social-help-type programs for the very people they were designed to assist is yet to be told. For example, we have yet to assess the damage done to the underprivileged family by hasty and unevaluated "programs," ranging from breakfast programs run by radical and even revolutionary groups to local, state, and federally funded programs such as community centers, where non-family adults do much to shape the thinking and attitudes of underprivileged children. Furthermore, such programs can encourage "delinquency" on the part of adult family members and weaken the family structure of the very families who need it strengthened. Such programs probably do not discriminate between children who actually have no such structure to start with or whose family members absolutely cannot care for them, and those whose parents and other close relatives are lured to the program as a means to escape traditional responsibility.

In one vastly important area which has been studied, the education of our children, we find examples of apparently less than the most responsible (and, one feels, not completely atypical, in the "social" program areas) experimentation at the recipients' and taxpayers' expense. Irving Kristol advances an interesting thesis of why we find ourselves in this situation (*New York Times Magazine*, November 14, 1971). He also discusses some of these "programs"; for example, on the issue of academic achievement and class size in our public schools, he contends (although for other purposes he approves of few students per teacher) that:

Whether a class has 20 pupils or 30 or even 40 simply doesn't matter. Students who do well in small classes will do well in large ones. Students who do poorly in large classes will do no better in small ones. This subject has been studied to death by generations of educational researchers, and the results are conclusive.

Not only do the extensive samples available for years in the Coleman Report bear this out, but such local studies as the *New York School Fact Book*, prepared by the Institute for Community Studies of Queens College, also show similar results. This work states:

170

We have recorded traditional variables that supposedly affect the quality of learning: class size, school expenditure, pupil/teacher ratio, condition of building, teacher experience and the like. Yet there seems to be no direct relationship between these school measurements and performance. Schools that have exceptionally small class registers, staffed with experienced teachers, spend more money per pupil, and possess modern facilities, do not reflect exceptional academic competence.

The study indicates that the very expensive saturation compensatory education program ("More Effective Schools Program"—with some schools having a student-teacher ratio as low at 7.5 to 1 and an expenditure of $2,152 per student per year) has not "shown any noteworthy results in this year's tabulation [1967–1968]. Of twenty-one schools measured in the MES program, pupils in only four, mostly middle-class white, read on grade level." The study adds, ". . . we are faced with the question that the variables we have been accustomed to measure are not the ones that should be studied" (pp. 2–6). It should be noted that the continuing emphasis on small student-teacher ratios is one of the chief reasons for the current extremely high school budgets and crushing school taxes all across the country. Furthermore, a lower student-teacher ratio often does not mean smaller classes in academic subjects even in the first through sixth grades. It often means additional teachers who take over the classroom teachers' chores in the non-academic areas (music, art, library, gym, etc.), while the classroom teachers get one period a day off away from the students.

On another currently fashionable, often expensive, and sometimes, from the students' point of view, disruptive practice, we read:

Team teaching has now been used in enough places for long enough periods to have been given a fair trial. The results of studies of its effectiveness (Gimpher and Shrayer, 1962; R. W. White, 1964) reflect Stephens' spontaneous schooling theory: they indicate that academic performance of students who learn under team teaching circumstances is about the same as those who learn under other circumstances.[*]

Yet student-teacher ratios continue to be cut, team teaching installed, and "old" proven methods discarded for "new," questionable ones; the resultant taxes continue to soar to crippling levels (even during this

[*] Robert F. Biehler, *Psychology Applied to Teaching* (Boston: Houghton Mifflin Company, 1971), p. 262.

recession period of tight money), and the youngsters in many of our largest school systems still cannot read as well as they used to.

If carried too far, particularly in light of many an average man's feeling of loss of traditional influence in political party structures, this whole imprudent "social engineering" process could cause something of a crisis in morale, that vague but vital ingredient to any successful society, particularly the sophisticated, free, democratic version in this country.

Chapter II

Today's Youth

"Youth" attitudes are among the most difficult to define. For one thing, young persons tend to be more unpredictable than adults. For another, there is the difficulty of discerning trends for any segment of society, if the evidence is of snapshot quality. Changes noted over a short period might be significant perturbations in the short run, but over a long period they may not be indicative of any true shift of opinion or change in value systems. Perhaps, as with analyzing adult attitudes, the only way to discern trends is to look at the American historical experience.

When analyzing "youth" as a segment—as when examining the population as a whole—we have to build up a data base from which to analyze historical trends. Our base of operation is, of necessity, influenced by our analysis of past occurrences. All "evidence" must be carefully sifted. This is particularly true when one deals with youth in the present and to some extent even in the recent past. However, the extent of this work allows only a cursory examination of primary data on youth.

This does not mean that a detailed, comprehensive work cannot be done on the subject. It is an area where primary-source information can outline certain trends that existed in previous eras. This in turn does not mean that there are no significant changes occurring today among the thinking and value systems of youth. It merely means that radical changes must be documented. One, of course, is aware of change over the years. Our society is not that of the Victorian era.

173

Today's youth are different. The basic questions are: How different are they? What significance will the difference have for the future?

Equally important in all analyses—but particularly where public opinion substantiates much of it—is that the issues involved must be clearly identified. Semantical differences, identification problems, and changes of identity of apparent sources of responsibility, particularly in dealing with minors—difficulties such as these can not only make it hard to describe trends, they can defy correlation with other data.

Our first point of consideration deals with the following questions: What is "youth" really like today in this country? What are the characteristics of various segments of youth? How are they acting today? Are they different from years ago, and if so, how much and in what ways? And what are they likely to do in the future?

A. *Overview of High School Students*

Traditionally, young people in this country have generally subscribed to the value systems of their parents. This is reflected in the voting patterns of the 21–25 and the 21-to-29-year-olds. It is also apparent in high school students' response to polls (which will be referred to later). This general trend of subscribing to the value systems of the parents is perhaps more discernible in high school students than in older ado-

Table 62

HIGH SCHOOL STUDENT RANKINGS OF "BEST" PRACTICES: 1954, 1965*

Rank	*Poll 38* *1954*	*Poll 74* *1965*
1—	Being courteous and friendly	Being dependable
2—	Being religious	Being courteous and friendly
3—	Showing sportsmanship	Being religious
4—	Being ambitious	Being ambitious
5—	Being dependable	Being healthful
6—	Keeping healthful	Being helpful and courteous
7—	Being helpful and courteous	Being patriotic
8—	Being patriotic	Being cheerful
9—	Being cheerful	Showing sportsmanship
10—	Driving safely	Driving safely
11—	Being industrious	Being industrious
12—	Seeking pleasure	Seeking pleasure

* *Report of Poll 74,* the Purdue Opinion Panel, Measurement and Research Center, Purdue University, March 1965, p. 5—hereafter cited as Purdue Opinion Panel, *Report of Poll.* Copyright, Reports of Polls Nos. 1-71 © H. H. Remmers, Nos. 72-93 © Purdue Research Foundation.

Table 63

HIGH SCHOOL RANKINGS OF
"WORST" PRACTICES: 1923, 1954, AND 1965*

Rank	Brogan 1923	Poll 38 1954	Poll 74 1965
1—	Killing or murdering	Killing or murdering	Killing or murdering
2—	Sexual misbehaving	Using or selling narcotics	Using or selling narcotics
3—	Stealing	Sexual misbehaving	Stealing
4—	Cheating	Stealing	Sexual misbehaving
5—	Lying	Drinking (alcohol)	Cheating
6—	Drinking (alcohol)	Cheating	Drinking (alcohol)
7—	Gambling	Lying	Lying
8—	Swearing, vulgarity	Being cruel	Being cruel
9—	Not being religious	Not being religious	Not being religious
10—	Being selfish	Reckless driving	Reckless driving
11—	Gossiping	Swearing	Swearing
12—	Idleness	Being undependable	Being inconsiderate
13—	Snobbishness	Gossiping	Being undependable
14—	Extravagance	Being inconsiderate	Gossiping
15—	Smoking	Smoking	Being conceited
16—	Being conceited	Being conceited	Smoking

lescents and young adults. The interesting question, of course, is how much change occurs between the time when people show so much similarity to their parents' thinking on values and politics and when they grow older. We will attempt to trace some "cohorts" from high school to college. We will also trace one "cohort" through the age brackets of the teens through the twenties, up to their late twenties and early thirties, by means of special polls taken of one group.** This is not possible with general poll data on nonstudents because they are not broken down as such, and age in general polls for the general public is only given in blocs; e.g., 21-to-24 year old, 21-to-29, 30-to-49, over 50.

1. PRE-1968

High school students' basic values on behavior and most moral issues apparently not only traditionally generally coincided with those of their parents, but have, at least up to the mid-sixties—and according to Tables 62 and 63—been more or less constant over the years.

* Ibid., p. 3.
** Appendix, "The Changing Attitudes of a College Class," traces a representative group of 1961 college graduates from high school to about age 30.

There have been some shifts in the "best" practices list: "showing sportsmanship" slipped from third to ninth, "being dependable" jumped from fifth to first place, "seeking pleasure" remained in the last place. On the whole, the rankings in both "worst" and "best" practices differ little between the 1954 and 1965 columns—or, for that matter, the 1923 column. For the items high on the list of "worst" actions, there is near-unanimity of opinion: for example, 89 percent chose "killing or murdering" in the worst four. But among "best" actions there is more variation. "Being dependable" drew a 52 percent rating in the first three in 1965, but about a fifth rated it in the last three. "Sexual misbehavior" had fallen below "stealing" by 1965; but it still ranked among the top three if the use and sale of narcotics (not emphasized as a youthful problem in 1923) is not considered. This rating in the mid-"swinging sixties" is interesting since it compares favorably to the "silent fifties" and the almost mid-"roaring twenties," over forty years earlier. This does not imply that there was no change over these years. As the comparison in Table 64 shows, the attitude toward those who are sexually promiscuous changed.

Nevertheless, polls taken indicate that the basic value system of students remained rather constant on most issues. Attitudes toward such traditional elements of our society as the government, the nation, and even the flag and patriotism (which—similar to the adult population—does not mean to them chauvinism or bellicosity), were slow to

Table 64

ATTITUDE TOWARD BEHAVIOR OF UNMARRIED PEOPLE*

High School Students

If I learned that some friends of mine had not followed the morals or rules relating to the behavior of unmarried people:

		Total Sample	*Boys*	*Girls*
I would not consider them good friends anymore	1952	57%	46%	67%
	1965	30	22	38
	Difference	27	24	29
It would not make any difference in our friendship	1952	43	54	33
	1965	69	77	60
	Difference	26	23	27

* Ibid., p. 4.

176

Figure 31

HIGH SCHOOL STUDENTS

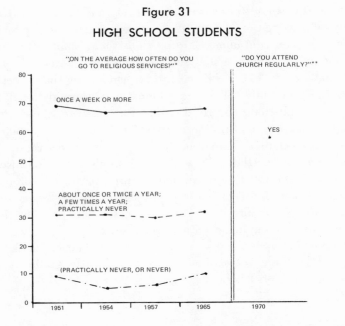

change. Church attendance was traditionally (and still may be) a stable element in their behavior (but a recent poll may indicate a change between the 1960s and the 1970s).

The drop in 1970 (to 58 percent) below the 1951–1965 average (66 to 67 percent) is perhaps slightly exaggerated because this sample eliminated sophomores under 15 years of age (the 1951–1965 sample included all tenth-, eleventh-, and twelfth-graders) and the students in tenth grade traditionally have a higher attendance than the eleventh- and twelfth-graders. Nevertheless, assuming this sample is of equal validity and, despite the slightly different question (which always makes some difference), the probability of a drop below the 1951–1965 level for all high school students must be considered, but it probably is still somewhat above 60 percent. This is not a drastic change, but it is significant when the stability of this percentage between 1951 and 1965 is considered.

An explanation must be inserted here about these polls. For example, about "9,000 students in public and private schools" are the samples used in the *Purdue Opinion Panel*, Poll #89, published in June 1970.

* Purdue Opinion Panel, *Report of Poll No. 74*, March 1965, p. 6.
** Louis Harris poll in *Life*, January 8, 1971.

177

About 2,000 of these forms were picked at random from each scientifically selected group representing regional, economic, ethnic, etc., distinctions. The continuous Purdue polls (and some other perhaps more intermittent high school student polls) are based on questionnaires that are sent to the subjects rather than having them interviewed by a pollster who fills out the questionnaire, as some national polls of adults are conducted. The results, therefore, can vary more for they depend on the degree of response. Some "weighting" can sometimes be done in this situation (and some polls do this on occasion); but in these few instances the polls will, for example, warn of insufficient response in certain areas and caution the user, particularly about making regional comparisons.* In my judgment, the polls are adequate for the purposes of this study. In many cases, independent polls are compared to substantiate or question the results.

In a typical sample, the percentage of students in each "achievement" category (the students classified *themselves* as to the grade scores they "*usually* get in high school") came out like this:**

Very low grades	2%
Below average grades	8
Average grades	51
Above average grades	31
Excellent grades	7

This is similar to the distribution of responses to this question in other Purdue polls; but, as can be seen, the distribution is skewed toward the above-average area. This makes it a far from even distribution.***

* See *Report of Poll No. 91* of the Purdue Opinion Panel, April 1971, pp. 34–35.
** Purdue Opinion Panel, *Report of Poll No. 89*, June 1970, p. 1a.
*** If this reflects high "self-esteem" it apparently may not be unusual. Trent and Medsker cite their own findings and those of several other studies over the years indicating that many youngsters also overestimate their abilities in vocational preferences (assuming they understand the complexities of the professions chosen). (James W. Trent and Leland L. Medsker, *Beyond High School* [San Francisco: Jossey-Bass, 1968], pp. 41–42.)

Bachman, in *Youth in Transition*, a study of tenth grade boys, isolates those groups with the higher self-esteem. He found his results "surprising: black males score noticeably *higher* than whites on our self-esteem scale, and when adjustments are made for other background factors the difference becomes larger." Jewish boys, from another minority with a history of discrimination, also score much higher in "self-esteem" than other students. (Jerald G. Bachman, *Youth in Transition,* [Ann Arbor: Institute for Social Research, University of Michigan, 1970], 2: 129–30.)

The last figure of 7 percent excellent grades may be accurate if it were based on being on honor rolls, etc. Those professing to get average grades were perhaps closer to what one would expect: 51 percent.

The percentage breakdown for post-high school careers as designated by the students on the June 1970 poll was as follows:

Go to college	50%
Special training other than college	15
Go to work	12
Enter military service	8
Other plans or don't know	15

In 1967 students answered questions on our American system in the following manner:

Table 65

FEELINGS TOWARD THE AMERICAN WAY OF LIFE*
High School Students

	Total
In these times, patriotism and loyalty to established American ways are the *most* important requirements of a good citizen.	
Agree	58%
Undecided	15
Disagree	25
We should firmly resist any attempts to change the American way of life.	
Agree	19
Undecided	13
Disagree	67
The American way of life is superior in nearly all respects to any other.	
Agree	57
Undecided	17
Disagree	26
The average citizen does not show enough respect for the United States flag.	
Agree	63
Undecided	11
Disagree	24

* Purdue Opinion Panel, *Report of Poll No. 81*, November 1967, p. 5a.

The response to the question, "resist any attempts," apparently reflects the normal, constant, and perhaps essential young person's attitude toward the world. Some emphasis must be placed on this issue if youth at any period is to be viewed in a normal perspective. The feeling that things can be changed for the better is essential for those with the future before them and no direct responsibility for the past. Without this feeling, there would be far less enthusiasm among the young. This enthusiasm and energy are apparent among the young today, as they have always been. In the adult category, above 21 years of age, the younger the person looking at the problem, the more likely he is to believe that large, immediate changes are desirable, if not essential, and the less likely he is to understand the difficulty, or even the counterproductivity, of quickly implementing certain changes. He is also more likely to show energy and flamboyance in defending traditions.

And all this is as it should be, for traditionally—if for no other reasons than those of health and stamina—younger people have provided, whenever needed, the energy to move the nation forward economically, politically, and even militarily. All persons take their turn at these tasks in their late teens and twenties, as apprentices, soldiers, and students, and learn about the difficulties of implementing programs. They generally gain the experience that is necessary to take their places as responsible guides for the next generation. The experiences of living, learning to get along with a wife, raising children, "meeting a payroll," etc., have sobering effects just when they are needed—when a man's decisions can have grave consequences. But these feelings are usually not so necessary or even desirable for the young with a zest for life and adventure.

The young man is also more likely to feel "exploited," since he sees the older artisan, political figure, scholar, etc., holding what appears to him to be a simple, easy, yet well-paid job; the young man has never performed it, although he knows how hard his own task is because he is doing it. This is not to say that the young are never exploited. Some graduate students have been shamefully exploited by professors who use the students' ideas and work in books published under the name of the professor. The same can be said for unscrupulous artisans, employers, commanding officers in the military, and so forth. But, the young have trouble understanding that exploitation is not only the burden of youth: older people are also exploited, and they sometimes produce more than the young that is exploitable. This is not to say that it is right or even endemic to the "system": it is only to say that the young can get a misleading view of the problems involved in changing the system. Without experience and without advice contrary to their own opinions, they have always been somewhat impatient with their lot. At times, some youth invariably feel that theirs is the worst lot in all history—and they might even be right. But without advice and education from older people, they are the *one* group which can't really judge. Nonetheless, this impatience, this desire for change *now* or, conversely, an extreme and energetic urge to prevent all change or even to go back to another age, are normal, healthy, traditional attitudes for the untempered raw material of the future adults of our society. Whether it reflects fundamental wrongs in our society and is the harbinger of a new, good or bad, feasible or infeasible foreign policy, cultural enlightenment, etc., are quite different questions. Traditionally, these youthful advantages and shortcomings (the former normally outweighing the latter) and their consequences have been understood for what they were: a normal and necessary phenomenon of any society. And, as mentioned earlier, youth generally followed their elders in value choices.

But the 1967 polls of high school students also indicate some apparent contradictions or uncertainties which cannot be ignored. One also gets the feeling that the 1968-1970 data (to be discussed later) also show some deviations, which might be explained by the way the questions were asked or it might indicate some recent changes in attitude. Answers to the last two questions below, for example, may seem to indicate that the very foundation of democracy is in question, and even that the left- and right-wing "vanguard-of-the-revolution" approach to political thought might be making inroads into the thinking of our youth. This would appear to be a hasty judgment, however, for not only are we probably running into the enthusiasm of youth for rather simplistic solutions, but a further analysis seems to indicate that when the adolescents were asked about more familiar fundamentals— again, they hadn't changed much since 1951.

Modern youth seem to parallel their parents on their outlook toward the future of the country. This does not mean that their satisfaction or dissatisfaction about the way things are going is identical with their parents'. They may not be so alarmed as their parents about

Table 66

FEELINGS TOWARD DEMOCRATIC PRINCIPLES*

High School Students

	1951	1967
Obedience and respect for authority are the most important virtues that children should learn		
Agree	75%	76%
Undecided	9	9
Disagree	16	15
Whatever serves the interests of government best is generally right		
Agree	22	20
Undecided	27	25
Disagree	51	53
What this country needs most is a few strong, courageous, tireless leaders in whom the people can put their faith		
Agree	64	56
Undecided	12	14
Disagree	24	26
A large mass of the people are not capable of determining what is and what is not good for them		
Agree	49	42
Undecided	19	16
Disagree	33	40

the apparent direction "things are going"; but one gets the feeling that many in the minority of those who support the New Left "movement" would be uncomfortable if suddenly they were faced with the reality of some of the proposals they support.

The following questions, asked in 1967, make an interesting comparison with adult feelings in this same period. Although the opinions of the students in most cases did not differ enough between groups to reverse a trend, the opinions of the different groups may be worth noting. The largest number of students in any category, according to their future plans, were (then as now), of course, in the college-bound group. This group (a) usually is quite close to the average of the total sample on all issues; and (b) in this case, as a distinct group, it varied from the others in being, on the whole, less pessimistic about the

* Purdue Opinion Panel, *Report of Poll No. 81*, November 1967, p. 3a; *No. 30*, November 1951, p. 2a, 6a, 8a.

Table 67

FUTURE—PERSONAL DIGNITY AND LOVE OF FELLOW MAN*

High School Students

Some people feel that personal dignity and love of fellow man will tend to *decrease* in the coming years. Do you agree that this will *happen?*

	Total Sample	Sex Boy	Sex Girl	Mother's Education Grade School	Mother's Education High School	Mother's Education College	Income Low	Income Middle	Income High	Political Preference Dem.	Political Preference Repub.	Political Preference Other	Political Preference Und.	Grade 10	Grade 11	Grade 12
Agree	36%	36%	36%	37%	35%	36%	37%	36%	36%	34%	37%	46%	38%	37%	34%	37%
Undecided; probably agree	20	20	20	20	21	17	18	20	20	19	22	17	19	18	22	20
Undecided; probably disagree	16	17	15	15	16	19	15	15	18	16	16	6	18	16	15	17
Disagree	26	25	28	26	27	26	26	27	25	29	24	23	24	28	27	24

	Course Grades Very Low	Course Grades Low	Course Grades Average	Course Grades High	Course Grades Excellent	Future Plans College	Future Plans Special Training	Future Plans Work	Future Plans Military	Future Plans Other Plan	Region East	Region Mid-West	Region South	Region West
Agree	39%	37%	36%	36%	38%	35%	37%	39%	33%	39%	34%	35%	36%	40%
Undecided; probably agree	22	19	18	24	19	21	21	18	20	16	16	22	20	21
Undecided; probably disagree	4	18	18	13	16	15	16	19	18	19	20	17	12	16
Disagree	30	26	26	27	25	28	26	21	28	23	29	24	30	21

* Purdue Opinion Panel, *Report of Poll No. 80*, April 1967, pp. 9a and 10a. A description was given earlier (previous to Table 65) of the way the "course grades" were determined and what percentage of students fell into each category in the 1970 polls.

183

Table 68

FUTURE—ANXIETY AND NERVOUSNESS*

High School Students

Some people think that in the future Americans will probably experience more anxiety and nervousness than they do now. Do you agree that this will happen?

	Total Sample	Sex		Mother's Education			Income			Political Preference				Grade		
		Boy	Girl	Grade School	High School	College	Low	Middle	High	Dem.	Repub.	Other	Und.	10	11	12
Agree	52%	49%	56%	48%	55%	55%	39%	53%	55%	49%	56%	65%	54%	51%	50%	57%
Uncertain; probably agree	25	25	26	29	24	21	32	24	26	26	23	15	28	27	27	22
Uncertain; probably disagree	9	10	8	10	10	7	11	10	8	10	9	4	8	10	9	9
Disagree	12	14	10	13	11	15	16	12	11	14	11	10	9	11	14	11

	Course Grades					Future Plans					Region			
	Very Low	Low	Average	High	Excellent	College	Special Training	Work	Military	Other Plan	East	Mid-West	South	West
Agree	48%	49%	50%	56%	61%	54%	54%	50%	44%	51%	53%	54%	46%	61%
Uncertain; probably agree	22	27	27	25	16	24	27	29	25	27	25	26	27	23
Uncertain; probably disagree	4	14	10	7	9	8	7	12	14	9	9	8	10	10
Disagree	22	10	13	11	14	13	12	8	16	11	12	12	15	6

* Ibid., pp. 9a and 10a.

184

Table 69

FUTURE—EFFECTIVENESS OF RELIGION*

High School Students

In the world in which you will live as an adult, do you think a church (or synagogue) will be successful or unsuccessful in helping you to solve such problems as "Why should I live?" or "What is my purpose in life?"

	Total Sample	Sex		Mother's Education			Income			Political Preference				Grade		
		Boy	Girl	Grade School	High School	College	Low	Middle	High	Dem.	Repub.	Other	Und.	10	11	12
Successful	59%	54%	64%	63%	58%	53%	58%	59%	57%	62%	59%	38%	54%	59%	59%	58%
Undecided; probably successful	20	21	19	21	19	20	26	20	18	21	18	15	20	21	19	19
Undecided; probably unsuccessful	9	11	7	7	10	12	4	9	11	8	10	15	11	9	9	10
Unsuccessful	11	13	10	9	12	15	9	11	14	8	12	29	15	10	12	12

	Course Grades					Future Plans					Region			
	Very Low	Low	Average	High	Excellent	College	Special Training	Work	Military	Other Plan	East	Mid-West	South	West
Successful	43%	44%	58%	63%	60%	61%	60%	60%	53%	48%	55%	54%	68%	56%
Undecided; probably successful	17	28	22	16	14	18	21	20	23	26	18	22	19	21
Undecided; probably unsuccessful	17	16	9	8	8	8	9	10	14	12	13	11	5	9
Unsuccessful	17	9	10	12	19	12	10	10	11	12	14	12	7	15

* Ibid.

185

Table 70

CHURCH ATTENDANCE—1980*

High School Students

As compared to today, I expect that church attendance, in 1980, will have	Total Sample	Sex		Mother's Education			Income			Political Preference				Grade		
		Boy	Girl	Grade School	High School	College	Low	Middle	High	Dem.	Repub.	Other	Und.	10	11	12
Increased greatly	13%	15%	12%	16%	12%	11%	24%	12%	12%	17%	11%	12%	9%	17%	12%	10%
Increased somewhat	23	24	21	24	23	19	20	24	22	25	22	15	21	24	23	21
Remained about the same as today	24	21	27	20	27	26	20	24	26	22	25	23	27	21	23	28
Decreased somewhat	28	26	29	27	27	34	23	27	30	27	31	17	28	25	29	29
Decreased greatly	11	13	10	11	12	10	14	11	11	9	11	31	14	11	11	11

	Course Grades					Future Plans					Region			
	Very Low	Low	Average	High	Excellent	College	Special Training	Work	Military	Other Plan	East	Mid-West	South	West
Increased greatly	35%	12%	15%	10%	11%	13%	13%	12%	17%	14%	8%	9%	22%	11%
Increased somewhat	17	23	24	23	15	23	23	20	25	22	23	24	23	18
Remained about the same as today	17	28	22	27	25	25	22	32	18	15	27	24	21	25
Decreased somewhat	4	23	27	31	33	28	31	22	25	31	30	31	22	32
Decreased greatly	13	16	11	9	14	10	11	13	14	15	11	10	11	13

* Ibid.

186

Table 71

DIVORCE RATE—1980*

High School Students

The divorce rate in 1980, compared to that of today, will be:	Total Sample	Sex		Mother's Education			Income			Political Preference				Grade		
		Boy	Girl	Grade School	High School	College	Low	Middle	High	Dem.	Repub.	Other	Und.	10	11	12
Greater	70%	70%	70%	69%	70%	69%	61%	70%	71%	66%	76%	75%	70%	71%	68%	70%
About as it is today	20	18	21	20	19	21	27	19	20	22	16	8	20	18	22	19
Less	7	8	6	8	7	6	8	7	6	8	5	10	7	7	6	7

	Course Grades					Future Plans					Region			
	Very Low	Low	Average	High	Excellent	College	Special Training	Work	Military	Other Plan	East	Mid-West	South	West
Greater	57%	63%	69%	73%	76%	72%	67%	68%	66%	65%	70%	73%	66%	71%
About as it is today	17	21	20	20	12	18	23	21	20	19	22	18	20	18
Less	13	13	7	4	9	7	4	7	11	10	5	5	10	8

* Ibid., pp. 11a and 12a.

fate of dignity and love of fellow man and the value of religion, in the future; and (c) its degree of pessimism about church attendance in the future was surpassed by all other groups, save one. It was by no means made up of Pollyannas; it appeared to be aware of the problems (note their answers to the probability of a high degree of nervousness and anxiety in the future), but it seemed somewhat more sold on the system than the other groups. It appears to be more in the center and less troubled by "right" or "left" defeatism.

The following table shows some "summaries" of attitudes at the end of 1967 as reflected in the form of answers to questions on some fundamentals. It shows concern for domestic and international problems, but a strong belief in the "basics" of the system: "religion, democracy and the free enterprise system." It shows a high degree of skepticism, but the weight of opinion falls on the side of the feeling that "people are basically honest."

Table 72

ATTITUDES TOWARD BASICS OF THE SYSTEM*
High School Students

I get tired of people constantly questioning governmental policies.	Total Sample	Boy	Girl
Disagree	38%	41%	36%
Unsure; but probably disagree	12	11	12
Unsure; but probably agree	12	12	12
Agree	36	36	38
Disobedience to any government is never justified.			
Disagree	48	54	42
Unsure; but probably disagree	12	10	14
Unsure; but probably agree	13	10	15
Agree	26	24	28
I am very worried about what is going on in national politics.			
Disagree	32	33	31
Unsure; but probably disagree	11	10	11
Unsure; but probably agree	17	16	18
Agree	40	41	40
I am very concerned with world problems.			
Disagree	21	20	22
Unsure; but probably disagree	8	8	8
Unsure; but probably agree	21	20	21
Agree	49	52	47

* Purdue Opinion Panel, *Report of Poll No. 82,* January 1968.

Table 72 (continued)

People should have more belief in religion, democracy and the free enterprise system.	Total Sample	Sex Boy	Girl
Disagree	7%	9%	6%
Unsure; but probably disagree	3	3	4
Unsure; but probably agree	15	16	14
Agree	73	71	75
Usually both sides of an issue are distorting the truth.			
Disagree	23	23	23
Unsure; but probably disagree	13	11	14
Unsure; but probably agree	18	16	19
Agree	45	49	42
The individual himself is the best judge of what is a moral act.			
Disagree	13	15	11
Unsure; but probably disagree	6	8	5
Unsure; but probably agree	11	11	10
Agree	69	65	72
People are basically honest.			
Disagree	29	28	28
Unsure; but probably disagree	12	13	11
Unsure; but probably agree	21	22	21
Agree	36	36	37
Most people would tell a lie if they could gain by it.			
Disagree	13	12	13
Unsure; but probably disagree	10	9	11
Unsure; but probably agree	16	15	16
Agree	60	62	59

The answers listed above would not always coincide with those that might be given by the parents of the students, but one cannot be sure. The heavy agreement on support of the basics ("religion, democracy and the free enterprise system") sounds like the results of an adult poll. Considerable cynicism was displayed by these adolescents, however, in supporting the thesis that "Usually both sides of an issue are distorting the truth" and their even heavier support of the proposition that "Most people would tell a lie if they could gain by it" (while at the same time subscribing to the idea that "People are basically honest"). This cynicism may or may not have run counter to parents' attitudes (or at least to their attitudes in cautioning children). It could have coincided with (and to some extent may have reflected) the far-from-sinister caveats drummed into children: "There are two sides to every story"; "Never buy anything expensive just because someone tells you it is a bargain"; "Don't believe everything you hear." Or it could have reflected more than that. Generally, however, these high school students do not seem to have been too different from adults in their attitudes.

2. YOUTH: 1968–1971

a. THE SIMILARITY AND DISSIMILARITY BETWEEN HIGH SCHOOL STUDENTS AND ADULTS

Answers limited to questions asked from 1968 to 1971, shown in the following table, reflected the attitudes of high school students toward their families, school, race relations, environment, and politics. Generally speaking, these attitudes also show a marked similarity to those of their parents, including, for example, such fundamental and, from a youngster's point of view, "pertinent" subjects (particularly if he intends to go to college) as feelings on law and order and discipline in high school. But there are some points where significant

Table 73

INFLUENCE IN FAMILY DECISIONS

High School Students

How much influence do you feel you have in family decisions that affect you?

| | | | | | July 1971**** | | |
	Dec. 1968*	May 1970**	Dec. 1970***	All	College-bound students	Above average students	Excellent students
A great deal of influence	22%	25%	24%	25%	28%	28%	38%
Considerable influence	30	28	33	29	33	32	28
Moderate influence	23	23	21	22	21	22	18
Some influence	15	15	15	15	11	12	4
Little or no influence	9	8	7	8	6	5	10

* Purdue Opinion Panel, *Report of Poll No. 85*, December 1968, p. 7a.
** Purdue Opinion Panel, *Report of Poll No. 89*, June 1970, p. 3a.
*** Purdue Opinion Panel, *Report of Poll No. 90*, January 1971, pp. 1a and 2a.
**** Purdue Opinion Panel, *Report of Poll No. 92*, July 1971, p. 4a.

Table 74

RELATIONSHIP WITH ADULTS*

High School Students

Relationships with parents and other adults (having too many decisions made for me; being too easily led by them; getting into arguments; hurting their feelings; being different; being talked about or made fun of; etc.)

	Total Sample	Sex		Grade			Father's Education			Mother's Education		
		Boy	Girl	10	11	12	Grade School	High School	College	Grade School	High School	College
Very much	14%	13%	15%	15%	12%	14%	17%	13%	12%	17%	13%	13%
Quite a bit	16	15	18	17	16	16	18	16	15	17	17	14
Some	23	25	20	22	24	21	22	23	23	21	23	25
A little	16	15	17	15	17	16	14	17	16	13	17	18
Not very much	29	30	27	26	28	31	26	29	30	28	29	27

	Course Grades					Region			
	Very Low	Below Average	Average	Above Average	Excellent	East	Midwest	South	West
Very much	28%	20%	13%	13%	12%	15%	15%	13%	12%
Quite a bit	13	15	17	16	15	15	15	16	23
Some	20	28	21	24	23	22	23	23	23
A little	13	10	17	16	20	15	17	16	16
Not very much	18	24	28	31	30	31	28	29	24

* Purdue Opinion Panel, *Report of Poll No. 88*, April 1970, pp. 15a and 16a.

191

differences exist.* These differences might arise for many reasons, including such mundane ones as confusion among the people polled or the way the questions were asked. On basic issues, such as their relationships with their family, there has been no significant change over the past three years.

Another poll showed 66 percent of youngsters between 15 and 21 having no trouble "communicating" with their parents and 80 percent of those who did, admitting to at least part of the fault in the breakdown. Of the same group, 73 percent said they accepted and agreed with their parents' values and ideals.** Nor do most students feel really put upon, "put down," or really annoyed by adults. This is particularly true, as one might expect, of the high achievers. With this kind of relationship one would expect students to continue to be influenced by their parents on many basic issues.

The following chart shows the interesting similarity of ranking of political parties over the years by high school students and the adult group that would include their parents, the 30-to-49 year olds. The students' opinions produce a sort of rough "shadow" of their parents' opinion; the lower position on the graph of the youngsters' choices results, as one would expect, from a higher percentage of them being "undecided" or preferring some other party. But, as the chart following this one indicates, even the increase in this category among high school students may reflect to some degree the thinking of their parents. The dates of the polls do not coincide exactly, but when they do, the choices are rather consistent. When parents change preference, students (when they show a preference) do, too; and they do so to a degree that a pattern of preferences that resemble each other is formed over the years.

Bar charts for the year 1970 show the similarity of patterns of high school students' and adults' political party choice. The 30-to-49-year-old group (which includes most parents of the high school students) is not included in this source; but this median-age age group of adults is likely to average within a few percentage points of the overall voters' opinion, so the pattern is still valid. As may be expected, the youngsters, again, are more likely to have no opinion on political issues than adults (and on average perhaps more for "liberal" than "conservative" reasons); but

* See the discussion following Table 75 in this chapter.
** Poll in *Life* Magazine, January 8, 1971, conducted by Louis Harris Associates, covering young people between the ages of 15 and 21.

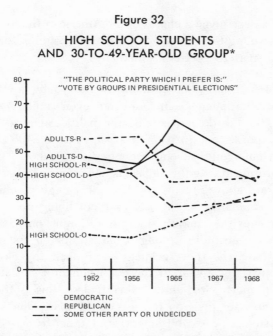

Figure 32

HIGH SCHOOL STUDENTS
AND 30-TO-49-YEAR-OLD GROUP*

"THE POLITICAL PARTY WHICH I PREFER IS:"
"VOTE BY GROUPS IN PRESIDENTIAL ELECTIONS"

ADULTS-R
ADULTS-D
HIGH SCHOOL-R
HIGH SCHOOL-D
HIGH SCHOOL-O

1952 1956 1965 1967 1968

———— DEMOCRATIC
- - - - REPUBLICAN
—·—·— SOME OTHER PARTY OR UNDECIDED

* Compiled from Purdue Opinion Panel *Reports of Polls: No. 47,* November 1956, p. 2; *No. 73,* January 1965, p. 1a; *No. 81,* November 1967, p. 1a; *No. 84,* November 1968, p. 1a; and *Gallup Opinion Index,* No. 42, December 1968, p. 5.

Figure 33

POLITICAL PARTY CHOICE

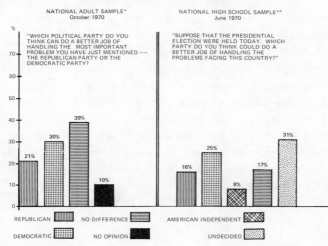

NATIONAL ADULT SAMPLE*
October 1970

"WHICH POLITICAL PARTY DO YOU THINK CAN DO A BETTER JOB OF HANDLING THE MOST IMPORTANT PROBLEM YOU HAVE JUST MENTIONED — THE REPUBLICAN PARTY OR THE DEMOCRATIC PARTY?"

21% 30% 39% 10%

NATIONAL HIGH SCHOOL SAMPLE**
June 1970

"SUPPOSE THAT THE PRESIDENTIAL ELECTION WERE HELD TODAY. WHICH PARTY DO YOU THINK COULD DO A BETTER JOB OF HANDLING THE PROBLEMS FACING THIS COUNTRY?"

16% 25% 8% 17% 31%

REPUBLICAN   NO DIFFERENCE   AMERICAN INDEPENDENT

DEMOCRATIC   NO OPINION   UNDECIDED

* Developed from *Gallup Opinion Index,* No. 64, October 1970, p. 3.
** Developed from Purdue Opinion Panel, *Report of Poll No. 89,* June 1970, pp. 21a and 22a.

had the adults been given a choice of the American Independent party, as were the youngsters, the "no difference" column for the adults might fit the "pattern" better. Nonetheless, the low "shadow" is still there.

This is not to imply that opinions of the young always coincide with their parents'; some feelings are not even similar to the degree indicated by the "shadow" curve on the political choice chart. What is more, in response to a question on basic values in 1968, although as a group the senior high school students did not show excessive concern, the confusion among the highest achievers was higher than among the average and above average students. The higher achievers might also set high standards for themselves ("not living up to my ideals," etc.) and perhaps they may be more questioning on most issues. On the other hand, attitudes among some adults on issues of values and morals (such as the "sociology" approach to religion) might have contributed somewhat to the confusion of these students with their closer rapport with adults. Nevertheless, this is the group—as we shall see in later polls on the use of the marijuana, belief in the American system, the establishment, and other issues—that usually reflected most strongly whatever "traditional value systems" were involved in these questions.

Differences in opinion between parents and high school students on some issues, however, is traditional, and as they get further into late adolescence, these differences increase. Perhaps the most interesting point these days is that under the combined pressure of such powerful "teaching" elements in a youngster's life as movies and other media, high school students are harder to stampede than some might think. Nevertheless, attitudes may have changed to a degree in some areas in recent years which might cause concern to many parents.

There have been some changes in such attitudes as the disapproval of sexual misbehavior. If restraints are not supported and young people get the impression (or, for that matter, some old "opinion-making" people are convinced) that the instant fulfillment of these very strong, normal desires is not out of line, then adolescents may be less likely to reject their friends when they do these things (see Table 64 for the change in attitudes between 1952 and 1965). A late 1970 poll of high school children over 15 years of age indicated that 78 percent felt that people "dating casually" should not have sexual relations; nor should those going steady (69 percent); nor should even those

194

Table 75

VALUES*
High School Students

Values (wondering how to tell right from wrong; confused on some moral questions; doubting the value of worship and prayer; not living up to my ideal; etc.)

	Total Sample	Sex		Grade			Father's Education			Mother's Education			Region			
		Boy	Girl	10	11	12	Grade School	High School	College	Grade School	High School	College	East	Midwest	South	West
Very much	14%	11%	17%	12%	15%	15%	12%	16%	15%	14%	14%	15%	14%	15%	14%	12%
Quite a bit	17	16	18	17	16	18	18	16	17	17	18	15	18	16	17	17
Some	23	24	21	22	23	23	23	24	22	24	23	22	21	23	22	26
A little	17	18	16	18	17	15	16	18	16	16	18	16	15	16	19	17
Not very much	27	28	25	27	27	27	29	25	27	26	27	28	29	27	25	27

Course Grades

	Excellent	Above Average	Average	Below Average	Very Low
Very much	23%	14%	12%	18%	18%
Quite a bit	21	18	16	19	3
Some	19	20	24	24	35
A little	17	18	17	10	18
Not very much	21	28	27	28	23

* Purdue Opinion Panel, *Report of Poll No. 88*, April 1970, pp. 19a and 20a.

195

Table 76

VIEWS ON MIDDLE EAST DISPUTE*
High School Students

In the dispute in the Middle East, do your sympathies lie more with the Israelis or the Arabs?	Total	Course Grades				
		Very Low	Below Average	Average	Above Average	Excellent
Definitely with the Israelis	25%	14%	19%	20%	31%	39%
Undecided; probably with the Israelis	50	36	51	52	52	38
Undecided; probably with the Arabs	13	12	15	16	8	12
Definitely with the Arabs	5	19	6	5	3	7

Should Great Britain, France, Russia, and the U.S. sell airplanes, guns and ammunition to Israel and the Arab countries?	Total Sample	Sex		Grade			Mother's Education			Father's Education		
		Boy	Girl	10	11	12	Grade School	High School	College	Grade School	High School	College
Definitely yes, to both	12%	11%	12%	12%	13%	11%	13%	11%	13%	13%	11%	11%
Yes, to the Israelis only	9	11	7	9	9	8	8	9	11	7	10	11
Yes, to the Arabs only	2	3	2	3	2	2	3	2	3	2	2	2
Definitely no, to both	72	71	73	70	71	74	71	74	68	72	73	70

* Purdue Opinion Panel, *Report of Poll No. 89*, June 1970, pp. 7a, 9a and 10a.

Table 76 (continued)*

	College	Future Plans				Course Grades					Region			
		Special Training	Work	Military	Other Plans	Very Low	Low	Average	High	Excellent	East	Midwest	South	West
Definitely yes, to both	11%	10%	13%	19%	12%	21%	13%	11%	11%	16%	11%	11%	15%	10%
Yes, to the Israelis only	10	9	5	13	6	12	9	8	9	10	3	9	9	9
Yes, to the Arabs only	2	2	5	1	2	7	3	2	1	3	3	2	2	2
Definitely no, to both	73	74	70	62	73	50	68	72	74	69	73	74	67	73

Adults**

"In this trouble, are your sympathies more with Israel or the Arab States?"

	Israel	Arabs	Neither	No Opinion
All	44%	3%	32%	21%
30–49 years of age [most parents of high school students]	41	4	33	22
Region				
East	48	5	32	22
Midwest	37	3	34	26
South	42	2	30	26
West	50	2	31	17

* Ibid., pp. 9a and 10a.
** Gallup Opinion Index, Report No. 58, April 1970, p. 13.

197

Table 77
VIEWS ON VIETNAM*
High School Students

How do you feel about the U.S. military involvement in the Vietnam war?	Total Sample	Course Grades					College	Special Training	Future Plans		Other Plans	Region			
		Very Low	Low	Average	High	Excellent			Work	Military Plans		East	Midwest	South	West
The U.S. should increase the military action there	42%	39%	47%	40%	43%	48%	40%	41%	44%	53%	44%	40%	38%	46%	45%
The U.S. should decrease the military action there	35	33	27	35	37	40	38	34	36	19	34	34	39	33	33
The U.S. should maintain military action at its present level	22	22	24	24	20	10	21	26	17	26	22	24	22	21	21

Adults**

People are called hawks if they want to step up our military effort in Vietnam. They are called doves if they want to reduce our military effort in Vietnam. How would you describe yourself, as a hawk or a dove?

	April 1968			March 1968		
	Hawk	Dove	No Opinion	Hawk	Dove	No Opinion
All	41%	41%	18%	41%	42%	17%
30–49-year-olds [most parents of high school students]	44	38	18			
Region						
East	34	47	19			
Midwest	43	40	17			
South	43	38	19			
West	46	37	17			

* Purdue Opinion Panel, Report of Poll No. 84, November 1968, pp. 3a and 4a.
** Gallup Opinion Index, Report No. 35, May 1968, p. 20.

Table 78

VIETNAM—HUMPHREY'S POSITION*
Adults

"If Humphrey were to take a
stronger peace position on
Vietnam, would this make
you more likely to vote for
him, or not?"

| | *Late September 1968* | | |
	Yes, would	*No, would not*	*No Opinion*
National	31%	60%	9%

VIETNAM—NIXON'S POSITION**
Adults

"If Nixon were to take a
stronger peace position on
Vietnam, would this make
you more likely to vote for
him, or not?"

| | *Late September 1968* | | |
	Yes, would	*No, would not*	*No Opinion*
National	35%	57%	8%

In December 1970 high school students were split on interventions to stop Communist take-overs in Asia, with a slight edge on the intervention side.***

| "The U.S. should intervene when the Communists attempt to take over an Asian country." | *Future Plans* | | Course Grades | | | |
	All	*College*	*Below Average*	*Average*	*Above Average*	*Excellent*
Definitely agree	25%	26%	23%	24%	27%	20%
Undecided, probably agree	28	28	23	28	29	23
Undecided, probably disagree	22	21	31	23	19	25
Definitely disagree	21	20	20	20	21	25

* *Gallup Opinion Index,* Report No. 40, October 1968, p. 17.
** Ibid., p. 16.
*** Purdue Opinion Panel, *Report of Poll No. 90,* January 1971, pp. 15a and 16a.

planning to marry (57 percent). A large minority (45 percent), however, felt it was all right if people were "formally engaged."* On the last issue, their approval is 35 percent and 25 percent higher than all adults as of 1965 and 1969 (see Figure 6). Recent increased opposition on the part of adults to permissive attitudes toward sexual behavior and pornographic material may result from a shift, or the fear of a shift, in the thinking of children.

Other issues on which high school students apparently deviate from the opinions of their parents are in areas that the young do not have very close contact with and have difficulty in evaluating by themselves. Most of what they learn about these issues outside the family comes from what they see on television, read in the press, or from what they are told by non-family adults who feel they should inform them about these issues. As one would expect, therefore, views on foreign policy (not only Vietnam, but on the Middle East and elsewhere), economic policy, and even racial problems (if students are not in the affected areas) may be held less strongly and/or deviate more from their parents' views than those on issues closer to home. Tables 76 and 77 are some examples of such thinking. The questions, as usual, are seldom identical and the possible answers almost always different, but a general comparison of attitudes may be evident from them. Nor do the differences of opinion between adults and high school students necessarily always go in the direction we might think. But a response to a question asked in a poll for *Seventeen* magazine (February 1971) indicated that among 14-to-17 year olds, 69 percent felt too much money was spent on the Vietnam War, 26 percent felt it was the right amount and 5 percent not enough. (This, of course, does not necessarily rule out the "intervention" position.)

It is interesting to note where the difference in opinion between adults (especially those who include most parents of the high school students) and high school students occurs. When adolescents were asked questions on Vietnam similar to the "hawk" or "dove" question asked their parents, the poll's results showed perceptible, though not significant, differences. And, as of 1968, when differences occurred, they were sometimes unexpected; that is, students with excellent grades were slightly more hawkish; boys were more hawkish than girls; students from the East more hawkish than adults in the East. But when adults were queried about their desires for a more peace-oriented

* Harris poll, *Life*, January 8, 1971, p. 27.

platform for presidential candiates in 1968, they came out strongly against it.

Another interesting area of comparison of opinions of adults and high school students on key issues is that of race relations.

Only 20 percent of the students endorsed "complete elimination of racial segregation in all regions of the country" in 1970. This appears low when compared to the adults' answers as to whether or not they objected to sending their children to integrated schools in September 1969: 89 percent of the adults in their parents' age bracket had no objection to schools with "a few" Negroes; 64 percent had no objection where "half of the children" were Negroes; and 33 percent had no objection where "more than half" were Negroes.* The reason, however, might have been because of the nature of the other choices with which senior high school students could respond to this question. In the context of these choices, this response could easily be viewed as one regarding enforced *busing* to achieve integration; and this was opposed by the 65 percent of the students who preferred other racial arrangements** (compared to 79 percent of adults in their parents' age bracket, 30-to-49, who were opposed to busing) and favored by

Table 78A

RACE RELATIONS***

High School Students

As a solution for race problems in public schools, which of the following would you strongly support: (Answer only one)

	Total Sample	Boy	Girl	10	11	12
		Sex			Grade	
Complete elimination of racial segregation in all regions of the country	20%	21%	19%	17%	20%	23%
Separate but completely equal schools	8	11	5	11	8	6
Freedom of choice to attend public school, integrated or segregated	57	51	62	58	57	55
No strong feelings; some other	12	13	11	12	11	13

* *Gallup Opinion Index,* Report No. 51, September 1969, pp. 5–7.
** "Separate but completely equal schools" plus "Freedom of choice to attend public school, integrated or segregated."
*** Purdue Opinion Panel, *Report of Poll No. 89,* June 1970, pp. 15a and 16a.

Table 78A (continued)

	Mother's Education			Father's Education			Future Plans				
	Grade School	High School	College	Grade School	High School	College	College	Special Training	Work	Military	Other Plans
Complete elimination of racial segregation in all regions of the country	17%	21%	22%	19%	20%	22%	22%	18%	17%	20%	16%
Separate but completely equal schools	10	8	6	10	7	8	7	10	12	8	8
Freedom of choice to attend public school, integrated or segregated	55	58	59	55	60	56	59	59	53	51	53
No strong feelings; some other	15	11	10	14	10	11	10	10	15	15	17

	Course Grades					Region			
	Very Low	Below Average	Average	Above Average	Excellent	East	Midwest	South	West
Complete elimination of racial segregation in all regions of the country	24%	20%	18%	22%	23%	29%	17%	18%	17%
Separate but completely equal schools	12	11	9	6	11	6	7	13	5
Freedom of choice to attend public school, integrated or segregated	29	47	58	61	51	51	60	56	60
No strong feelings; some other	31	19	12	8	12	10	14	12	13

20 percent of the students (compared to 16 percent of the adults in that bracket favoring busing). On the other hand, as some students might have found it hard not to subscribe to the "elimination of racial segregation," the question might have attracted more than a straight busing response. In any event, in all sections of the country, the majority response was for "freedom of choice" (a catching phrase too) to attend integrated or segregated schools. The highest percent approval

Table 73B

SCHOOL INTEGRATION*
Adults

"Would you, yourself, have any objection to sending your children to a school where a few of the children are Negroes?"

	July 1969	
	Yes	No
National	11%	89%
Age		
21–29 years	9	91
30–49 years	11	89
50 and over	8	92

"Would you, yourself, have any objection to sending your children to a school where half of the children are Negroes?"

	July 1969		
	Yes	No	No Opinion
National	32%	64%	4%
Age			
21–29 years	25	70	5
30–49 years	32	64	4
50 and over	36	61	3

"Would you, yourself, have any objection to sending your children to a school where more than half of the children are Negroes?"

	July 1969		
	Yes	No	No Opinion
National	55%	36%	9%
Age			
21–29 years	44	47	9
30–49 years	59	33	8
50 and over	52	40	8

* *Gallup Opinion Index*, Report No. 51, September 1969, pp. 5–7.

203

Table 78C
BUSING OF SCHOOL CHILDREN*
Adults

"In general, do you favor or oppose the busing of Negro and white school children from one school district to another?"	March 1970		
	Favor	Oppose	No Opinion
National	14%	81%	5%
Race			
White	11	85	4
Nonwhite	37	48	15
Age			
21–29 years	17	80	3
30–49 years	16	79	5
50 and over	10	84	6
Region			
East	19	73	8
Midwest	15	81	4
South	8	87	5
West	13	84	3

came from the "above average" students (61 percent), "average" (58 percent), and "excellent" students (51 percent).

In answer to a straightforward question on whether they approved of a law aimed at "achieving racial balance in schools by busing," 66 percent of the 15-to-21 year olds (a broader group of young people than tenth-eleventh-twelfth-graders) in the late 1970 Harris poll said no.** The *Seventeen* poll,*** taken at the same time and covering a 14-to-22-year age group, shows only 53 percent against "compulsory busing to end school segregation" (a somewhat different proposition). It shows the opposition of the 14-to-17 year olds as 51 percent and the 18-to-22 year olds as 55 percent.

The *Purdue Opinion Panel* poll given in Table 78A showed the answers getting slightly more "liberal" as the grade level went up: The eleventh grade was more "liberal" than the tenth, and twelfth more "liberal" than the eleventh. This is usually the case on most issues, so this would indicate that if the 14 year olds (most freshmen) were

* *Gallup Opinion Index*, Report No. 58, April 1970, p. 9.
** Harris poll in *Life*, January 8, 1971, p. 25.
*** *Seventeen*, February 1971, p. 125.

added, the objection should be higher. The questions were different—one asked about "racial balance," the other, a program to "end school segregation." The latter point is stronger and if the students understood the point (and perhaps even thought it only applied to legally segregated schools in the South), this might account for the difference. But one is still not convinced that this is the full explanation.

In Table 79, in which a more direct question dealing with specific, well-understood situations, is asked of the high school students, the student opinion is clear, as was that of the adults when asked if they would send their children to schools that had Negroes. The 70 percent of the students with no strong objections closely resembles the 64 percent of "no objection" to the 50–50 level of integration with which their parents responded. The somewhat greater liberalism (73 to 74 percent) of the students with college-educated parents coincides with the greater "tolerance" of college-educated adults in their poll (67 percent compared to 64 percent overall). As indicated earlier, however, many things are not easily predictable with these children. For example, one might expect (because of, among other things, "the uninvolved, lily-white districts" from which we might expect these "high achievers" to come) the increase in tolerance with an increase in grade scores, which consistently occurs—until one reaches those with "excellent" grades, when it suddenly drops nine points from the "above average" group. This is not likely to be the result of statistical variations; and it is only one of so many such occurrences that one gets the feeling that, as with the adults, one must be constantly on the alert for deviations from what we have come to "expect" from our population.

b. A NEW SET OF CATEGORIES

In June 1970 the Purdue group began to record high school student responses from the point of view of their political "philosophy," in addition to their family background, grade, and level of competence. From here on these categories will be occasionally referred to; and since their make-up is not as obvious as others, some effort should be made to describe them and give a sample of which other students' categories they fall within, and vice versa.

The political "philosophy" of the students was based on their choice of responses to the question, "Which of the following do you believe most strongly?" The students who responded that, "There are serious

Table 79

RACE RELATIONS*

High School Students

If you do have strong objections to working closely in school with a student of some other race or color than you, check any of the following activities in which you would object to work closely with this student. (You may answer more than one).

	Total Sample	Sex		Grade			Mother's Education			Father's Education		
		Boy	Girl	10	11	12	Grade School	High School	College	Grade School	High School	College
In classroom work	5%	6%	3%	6%	5%	4%	5%	4%	6%	5%	4%	5%
Riding the school bus	5	7	3	6	5	4	6	4	4	6	4	4
Sharing the same locker	12	15	10	14	12	12	14	13	9	14	11	12
Attending school assemblies	4	6	3	5	5	3	4	4	3	5	4	4
Participating in physical education	5	7	4	6	5	4	5	5	5	5	4	4
Participating in extra-curricular activities	5	7	2	5	4	4	4	4	6	5	3	5
Attending school affairs (dances, etc.)	11	12	9	13	11	8	10	11	9	10	11	9
Eating in school cafeteria	7	8	5	8	6	5	7	6	5	8	5	5
Making friends, sharing friendships	7	7	6	7	7	5	7	6	5	7	6	6
No strong objections	70	66	74	68	69	73	67	72	73	68	71	74

* Purdue Opinion Poll, *Report of Poll No. 89*, June 1970, pp. 15a and 16a.

Table 79 (continued)*

	Future Plans					Region				Course Grades				
	College	Special Training	Work	Military	Other Plans	East	Midwest	South	West	Very Low	Below Average	Average	Above Average	Excellent
In classroom work	4%	5%	5%	10%	4%	5%	3%	6%	5%	19%	8%	4%	4%	10%
Riding the school bus	3	7	8	6	7	3	4	8	3	24	8	4	4	6
Sharing the same locker	9	13	19	17	15	11	11	18	7	26	14	12	12	14
Attending school assemblies	3	5	5	8	5	3	3	6	4	26	5	4	3	6
Participating in physical education	4	5	8	10	5	6	4	7	5	26	9	4	5	9
Participating in extra-curricular activities	3	4	6	8	6	5	4	5	3	24	6	4	3	6
Attending school affairs (dances, etc.)	9	12	12	12	10	9	9	16	4	24	7	10	10	16
Eating in school cafeteria	4	7	11	10	8	6	5	10	4	21	11	5	5	10
Making friends, sharing friendships	5	8	8	12	7	6	7	8	4	24	10	6	5	7
No strong objections	76	65	63	67	65	75	74	58	76	57	63	70	75	66

* Ibid.

flaws in our society today, but the system is flexible enough to solve them" were labeled the *Middle Group*; those that reported, "The American way of life is superior to that of any other country" were labeled the *Conservative Right;* and those that chose "The American system is not flexible enough; radical change is needed" were labeled the *Radical Left.**

This categorization may well have flaws in it (and I feel there are some significant ones); but if we accept it as a rough guide (which I also feel is valid) it is interesting and perhaps helpful for the later portions of this work to see how the students fall into these categories. Table 80 gives the total and the breakdown for each category.

A comparison of high school students with their parents according to this method is not possible because adults are not categorized by their answers to philosophical questions, but are merely asked to categorize themselves. Furthermore, the categories for adults (they were given only two choices) do not match those used for the students; but, for what it is worth, this is the breakdown on adults for the same time periods:**

Conservative	52%
Liberal	34
No opinion	14

Normally this national average equates roughly to the "center" group of 30-to-49 year olds, which incorporates the parents of the high school students.

Of perhaps more interest are the grades of the students in the various "ideological" categories. According to the Purdue polls of April and November 1970, the "excellent" students have the fewest in the Radical Left (11 percent and 15 percent); the second largest group of excellent students are Conservative Right (21 percent and 17 percent); and the largest number (51 percent and 59 percent) are in the Middle Group. The above-average (high) student broke down the same way: Radical Left, smallest (16 percent and 12 percent); Conservative Right next (18 percent); Middle Group (54 percent and 53 percent). So did the average students (18 percent and 15 percent;

* Purdue Opinion Panel, *Report of Poll No. 89,* June 1970, p. 9.
** *Gallup Opinion Index,* No. 60, June 1970, p. 15.

Table 80

POLITICAL PHILOSOPHY OF HIGH SCHOOL STUDENTS—APRIL AND NOVEMBER 1970*

For each category the first (left) figure is from the June 1970 survey (Poll No. 89) and the second from the later survey (Poll No. 90); "Father's Education" and "Very Low" course grades have a single figure only.

Total Sample, Sex, Grade, Mother's Education, Father's Education

	Total Sample		Sex: Boy		Sex: Girl		Grade 10		Grade 11		Grade 12		Mother's Ed. Grade School		Mother's Ed. High School		Mother's Ed. College		Father's Ed. Grade School	Father's Ed. High School	Father's Ed. College
Conservative Right	19%	18%	20%	23%	16%	15%	20%	21%	20%	16%	18%	17%	20%	20%	19%	18%	18%	15%	19%	20%	19%
Middle Group	46	46	46	45	46	47	43	42	47	46	48	49	40	39	49	46	53	48	44	45	52
Radical Left	18	15	15	16	15	19	19	14	15	16	18	15	20	16	16	14	17	18	18	19	15
Undecided	17	20	18	15	23	19	17	22	18	21	16	18	20	24	16	21	15	13	20	16	14

Future Plans

	College		Special Training		Work		Military		Other Plans	
Conservative Right	20%	17%	15%	11%	20%	26%	28%	27%	15%	19%
Middle Group	52	51	44	48	36	32	38	41	36	34
Radical Left	16	13	21	19	21	13	14	11	18	19
Undecided	11	18	20	20	22	26	18	19	29	28

Course Grades and **Region**

	Very Low	Below Average		Average		Above Average		Excellent		East		Midwest		South		West
Conservative Right	33%	13%	19%	19%	19%	18%	18%	21%	17%	17%	12%	20%	19%	23%	14%	17%
Middle Group	17	31	37	42	42	53	54	51	59	46	52	48	48	40	49	43
Radical Left	21	25	24	18	15	12	16	11	15	18	17	15	13	18	20	18
Undecided	29	30	18	20	23	17	12	15	9	18	18	16	19	17	16	22

* The first column of figures under each category was taken from the June 1970 Purdue Opinion Panel Report of Poll No. 89, pp. 5a and 6a, and the second was reported seven months later in the Purdue Opinion Panel Report of Poll No. 90, January 1971, pp. 3a and 4a. The categories "father's education" and "very low" course grades were not reported in January 1971.

** See the tables on the following pages for the percentage of the student body included in each "future plans" and "course grades" group, and how these figures were arrived at.

42 percent; 19 percent). In fact, as Table 84 and the graph below show, as one goes down the estimated achievement levels of senior high school students in 1970, the Middle Group percentages decrease. At the below-average level there is a scattering of results with a drop in the Conservative Right and the Middle Group percentages, and the largest increase in the no opinion category (from 18 to 30 percent). The relatively high reading (25 and 24 percent) for the Radical Left in the below-average category remained the same.

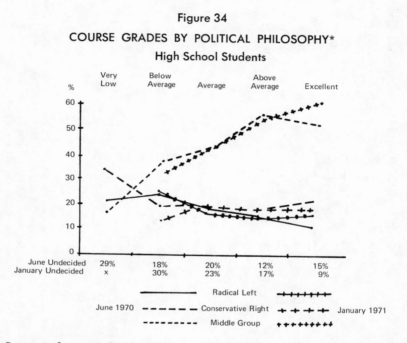

Figure 34

COURSE GRADES BY POLITICAL PHILOSOPHY*

High School Students

In my judgment, the argument is still rather convincing, that normally there is likely to be a recognizable comparison between intelligence and achievement in primary and even secondary schools of selected groups of students; that is, a higher average I.Q. score is more likely to be found in an excellent group than in a low one, or even in an above-average group rather than in an average one. Assuming that the relative standing which the students picked for themselves bears some relationship to their real relative standing, the above data are interesting. A majority (51 and 59 percent) of the students in the "excellent"

* Developed from Table 80.

category and "above average" category (54 and 53 percent) were in the Middle Group; a minority (21 and 17 percent) of the "excellent" students and "above average" students (18 percent) were Conservative Right; and a smaller minority of these high-achievers (11 and 15 percent "excellent," 16 and 12 percent "above average") fit into the Radical Left. This is not to imply that the relationships between intelligence and high-school grades hold in all cases; there are some intelligent students whose grades do not reflect their intelligence because they cannot, or will not, adjust to the structured curriculum and regulations of the school. These students may well be found within the Radical Left or Conservative Right. Nevertheless, the intelligence/grades relationship is probably the best measure available to apply to most students.

This mid- and late 1970 evidence, as well as the trends indicated by the slopes of the curves mentioned earlier, cannot be completely ignored when evaluating "ideological" groups of high school students or even college students. It seems clear that the better-achievers in high school either are more influenced by moderate adults (parents?), or that they are more likely to reject the "Radical Left" and "Conservative Right" based on their own independent conclusions, or both. And these high school groupings apparently have some significance. For example, they seem to think somewhat differently about some basic educational and family issues.

Table 81
THE AMERICAN WAY OF LIFE AND NEED FOR DISCIPLINE*

Need for discipine	Conservative Right	Middle Group	Radical Left	Undecided
From parents and school	36%	32%	22%	33%
From parents only	30	26	22	20
From schools only	2	1	2	2
From themselves only	21	30	36	27
Have enough now	10	9	17	17

C. THE "GENERATION GAP" AND ANTI-ESTABLISHMENTISM

Since the vast majority of students fall under the categories of Conservative Right, Middle Group and Undecided, the above chart indicates that the students are not that averse to advice, or even "discipline," from the two groups of adult "authority figures" in their

* Purdue Opinion Panel, *Report of Poll No. 89*, June 1970, p. 13.

lives—their parents and teachers. Furthermore, even in late 1969, there is some evidence that senior high school students did not differ as much from their parents as some might think on problems of youth. The following table shows the results of asking students what their gripes about young people were, having them rank them, and then having the students rank what they thought their parents' gripes about young people were.

Table 82

BIGGEST GRIPE ABOUT YOUNG PEOPLE TODAY*

Rank	Students' Gripe		Parents' Gripe	
1	use of drugs	50%	use of drugs	43%
2	lack of respect for authority	29	lack of respect for authority	37
3	undisciplined behavior	25	irresponsible	35
4	irresponsible	14	manner of dress, appearance	30
5	manner of dress, appearance	11	undisciplined behavior	24
6	overindulged	7	overindulged	15
7	impatience	6	impatience	9
8	no complaints	11	no complaints	3

The study stated that despite higher percentages of parents registering on specific gripes, "no evidence for a generation gap was revealed by these results."**

The above vote probably reflects, to a large degree, the "perceptions" of the parents' "value systems."

Parents may communicate their value systems to their children; children may or may not perceive this communication. If values have been communicated in some way by parents, and have been perceived by their children, then children should be able to report these perceptions. Children may acquire their parents' value system to some degree, ignore it, or reject it.***

With similar value systems and apparent respect for parents and teachers in late 1969 (the recognition for the need for their discipline as well as those other indicators mentioned earlier are examples of such respect), it was still difficult to fit most students into a rebel (or

* Purdue Opinion Panel *Report of Poll, No. 87*, January 1970, p. 3.
** Ibid.
*** Ibid., p. 4.

radical) mold. However, a new "indicator," that may create a way for some students to by-pass the commonly held value systems, has gained currency in recent years. This new twist is the idea that there is something other than the family and the country—and perhaps even all the economic, governmental and social things that make it up—which can be identified as part of the environment, and perhaps an evil part of it. This is the idea of "the establishment." As indicated before, most students thought our way of life was the best, or that the country was flexible enough to change and right any existing wrongs. On this "establishment issue," however, 6 to 8 percent of the students appeared to be very anti-establishment and another 12 to 15 percent were "probables" on the anti-establishment scale. An even larger percentage (41 to 45 percent) were undecided whether or not they would ever "hold the same beliefs" or "work within" the establishment ("maybe and maybe not; I don't know"). Only 13 percent identified strongly with "the establishment," and another 21 percent were "probables" for the pro-establishment scale.* This was a smaller percentage than those shown in favor of the country, the home, business, etc., in other charts.

There is apparently, however, some confusion about exactly what this establishment is (41 to 45 percent were undecided), as well as apparent opposition to it for being both too far right and too far left. The following bar chart, devised from *Purdue Opinion Panel* data (Poll No. 89, cited earlier), shows that even those high school students who, after graduation, intend to become part of some of the most important segments of the establishment, say they will never have anything to do with it, or that they doubt they will have anything to do with it. For example, many students who will be taking specialized training, mainly girls who will be secretaries or nurses, but one assumes also some probably taking such things as computer programming, and so forth (which means they are going to work for a hospital, doctor, the government or for a business concern, probably often a large one) say they are *not* going along with the establishment. Those intending to enter the military after graduation post the highest percentage— 14 percent of them say they will *never* have anything to do with the establishment and a like amount are doubtful about it. They may feel that the "establishment" is too far left, since this group had a stronger preference for Wallace in 1968. Those who intend to go on to college show only 6 percent who say they will never have anything to do with

* Ibid., pp. 5a and 6a; *Report of Poll No. 89*, June 1970, pp. 9a and 10a.

213

the establishment, and a somewhat larger percentage saying they doubt they will have anything to do with it. For purposes of this chart, as well as the graph that follows it, we have lumped the "certains" and the "probables" both "pro" and "anti" together.

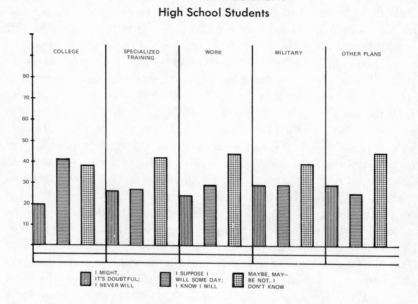

Figure 35
JOIN THE ESTABLISHMENT*
High School Students

There are some groups that may have a better idea as to what the establishment is, and why they oppose it. One of these groups, the Negroes, has a bias toward the Radical Left and also is anti-establishment. Perhaps many Negroes believe the white, upper middle class *is* the establishment and that they are not part of it. Nevertheless, we are left with the belief that there may be some confusion on the part of many other students as to exactly what it is they are opposing and why.

As indicated on the following graph, as one goes up the levels of achievement—and presumably the intelligence—of the students, support for the establishment increases. In fact, among students with excellent grade scores, support for the establishment touches 49 to 50 percent. Conversely, as one goes down the achievement levels, the acceptance of the establishment decreases. There is a slight exception

* Purdue Opinion Panel, *Report of Poll No. 89*, June 1970, pp. 9a and 10a.

214

to this last phenomenon among the excellent students, where there is a two-point variation of this 7 percent of the student body. The following graph shows the results of two surveys in January and June 1970.

Figure 36

JOIN THE ESTABLISHMENT*
High School Students
According to Course Grades

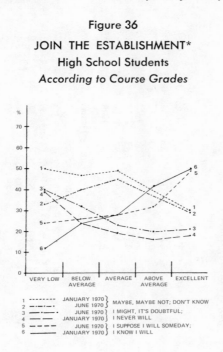

d. DRUGS

If the establishment is vague, and perhaps relatively remote, other things closer to home are not. The high school students' feelings about the use of drugs, including marijuana, exemplify this. The phenomenon of the "under-use" of drugs among high school students was evident in an October 1969 survey of all forty-five high schools in Montgomery County, Maryland (a county bordering Washington, D.C.). Almost half of the students polled believed that "more than one of their closest friends used marijuana." The study's sponsors considered that this "constitutes a dramatic overestimate" which they interpreted to indicate a trend toward more drug use and abuse. The study showed that

* Developed from Purdue Opinion Panel, *Report of Poll No. 87* and *Report of Poll No. 89*, January and June, 1970. Note the similarity to the previous graph in Figure 34 in the comparison of the degree of "radicalism" or "conservatism" with grade scores.

215

Table 83

SELF-REPORT ON USE OF DRUGS, ALCOHOLIC DRINKS, AND CIGARETTES*

In Montgomery County Schools

USE OF PRODUCT	Marijuana			Heroin			Amphetamines			LSD		
	Junior High	Senior High	Total	Junior High	Senior High	Total	Junior High	Senior High	Total	Junior High	Senior High	Total
I've never tried it	93.28%	79.67%	86.63%	96.57%	95.10%	95.86%	96.38%	90.28%	93.41%	96.71%	91.06%	94.45%
I've tried but quit	2.73	7.27	4.93	0.42	1.19	0.79	1.12	4.53	2.77	0.70	2.15	1.40
I use it almost once a month	1.54	4.30	2.68	0.07	0.15	0.11	0.42	2.08	1.22	0.28	2.08	1.15
I use it almost once a week	0.68	4.30	2.41	0.0	0.22	0.11	0.07	0.82	0.43	0.07	1.19	0.61
I use it almost every day	0.0	2.82	1.37	0.0	0.37	0.18	0.0	0.37	0.18	0.07	0.37	0.22
No response	1.82	1.63	1.73	2.94	2.97	2.95	2.03	1.93	1.98	2.17	2.15	2.16

USE OF PRODUCT	Barbiturates			Glue			Alcoholic Drinks			Cigarettes		
	Junior High	Senior High	Total	Junior High	Senior High	Total	Junior High	Senior High	Total	Junior High	Senior High	Total
I've never tried it	96.71%	90.80%	93.84%	91.74%	90.73%	91.25%	67.81%	35.01%	51.89%	55.42%	33.16%	44.62%
I've tried but quit	0.77	4.82	2.74	5.25	6.38	5.80	15.82	19.44	17.57	29.39	39.24	34.17
I use it almost once a month	0.28	1.85	1.04	0.77	0.59	0.68	9.03	26.85	17.68	3.71	3.41	3.56
I use it almost once a week	0.07	0.22	0.14	0.35	0.22	0.29	4.48	14.47	9.33	2.31	2.82	2.56
I use it almost every day	0.0	0.30	0.14	0.21	0.22	0.22	1.05	2.52	1.76	8.05	20.25	13.97
No response	2.17	2.00	2.09	1.68	1.85	1.76	1.82	1.71	1.76	1.12	1.11	1.12

* "Use of Drugs in Montgomery County Found Less Than Predicted," Washington Post, March 11, 1970, p. 70.

216

actually about a fifth of high school students and 7 percent of junior high school students had tried marijuana. (The study group did not suggest that the "under-use," compared to the estimates, was due to students' reluctance to admit to drug use, even in an anonymous survey. But this is such an obvious possibility that one assumes they had a good reason not to indicate this had been a significant factor.)

The assumption of relatively high use, apparently a worry to parents, seems also to be reflected by the opinion of the senior high school students in the Purdue surveys, and the estimates went up drastically in two years.

When they were asked about the use of marijuana in their own school, they gave different answers, but the estimates rose significantly between 1969 and 1971 (see Table 85).

In the second half of 1970, the parents' attitudes had begun to signal that something might have changed since the 1969 polls of high school students. Furthermore, despite the great increase in their own estimates of those who had tried drugs in their own schools, there was a great difference of opinion between high school juniors and seniors and their parents on the issue of whether this constituted a "serious problem" in their public schools.*

Marijuana and other drugs are increasingly being used by students. Do you think it is a serious problem in your public schools?	Public School Parents	Parochial School Parents	High School Juniors and Seniors
Yes	56%	69%	39%
No	31	18	59
Don't know	13	13	2

The judgment of the mass of generally loving, concerned parents is not a trivial thing (even when it runs counter to the judgment of the high school students themselves). One also gets the feeling from some of the discussions on marijuana usage by some adults, especially in the media, that they know little more and perhaps even less than the parents.

In 1969, between "a third and one-half of the junior high, and between one-fourth and one-third of high school students, said they did not know" what factors lead to drug use. Those who did know rated

* Gallup Opinion Index, No. 66, December 1970, p. 17.

217

Table 84

USE OF DRUGS IN HIGH SCHOOL

High School Students

Among all high school students everywhere, how many do you think have tried using marijuana or another drug, as much as once?

	Total Sample		Sex Boy		Sex Girl		Grade 10		Grade 11		Grade 12		Mother's Education Grade School		Mother's Education High School		Mother's Education College	
	1969*	1971**	69	71	69	71	69	71	69	71	69	71	69	71	69	71	69	71
Very few (about 1 in 100)	16%	3%	21%	4%	11%	2%	18%	4%	15%	3%	14%	3%	20%	5%	15%	3%	9%	2%
Few of them (less than 10 percent)	31	9	35	11	27	6	31	11	30	9	33	6	29	11	33	8	30	5
Several of them (more than 10 percent)	38	32	33	36	43	28	35	35	38	33	40	29	36	31	37	34	44	29
Approximately half	15	20	11	18	19	21	15	17	16	18	13	24	15	18	15	19	17	22
At least half, maybe more		35		28		41		32		35		37		34		34		38

	Family Income (1969)		
	Low	Average	High
Very few (about 1 in 100)	19%	16%	12%
Few of them (less than 10 percent)	33	31	31
Several of them (more than 10 percent)	33	38	41
Approximately half	14	14	16

* Purdue Opinion Panel, *Report of Poll No. 86*, March 1969, pp. 13a and 14a.
** Purdue Opinion Panel, *Report of Poll No. 91*, April 1971, pp. 15a and 16a. The choice, "At least half, maybe more" was not given in 1969; added to "Approximately half," this jumps the total for this category to 55 percent in 1971 from 20 percent in 1969.

218

Table 84 (continued)

	Course Grades								Region							
	Below Average		Average		Above Average		Excellent		East		Midwest		South		West	
	69	71	69	71	69	71	69	71	69	71	69	71	69	71	69	71
Very few (about 1 in 100)	18%	4%	17%	5%	13%	1%	15%	2%	14%	2%	17%	3%	20%	5%	8%	2%
Few of them (less than 10 percent)	31	8	33	9	31	7	20	11	30	4	38	6	31	14	21	9
Several of them (more than 10 percent)	30	27	33	32	43	34	55	35	39	18	34	36	36	41	45	30
Approximately half	18	19	16	17	13	22	9	24	17	24	11	21	11	15	26	19
At least half, maybe more	41		35		35		28		51		31		24		38	

Influence on Family Decisions (1969)

	Great	Considerable	Moderate	Some	Little/No
Very few (about 1 in a 100)	15%	12%	16%	19%	20%
Few of them (less than 10 percent)	27	34	33	30	25
Several of them (more than 10 percent)	41	42	36	33	31
Approximately half	16	11	15	17	21

Table 85

USE OF DRUGS IN OWN SCHOOL

High School Students

In your own school, how many students do you think have tried out marijuana or another drug?

| | Total Sample | | Sex | | | | Grade | | | | | |
| | | | Boy | | Girl | | 10 | | 11 | | 12 | |
	1969*	1971**	69	71	69	71	69	71	69	71	69	71
Very few (less than one percent)	50%	14%	55%	18%	45%	10%	51%	17%	51%	12%	47%	13%
Few of them (less than 10 percent)	28	25	25	26	30	23	29	27	28	25	26	21
Several of them (more than 10 percent)	14	27	13	25	16	28	12	26	13	29	19	25
Approximately half	6	13	5	10	7	15	6	12	7	11	7	15
At least half, maybe more		19		17		21		14		19		23

In your own school, how many students do you think have tried out marijuana or another drug?

| | Mother's Education | | | | | | Family Income (1969) | | |
| | Grade School | | High School | | College | | Low | Average | High |
	69	71	69	71	69	71			
Very few (less than one percent)	55%	20%	50%	13%	37%	10%	55%	54%	40%
Few of them (less than 10 percent)	26	25	28	26	32	19	26	26	31
Several of them (more than 10 percent)	11	25	16	27	16	29	11	13	20
Approximately half	5	12	5	12	13	15	5	5	8
At least half, maybe more		16		19		23			

Table 85 (continued)

Course Grades

	Below Average		Average		Above Average		Excellent	
	69	71	69	71	69	71	69	71
Very few (less than one percent)	52%	14%	49%	15%	50%	13%	50%	15%
Few of them (less than 10 percent)	26	24	28	25	28	25	26	24
Several of them (more than 10 percent)	14	29	14	26	15	27	13	28
Approximately half	7	8	6	12	6	13	9	15
At least half, maybe more		20		18		20		15

Region

	East		Midwest		South		West	
	69	71	69	71	69	71	69	71
Very few (less than one percent)	41%	4%	51%	14%	66%	26%	33%	8%
Few of them (less than 10 percent)	31	10	30	27	21	33	29	26
Several of them (more than 10 percent)	17	23	14	28	7	25	25	34
Approximately half	10	22	3	13	3	7	12	11
At least half, maybe more		38		16		7		17

Influence on Family Decisions (1969)

	Great	Consider-able	Moderate	Some	Little/No
Very few (less than one percent)	46%	48%	50%	57%	51%
Few of them (less than 10 percent)	31	32	27	22	18
Several of them (more than 10 percent)	15	13	14	15	20
Approximately half	8	5	6	6	7
At least half, maybe more					

* Ibid., *Report of Poll No. 86*, March 1969, pp. 17a and 18a.
** Purdue Opinion Panel, *Report of Poll No. 91*, April 1971, pp. 19a and 20a.

"the desire to be 'turned on' " first; "factors such as 'being bored in school,' 'preparing for exams,' and 'worries about war and riots' received little support."[*]

Perhaps more interesting in the Purdue data is how the students felt about the "drug environment" in 1969 and at present—for example, their attitude toward others using drugs. The weight of opinion now seems to have definitely shifted from a feeling that their friendship would be adversely affected if they discovered that a friend used marijuana to one that it would not.

There seemed to be a greater tolerance among the children of higher-income families in 1969, and among families where the mother had some college in both 1969 and 1971, compared with those where the mother had only a grade-school education. This tendency toward tolerance may be due to liberal ideas, but it may also be due to a relative lack of experience with drug-users in the neighborhoods where the children in this category live, compared with the lowest educational group (which also contains many Negro mothers)—see 1969 family income column on the following Table. Students' tolerance of drug use by their friends is inversely proportional to their achievement levels; those with the highest grade scores indicate the lowest tolerance. On the other hand, in a 1969 survey, with the exception of the "very poor" students, as the grade score category decreased, the percentage of students supporting drug use as the top gripe increased.[**] The lower-achievers may be more tolerant of their user friends (and may have more such friends), but they apparently didn't like the situation.

There is some evidence in the 1969 survey of regional dependency and its relationship to the number of drug-users in the area. Parents in the East and West showed the highest percentages (45 and 51 percent respectively), naming drug use by children as their "biggest gripe about young people today" (according to the estimates of their children in senior high school), concerned parents in the Midwest rated it second (37 percent) after "irresponsibility" (38 percent).[***] (The regional data particularly for the East is less reliable in the 1971 poll

[*] *Washington Post*, March 11, 1970, p. 70. This desire to be turned on was given for the reason for the increasing switch to hard drugs on the college campuses . . . "It's the greatest high there is." *New York Times*, January 17, 1971, p. 52.
[**] Purdue Opinion Panel, *Report of Poll No. 87*, January 1970, pp. 1a and 2a.
[***] Ibid.

because of fewer returns of the survey in that area.) The probability of "tolerance" in 1969 was greatest among the children with the lowest rapport with their parents.*

The most significant item, however, is that apparent reversal in attitude of the majority toward their friends who would use drugs, which probably indicates a divergence of opinion from their parents.

The percentage of those students who feel that "social pressure" is likely to influence young people to try drugs increases somewhat as the survey moves from the lower to the higher achievers. There was no obvious pattern in 1969 relating to rapport with their parents or family income on the "social pressure" issue.

Hard data on the students' attitudes toward drugs and even on the numbers of high school students who have tried marijuana at least once are somewhat less than satisfactory. Surveys made—the Purdue polls, the Montgomery County study, several 1967 and 1968 studies of San Francisco area high schools, two high schools in the suburbs of New York City and high schools in the state of Michigan—vary from reported use to students' estimates of use, and in some urban San Francisco area schools poll results ranged from zero to as high as 33 percent having said they tried it.** Today there may be many schools with much higher numbers of users, and the Purdue Panel Poll estimates by the students of the number of drug users in the same schools as the students polled—shown previously in Table 85—show a distinct difference in students' estimates of drug use between the East and the West compared to the rest of the country. In 1969, however, very heavy experimentation and/or use apparently was going on in a relatively small number of schools; only 10 percent of the Eastern students and 12 percent of the Western students estimated that half the student population had "tried marijuana or another drug." Overall, half of the students estimated less than 1 percent of the students in their school had tried "marijuana or another drug," and another 28 percent estimated that less than 10 percent had done so. Two years later the estimate that half or more of the students had tried "marijuana or another drug" had jumped to 60 percent in the East, 27 percent in the West.

The disapproval of drugs, including marijuana, which was indicated

* Purdue Opinion Panel, *Report of Poll No. 86*, March 1969, pp. 13a and 14a.
** *Extent of Illicit Drug Use: A Compilation of Studies, Surveys and Polls*, by Dorothy F. Berg, Division of Drug Sciences, Bureau of Narcotics and Dangerous Drugs, United States Department of Justice.

Table 86

TOLERANCE TOWARD THOSE USING DRUGS
High School Students

March, 1969*

If you discovered that a person with whom you had associated was using marijuana or drugs, would it change the relationship between you?

	Total Sample	Sex		Grade			Region				Mother's Education			Family Income		
		Boy	Girl	10	11	12	East	Mid-west	South	West	Grade School	High School	College	Low	Average	High
Yes, it would	43%	43%	44%	47%	45%	39%	35%	41%	56%	39%	49%	42%	35%	49%	44%	39%
Undecided; probably would	22	21	22	22	20	23	22	23	21	21	20	22	24	21	22	33
Undecided; probably would not	13	13	14	11	13	16	17	15	9	14	11	14	17	11	13	14
No, it would not	20	21	19	19	20	21	25	20	12	25	19	20	22	18	19	23

	Course Grades				Influence in Family Decisions				
	Below Average	Average	High	Excellent	Great	Considerable	Moderate	Some	Little/No
Yes, it would	39%	44%	44%	42%	49%	41%	43%	47%	35%
Undecided; probably would	16	21	23	23	16	24	26	21	13
Undecided; probably would not	13	12	14	18	12	15	12	12	17
No, it would not	30	21	17	17	22	18	17	19	33

* Ibid.

224

Table 86 (continued)

April, 1971**

If you discovered that a person with whom you had associated was using marijuana or drugs, would it change the relationship between you?

	Total Sample	Sex		Grade			Mother's Education			Course Grades				
		Boy	Girl	10	10	12	Grade School	High School	College	Very Low	Below Average	Average	Above Average	Excellent
Yes, in the direction of a better relationship	9%	10%	8%	8%	10%	9%	14%	7%	8%	13%	13%	11%	6%	8%
Yes, in the direction of a worse relationship	33	35	30	35	33	30	34	33	29	26	30	29	35	46
No, not as long as others (parents, friends, etc.) don't make a big issue out of it	19	20	18	20	18	19	18	19	19	13	14	20	20	11
No, it definitely would not	37	33	41	35	37	39	32	38	41	45	40	37	36	33

	Future Plans					Region			
	College	Special Training	Work	Military	Other Plans	East	Midwest	South	West
Yes, in the direction of a better relationship	8%	9%	16%	13%	9%	7%	8%	12%	9%
Yes, in the direction of a worse relationship	33	40	28	24	29	23	35	40	29
No, not as long as others (parents, friends, etc.) don't make a big issue out of it	19	15	15	29	21	21	17	18	21
No, it definitely would not.	37	34	36	32	40	48	37	28	38

** Purdue Opinion Panel, Report of Poll No. 91, April 1971, pp. 15a and 16a.

225

Table 87

SOCIAL PRESSURE TO USE DRUGS

High School Students

How many high school students do you think would try using a drug or a narcotic if they knew they would be called "chicken" or "baby" for refusing?

	Total Sample 1969*	Total Sample 1971**	Boy 69	Boy 71	Girl 69	Girl 71	Grade 10	Grade 11	Grade 12	Grade School 69	Grade School 71	High School 69	High School 71	College 69	College 71	Income Low	Income Average	Income High
			Sex				Grade (1969)			Mother's Education						Family Income (1969)		
Very few of them	36%	21%	44%	25%	28%	17%	35%	34%	38%	35%	23%	38%	21%	31%	18%	35%	36%	35%
Some, but not very many	40	34	38	35	41	33	37	42	40	38	32	39	35	44	34	40	40	41
Not more than half	14	18	9	16	19	21	14	14	14	15	17	14	19	15	19	13	15	15
At least half, maybe more	6	17	4	14	8	20	8	6	4	7	17	6	17	4	18	8	5	5
Most of them	4	9	4	10	4	8	5	3	3	5	10	3	8	4	9	4	4	3

Course Grades / Region

	Very Low 71	Below Average 69	Below Average 71	Average 69	Average 71	High 69	High 71	Excellent 69	Excellent 71	East 69	East 71	Midwest 69	Midwest 71	South 69	South 71	West 69	West 71
		Course Grades								Region							
Very few of them	19%	40%	26%	37%	24%	35%	17%	22%	19%	35%	17%	35%	19%	40%	26%	32%	21%
Some, but not very many	35	38	27	39	34	41	37	44	29	41	32	44	33	35	34	40	38
Not more than half	26	9	20	14	18	15	19	21	18	14	20	13	21	13	16	18	16
At least half, maybe more	6	5	17	6	14	7	19	4	22	6	19	6	16	6	16	6	16
Most of them	13	8	9	4	10	2	7	7	12	3	10	2	10	6	8	3	7

Influence in Family Decisions (1969)

	Great	Considerable	Moderate	Some	Little/No
Very few of them	36%	33%	36%	39%	38%
Some. But not very many	36	45	42	33	35
Not more than half	16	12	14	16	13
At least half, maybe more	6	6	5	6	8
Most of them	4	2	2	6	6

* Purdue Opinion Panel, *Report of Poll No. 86*, March 1969, pp. 13a and 14a.
** Purdue Opinion Panel, *Report of Poll No. 91*, April 1971, pp. 15a and 16a.

by rating their use as top on the students' "worst habits" list in 1970, had been reflected in their overwhelming disapproval of the legalization of the possession and sale of marijuana in an early 1969 poll. Two years later, though a majority still tended to disapprove, a similar poll showed a significant alteration of this stand among high school students, an issue which might tend to worry parents and all adults (whose overwhelming opposition has not altered at all—see Table 91), and lead one to ask who is being convinced by the pro-legalization efforts.

The tendency for the majority to disapprove legalization of marijuana (including "undecided; probably disapprove"), however, still cuts across all grade categories except students with very low grades, who show more approval. The degree of solid approval drops as one surveys the higher achievement groups and the disapproval generally grows, but this does not hold for the "probable" approval line when one reaches the excellent students. Here again, opposition in 1969 was somewhat less among the children from families of higher income and mothers with college education.

In answer to a slightly different but very similar question, "Should marijuana be legalized?" in a late 1970 Harris poll, 15-to-18-year-old high school students registered 70 percent "No."* As Table 82 indicates, even if we eliminate the tenth-graders—who include the 14-year-old students—the juniors and seniors in 1969 (almost all over 15 years of age) showed 80 and 77 percent "disapproving" or "undecided; probably disapproving." By 1971, these figures had dropped to 61 percent for both, which continues the drop indicated in the 1970 Harris poll. The drop for tenth- eleventh-, and twelfth-grades combined was from 79 to 64 percent disapproving and probably disapproving. A shift of 15, 16, or 19 points in two years is significant, and if it is "real" and if it continues, could prove to have serious consequences.

In the same 1970 Harris poll, some other interesting questions were asked.**

"Why don't even more young people use marijuana?"
 1. fear of damaging their health
 2. fear of arrest
"What reasons for not using it impress you least?"
 1. fear of school authorities
 2. parental disapproval

* Louis Harris poll, *Life,* January 8, 1971, p. 26.
** Ibid., p. 26.

Table 88

LEGALIZATION OF MARIJUANA
High School Students

Some people urge that the sale and possession of marijuana, which is now illegal, should be legalized. How do you feel about this?

	Total Sample		Boy		Girl		Grade 10		Grade 11		Grade 12		Grade School		High School		College	
	1969*	1971**	69	71	69	71	69	71	69	71	69	71	69	71	69	71	69	71
Approve	11%	22%	14%	23%	8%	21%	10%	17%	11%	24%	13%	25%	10%	21%	11%	21%	15%	27%
Undecided; probably approve	7	13	7	12	7	14	6	13	7	13	9	13	12	14	7	13	9	13
Undecided; probably disapprove	13	14	14	14	12	13	13	14	13	14	14	13	12	12	14	13	14	16
Disapprove	66	50	62	49	71	51	69	54	67	47	63	48	69	52	66	53	60	39

(Grade = school grade; last three groups = Mother's Education)

Family Income (1969)

	Low	Average	High
Approve	12%	9%	15%
Undecided; probably approve	6	7	8
Undecided; probably disapprove	12	13	15
Disapprove	68	70	61

Course Grades

	Very Low		Below Average		Average		High		Excellent	
	69	71	69	71	69	71	69	71	69	71
Approve		45%	24%	29%	11%	22%	9%	20%	10%	18%
Undecided; probably approve		23	11	10	7	14	6	11	7	17
Undecided; probably disapprove		10	10	9	14	14	12	14	16	11
Disapprove		23	56	48	66	48	71	53	64	54

Region

	East		Midwest		South		West	
	69	71	69	71	69	71	69	71
Approve	13%	31%	12%	21%	7%	15%	15%	22%
Undecided; probably approve	10	15	7	13	4	10	7	15
Undecided; probably disapprove	14	15	15	15	9	12	16	12
Disapprove	62	35	64	50	76	62	60	48

Influence in Family Decisions (1969)

	Great	Considerable	Moderate	Some	Little/No
Approve	13%	8%	8%	13%	23%
Undecided; probably approve	6	6	7	7	8
Undecided; probably disapprove	11	15	14	12	12
Disapprove	69	69	68	66	54

* Purdue Opinion Panel, *Report of Poll No. 86*, March 1969, pp. 17a and 18a.

** Purdue Opinion Panel, *Report of Poll No. 91*, April 1971, pp. 19a and 20a.

Table 89

If you could be sure that you could use a drug or narcotic without becoming addicted or arrested, do you think you would like to try it?

	Total	Sex		Grade			Mother's Education			Course Grades				
		Boy	Girl	10	11	12	Grade School	High School	College	Very Low	Below Average	Average	Above Average	Excellent
Yes	21%	22%	21%	21%	21%	22%	21%	20%	25%	52%	24%	22%	20%	16%
Undecided; probably yes	10	11	9	9	11	10	10	10	12	6	8	10	11	13
Undecided; probably no	10	11	9	11	9	11	9	10	14	0	9	10	11	11
No	55	52	58	55	55	55	56	58	46	35	54	55	57	57

	Future Plans					Region			
	College	Special Training	Work	Military	Other Plans	East	Midwest	South	West
Yes	21%	17%	21%	25%	25%	32%	23%	11%	21%
Undecided; probably yes	12	9	10	8	8	10	11	9	10
Undecided; probably no	10	12	7	7	12	11	10	9	12
No	55	59	60	54	51	45	52	68	53

"If legalized, would not pot smoking become as common as drinking?"
Yes—71%

Also, 62 percent of high school students and 53 percent of college students said they believed marijuana leads to "hard drinking and addiction."

The 1971 Purdue poll asked a different question about the use of drugs free from the threat of arrest or addiction, in that it did not specifically name marijuana, but used the terms "drug and narcotic." It also inquired about the student himself, not his opinions of what others would do. This leaves open the question whether the student considers marijuana a drug or narcotic and, of course, asks him personally what he would do (see Table 89).*

The indicators here seem to be that when students are asked about themselves the majority say they would not "like to try" a "drug or narcotic," even without fear of arrest or addiction. Only 21 percent say "yes" and 10 percent say "probably yes." Another question, asking about trying "a drug" without these assurances, however, shows an even larger majority saying they disapprove (see Table 90).**

While keeping in mind (but not necessarily agreeing with) all the arguments why current U.S. laws (though more lenient than those in many other countries) are excessively hard on pot *users*, removing the fear of arrest seems, according to this data, to be an ill-advised move as far as the battle to deter youngsters from *starting* (or even continuing) to use marijuana is concerned. Stressing the "realistic" points that it is really quite "harmless" physically and "non-addicting" (both still somewhat less than conclusive, particularly for young people) also seems ill-advised from the point of view of this battle against starters and users.

From this overall data, either the youngsters see marijuana as something other than a "drug" or "narcotic," or some are over-estimating the number of their classmates who have used the drug, or those who think many students use it are in groups that contain many users—or use *is* heavier than we think. Those who favor legalizing marijuana (22 percent) and who say they would try a drug or narcotic if it were not illegal and addicting (21 percent), may be the users plus the most "broad-minded" or rebellious nonusers. The users may be those who think about half or more than the students in their school use it (19

* Purdue Opinion Panel, *Report of Poll No. 91*, April 1971, pp. 19a and 20a.
** Ibid., pp. 17a and 18a.

Table 90

Some people say it is all right to try a drug to see what its effect is like, so long as you do not use it regularly. How do you feel about this?

	Total Sample	Sex		Grade			Father's Education			Course Grades				
		Boy	Girl	10	11	12	Grade School	High School	College	Very Low	Below Average	Average	Above Average	Excellent
Approve	12%	14%	10%	11%	11%	14%	13%	10%	16%	29%	12%	13%	10%	13%
Undecided; probably approve	10	10	10	9	12	10	10	11	9	29	13	10	10	7
Undecided; probably disapprove	15	15	16	15	15	17	14	15	17	6	13	15	17	13
Disapprove	61	59	62	64	61	58	62	62	56	35	59	60	63	68

	Future Plans					Region			
	College	Special Training	Work	Military	Other Plans	East	Midwest	South	West
Approve	10%	10%	15%	14%	17%	14%	13%	8%	14%
Undecided; probably approve	9	9	13	14	13	15	11	6	10
Undecided; probably disapprove	17	16	10	12	12	17	18	13	14
Disapprove	62	65	61	57	56	53	57	71	60

231

percent), or they may be closer to the 12 percent who feel they should try a drug "to see what its effect is," which would put it close to the 1969 figure for the Montgomery County schools. These may or may not be "typical" junior or senior high schools; if they are, it means the number of those who have tried marijuana (if we have isolated those 12 percent in the Purdue senior high school survey) has not increased. But then this would mean that the students have no feeling for whether or not use is increasing in their schools. Of course, if the Montgomery County schools were far above average in the number of those who had tried marijuana, then the numbers could have gone up nationally to meet that level. In any event, one gets the feeling that there has been an increase in the number of students who have tried marijuana—perhaps less than that in the colleges, but a significant increase, nonetheless.

These answers in student surveys may speak volumes, not only about drug abuse, but about basic issues of child rearing, effective constraints, school administrations, and so forth. They also tend to support the opinions of the average citizen on these issues. Indications of the possible effects of *de facto* immunity from prosecution for possession of marijuana in such places as college campuses are now numerous.* The difficulties in keeping it away from minors in such a milieu (even in the Army) are also becoming apparent.

Actual numbers of drug users in 1969 and in the spring of 1970 could have been higher than the polls indicate (though this is not likely to have a high probability), or there could have been a vast increase in drug experimentation and use over the last year.** A late 1970 survey

* "Marijuana is the common denominator among all groups. The acceptance it has gained is so widespread that prosecution for possession has relaxed at a number of colleges. In the minds of many, it has been declassified as a narcotic." (*New York Times*, January 17, 1971. See p. 52.) This article goes on to point out that some of the "way-out" students are now shifting to alcohol, both to enhance the effects of marijuana and to substitute for it. The less "far-out" students, on the other hand, are now taking to marijuana in ever-increasing numbers.

** Some data, such as answers to questions like the following, are of value if compared to other years to show possible trends. They are not the same as the foregoing use data, however. A blatant heroin user, for example, would cause a big splash and be known by everybody in a very conservative school where no one else used it.

Do you personally know anyone who has used

	High School		College	
Marijuana	Yes	62%	Yes	83%
Amphetamines	Yes	41%	Yes	62%
LSD	Yes	35%	Yes	57%
Heroin	Yes	19%	Yes	35%

(Louis Harris poll, *Life*, January 8, 1971, p. 26.)

of Pennsylvania high schools reportedly lists one of every five high school seniors as a "high user" and states that one in every ten students is "regularly using drugs in large amounts."[*] Polls of college students—which will be discussed later—show a spectacular increase in the use of drugs of all types on our campuses in a year and a half. But what might be even more important is the "self-fulfilling prophecy" possibility here. One cannot ignore the overall concern about drug use perhaps being higher than it is, the "legitimacy" which goes with widespread use, and the "approval" (or at least non-condemnation) of "influential" adults—all this affects the way some people behave. Furthermore, this could be a high-risk (even if not as high a probability) situation. Drug addicts lead terrible lives and often come to horrible deaths. The public does not welcome the probability of this increasing; majority opinion favors reducing it.

e. ALIENATION AND DECISION-MAKING

The current changes in attitudes in our society that may be significant are those that could alter or circumvent the value systems of the young. Whether the changes are for better or worse depends to some degree on the value system of the one making the judgment. There are, however, some "absolutes" which any prudent man, regardless of his persuasions, cannot ignore. If there are real signs of a breakdown in the value system of a significant segment of our youth, or even signs of acceptance of a substitute value system that later will not withstand scrutiny by a twenty year old, we must be concerned. If there is any chance of such a breakdown, there is also a chance—perhaps even a better one than that of a drastic, harmful change in our society—that we may be encouraging a situation which is more likely to increase the probability of rearing a number of somewhat disturbed minors. Under normal circumstances, the danger of such a situation is insignificant; and even in the recent (and to some extent continuing) somewhat odd situation, it is not great. The "normal," traditional situation finds truly concerned family adults calming the fears of the young facing an uncertain world and helping them over the rough spots. This brings with it all the problems of such an association (including, eventually, the "in-law" problem), with adults often attempting to be helpful in areas that, despite their love and concern, are not analagous to their own experiences. Overall, however, there still may be a real question today

[*] *Philadelphia Inquirer,* November 28, 1970, p. 6.

about which method has more shortcomings—the old, family approach (perhaps less effective than of old) or the recent extreme, and even not-so-extreme, independent, "youth-cult" or "counter culture" approach. It remains to be seen whether significant numbers of educators, members of the media, and public figures chose wisely when they apparently read great benefits into the latter "life style" and to some extent even supported it.

A hesitancy to subscribe to the recent "new" youth-cult approach need not be based solely on the alarm over it demonstrated by parents (although any researcher ignores the overwhelming concern by parents on family issues at his peril), but from lack of convincing evidence that it is a wise approach from a purely "horse-sense" point of view. Young people were (and to some extent still are) being asked to make decisions in areas in which they may not be emotionally stable enough to do so. Furthermore, they are simultaneously being discouraged from getting the competent, truly concerned, loving adults to help them over the rough spots. They (and we) are often told that they are more intelligent and better educated than earlier students moving through the school systems. But even if true, this may not be that relevant. Emotional stability may not have improved, and the new "youth-cult" milieu may be full of pitfalls with which earlier generations did not have to cope. For example, making an honest, unbiased decision "based on conscience" about the validity of a war in which one has such possible personal involvement as fighting in that war, is a big order for any man, let alone a teen-ager. If one then offers an interesting circumvention of this duty, based on the idea that the one with *real* courage is the one who refuses to serve, not the one who gets shot at, life may really get difficult for some young men. They may attempt to rationalize themselves into accepting the above premise if they are called up; but when they look at themselves in the mirror in the morning, they may have difficulty in suppressing other insights into their motives.

The results of the following poll of college students taken in 1968, a year when casualties in Vietnam (though relatively very light compared to our other wars) were heavy enough to generate a massive publicizing of them, complete with detailed pictures and interviews, raises some interesting questions:

"If [you] plan to avoid military service which *one* of the three reasons is most important to you in trying to avoid military service—because you feel we are involved in an illegal and immoral war in Vietnam, or because you have better things to do than wasting two years of your life, or because you frankly want to avoid the possibility of getting yourself killed?"*

	Freshmen	Seniors
1. Immoral war	35%	29%
2. Have better things to do	46%	54%
3. Don't want to get killed	14%	13%
4. No answer	5%	3%

If a man really believes choice number one without a selfish motivation, and does not wish to further an immoral cause (that is, war and killing), he is probably in the same category with other conscientious objectors. These are well-adjusted, honest men who, primarily for religious reasons, do not believe in war. (Some of these conscientious objectors have served valiantly under fire as unarmed, combat medical men, helping the wounded of both sides.) It is harder on the selective objection to a specific war; one has to know a good deal about the issues and both the long- and short-term good resulting from, or evil reduced or eliminated through, the war, versus the destruction from the battles. Men have refused to serve in all our wars and in great numbers, no matter how "righteous" the wars were. This was so in World War II and in our Civil War, when Union troops felt they were fighting to save the Union and abolish slavery. The one thing all wars have in common is that one can get hurt in them; and every man in his right mind is afraid of getting hit in a war. One must ask if this idea is really so obscure or immaterial to over 30 percent of those who planned "to avoid military service" in 1968.

Such possible rationalizations may also hold true, but to a lesser degree, for many of those who "drop out" of, or simply won't try, difficult jobs, school, and so forth, because the "establishment is corrupt" and the tasks are "irrelevant." Maybe so. But often the quizzes and tasks were also difficult for them. And, unless they are complete charlatans, even with themselves, they may end up with more self-doubts than ever. Many of these problems, therefore, may be traced to parents and high school and college instructors who provided insufficient training and guidance, and forced decisions on the youngsters

* The Beliefs and Attitudes of Male College Seniors, Freshmen and Alumni, a Study by Roper Research Associates, Inc., prepared for Standard Oil Company, New Jersey, May 1969.

before they were ready for them. Decisions involved in "doing your own thing" are not necessarily easily made; they can be *very difficult* and even disturbing, especially to the young. But apparently, for the usual, obvious reasons, many of the young seem to be the last to admit that they fear to (or cannot) cope with the decisions.

The assistance which the "straight" parent, clergyman, teacher, foreman, and even military officer used to provide is often missing today. I am referring to the role as "lightning rod" for abuse from the peer groups of the youngsters in their charge. If a parent adamantly, and if necessary publicly, refuses to allow a youngster to do things which the youngster himself often has misgivings about, the parent helps to relieve the peer group pressures on his charge. The young person does not lose face, and the parent gets the bad reputation among the youngster's peer group. This is a much more desirable situation than forcing the youngster to choose, because he is often in a bind. If he refuses, he may be in trouble with the group; if he goes along, often against his better judgment, he could get into real trouble. Even forcing him into situations where he must make such decisions can be disturbing. Adults in positions of responsibility get few thanks from anyone these days for keeping young people out of such situations, either from those in their charge, the youngsters' peer group, or often even their own peer group. Nevertheless, it is a vital function and one of the most difficult to perform, for one must not be over-protective yet must sense when a youngster is getting in over his head, despite his protests to the contrary. It is a thankless, selfless task that only a truly loving adult can perform.

In a 1968 survey by the Purdue group in January 1968, there were some indications that high school students (particularly girls) might be somewhat less likely to be influenced by their parents than by their teachers (see Table 91).

This far-from-unusual attitude toward teachers might be very important today. Teachers have always been rallying points for some adolescents, particularly those who were having difficulties with their parents. Traditionally this was not in the least disturbing. Teachers were, to an exceptional degree, stable people who had a genuine interest in the young and who gently, but firmly guided them through the difficult periods and toward the influence and value system of their families and the world in which they must live. Today, the vast majority of adults still understand the necessity of such action; but some

Table 91

INFLUENCE BY PARENTS AND TEACHERS*
On High School Students

I question many of my parents' attitudes and beliefs.	Total Sample	Sex Boy	Sex Girl
Disagree	30%	33%	28%
Unsure; but probably disagree	8	9	8
Unsure; but probably agree	11	13	10
Agree	50	46	53
I question many of my teachers' attitudes and beliefs.			
Disagree	35	33	36
Unsure; but probably disagree	11	12	11
Unsure; but probably agree	13	13	13
Agree	40	42	38

adults, other than the members of their families, apparently feel that acquiescing in, or even abetting, the resulting degree of alienation of some youth from their families is justified on the basis of political or social reasons. A small, but apparently not insignificant minority of high school teachers (but not nearly so much as college instructors) seem to have fallen into this category; they seem to have seen (and perhaps still see) their role as propagating secular humanist-Left values. The objections to this are the same as those to right-wing (even racist) teachings that used to be found in some of our schools. Doctrinaire teaching espoused by "authority figures" in classrooms tends to be factually incomplete and/or incorrect, has a strong tendency to be almost overwhelmingly simplistic and, of course, is usually misleading. The recent brand of such teaching, when it occurs, apparently is no exception. Not only does this teaching ill-prepare students for the post-school life, but it could encourage the alienation of children from their families at the very time they need help and guidance in adjusting to growing up.

To some degree, non-family adults have been aided in abetting the alienation of children from their families by the attitudes of some people in the public media and even by some public figures. This has occurred (and to a much lesser degree still occurs) not so much by outright approval of radical youth, but rather by "praising with faint

* Purdue Opinion Panel, *Report of Poll No. 82,* January 1968. Girls also registered slightly more "Radical Left" and significantly less "Conservative Right" in the June 1970 poll mentioned earlier in this section.

damning," which tends to transmit approval to the youngsters: "I don't agree with their actions, but in the environment of what they consider to be the immoral Vietnam war, nuclear weapons, etc . . ." In short, the focus has been (and to some extent still is) on the *political* statements of the young. Presumably the adults who agree with them feel that they reach these positions for the same reasons and in the same way adults do.

Not surprising are indications that, as one goes down the scale of student competence, measured by grade scores (intelligence?)—at least to the "below-average" category—students tend to have less rapport with their parents and to have fewer opinions on issues. This is a general phenomenon which has been noticeable over a long period of time; students having difficulties in school are more likely to have them at home. Many "underprivileged" students, however, have generally good rapport with their parents, as indicated by the percentage of Negro, Puerto Rican, and Indian children who rate their influence on family decisions as high.

Table 92

RACE AND AUTONOMY IN THE FAMILY*

High School Students

		Race		
Influence—Family	White	Negro	American Indian	Puerto Rican
Great deal	24%	32%	32%	42%
Considerable	30	22	11	0
Moderate	23	19	18	8
Some	15	18	21	33
Little or no	7	8	18	17

These parents may have less time to spend with their children (the fathers frequently "moonlight" on a second job and many mothers work) and, furthermore, the children may be less likely to get assistance from the parents on more complicated school work (to say nothing of decisions on complex domestic and foreign policy issues). The relationship of the school to these students is important, but also a little hard to define. These children and their parents may be less able to impress teachers and school officials. Yet these youngsters, like all of

* Purdue Opinion Panel, *Report of Poll No. 89*, June 1970, p. 12. Of course, many alienated youth will have dropped out of school as soon as legally possible and will not appear in the Purdue data.

their age group, are unlikely to be able to judge what type of training is best for their post-school life, and are likely to be more dependent on teachers guidance, particularly if they want to go on to higher education, than are children of parents with a college education.

On school autonomy (in school, how much influence the students feel they have in decisions about courses to take; what, how, and how much to study; and so forth) the opinion splits, with Negroes quite close to the whites in feelings of autonomy:

Table 93
RACE AND AUTONOMY IN SCHOOL*
High School Students

Influence—School	White	Negro	Race American Indian	Puerto Rican
Great deal	31%	28%	18%	8%
Considerable	26	22	16	17
Moderate	18	16	24	25
Some	14	18	13	8
Little or no	10	15	26	42

In the matter of discipline, one gets some feeling for the attitudes of these students.

Table 94
RACE AND NEED FOR DISCIPLINE**
High School Students

Need for Discipline	White	Negro	Race American Indian	Puerto Rican
From parents and school	31%	34%	24%	8%
From parents only	25	22	18	25
From schools only	1	2	8	8
From themselves only	30	24	24	25
Have enough now	11	16	26	33

The stronger feeling for the need for discipline from the schools and parents expressed by Negro students was reflected by the opinion of nonwhite adults.***

* Ibid., p. 12.
** Ibid., p. 13.
*** Gallup Opinion Index, December 1970, p. 17.

239

	Not strict enough	Just about right	Don't know
White	52%	32%	14%
Nonwhite	62	21	13

It is interesting to compare this approach to the issue by all Negro high school students and their parents with the somewhat different opinions of the "Radical Left" minority of students shown in Table 81. The vast majority of students, in fact, apparently show a good adjustment to their parents (as do all youth: late in 1970, only 10 percent said their parents were "too strict" and 8 percent thought they were "too permissive"), as well as to their school and surroundings.* Most students did not seem to endorse the very "permissive," unstructured approach to learning and upbringing, which are fundamental issues on which their opinions may be felt to be of more value than on some more complicated and remote subjects.

Even an "anti-establishment" attitude does not necessarily mean that high school students are alienated from their families. In fact, among those students who are "right-wing" there tends to be a close rapport with their families; but some groups which showed right-wing tendencies (like those choosing the military for post-school plans) also showed higher "anti-establishment" feelings. The Radical Left—"the American system is not flexible enough; radical change is needed" —seems more likely to contain the highest percentage of students who are likely to be "alienated."

The following are descriptive summaries of characteristics of each "political" group, which indicate a higher probability of finding students with the characteristics described in the group under which they are listed rather than another. The Middle Group, which felt the American way of life was flexible enough to work within, "reported very much interest, excitement and stimulation from their family, their friends and their teachers."**

. . . the Conservative Right (19 percent) reported that the American way of life is superior to that of any other country. The Conservative Right also reported:
1. jobs, the Establishment and society are very interesting, exciting, and stimulating,

* Louis Harris poll, *Life*, January 8, 1971, p. 22.
** Purdue Opinion Panel, *Report of Poll No. 89*, June 1970, p. 10.

2. their family, friends, and teachers are very interesting, exciting, and stimulating,
3. in their family, they feel a great deal of autonomy in decisions that directly affect them,
4. most children and high school students need more discipline these days from their parents and school,
5. they know they will hold the same beliefs as the Establishment and work within the authority of the Establishment.

Students described . . . as the Radical Left (18 percent) reported that the American system is not flexible enough; radical change is needed. The Radical Left also reported:
1. more are Negroes (than in other categories),
2. their community and school are not very interesting, exciting, or stimulating,
3. their family, friends, and teachers are not very interesting, exciting, or stimulating,
4. jobs, the Establishment, and tradition are not very interesting, exciting, or stimulating,
5. the following individual referents are not very interesting, exciting, or stimulating: the future, ambition, communication, criticism, competition, making decisions, and taking risks,
6. in their family, they feel little or no autonomy in decisions that directly affect them,
7. children have enough discipline now; if more is needed, it is from themselves only,
8. they never will join the Establishment.*

The latter group of youngsters appears to be more likely to have difficulties adjusting to society. Some of this group may be very "advanced" intellectually and emotionally; but there is no reason to believe that there is a higher percentage of such children in this group than in the others. In fact, the large majority of students at the higher end of the achievement scale have closer rapport with their parents, indicate a very open mind to change, but are also apparently willing to live under the American system and are reluctant to jettison the value systems of their society.

This, of course, leads one to look again at some of the attitudes that apparently are accepted by some secondary school educators and observers. When high school students are considered to be "hopeful" because they are against the Vietnam war and pollution, and so forth,

* Ibid., pp. 14–15.

this judgment cannot be faulted if it is taken to indicate that the students have a sense of responsibility and are loving and charitable. But the assumption may also be that the students arrived at these opinions in the way an adult would; and this might begin to raise doubts about the adult judgment of their opinions.* The *reasons* why, and which groups of the young arrive at these opinions could be important. Today's "alienated" are apparently more likely to be included in the group that accepts the *au courant* causes. It is but a short step from admiring the conclusions of a student because he agrees with us to assuming that he has "sound judgment" and is "intelligent" and "good." If the student reaches a conclusion with which we agree before the other students do, we may even consider him a pace-setter, a prophet of what is to come. As indicated above, the "alienated" activist student need be none of these. Furthermore, accolades might only encourage his alienation at a time when he needs help to increase contact with his family and his surroundings. In fact, since alienated high school students normally make up a higher percentage of the lower scholastic categories, putting the alienated from this group in a position where they stand a high chance of being asked to make decisions on complicated social and foreign policy issues, might be quite disturbing to some already somewhat confused and not-too-talented youngsters. On the other hand, the student who is slow to reach "correct" conclusions on complicated issues and refuses to be pushed into doing so, need not necessarily be obtuse; he may actually be more analytical and mature. Those high school students who rejected the extreme "youth-cult" ideas, according to the data, made up a larger percentage within the higher-achiever groups than those who accepted it.

In fact, the whole new "involvement" teaching atmosphere, at least the way it is often applied today, may have some questionable effects on students over the whole spectrum of potential. Some intelligent, highly motivated learners—the traditional "sponges" with an insatiable

* An interesting example of how students do not conform to the adult assumptions of their pattern of thinking was done in 1970 by Simon Wittes. In this study, the author attempted to evaluate the effect of the "power structure" (an adult concept, like the idea of the "establishment") on the alienation or non-alienation of youth. He established criteria which he felt should indicate this impact, only to find that numerous answers came out differently from what he had hypothesized. In the final analysis, only one significant relationship was found: Students who feel closer to their peer group feel more secure when attending a well-ordered, powerfully administered school. (Simon Wittes, *People and Power* [Ann Arbor: Center for Research on Utilization of Scientific Knowledge, Institute for Social Research, University of Michigan, 1970].)

242

thirst for information—may be repelled by a process which, every time they have absorbed a few drops (or even before they have been taught anything on the subject), tries to squeeze it out of them prematurely through "inquiry-learning" techniques. Furthermore, these bright children may know the futility of the blind leading the blind, and may not like to discuss complex issues with uninformed youngsters. They may prefer to learn some facts on which they can base an opinion before they want to discuss "issues," let alone become actively "involved" in the "solution" of all types of social and political problems. This new "inquiry process" is like constantly pulling up a plant to see how its roots are growing. Furthermore, many bright students may not respect a specialist teacher who keeps acting as though the students knew as much about his specialty as he does; and they may dislike the almost "group encounter" sessions which some classes tend to become. What may be worse, in this new atmosphere in high schools, some students are perhaps being "prepared," through a process of "social education," for a world that might exist only in the minds of a minority of "social engineers" in our school systems and furthermore, a world that may never be.

A less portentous situation from society's point of view, but a serious one from the point of view of many students, is one mentioned earlier in which the less-fitted and somewhat-confused students may be encouraged to jump into a much too complex and disturbing decision-making arena. The result may be that they often end up not making the decision, while rationalizing that they have, but are really having it handed to them, either directly or indirectly, as it often was in former times, by adults; but now, recently, for the "alienated," there has been a good chance that these adults would be non-family members, some of whom may have what some parents would consider ill-conceived motivations. This is not to say that students should "be seen and not heard"; on the contrary, it is saying perhaps students should be objectively taught more facts so that when they are asked to make a judgment they are equipped to do so.

There have been some signs in the recent past that some of the alienated youngsters have become susceptible, not only to some apparently misguided high school and college instructors and other adult "activists," but in some cases, to aberrant, irresponsible, and even vicious groups. In fact, the disquieting thing about much that has been accepted and even approved by the New Left (particularly to those of us who remember the activities of the Nazis) is the irresponsible mind-lessness of many of their statements, to say nothing of the evidence of apparently somewhat psychologically inadequate adolescents in the groups that have accepted and chanted equally mindless slogans on cue from abusive (often adult) "directors."

The epitome of such irresponsibility was the "counter-culture" adula-tion of the Charles Manson clan and its deeds. This reaction may bear a vague, but only a vague, resemblance to the feelings for Robin Hood, Jesse James and even John Dillinger in the 1930s. All were thought by some to have fought the "establishment"; but the mysticism surrounding the Manson group and the mindlessness, by normal stand-ards, of the killings, puts their crimes more in the category of Leopold and Loeb (no heroes to anyone) than to Robin Hood.

The *New York Times* reported:*

Among the counterculture, Manson achieved almost instant star status. He became the cover boy of the underground press, one of "us" merely be-cause he was not one of "them."

Manson's popularity on the Left paled a bit when it became clear that his political views were at best underdeveloped, and at worst, absurd. He also fell victim to the growing feeling that random violence is counterproductive "adventurism." Nevertheless, long articles by and about him still appear in the underground press.

Note that, according to this source, the reason "Manson's popularity on the Left paled a bit" was not because of the utter brutality and viciousness of the acts, but because his political views were not ortho-dox and because "random violence is counterproductive."

As suggested by previous data, "activist"-oriented high school stu-dents have been, and probably still are, a minority of that category of youth and would normally not call for the attention given them here. It may be interesting, however, to try to determine what effect, if any, educators, mass media, and even public figures—who to some extent inspired and supported this minority—have had in setting the "style" and shaping the milieu for youth. More important is the question of whether attempts have been made to stack the deck against the "non-conformist" youth who resists non-family adult and minority youth pressure from the Right or Left. The technique mentioned above, of

* *New York Times* "News of the Week in Review," January 31, 1971, p. 2.

singling out the vague, non-associable, but "evil" establishment or power structure to begin the alienation process, may be one of these.

B. *Overview of University Students*

The formal, identifiable segment of society with the most obvious recent "alienation environment" seems to be some parts of the universities. The universities merit attention because an ever-larger number of minors enter them each year. Their instructor and student "dissenters" receive exceptional and, at least up until the second half of 1970, generally sympathetic news coverage in the national media; and the universities themselves have been one of the traditional sources of upward mobility in the nation. Particularly in the past decade, these institutions have been influential in government and the national media to a degree disproportionate to their size. Nonetheless, the high school environment may have been much more important than college in enveloping and directly affecting virtually all of our youngsters; and, in addition, it forms the basis of the college-bound student's ability to cope with college.

We must keep in mind that the college system may be changing. With over half of all high school graduates entering college in 1971 and a lowering of the standards of the system becoming a definite possibility, we may have not only a larger, but a different group of people to consider. Open-admissions programs, though inordinately hard on parents' pocketbooks (no college education is free—a potential worker to supplement the family income is lost) and even morale (when the child who went off with high hopes and parental pride comes home a "flunk-out"), may or may not damage the educational system, depending on whether or not they are accompanied by the normal high "mortality" rate in the freshman year. Without this filter system, which may be starting to disappear, college graduates simply may not be college-educated. Jobs for all of them will probably not be available at the salary levels they now expect. There will, in any case, probably be too many graduates; and if the filter system is reduced, they may be less likely to be high caliber people.

Nevertheless, the instructors and students may still look on themselves as "elites" and perhaps "pace-setters" for the future; and many others will believe them. The lofty "union-card" status of the college degree will not disappear overnight. These schools will still be im-

245

portant to individuals who need these "union cards," to those persons who are influenced by the academy, and to many who have had some college education and may be affected by it.

The students are obviously the first concern in the college situation, so a survey of possible effects of the college milieu on them may be in order. This task is by no means easy, particularly if one tries to determine whether what he is seeing is the effect of the influence of the campus or a changing local or national environment from which students come. Nonetheless, a comparison of a high school and a college group (or perhaps this same group at different times, if the samples truly indicate the feelings of a "cohort") may be interesting to look at. High school students who indicated they would go to college in the 1967 and 1968 Purdue Opinion Panel polls of high school sophomores, juniors, and seniors are contemporaries of the college students polled by the Gallup organization in 1969 and 1970. Perhaps these two groups may be compared validly.

The comparison quickly brings to light some changes in opinion of youngsters from the same "cohort." The political philosophy of the "cohort" changed somewhat (37 percent Democrat, 32 percent Republican, 9 percent other, 21 percent undecided, for college-bound high school students in 1968, compared to 25 percent Democrat, 25 percent Republican, 50 percent independent for college freshmen in the spring of 1969). Those on the right, the Republicans, seem to have held more firmly in college than the Democrats. One might assume that this reflects a return to normal after the enthusiasm of the campaigns for Democratic "peace" candidates in 1968. There was a temporary Democratic "surge" in the May 1968 choices of college-bound high school students—45 percent Democrat, 25 percent Republican, 3 percent other parties, 25 percent undecided—but this had already subsided by late 1968. Things were already back to normal directly afterward; i.e., 37 percent Democrats, 32 percent Republicans, 9 percent some other party and 21 percent undecided. In November 1967, 38 percent of college-bound high school students had considered themselves Democrats and 31 percent Republicans; 2 were for some other party; and 28 were undecided. In 1969, the sophomores in college, who belong to the same "cohort" as those included in the 1967 high school figures, differed somewhat from the college freshmen listed above: the percentage of college students who considered themselves Democrats increased as the class level went up (freshmen 25 percent;

sophomores 31 percent), and this was evident right through to graduate school.†

In the spring of 1970, the political preference makeup of college students shifted significantly. There was a big jump in the number of independents and a drop in both major parties, especially the Republican party.

The following polls (the second presumably taken in late April or May 1970) show the 1969 and 1970 college political preferences.

Table 95
POLITICAL PARTY AFFILIATION
College Students

"In politics, as of today, do you consider yourself a Republican, Democrat or Independent?"

	Republican		Democrat		Independent	
	1969*	1970**	1969*	1970**	1969*	1970**
NATIONAL	24%	18%	32%	30%	44%	52%
SEX						
Men	23	19	32	27	45	54
Women	25	18	33	34	42	48
AGE						
18 years and under	24	21	25	33	51	46
19 years	26	20	31	27	43	53
20 years	28	18	29	28	43	54
21–23 years	18	16	38	29	44	55
24 years and over	26	14	39	40	35	46
REGION OF COLLEGE						
East	18	12	32	29	50	59
Midwest	25	22	31	26	44	52
South	29	20	36	38	35	42
West	22	18	30	26	48	56
PARENTS' INCOME						
$15,000 and over	29	18	25	21	46	61
$10,000–$14,999	26	23	31	26	43	51
$ 7,000–$ 9,999	16	17	36	41	48	42
Under $7,000	15	10	47	48	38	42
CLASS IN SCHOOL						
Freshman	25	19	25	31	50	50
Sophomore	25	21	31	25	44	54
Junior	26	17	35	31	39	52
Senior	19	18	40	30	41	52
Graduate	23	8	42	42	35	50

† Purdue Opinion Panel, *Report of Polls No. 81*, November 1967, pp. 1a and 2a, *No. 83*, May 1968, pp. 1a and 2a, *No. 84*, November 1968, pp. 1a and 2a. *Gallup Opinion Index*, No. 48, June 1969, p. 39, No. 60, June 1970, p. 21.

* *Gallup Opinion Index*, No. 48, June 1969, p. 39.

** *Gallup Opinion Index*, No. 60, June 1970, p. 21.

247

Table 95 (continued)

	1	2	3	4	5	6
TYPE OF COLLEGE						
Public	23	16	32	31	45	53
Private	29	23	31	29	40	48
Denominational	15	23	43	25	42	52
DEMONSTRATORS	11		36		53	
NON-DEMONSTRATORS	29		31		40	
RELIGIOUS PREFERENCE						
Protestant	36	29	29	32	35	39
Catholic	15	11	39	37	46	52
POLITICAL PHILOSOPHY						
Extremely Conservative	59		18		23	
Fairly Conservative	45		22		33	
Middle-of-the-Road	35		28		37	
Fairly Liberal	12		39		49	
Extremely Liberal	3		40		57	
STUDENTS WHO HAVE:						
Done social work	22		34		44	
Been drunk	26		29		45	
Tried barbiturates	15		20		65	
Tried marijuana	15		25		60	
Tried LSD	12		6		82	

In a more recent poll (December 1970) 13 percent of the students indicated that they were "highly favorable" to the Republican party while 15 percent said they were "highly unfavorable." For the Democrats the reading was 19 percent and 7 percent respectively.* On the assumption that the students could rate both parties unfavorably if they chose, and based on the ratio of "fairly favorable" to "very favorable" on other questions (it runs from a minimum of two to one to eight to one), these figures may show some current increase in support of the regular parties. Since the questions are different from those asked in the above polls, however, we cannot use this information to find a trend, but only for what it actually says.

In addition to classifying themselves according to political party preference, college students also classified themselves as conservatives or liberals; their choices make an interesting contrast with those of high school students. In the spring of 1970, high school students were categorized according to their responses to three questions descriptive of their political orientation. The answers by percentages of college-

* Gallup Opinion Index, No. 68, February 1971, p. 18.

bound high school students are listed in Table 96. As a comparison, directly below them, under the same categories, are the answers of college students who were asked their preference among virtually identical statements in 1969 and 1970 by Daniel Yankelovich, Inc.*

Table 96
POLITICAL PHILOSOPHY
College-Bound High School Students and College Students

Conservative	Middle Group	Radical Left	Undecided
"The American way of life is superior to that of any other country."	"There are serious flaws in our society today, but the system is flexible enough to solve them."	"The American system is not flexible enough; radical change is needed."	

College-Bound High School Students—1970 **

	Conservative	Middle Group	Radical Left	Undecided
May	20%	52%	16%	11%
December	17	51	13	18

College Students—1969 and 1970 ***

Conservative		Middle Group		Radical Left		
1969	1970	1969	1970	1969	1970	No undecided
17%	10%	70%	68%	13%	22%	category offered

Another survey in the spring of 1969, which included the responses of college freshmen (the high school seniors of the spring of 1968), classified the political orientation of all college students as follows:****

Table 97
POLITICAL ORIENTATION
College Students—1969

	Extremely Conservative	Fairly Conservative	Middle of the Road	Fairly Liberal	Extremely Liberal	Don't Know
National	2%	19%	24%	41%	11%	3%
Freshmen	2	17	24	43	11	3
Sophomores	3	21	23	41	9	3
Juniors	2	18	28	40	11	1
Seniors	1	22	21	39	16	1
Graduate Students	1	18	24	40	14	3

* There was a small dissimilarity in the first statement of the Purdue Opinion Polls (". . . to that of any other country"), as used in Table 96, and that used by Daniel Yankelovich, Inc., in *Youth and the Establishment,* A Report on Research for John D. Rockefeller, 3rd, and the Task Force on Youth, by Daniel Yankelovich Inc., February 1971, p. 36. (". . . to that of other countries").

** Purdue Opinion Panel, *Report of Poll No. 89,* June 1970, pp. 5a and 6a, and *Report of Poll No. 90,* January 1971, pp. 3a and 4a.

*** *Youth and the Establishment,* p. 36.

**** *Gallup Opinion Index,* No. 48, June 1969, p. 40.

Table 98

POLITICAL ORIENTATION*

College Students—1970

"This card lists political positions from the far left to the far right. Considering your own political views, where would you place yourself on this scale?"

December 1970

	Far Left	Left	Middle-of-Road	Right	Far Right	Don't Know
NATIONAL	7%	30%	40%	15%	2%	6%
SEX						
Male	7	30	37	18	2	6
Female	5	29	47	11	2	6
AGE						
18 years and under	7	30	40	15	2	6
19 years	4	32	42	14	2	6
20 years	4	34	37	18	3	4
21–23 years	11	30	41	12	1	5
24 years and over	6	38	31	17	–	8
REGION OF COLLEGE						
East	8	39	39	5	2	7
Midwest	8	29	38	17	3	5
South	5	21	53	17	1	3
West	6	29	32	21	2	10
TYPE OF COLLEGE						
Public	7	27	42	15	2	7
Private	7	37	36	14	2	4
Denominational	4	31	41	17	4	3
PARENTS' INCOME						
$15,000 and over	7	34	36	17	2	4
$10,000–$14,999	4	29	44	14	3	6
$ 7,000–$ 9,999	6	30	44	15	1	4
Under $7,000	8	27	37	19	2	7
CLASS IN SCHOOL						
Freshman	6	22	48	15	2	7
Sophomore	5	34	36	17	2	6
Junior	6	29	41	15	3	6
Senior	7	36	36	16	1	4
Graduate	15	44	32	6	–	3
RELIGION						
Protestant	3	22	48	20	2	5
Catholic	3	27	45	18	2	5

It is interesting to compare Table 97 to one taken in December 1970 by the same organization, but in which the question was worded differently. "Left" and "Far Left" might be prejudicial terms compared to "Fairly Liberal" and "Extremely Liberal," even on the campuses. This should hold (or even be more true) for the terms "Right" and "Far Right" compared to "Conservative" and "Extremely Conservative."

° *Gallup Opinion Index*, No. 68, February 1971, p. 36.

The result, as one might suspect, is a large increase in the "Middle-of-the-Road" group (the only title which was not different from the 1969 poll), but with the "left" still outnumbering the "right" by two to one. Without trying to see a "trend," because of this change in semantics, the information on where the students place themselves on the political spectrum is interesting.

The liberal-conservative breakdown among all college students by their own estimate in the spring of 1970 was as follows:*

Table 99
LIBERAL-CONSERVATIVE ORIENTATION
All College Students—1970

	Liberal	Conservative	No Opinion
Freshmen	60%	28%	12%
Sophomores	59	29	12
Juniors	59	23	18
Seniors	59	28	13
Graduate students	69	22	9
All students	61	26	13
General Public	34	52	14

Here is a real "gap," a political orientation gap, between the young, "decoupled" university students—particularly graduate students—and the public. Even among the 21-to-29-year-old "youth" on the "outside" the weight of opinion was conservative. (See Table 36.)

Graduate students today are almost invariably further left on most subjects than undergraduates. But they seem to be more practical in their estimates of the probability of a revolution actually occurring; in late 1970, less of them (23 percent) felt change in the next twenty-five years in the United States would come through revolution than college students as a whole (43 percent). (See footnote following Table 140.) This Left-liberalism is not surprising, however, for graduate students tend to be similar to young instructors (who traditionally have more liberal ideas, particularly those who are in the social sciences); in fact, not only do many graduate students become instructors, but some already teach while they are still students.

If one wishes to pinpoint possible factors in college environment that

* *Gallup Opinion Index,* No. 59, May 1970, p. 8.

251

might be useful in determining why and which students at which universities are likely to dissent, instructors may be a good "indicator" group in our universities. With the exception of the years of the G.I. Bill "explosion" and the decrease thereafter, there has been a steady and growing increase in students since World War II (see Table 108); this has led to an unparalleled increase in instructors, too. The curve reached its steepest incline only a very few years ago, so many of these men are young, only a few years out of—and some still in—their doctoral work. The make-up of this body of instructors is interesting. The following tables on the "political" orientation of college faculty members are the results of a study by the Carnegie Commission on Higher Education, with the cooperation of the American Council on Higher Education, completed in the spring of 1970 (as reported by Seymour Lipset and Everett Carll Ladd Jr. in the November 1970 issue of *Psychology Today*).

Table 100

POLITICAL SELF-APPRAISAL OF THE FACULTY AND 1968 SUPPORT
FOR NIXON, BY FIELD OF STUDY

Field of Study	Left or Liberal	Conservative	Nixon Support
Social Sciences (n=6,845)*	71%	11%	19%
Humanities (n=9,546)	62	17	23
Fine Arts (n=3,732)	52	22	36
Education (n=3,277)	41	27	40
Physical Sciences (n=7,599)	44	26	38
Biological Sciences (n=4,403)	44	27	40
Business (n=2,080)	33	36	53
Engineering (n=4,165)	29	41	60
Agriculture (n=1,348)	18	50	61
General Public (Gallup)	34	52	

* The numbers in parenthesis in Tables 100, 101, 103, and 104 refer to the number of faculty members in each category responding to the poll.

Table 101

FACULTY SUPPORT OF STUDENT ACTIVISM, BY FIELD OF STUDY

Field of Study	Approve of Student Activism	Approve of Student aims— 1968 Columbia Student Revolt	Agree no Place for Student Demonstrations On Campus
Social Sciences (n=6,845)	63%	67%	13%
Humanities (n=9,546)	56	60	22
Fine Arts (n=3,732)	51	57	26
Education (n=3,277)	45	54	28
Physical Sciences (n=7,599)	40	48	27
Biological Sciences (n=4,403)	40	51	28
Business (n=2,080)	29	42	33
Engineering (n=4,165)	26	36	36
Agriculture (n=1,348)	19	29	47

Table 102

CONSERVATIVE
ATTITUDE TOWARD VIETNAM WAR AND POLITICAL SELF-APPRAISAL BY FIELD OF STUDY AND RELATIVE ACADEMIC STATUS OF SCHOOL
Nonweighted Percent

	High*		Medium*		Low*	
	Resist Communism in Vietnam	Conservative	Resist Communism in Vietnam	Conservative	Resist Communism in Vietnam	Conservative
Social Science	15%	8%	20%	10%	28%	14%
Humanities	16	11	24	14	31	20
Fine Arts	23	17	32	19	39	26
Education	28	15	42	23	46	28
Physical Science	22	16	36	24	52	39
Biological Science	25	19	42	29	59	38
Business	32	24	54	39	67	50
Engineering	41	29	55	45	67	52
Agriculture	53	38	68	53	50	65

* These three column headings refer to colleges of "high," "medium," and "low" prestige.

Obviously the social sciences and humanities are the disciplines in which liberal and humanist-left thought prevails, and in which left-liberal "activism" is more likely to be accepted. And "high" prestige schools have fewer conservatives. What is interesting is the breakdown, based on the questions indicated, according to fields within the social sciences. Perhaps even more striking is the large difference of opinion between age groups of professors within disciplines:

Table 103

SUPPORT FOR STUDENT ACTIVISM,
BY FIELD WITHIN THE SOCIAL SCIENCES

	Approve of student activism	Agree, most American colleges are racist
Sociology (n=1,009)	71%	58%
Social work (n=451)	71	58
Psychology (n=2,046)	63	48
Social psychology (n=263)	79	60
Clinical psychology (n=415)	65	52
Experimental psychology (n=566)	62	44
Political Science (n=1,230)	63	46
Anthropology (n=402)	56	51
Economics (n=1,439)	58	42
All Social Scientists (n=6,845)	63	49

The authors noted that "differences associated with age were surprisingly large. In each discipline, as age increases, support for student activism decreases. It is almost too neat: we are accustomed to more vagaries in opinion distributions when the control variable is one so generally inclusive as age."[*] This was apparently so even though the authors "expected to find big generational differences in support for campus activism among the social scientists." Perhaps we are seeing the results of a survey taken in an environment where experience with reality simply made persons skeptical of the objectives and tactics of the activists. The authors further felt that "young untenured assistant professors are obviously closer to the interests, insecurities and perspectives of student dissenters than are older, tenured professors."[**] A concentration of such instructors, particularly in the social sciences,

[*] Seymour Martin Lipset and Everet Carll Ladd, Jr., "And What Professors Think," *Psychology Today*, November 1970, p. 106.
[**] Ibid.

Table 104

SUPPORT FOR STUDENT ACTIVISM,
SELECTED SOCIAL SCIENCE DISCIPLINES, BY AGE

Field and age	Approve of student activism	Agree, student disrupters should be expelled
Sociologists		
20s (n=174)	81%	40%
30s (n=347)	73	56
40s (n=288)	72	58
50s (n=144)	59	67
60s (n=56)	55	75
all ages (n=1009)	71	56
Psychologists		
20s (n=358)	67	60
30s (n=811)	68	61
40s (n=533)	63	65
50s (n=232)	56	75
60s (n=112)	38	76
all ages (n=2046)	63	65
Political scientists		
20s (n=267)	76	52
30s (n=470)	66	64
40s (n=284)	58	77
50s (n=154)	44	82
60s (n=55)	39	95
all ages (n=1230)	63	67

would seem to be one element in determining the potential level of student dissent (even though they feel less sympathy for actual disrupters).

This may be a key problem: The prudent person must wonder if it is wise to have many ill-prepared, some even confused and somewhat "psychologically inadequate" late adolescents exposed to authority figures who are "closer to" and, possibly themselves still beset by the "insecurities and perspectives of the student dissenters." It should be more likely under these conditions that questionable groups on campus will be glorified, and alienation from parents and society, in some cases, perhaps even deliberately promoted.

In a survey of 1961 college alumni, taken in 1968, alumni were shown to have mixed feelings toward student activists. The alumni generally thought that there had been a good deal wrong with the university when they had attended, and felt that these things should be changed. However, they expressed moderate opinions on student involvement, and on militancy as a whole, and tended to differentiate between acceptable and unacceptable forms of activism, involvement and militancy. They were very much against student involvement in the administration of colleges, but were for students having a voice in the curriculum and in determining their own behavior. Those who were younger, who were from high-quality private colleges, who had majored in social sciences or humanities, who had had good grades and had spent some years in graduate school (a third of the alumni did) were more likely to support activism.* One senses, however, that perhaps these alumni may not have truly grasped what the new activists were really like. Furthermore, as the preceding charts indicate, a majority of each age group of the strongest faculty supporters of the activists were not prepared to accept the problems which are almost bound to follow on the campuses themselves when such people are encouraged—with one exception, a majority of each category of these "supporters" wanted to expel "student disrupters."

In June 1969, the "gripes" of the student demonstrators were thought by the students as a whole to be as follows:

Table 105

GRIPES OF STUDENT DEMONSTRATORS
AS DESCRIBED BY ALL COLLEGE STUDENTS**

Not enough say in running of college	42%
Current inadequacies of society	22
Adult and governmental authority	16
Vietnam war	11
Want to have their voices heard	7
Civil rights	6
They have no real gripe	8
Other responses	5

"All persons interviewed were then asked if they agreed or disagreed with the complaints named. In each case large majorities expressed agreement."

* Joe L. Spaeth and Andrew M. Greeley, *Recent Alumni and Higher Education* (New York: McGraw-Hill Book Company, 1970), pp. 99–110. Also see the Appendix, "The Changing Attitudes of a College Class."
** *Gallup Opinion Index*, No. 48, June 1969, p. 8. Table adds to more than 100 percent because of multiple responses.

Note that the Vietnam war drew only an 11 percent vote for the "biggest gripe," which might say a good deal for how the student activists and perhaps even significant sections of the student bodies felt: They saw bigger "problems" and were out to get more power in the colleges, to change "society," and may have even have been more interested in reducing "adult and governmental authority." In the same time period, polls of students and the general public on some of these issues showed the following results:

Table 106

MORE SAY IN RUNNING OF COLLEGES*

"Do you think college students should or should not have a greater say in the running of colleges?"

	All Students	Demonstrators	General Public
Yes, should	81%	92%	25%
No, should not	17	6	70
No opinion	2	2	5

Table 107

MORE SAY ON ACADEMIC MATTERS?**

"Do you think college students should or should not have a greater say concerning the academic side of colleges—that is, the courses, examinations, and so forth?"

	All Students	Demonstrators	General Public
Yes, should	75%	86%	33%
No, should not	23	13	55
No opinion	2	1	12

Today some feel that the basis of student protest is legitimate, and that their wish for more to say in running the colleges lies in their desire to eliminate the dehumanizing, factory-like approach to education, in which the student is "just a number." There are many things wrong with our university system. There may be little doubt, for example, that many required subjects act as "filters" that, together with some equally rigid syllabi, tend to screen out people who are clearly not the ones who should be eliminated. This probably holds for

* *Gallup Opinion Index*, No. 48, June 1969, p. 7.
** Ibid.

all colleges, but it may be more true for schools that specialize in training for jobs requiring spontaneity and creativity, as well as intelligence and persistence. Our military academies come first to mind, followed closely by universities that house our foreign service schools, operations analysis departments, management schools, and so forth. We have all felt that some good people were being eliminated by this process, and there is evidence that tends to substantiate this belief.* But the difficulty for the young in college (as well as for the adults) is judging how capable the students are who are being filtered out, how and why it is happening, and how they can be helped.

One gets the feeling that many of the students' ideas even on these issues may not be very relevant. They cry out against the motivation and learning problems, but seem at times to assume that they will be solved by such things as a more "personalized" school. Insofar as this only means something like a lower student/instructor ratio, we must be cautious; for this may be a simplistic, perhaps even counterproductive, "solution" for a real, but much more complex, problem. For example, based on what precedent we have, under the current situation, it would be hard to make the case that the instructor/student ratio alone is the key to the degree of undergraduate learning. As the following chart shows, the student population did not exceed the post-World War II G.I. Bill "hump" until the early 1960s, but the faculty population had doubled by 1964.

Table 108

NUMBER OF COLLEGE STUDENTS
AND FACULTY 1940–1969**
(in thousands)

Year	Faculty	Students
1940	147	1,708
1950	247	3,508
1960	381	3,466
1964	495	4,508
1966	658	5,526
1968	745	6,912
1969	836	6,928

* Arthur W. Chickering, *Education and Identity* (San Francisco: Jossey-Bass, 1971), pp. 285–287, 302–305.
** Statistical Abstract of the United States, Bureau of the Census, U.S. Department of Commerce, 1970, p. 127; 1971, p. 126.

There have recently been about 50 or 60 percent more faculty available for a given number of students than for the veteran and non-veteran students during the G.I. Bill surge. Nevertheless, despite the unparalleled large classes, fantastic overcrowding and lack of "personal attention," the "creativity" and scholastic achievement of students in that period was far from inferior.* I am reluctant to accept quickly the idea that in undergraduate school, small classes with much communication between students, and many less-than-excellent instructors (the need for great numbers of them almost guarantees this) is preferable, from the point of view of learning, to straight lectures to large classes by fewer superior men. This latter way of learning is based on the assumption that there are those in the world who are better informed than others, and that one way to learn is simply to listen a good deal to the better informed, if they are in a position and desire to enlighten us. This, of course, raises entirely different issues than those stressed by most student activists.

The real question again, however, is what is it that the dissenters really want? Is it really the desire but lack of opportunity to learn that drives the activists to demand more and more attention? Even if one were to grant that the "gripes" were legitimate, it soon becomes apparent that the appearance of radical activists could be a symptom of something more than long-standing campus problems. Some new kind of activist mode seemed to be forming in the late 1960s. One gets some sense of what the demonstrators (28 percent of the students) were becoming when questions such as that below were answered in the following way:

Table 109

EXPEL CAMPUS LAWBREAKERS?**

"Do you think college students who break laws while participating in campus demonstrations should be expelled?"

	Demonstrators	All Students	General Public
No, should not	62%	40%	11%
Yes, should	31	54	82
No opinion	7	6	7

* See Peter F. Drucker's statement on these "incredibly superior" students, in *The Age of Discontinuity* (New York: Harper and Row, 1969), p. 324.

** *Gallup Opinion Index*, No. 48, June 1969, p. 7.

And in 1969, over two and one-half times as many student demonstrators (40 percent) had tried marijuana than non-demonstrators (15 percent); over three times as many (21 percent) had taken barbiturates (non-demonstrators, 6 percent); over twice as many (7 percent) had tried LSD (non-demonstrators, 3 percent); considerably more (67 percent) had been drunk (non-demonstrators, 53 percent); and less than half as many (16 percent) thought that premarital sexual relations were wrong (non-demonstrators, 34 percent).* The "profile" in Table 110 contains some further information on student demonstrators and compares the demonstrator and non-demonstrator of 1969.

The demonstrators apparently often considered themselves the vanguard of the students, if not all youth; but more of their importance may stem from what other people think they are than from their actual potential. We have mentioned the significant numbers of young instructors who at least until recently supported them. There was also a strong indication that social science departments on the East and West coasts were highly affected by pro-activism. College administrators feared the demonstrators and many in the media seemed to feel that they really spoke for youth. I have yet to see a convincing argument to substantiate the position that they (and almost they alone) voice the spontaneous and deep, long-term hopes and desires of youth, or even of college students. And the least that one could say from the sample of the credentials of those instructors who were the most active supporters of the demonstrators (compared to the professors who opposed them), is that it would be hard to endow these supporters with a strong sense of historical perspective.

1. WHO ARE THE ACTIVISTS?

The question still remains, who are the demonstrators? Are they the smarter people, those better qualified to make judgments? We may be able to gain some feeling in gross terms for the probable percentage of naturally bright people in this group, and even for the likelihood of finding which types of people are among them.

First of all, how intelligent are the students in this group? At first glance, and according to many deeply held convictions, one might have felt that they were (and are) the very bright students. An unusually high percentage of graduate students of 1969 (41 percent) had joined

* Ibid., pp. 19, 32.

Table 110

PROFILE OF THE STUDENT DEMONSTRATOR AND THE NON-DEMONSTRATOR*

	Have Demonstrated	Have not Demonstrated
All students	28%	72%
Sex		
Men	31	69
Women	24	76
Age		
18 years and under	27	73
19 years	24	76
20 years	33	67
21–23 years	28	72
24 years and older	32	68
Region of college		
East	34	66
Midwest	29	71
South	22	78
West	28	72
Politics		
Republicans	13	87
Democrats	31	69
Independents	34	66
Political philosophy		
Extremely conservative	22	78
Fairly conservative	16	84
Middle–of–the–road	15	85
Fairly liberal	33	67
Extremely liberal	61	39
Parents' income		
$15,000 and over	32	68
$10,000–$14,999	27	73
$ 7,000–$ 9,999	31	69
Under $7,000	30	70
Class		
Freshmen	28	72
Sophomores	28	72
Juniors	25	75
Seniors	24	76
Graduate students	41	59
Type of college		
Public	28	72
Private	30	70
Denominational	27	73

* Ibid., p. 13.

261

the ranks of the demonstrators, and traditionally graduate students have been thought to be among the better students. Graduate students probably make up about 12 percent or more of the student body, and in 1969 about 5 percent of this 12 had been demonstrators. If we assume that activists will also be found in a similar percentage of potential graduate students in the undergraduate school (which admittedly depends on a further, even more questionable, assumption of a "constant state" of political thought throughout college), we must conclude that perhaps a half (12 or 15 of 28 percent) of the demonstrators is made up of graduate and potential graduate (i.e., supposedly bright) students. This is a sizable number of bright activists, and it might be worth considering (1) where the demonstrating undergraduates come from and (2) where the demonstrating potential and actual graduate students come from.

About 9 percent of college-bound high school students with above-average and excellent grades (these two categories contain 56 percent of all college-bound students) fit the Radical-Left category in June 1970. About 8 percent of these radicals were above average and 1 percent were excellent students. In years gone by, with fewer people going to college, Radical-Left students with higher grades might have made up a larger percentage of the college-bound students; but one has doubts about this from the record of the "silent fifties," for example.

Scholarships for merit to students whose fathers had incomes low enough to qualify for them (an increasing number of students in recent years) should bring in more sons and daughters of parents of high school background. College-bound, Radical-Left children with good scholastic ratings from such families are likely to account for about 4.5 percent of the college freshmen (4 percent average and about .5 percent excellent students). Open admission programs will probably increase the numbers of less-talented undergraduates who are more likely to be Radical Left; but they are less likely to be what is normally considered graduate school material.

Of the high school group entering college, probably somewhere between 5 and 8 percent are Radical-Left students whose mothers and fathers went to college. (The total percentage of Radical-Left high school children whose parents went to college is between 15 and 18 percent.) These Radical-Left students are likely to be in the average or above-average category, but less likely to be in the excellent one. We found earlier that the high school students who chose the Radical-

262

Left as their political orientation contained a higher percentage of who were disinterested in their environment, and who perhaps tended to be somewhat alienated, possibly unhappy adolescents. In order to get some feel for the number of Radical-Left students entering college who are not alienated from their parents and environment, I first looked at the number of excellent and above-average high school students with college-graduate parents on the premise that more parents with this background would be sympathetic to—or at least would not strenuously oppose—Radical-Left ideas of their children. Presumably, if this were the case, these Radical-Left high school students would be less alienated from their families and might be more psychologically "adequate" (stable?). Even this situation, however, might prove inefficacious; for there is some expert opinion that parents who are loathe to take on their children in a head-on confrontation could be unknowingly abetting their instability.* Furthermore, college-educated adults as a whole, as we have seen, contain a higher percentage of people who rate themselves politically as conservatives, even though there are more in this group who tend to be liberal on behavioral issues.

As indicated above, only about 1 percent of college-bound high school students are Radical-Left *and* excellent students. About 11 percent of the excellent high school students are Radical-Left, but the excellent category includes only 7 percent of the total number of high school students. Seventy-three percent of children of college-graduate parents who are making excellent course grades go to college, but they comprise only about 5 percent of all college-bound high school students. Children of college-graduate parents who are excellent scholastically *and* Radical-Left are only about one-half of 1 percent of all college-bound high school students.

A smaller percentage of college-bound high school students with college-graduate parents fall into the above-average and average groups than are found in the excellent one; but the former groups are larger, and Radical-Leftism is, as we have seen, greater among the less-gifted students. Radical-Left, above-average high school students with college-graduate parents make up about 2.3 percent of the college-bound students. The total percentage of all college-bound, above-average

* Herbert Hendin, "A Psychoanalyst Looks at Student Revolutionaries," *New York Times Magazine*, January 17, 1971, p. 19; Bruno Bettelheim in an address as reported in "Youth in Turmoil," *Philadelphia Inquirer*, February 4, 1971, p. 1.

high school students of college-graduate parents, without regard to political orientation, is about 14 percent. About 45 percent of all college-bound students fall into the above-average category, but only 20 to 27 percent of students with college-graduate parents are in this group. Since there are only 15 to 18 percent of all children of such parents who consider themselves Radical-Left, about 2.3 percent of them should be in this group.

The high school students making average grades include 40 percent of those going to college; about 6 of that 40 percent represents students who have parents who are college graduates. Of these 6 percent, about 1 percent are likely to be Radical-Leftists.

In summary, in 1970 a total of less than 4 percent of the college-bound high school students were Radical-Left, excellent, above-average, or even average students *and* came from homes where the parents are college graduates.* Even presuming that the great majority of these parents and students agree in outlook (which is somewhat doubtful since half the college-educated adults said they were conservatives), and assuming that this is an indicator of a higher likelihood of better adjustment of youngsters, the actual figure for "well-adjusted" radicals will be smaller than 4 percent. If we then eliminate the average students, we are left with about 3 percent excellent and above-average, college-bound, Radical-Left students who may also be the most well-adjusted of this group.

Obviously we are not isolating the source of college demonstrators by this method. (In 1969, 28 percent of the student body had demonstrated, almost always for Leftist causes.) We are not even isolating demonstrating graduate and potential graduate students. If we include college-bound students from non-college-graduate parents—who may be likely to be politically liberal (in the old sense), but who are less likely to be liberal on behavioral issues than the college-educated parents—we cannot come up with more than 4 percent at the most who are Radical-Left and have excellent and above-average grades. Moreover, if we are looking for the percentage of bright Radical-Leftists who are also well-adjusted in their family relationships, etc.,

* The above data is derived primarily from Purdue Opinion Panel reports cited earlier, particularly *Report of Poll No. 89*, June 1970, pp. 1a, 2a, 5a and 6a, and *Report of Poll No. 90*, January 1971, pp. 3a and 4a. (Low-income fathers were assumed to be more numerous among men with only a grade-school or high-school education than among men with college degrees.) The basic rough breakdown given above is not likely to have changed radically in the past two years.

when they leave high school, then that 4 percent must be further reduced. As we have shown, the Radical-Left group seems to contain the most high school students who are unstimulated by their families, their friends, school, community and almost anything else; they also have little feeling of autonomy in making decisions within the family. This might even emphasize some personality problems. In addition, we assume that some of the 4 percent of Radical-Left students will have parents who strongly disapprove of Radical-Left ideas, thereby possibly further alienating students from their families and reducing their confidence, and consequently perhaps affecting their personalities.*

On this basis, one could make the argument that there are just too few bright Radical-Leftist adolescents (particularly "well-adjusted" and happy ones) in their natural state in the high school population to be the source of even a sizeable portion of the 28 percent of college student demonstrators. This means one of several things: (a) some young are radicalized when they reach the campuses, so that activists are recruited from the large majority of bright, moderate, non-alienated students (and if so, in the process, many apparently tend to become more alienated from their parents and possibly become somewhat less "stable");** (b) they are largely made up of the more alienated, *not* so bright, and perhaps psychologically "inadequate" students; (c) a large percentage are bright, but are alienated and emotionally "inadequate" students; (d) a combination of these. If as many as 41 percent of the graduate students are demonstrators, we may assume

---

* As can be imagined, finding terms acceptable to all for the description of the different characteristics of students is an almost insurmountable task. In fact, providing an analytic description in any terms is extremely difficult. Students who look irresponsible to some look extremely responsible to others; the value of a student's ability to adjust to a given system is looked on as very commendable and a sign of a stable person by some, but almost reprehensible by others. Some seem to subscribe to this latter idea because of feelings that our society and its systems are themselves sick, and one must be somewhat unhealthy to adjust to them. The judgments about whether these young people are truly happy or not, or are likely to be well adjusted or emotionally "adequate," are based on the idea that alienated, very dissatisfied people are normally not as happy as more satisfied people. This does not ignore the point that, as mentioned earlier, it is quite normal for young people to reject some adult opinions and beliefs; it merely assumes that an abnormally high degree of rejection, disinterest, and activist dissent can indicate an unhappy adolescent for other than "political" reasons.

** This process of "conversion" is described excitedly by Charles A. Reich in *The Greening of America* (New York: Random House, 1970), p. 224: "In a brief span of months a student, seemingly conventional in every way . . . transforms himself into a drug-using, long-haired, peace-loving 'freak.'"

265

that their unexpectedly great numbers are largely due to something such as a change of attitude on the part of bright, moderate students in the campus milieu. But if this does not account for all of them (and one doubts that it does) then something like (b) or even (c) might also partially explain the source of activists.

The important questions about the whole activist-demonstrator issue, therefore, might be: what was (and perhaps still is) deemed more important in the "demonstrators' club"—the ideology of the student or his intelligence? How are activists recruited, or do they spontaneously join? How much do the followers believe? Are many bright students convinced by fellow students? Do they succumb to the instructor "authority figures" and the persuasive atmosphere of the university? ("We all agree because we are all intelligent men. No intelligent man thinks otherwise.") Were (and are) bright, potential opposition students intimidated by them? Do good students with less than ultra-liberal ideas get turned off by a hostile environment in the graduate schools? There are indications that some of all the above additional elements play a role.*

There is no doubt that college students as a group react differently than high school students. And individually they react differently in college from when they were in high school; that is, they change as they get "older" (but traditionally—particularly among the actual radicals —they tend to change back after they leave the campuses, see Table 140A and the discussion before and after it). How much they change, and why, is another question. In comparing some of their basic attitudes between high school and college years we are able to see some changes. Some of the issues are hard to compare because of the difficulties in using the polls mentioned earlier. For example, the two charts which are given in the portion "Generation Gap Seen by Young and Old" of the June 1969 *Gallup Opinion Index* were not meant to be, and cannot be, used as a comparison with the Purdue charts on high school student opinions at the beginning of this sec-

*The International Committee on University Emergency, including such prestigious, far from reactionary scholars as Harvard's Edwin O. Reischauer and Paul Freund, Chicago's John Hope Franklin and Yale's Alexander Bickel, said in 1970 that it wanted "to alert campus and public" to the fact that "increasingly from Berkeley to Berlin, political criteria are being used to evaluate academic performance. . . ." (Fred M. Hechinger, "For Campus Freedoms," *New York Times*, November 22, 1970, Section IV, p. 7.)

There has also been much anecdotal evidence of, but no comprehensive data on, the forcing of a "low profile" on bright conservatives, middle-of-the-roaders, and even less radical liberals on our campuses; and there are, as we have seen, a great number of them leaving the high schools for college.

tion. The Purdue charts, which led that group to conclude in late 1969 that there was no generation gap, compared the young peoples' gripes about *young people* with their estimate of their *parents'* gripes about *young people*. The two Gallup charts in the tables below compare the gripes of *each* about the other. In any event, this poll was not intended to be used to find out if there was a gap, but rather to see if people *thought* there was. As indicated earlier, they did; and this poll tended to confirm it: "Seven in ten college students think a 'generation gap' exists, and the same proportion of older persons in the populace hold this view."*

Table 111
BIGGEST GRIPE OF COLLEGE STUDENTS ABOUT PARENTS' GENERATION?

Too set in their ways	36%
A lack of communication (they won't listen to us)	18
Too conservative	8
Indifferent, apathetic	8
Materialistic	6
Too strict	6
Their views on morals	4
Racial prejudice	4
They stereotype young people	4
Other responses	6
No gripe about them	11
No opinion	3
	114%

Table 112
BIGGEST GRIPE OF PARENTS ABOUT YOUNG PEOPLE?

Undisciplined behavior	30%
Lack respect for authority	16
Youth are overindulged	10
Irresponsible	7
Parents too permissive	7
Smug, too self-assured	6
Use of drugs	4
Too idealistic, naive	2
Other responses	4
No gripe about them	12
No opinion	6
	104%

* *Gallup Opinion Index*, No. 48, June 1969, pp. 19, 20. Totals add to more than 100 percent because some persons gave more than one response.

267

It is noteworthy that only 4 percent of the parents listed drug use as their biggest concern in 1969. Compare this to the responses in 1970 and 1971 of adults when asked about our biggest problems today (see discussion following Table 51).

There are questions, however, on which college and high school students can be more directly compared. One of these is the legalization of marijuana. In March 1969, high school seniors overwhelmingly disapproved—by almost eight to two—the legalization of marijuana;* yet, in the spring of 1970, these same young people, as college freshmen, were 46 percent *for* and 49 percent against it.** In a late 1970 poll, college students as a whole registered 53 percent in favor of legalizing marijuana.*** In October 1969, 84 percent of all adults opposed it, and in another poll in late 1970 were again against it by 86 percent.****

The detailed breakdown of the spring 1970 poll which showed college students 50 percent in favor of legalization, is found in Table 113.

Some change was, of course, to be expected as these adolescents became "young adults." (A change through the years was even evident in a 1969 Purdue poll of high school students; tenth-graders were somewhat less lenient—16 percent for, 82 percent against the legalization of marijuana—than twelfth-graders.) Of course, there was a general shift in attitudes among all high school students in the country as a group: There was an 11-to-17 percent increase in their approval of the legalization of marijuana between 1969 and 1971 (the actual amount depends on whether we count only those who said they "approve" of legalization, or also count those who answered "undecided, probably approve"). In 1971, high school seniors showed 38 percent "approving" or "undecided, probably approving" legalization (see Table 88). But the increase of more than 25 percent solid approval in the one year between their senior high school and college freshman years is significantly greater.†

* The opinions of the college-bound high school seniors should not be too different from the overall view. The excellent, above-average, and average students all register 80 percent or more against legalization; those with college-graduate parents and high-income families disapproved 74 and 76 percent respectively. Purdue Opinion Panel, *Report of Poll No. 86,* March 1969, pp. 17a and 18a.

** *Gallup Opinion Index,* No. 60, June 1970, p. 22.

*** Harris poll in *Life,* January 8, 1971, p. 26.

**** See Table 9 for the polls.

† As can be seen from many of these charts, there is a measurable, but not drastic change of opinion of college students as they proceed from the freshman through the senior year. Generally, this is a liberalizing change up through the junior year and then, often, a slight shift back toward conservatism in the senior year. These changes can be expected because people pass from late adolescence to adulthood *in* as well as *out* of college. Undoubtedly, when students first enter col-

Table 113

LEGALIZE MARIJUANA?*
Asked of College Students

"Do you think the use of marijuana should be made legal, or not?"

April 24—May 3, 1970

	Should	Should Not	No Opinion
NATIONAL	50%	44%	6%
SEX			
Men	54	40	6
Women	45	49	6
AGE			
18 years and under	45	52	3
19 years	48	45	7
20 years	49	44	7
21–23 years	58	37	5
24 years and over	46	46	8
REGION OF COLLEGE			
East	60	33	7
Midwest	53	41	6
South	38	57	5
West	51	42	7
POLITICAL AFFILIATION			
Republican	36	59	5
Democrat	43	52	5
Independent	58	34	8
PARENTS' INCOME			
$15,000 and over	58	37	5
$10,000–$14,999	45	46	9
$ 7,000–$ 9,999	50	45	5
Under $7,000	42	53	5
CLASS IN SCHOOL			
Freshman	46	49	5
Sophomore	50	43	7
Junior	55	37	8
Senior	54	41	5
Graduate	52	40	8
TYPE OF COLLEGE			
Public	51	42	7
Private	55	40	5
Denominational	36	60	4
RELIGIOUS PREFERENCE			
Protestant	37	58	5
Catholic	52	42	6

lege, they receive a sense of change, apparently enough to alter drastically some, but not all, of their basic attitudes. More changes take place as they become sophomores and juniors. Much of the personality change and growth through the college years has been analyzed from a sizeable sample of students from diverse colleges in Chickering, op. cit.

* *Gallup Opinion Index,* No. 60, June 1970, p. 22.

269

A similar shift seems to occur in regard to the attitude toward extramarital sexual relations. In the March 1965 Purdue survey of the "worst practices," "sexual misbehaving" was high on the list of high school students. Yet, as the following chart shows, people from the same "cohort," who were college juniors in the spring of 1969, felt that extramarital sexual relations were not wrong (67 to 28 percent). Unlike the situation with adults (see Figures 6 through 12), the "new morality" may have been having some effect on the high school students' attitude toward those who "had not followed the morals or rules relating to the behavior of unmarried people," at least as early as 1964. (See Table 64.) As young people "go on their own" when they leave high school, they are perhaps more likely to begin that "liberal perturbation" on personal behavior, but the campuses seem particularly to stimulate it.

Table 114

PRE-MARITAL SEX RELATIONS*
Asked of College Students

"There's a lot of discussion about the way morals and sex are changing in this country. Here is a question that is often discussed in women's magazines . . . what is your view on this—do you think it is wrong for a man and woman to have sex relations before marriage, or not?"

	Yes	No	No Opinion
NATIONAL	29%	66%	5%
SEX			
Men	24	72	4
Women	37	55	8
AGE			
18 years and under	32	62	6
19 years	35	59	6
20 years	26	69	5
21–23 years	28	67	5
24 years and older	21	74	5
REGION OF COLLEGE			
East	24	71	5
Midwest	33	59	8
South	33	65	2
West	25	70	5
POLITICAL AFFILIATION			
Republican	38	56	6
Democrat	30	66	4
Independent	25	69	6

* *Gallup Opinion Index,* June 1969, p. 32.

Table 114 (continued)

PARENTS' INCOME

$15,000 and over	23	74	3
$10,000–$14,999	33	63	4
$ 7,000–$ 9,999	31	64	5
Under $7,000	38	58	4

CLASS IN SCHOOL

Freshman	30	65	5
Sophomore	29	67	4
Junior	28	67	5
Senior	28	65	7
Graduate	30	63	7

TYPE OF COLLEGE

Public	29	66	5
Private	20	74	6
Denominational	56	36	8
DEMONSTRATORS	16	80	4
NON-DEMONSTRATORS	34	60	6

RELIGIOUS PREFERENCE

Protestant	36	57	7
Catholic	39	55	6

POLITICAL PHILOSOPHY

Extremely conservative	50	44	6
Fairly conservative	41	55	4
Middle–of–the–road	38	54	8
Fairly liberal	25	71	4
Extremely liberal	4	92	4

STUDENTS WHO HAVE:

Done social work	32	62	6
Been drunk	19	77	4
Tried barbiturates	9	89	2
Tried marijuana	5	94	1
Tried LSD	1	95	4

When a late 1970 poll of young people 15-to-21 asked a question regarding the *degree* of promiscuity, the results were as follows:*

"Is it all right to have sexual relations if you are:"

	High School	*College*
Dating casually?	No 78%	No 68%
Going steady?	No 69	No 51
Planning to marry?	No 57	Yes 52
Formally engaged?	Yes 45	Yes 72

* Louis Harris poll in *Life,* January 8, 1971, p. 27.

Here, again, the change between high school and college opinion is considerable; but the difference in attitude on this subject between the general public and college students is so striking that one has to question whether, on a growing number of issues, the college campus is not becoming a more and more detached segment of our society. What we see by comparison of the data on this issue is the difference of opinion between the college students and their parents. Adults over the years have become *more* opposed to such practices. Even when the question, "Do you think that two people who are in love and engaged to be married should wait until marriage to have sexual relations or not?" was asked in 1965, 64 percent of the adults said they should wait. This compares strikingly to the 1969 question above, in which 72 percent of the college students said under these circumstances it was all right. In 1937, 57 percent of adults polled felt it was wrong to indulge in extramarital relations, and in 1954, 53 percent felt the same way. But in 1969, 68 percent of adults opposed it, 21 felt it was all right, 11 had no opinion or wouldn't answer.* Yet, as we have seen, in June 1969, 66 percent of college students felt such behavior was *not* wrong, 29 felt it was wrong, and 5 held no opinion. Also noteworthy are the extremes of opinion between the politically more conservative students and those who have not used drugs, on the one hand, and the fairly liberal and extremely liberal students and those who have tried barbiturates, marijuana, and LSD, on the other. Despite the contraceptive pill, there are still a great number of pregnancies among the young, and because of promiscuity and the pill, venereal disease has been on the rise.

Probably the most disturbing aspect of the college campus milieu, and one which no doubt contributes substantially to the problems mentioned above and to many others, is the enormous increase in drug use on our campuses in the period between the surveys shown in Table 115. Extreme opposition to the legalization of marijuana seems justified if the *de facto* immunity from prosecution for possession on many campuses, which has been in effect in the past two years, shows such results. Furthermore, the worries of parents (and perhaps high school students) seem justified. The increased use of more dangerous drugs, and the much higher probability of experimenting with them among people who have used marijuana, is alarming.

* See Figure 6.

Table 115
FREQUENCY OF MARIJUANA USE
College Students

	Ever used 1969*	Ever used 1970**	Used in last 12 Months 1970**	Used in last 30 Days 1970**
ALL STUDENTS	22%	43%	39%	28%
SEX				
Male	25	49	44	31
Female	18	35	33	23
CLASS IN SCHOOL				
Freshman	23	38	35	24
Sophomore	25	46	43	32
Junior	23	50	44	27
Senior	19	40	40	30
Graduate	13	54	43	31
AGE				
18 years and under	21	35	32	22
19 years	21	49	46	32
20 years	24	53	48	35
21–23 years	23	40	36	25
24 years and over	20	43	33	19
TYPE OF COLLEGE				
Public	24	43	39	26
Private	24	49	44	32
Denominational	4	34	32	26
POLITICAL PHILOSOPHY				
Extremely conservative	11			
Fairly conservative	9			
Middle–of–the–road	15			
Fairly liberal	25			
Extremely liberal	49			
AREA OF STUDY				
Humanities		47%	44%	31%
Math and Science		41	40	26
Social Science		57	52	36
Engineering		40	30	21
Business Administration		41	35	24
Education		26	23	15
SPECIAL ANALYSES (of those who have:)				
Used amphetamines in last 30 days		87	86	82
Used hallucinogens in last 30 days		100	100	98
Drunk beer in last 30 days		51	47	33

* *Gallup Opinion Index*, No. 48, June 1969, p. 30.
** *Gallup Opinion Index*, No. 68, February 1971, p. 2.

Table 115 (continued)

SPECIAL ANALYSES (continued)

Drunk wine in last 30 days	58	53	39
Drunk hard liquor in last 30 days	51	47	31
Used barbiturates in last 30 days	88	86	84

Table 116

FREQUENCY OF BARBITURATE USE
College Students

	Ever used 1969*	Ever used 1970**	Used in last 12 Months 1970**	Used in last 30 Days 1970**
ALL STUDENTS	10%	14%	10%	5%
SEX				
Male	11	17	12	6
Female	9	10	6	4
CLASS IN SCHOOL				
Freshman		15	9	4
Sophomore		17	15	9
Junior		10	5	4
Senior		17	10	2
Graduate		12	7	3
AGE				
18 years and under	11	12	7	4
19 years	10	18	15	6
20 years	9	16	12	8
21–23 years	11	13	7	3
24 years and over	10	15	11	7
TYPE OF COLLEGE				
Public	12	15	9	5
Private	9	12	8	3
Denominational	1	22	20	10
POLITICAL PHILOSOPHY				
Extremely conservative	6			
Fairly conservative	7			
Middle–of–the–road	6			
Fairly liberal	12			
Extremely liberal	21			
AREA OF STUDY				
Humanities		16	11	6
Math and Science		13	10	7

* *Gallup Opinion Index,* No. 48, June 1969, p. 29.
** *Gallup Dpinion Index,* No. 68, February 1971, p. 5.

Table 116 (continued)

AREA OF STUDY (continued)

Social Science	21	14	5
Engineering	12	7	7
Business Administration	11	7	4
Education	6	3	1

SPECIAL ANALYSES (of those who have:)

Used marijuana in last 30 days	36	28	14
Used amphetamines in last 30 days	70	65	39
Used hallucinogens in last 30 days	55	48	30
Drunk beer in last 30 days	18	13	7
Drunk wine in last 30 days	22	16	8
Drunk hard liquor in last 30 days	19	15	8

Table 117

FREQUENCY OF HALLUCINOGEN USE

College Students

	Ever used 1969*	Ever used 1970**	Used in last 12 Months 1970**	Used in last 30 Days 1970**
ALL STUDENTS	4%	14%	12%	6%
SEX				
Male	5	17	14	7
Female	3	11	9	4
CLASS IN SCHOOL				
Freshman	6	13	11	5
Sophomore	4	16	15	8
Junior	2	17	12	6
Senior	5	16	12	4
Graduate	1	12	7	4
AGE				
18 years and under	4	11	11	5
19 years	5	16	16	7
20 years	3	20	16	8
21–23 years	5	13	9	3
24 years and over	4	10	7	7

* *Gallup Opinion Index*, No. 48, June 1969, p. 31.
** *Gallup Opinion Index*, No. 68, February 1971, p. 6.

Table 117 (continued)

TYPE OF COLLEGE				
Public	5	13	10	5
Private	2	15	13	5
Denominational	1	23	20	16
POLITICAL PHILOSOPHY				
Extremely conservative	6			
Fairly conservative	1			
Middle–of–the–road	3			
Fairly liberal	4			
Extremely liberal	12			
AREA OF STUDY				
Humanities		20	17	9
Math and Science		17	13	8
Social Science		17	15	7
Engineering		12	9	7
Business Administration		8	6	3
Education		6	4	2
SPECIAL ANALYSES (of those who have:)				
Used marijuana in last 30 days		46	39	21
Used amphetamines in last 30 days		59	54	34
Drunk beer in last 30 days		16	13	7
Drunk wine in last 30 days		21	18	9
Drunk hard liquor in last 30 days		15	13	6
Used barbiturates in last 30 days		61	57	37

We see here once more the increased tendency to have more users of all drugs within the extremely liberal group. Surely here is a "gap" in attitude between the worried parent and the experimenting student: Better than four in ten college students have used marijuana, and as many as almost three in ten may use it at least once a month. One out of seven students is willing to experiment with drugs that are classified as harmful to him, and one in sixteen is perhaps willing to do it once a month. And the increase of drug use in the denominational colleges has been phenomenal: They are now far ahead of the public and private schools in the use of hallucinogens and barbiturates. Apparently the campuses are full of optimistic pot users: Of the students who have used marijuana within the last thirty days, 85 percent feel it is not injurious to the health (versus 8 percent who think it is), and 92 percent do not think it will lead to hard drugs (versus 2 percent who think it will). (The obviously much higher probability of marijuana users turning to LSD or some other hallucinogen, so clearly indicated in the charts, has either not been impressed on the students, or they do not classify LSD and other hallucinogens as "hard," a colloquial term which has meant heroin—now also used on campuses—cocaine, and so forth, and which continues to be applied only to these drugs, and often not to the new powerful hallucinogens.) These opinions diverge widely from those of the overwhelming majority of the general public (including non-college youth) and the students' parents.

On other issues, however, college students are still quite close to their parents. On two very basic ones—the relevancy of religion and faith in the system's reward for ability—the students sound like their parents. If we compare the relevance of religion to college students in 1970, the subject of Table 118, with the church attendance of adults and college students in 1969 (see Table 31), we find that in 1969, 42 percent of the adults and 47 percent of the college students attended church during the week they were questioned, and in the spring of 1970, 42 percent of the college students found religion relevant. In late 1970, 43 percent of the college students said they attended church regularly, and 56 percent felt religion was important to them.* Table 118 has a breakdown on the feelings of students toward the relevance of organized religion according to age, class, and other factors.

It is interesting to compare the somewhat more conservative feeling toward religion among graduate students, and toward many of the issues given previously, with the views of undergraduates. This leads to speculation over a greater gap between the more "liberal" and "conservative" factions of the (older) graduate students. In light of the large number of demonstrators, and the greater representation of the Left among graduate students, it is possible that the dichotomy is sharper in this class than in any other.

Students show a strong belief in the value of ability and hard work (see Table 119).

According to a Harris poll in late 1970, 52 percent of the college

* Louis Harris poll, *Life*, January 8, 1971, p. 26.

Table 118

RELEVANCE OF RELIGION*

College Students

"Is organized religion a relevant part of your life at the present time, or not?"

	April 24—May 3, 1970	
	Yes	*No*
NATIONAL	42%	58%
SEX		
Men	38	62
Women	50	50
AGE		
18 years and under	51	49
19 years	43	57
20 years	39	61
21–23 years	38	62
24 years and over	41	59
REGION		
East	38	62
Midwest	39	61
South	50	50
West	41	59
POLITICAL AFFILIATION		
Republican	56	44
Democrat	56	44
Independent	30	70
PARENTS' INCOME		
$15,000 and over	32	68
$10,000–$14,999	42	58
$ 7,000–$ 9,999	49	51
Under $7,000	56	44
CLASS IN SCHOOL		
Freshman	46	54
Sophomore	44	56
Junior	37	63
Senior	38	62
Graduate	41	59
TYPE OF COLLEGE		
Public	39	61
Private	38	62
Denominational	69	31
RELIGIOUS PREFERENCE		
Protestant	51	49
Catholic	57	43

* *Gallup Opinion Index,* June 1970, p. 18.

278

Table 119

REASON FOR SUCCESS*

College Students

"Do you think people who are successful get ahead largely because of their luck or largely because of their ability?"

| | April 24—May 3, 1970 | | |
	Luck	*Ability*	*No Opinion*
NATIONAL	9%	88%	3%
SEX			
Men	9	87	4
Women	9	89	2
AGE			
18 years and under	9	89	2
19 years	11	86	3
20 years	8	91	1
21–23 years	8	87	5
24 years and over	9	88	3
REGION OF COLLEGE			
East	13	82	5
Midwest	7	90	3
South	9	90	1
West	6	90	4
POLITICAL AFFILIATION			
Republican	5	93	2
Democrat	8	91	1
Independent	11	85	4
PARENTS' INCOME			
$15,000 and over	10	87	3
$10,000–$14,999	10	85	5
$ 7,000–$ 9,999	6	92	2
Under $7,000	6	93	1
CLASS IN SCHOOL			
Freshman	9	88	3
Sophomore	11	87	2
Junior	9	88	3
Senior	7	89	4
Graduate	8	88	4
TYPE OF COLLEGE			
Public	9	89	2
Private	11	83	6
Denominational	6	92	2
RELIGIOUS PREFERENCE			
Protestant	6	93	1
Catholic	9	88	3

* Ibid., p. 23.

279

Table 120

Importance of money to the respondent:	Total	Sex		Age				Education						Race		Financial Background				
		Male	Female	Under 17	17–18	19–21	22–24	Out of School-Not H.S. Graduate	In High School	Out of School-H.S. Graduate	Out of School-Some College	In College	College Graduate	White	Nonwhite	Prosperous	Above Average	Average	Below Average	Poor
A most important thing	11%	13%	9%	16%	14%	9%	5%	12%	17%	10%	5%	6%	4%	10%	23%	8%	11%	11%	18%	9%
A very important thing	32	33	30	28	29	32	38	31	27	36	36	34	28	32	28	36	35	30	24	32
Moderately important	50	45	55	49	47	50	52	48	48	47	51	53	63	51	43	44	48	53	49	32
Relatively unimportant	7	8	7	7	9	9	4	10	7	7	9	8	5	8	6	11	6	7	9	29

students felt that "success and wealth" were worth striving for.* Another poll at the same time showed that 53 percent of a different sample felt "material things people work hard for" are "worth the time" it takes to get them.** An extensive survey of youth conducted in October 1970 was published in *Finance-Related Attitudes of Youth,* A Report on a Nationwide Survey of Today's Young Americans between the ages of 14 and 25 (Gilbert Youth Survey), Institute of Life Insurance, Division of Statistics and Research: New York 1970. (See Table 120.) This survey also included some questions on life style, which is what we may be concerned with here and certainly will be concerned with in the next section.

That students were also interested in careers for other reasons than merely making money was evident in the beginning of 1969. In the following Gallup poll, students were notably interested in going into what Gallup calls the "helping" professions.

Table 121

PREFERRED FIELD OR OCCUPATION BY AGE 40***
Asked of College Students

"What field or occupation do you expect to be in when you are age 40?"

Teaching	29%
Business Management	8
Housewife	8
Law	5
Clergy	5
Engineering	4
Social Work	4
Medicine	2
Others	24
Don't Know	11

It is essential to have the "helping" professions, but there is a question whether large numbers of students have true "callings" to them. Some of these professions could also be considered to be "decoupled"— that is, they are only indirectly attached to the system; rules of meas-

* Louis Harris Poll, *Life*, January 8, 1971, p. 22.
** Survey in *Seventeen*, February 1971, p. 123. This sample included non-college students between 14 and 22 years of age.
*** *Gallup Opinion Index*, June 1969, p. 18.

urable productivity are difficult to apply to them; and the hard decisions and discipline essential for maintaining standards can more easily be avoided.

Some persons, however, apparently did not (and perhaps still do not) recognize the need for discipline and productivity; in fact, they see them as just another indication of the outdated thinking associated with the current system which is the real villain. The best-selling *The Greening of America* is an extreme exposition of this approach. The book abounds with hyperbole describing the catastrophe that is now American society: "Americans have lost control of the machinery of society"; "disintegration of the social fabric, and the resulting atmosphere of anxiety and terror in which we all live"; "less than two hundred years later almost every aspect of the American dream has been lost"; "the family, the most basic social system, has been ruthlessly stripped of its functional essentials"; "beginning with school, if not before, an individual is systematically stripped of his imagination, his creativity, his heritage, his dreams, and his personal uniqueness . . . instinct, feeling and spontaneity are repressed by overwhelming forces"; "for most Americans, work is mindless, exhausting, boring, servile, and hateful."*

If, despite all the evidence to the contrary (see Tables 52–60), one believes that this extremely pessimistic counter-culture analysis is truly the state of affairs, even a sensible man would have to think that drastic changes are necessary; he might be looking desperately almost anywhere for answers. Professor Reich recommends a change of "consciousness" to understand and to cope with our new technological "corporate society," a "mindless juggernaut . . . obliterating human values," which leads not only to domestic disaster, but to things such as the Vietnam war, "with its unprincipled destruction of everything human." The hope is in a new form of revolution, spearheaded by a vanguard of certain youth who follow a philosophy "which will in time include not only all youth, but all people in America." Only a new culture can control the machinery of society, but "its emotions can be comprehended only by seeing contemporary America through the eyes of the new generation." After a man has saved himself from his "present danger" he must learn to live in a new way: It requires the creation of a new "reality . . . . the process of creation, which has

* Charles A. Reich, *The Greening of America* (New York: Random House, 1970), pp. 5–21, passim.

already been started by our youth in this moment of utmost sterility, darkest night and extremest peril. . . ."*

When one gets to this new "reality" in Reich's book, it is rather disappointing. Much of what Reich claims for the special insight of his type of youth is either contrived or is probably nothing new to most people, and might stem from an underestimation and unknowing caricature of his fellow citizens. His "solutions" are based on his people not being like the rest of men—hypocritical, materialistic exploiters of their fellow man, "plastic," artificial—but rather on their being "truthful," true to one's self first and foremost, sticking firmly to principles, wearing one's heart on one's sleeve, only working at what one wants to, not being bound by unpleasant obligations (legal or otherwise), being free to enjoy life and beauty.

This new philosophy strikes one as not being new. A faint, yet clear and familiar echo of the young European Romantics of the late eighteenth and early nineteenth centuries can be heard in it, and it is difficult to miss:

Disciplined individualism was no longer enough for the Romantics. It came to mean to them no more than individually bowing to the same "fixities" and"definities." And the Romantic craved not to find the same universal truth, but to experience reality in a way wholly his own. This was to be done not by reasoning, but through feeling, sentiment, imagination, instinct, passion, dream and recollection. These, unlike syllogistic reasoning, were modes of experience in each case spontaneous and unique. . . .**

But there are other points of view which bring into question the previous perception of the virtues of college youth, particularly the virtues of student activists. In 1969, Professor Joseph Schwab of the University of Chicago, a sympathetic analyst of college-student protest, identified this specific issue as related to one of the "radical privations" which many students must endure. (Analysts such as Schwab also make some rather broad statements, but about a much narrower and presumably familiar subject—in Schwab's case, the college students.)

Students are ignorant of defensible grounds of morality, using, instead, three platitudes: "sincerity," "self-integrity," and "service to others." Two

* Ibid., pp. 19, 20, passim.
** J. L. Talmon, *Romanticism and Revolt* (New York: Harcourt, Brace and World, 1967), p. 139.

283

of these are good platitudes (integrity and service), but until the complexities and interconnections of "self," "other," "integrity," and "service" are understood, they can only dazzle and mislead.[*]

Professor Schwab also writes that, contrary to suggestions by some, he found no valid differentiation between college activists as "the best or better students" and the non-activists as "the poor and average students." The activists, he asserts, "appear to be drawn from and to represent well, almost the entire spectrum of student competence. . . . In short, student activists are *students*."[**] For example, Scholastic Aptitude test scores of 46 identified activists were found to be distributed in a similar pattern to students as a whole:

Table 122
DISTRIBUTION OF SCHOLASTIC APTITUDE SCORES[***]

	Verbal		*Quantitative*	
	Activists	*All*	*Activists*	*All*
750–800	11%	13%	15%	13%
700–749	33	26	22	24
650–699	30	25	28	24
600–649	13	18	22	19
550–599	11	12	4	12
500–549	2	4.5	9	5
Below 500	0	1.5	0	3

For the entire group (All) N=700; for Activists, N=46

[*] Ibid., p. 32.

Professor Schwab points out that these data show that the student activists do include some of our "best students . . . with respect to mathematical as well as verbal competence."[****] (One need not stress the obvious point that if the activists are a standard minority of students [in June of 1969 only 28 percent of students had demonstrated, see Table 110] they do not include the majority of the best students, and by concentrating on the activists we may tend to disenfranchise this majority of the best students.) On the other hand, he states that the "audible leaders" and "doctrinal theorists" of the activists do not come

[*] Joseph J. Schwab, *College Curriculum and Student Protest* (Chicago: University of Chicago Press, 1969), p. 37. I will refer at length to this study which was partially done under a Ford Foundation grant.
[**] Ibid., p. 33.
[***] Ibid., p. 32.
[****] Ibid., pp. 33, 34.

from these superior students but "mainly from the 600 to 699 group." He further states:

Neurosis, unfortunately, is no respecter of intellectual potential; the superior group has its full share of serious symptoms, generalized hostility, and difficulty in establishing effective relations with over-thirties.

But the professor feels that if one subtracts the "seriously ill"—and "even if we stretch the meaning of 'hostility' and 'difficulty in establishing relations' about as far as they will go," and discount the recovery rate after mid-adolescence—"a substantial proportion of the superior group [of activists] remains: highly intelligent, flexible, potentially capable of effective relations with a variety of people."* He feels strongly that they should not be abandoned by other youth and adults. The vast bulk of his work is devoted to recommendations on how the universities can make these students and others feel part of the university community and realize their potential as scholars.

The following discussion might shed some light on the make-up of the 1969 demonstrators that we discussed earlier, particularly regarding their relationship to the numbers of Radical Left and other "political" categories of college-bound high school students. Professor Schwab states that the majority of student activists were "not sick, not demagogues, imitators of demagogues or members of the New Left." Most of them, "occasional protesters," were (are?) moved by everything from "the ordinary impulse of any late adolescent to use an opportunity to thumb a nose at (*not* kick in the teeth) the parental generation," to "a sense of generational loyalty," to a sheeplike attitude, for fear of being left out, which exceeds the fear of "what they are being led to do."** He makes the point, however, that many "occasional" protesters become "regulars" for reasons that have nothing to do with the issues. Based on the statements of "dozens" of student sit-in attendees, he states, "for most it is one thing and very clear: they discover community." But the brighter ones soon decide that the euphoric "religious" experience of a sit-in is lacking something and, further, that the experience cannot be repeated by repeating the same happening. He concludes that they discover that "community is much more than a warm, crowded nest with lots of cheeping." This "hunger for community," he

* Ibid., p. 33, 34.
** Ibid., p. 30.

285

claims, is not confined to the activists, but to a "majority of students generally."*

This means that we are talking about a student group that for many of us includes our own children and the children of our friends. They are, on the whole, ignorant, misinformed and confused; but they are also intelligent, serious and of decent, primitive habits. . . .

He asserts, however, that the university is ill-suited to fill this gap completely, and it should not attempt to.

That many students have this hunger, even that it is a legitimate hunger, constitutes no necessary reason why we should assuage it. That the university is Alma Mater is no reason for her becoming Omna Mater. The university is only one of many agencies that affect students' lives; it has a character derived from its social functions; and this character can unsuit it to some other functions.**

Professor Schwab proposes changes in the college curriculum to correct a condition stemming largely, he asserts, from "six classes of radical privation requiring curricular attention."*** The statement on the three platitudes, mentioned earlier, was part of a subset of one of these six. A few more are worth mentioning to give some feel for one analyst's observations of students in 1969 that differ greatly from Professor Reich's.

Our students lack resources of durable satisfaction and pleasure.

They are untrained in the arts and disciplines of looking, listening, and reading with respect to form and structure, coherence and cogency. Hence they find little satisfaction in these acts and no impetus toward further development of the competencies involved. This indicates a special obligation of the humane disciplines.

Our students lack knowledge of the character and location of meaning and are consequently irresponsible in their use and reception of language. They are ignorant of canons of evidence and argument, and hence poorly equipped to judge solutions to problems.****

* Ibid., pp. 30–32.
** Ibid., pp. 32–33.
*** Ibid., p. 36.
**** Ibid., p. 40.

286

In the area of decision-making, he says of the students:

They are ignorant of what is involved in the processes of decision and choice.

Most students are under the impression that good decisions are immediately derivable by simple matching of "principles" and cases; that decisions otherwise constructed are products of compromise out of cowardice and self-interest—all these terms, including "compromise," being used invidiously. They are unaware of the complexity of actual cases: the conflict of principle which exists in almost all cases and inevitably requires compromise; the difficulty of bringing even one principle to bear on the ambiguities of real cases.

They lack experience in collaboration toward *proximate* goals. They believe that cooperation is possible only among persons who agree in all respects (doctrinalism). They are self-conditioned to behave accordingly, feeling uneasiness and distraction among persons whom they suspect of differing from themselves in "values," commitments, and ultimate goals. They have had little conscious experience of the fruitful collaboration that can result from discovery of common proximate goals among persons otherwise differing.*

He suggests a curriculum to help dissipate, to the degree that it can, the feeling among radical and other students that they are aliens on the campus. He would rectify other wrongs to the young and through them the wrongs to the university. He feels strongly that the curriculum at present does not give the students sufficient opportunities to exercise their competence. This he would change.**

We may or may not agree with Professor Schwab's conclusions, and we need not agree with his proposed solutions. We cannot, however, easily ignore his estimate that students (at least as of 1969) were not equipped to cope with the learning process there—let alone make judgments on difficult policy decisions. Nor can we ignore the impression one gets that Schwab feels there are things wrong with some recent student activists, particularly among those who are committed activists, which might be traced to neurosis, for the warnings are not confined to his study.

For example, Dr. Herbert Hendin, a research psychiatrist at St. Luke's Hospital and a member of the faculty of the Columbia Univer-

* Ibid., pp. 37, 38.
** Ibid., p. 40–41.

287

sity Psychoanalytic Clinic, has worked with a number of student revolutionaries who, for a fee, agreed to be subjects for an experiment (none had come to the clinic on their own for treatment). A series of interviews with fifteen such students obviously caused him to have sincere concern for these young people, who had considerable inner turmoil. The examples cited in an article* indicate that the political rebellion of these young people is often really a manifestation of rebellion against personal difficulties. These ranged from an apparent need for greater restraints by parents and other adults to personal rejection by friends, much of which emerged in political symbolism. There was also an indication that these students suffered because their parents had abdicated their positions of responsibility. Often their parents had failed to meet the students' problems head-on; other times they had devoted too much attention to the political positions of students and not enough to their psychological needs. Many times parents had capitulated to students' demands out of fear.

Hendin contends, however, that the "existence of inner turmoil does not invalidate" the students' critique of society—on the contrary:

But to discuss the historical and social forces that produce revolutionaries without knowing who student revolutionaries are or what they feel is misguided. However, even analysts and social scientists have ignored this inner dimension because of their involvement in the politics of the students. Agreeing with many of the students' criticisms of society, many psychoanalysts and social scientists try to become students' advocates and allies.**

He says, furthermore, that students can see through, and have a "benign contempt" for, "compassion that has its source in fear and sentimentality." His final sentence relates the remark of an arraigned student after a judge had given a "sympathetic talk on the problems of students today," and suspended sentence: " 'He means well, but with fools like that running the system, how can the revolution help but succeed?' "***

A speech given in Philadelphia by Dr. Bruno Bettelheim, noted psychiatrist and professor at the University of Chicago (with whom Dr.

* "A Psychoanalyst Looks at Student Revolutionaries," *New York Times Magazine*, January 17, 1971, p. 16.
** Ibid., p. 30.
*** Ibid.

288

Hendin differs somewhat), tended to corroborate Hendin's point on the role of "permissiveness."

Many parents are failing to "explain, understand and help" their children resolve "identity crisis" which underlie much of the unrest of today's young generation, he said.

He cited case studies in which a parent's refusal to put his foot down— impose his views on his child—resulted in the child's growing up confused, emotionally abandoned and radical. He urged parents to reason with their children. . . .

[He] told of a father who even refused to "advise" his daughter whether to participate in a campus riot.

Parents would "rather risk killing" their children than have "an exchange" with them, he said.

As a result, these children . . . are forever acting out unresolved Oedipal complexes, they have been robbed of adult figures with which to positively identify, he said. . . .

[They] oversimplify issues like poverty, through which they seek escape from their own deprivation, he said.*

Despite the small size of these samples and the possibly less than optimum study efforts, I would argue that a prudent man must conclude, on the evidence, that he should take a cautious approach toward the political and social proclivities of activist students. Also, from this same evidence, it would seem that responsible people should be careful when involving activists in the analysis- and decision-making processes, whether in school or out. As indicated earlier, such involvement may have undesirable consequences, not only for society, but, perhaps even more importantly, for these young people themselves. A group which is likely to contain a high percentage of the "decoupled," impractical, apparently often unhappy and humorless—and possibly even somewhat disturbed—activists of the colleges and Radical Leftists of the high schools, is perhaps injured by being told it is an elite "vanguard." The added responsibility of making decisions on complex issues (a task at which, in the realm of reality, many apparently are likely to have little competence), without being able to seek the advice of several categories of competent adults (which seems to be hardest for this group), may be very disturbing to them. One must also be concerned

* *Philadelphia Inquirer*, February 4, 1971, p. 1.

when such persons, with their probable bad judgment and lack of decision-making competence, are turned to for leadership in developing campus modes and mores, college courses and curriculum—to say nothing of "life styles" for youth, political policy, or cures for social ills.

2. NON-STUDENTS, TYPES OF STUDENTS, LIFE STYLES AND TRENDS

There are different types of youth just as there are different types of adults, and as with adults, their opinions vary with age and other factors. This becomes clear in polls that categorize youth. We find, again as one would expect, large differences in outlook between college student youth and non-student youth. (It is well to recall that as of June 1970, when half of the high school graduates went to college, those youths who finished high school and did not go to college represented about 28 percent of the excellent, 29 of the above-average, and 62 of the average high school students. The capability of high school students in this last category should not be underestimated because 40 percent of the college students came from it. Among the young people who do not go to college, 29 percent have mothers who are college graduates, 46 percent have mothers who are high school graduates, and the same percentages have fathers with those levels of education.)* There are, as we have also seen, differences between college students. A survey conducted by Daniel Yankelovich, Inc., for *Fortune* (based on 1968 data) breaks down non-students from its sample of youth and divides college students into two new categories: the "forerunners" and the "practical-minded." According to *Youth and the Establishment,***

The Yankelovich/Fortune study of 1968 identified a large segment of college students (44 percent) whose motivation in going to college contrasted with

* Several studies of high school students in 1954 and 1959 indicated that "a very large proportion of the sample's brightest students did not enter college." Furthermore, in 1959 the probability of the "academically able" children of lower-income families going to college was highly dependent on many factors; for example, whether there was a college in their home town (53 percent went if there were; only 22 percent if there weren't); but their more affluent, equally competent peers were not so affected: 82 percent of these children went to college regardless if there were a local college or not. (James W. Trent and Leland L. Medsker, *Beyond High School* [San Francisco: Jossey-Bass, 1968], pp. 25, 27.)

** *Youth and the Establishment*, A Report on Research for John D. Rockefeller, 3rd, and the Task Force on Youth, by Daniel Yankelovich, Inc., February 1971, p. 16.

the more career-minded majority. These young people stated that they took the practical advantages of college for granted (e.g., earning more money, having a successful career, enjoying a better position in society). For them college meant something more intangible such as "the opportunity to change things rather than make out well within the existing system." Subsequent research has shown that this motivation for going to college, and the post-affluent attitude it reflects, symbolizes a whole set of new values, attitudes and beliefs we have come to associate with the college rebellion. The gradual dissemination of these new values throughout the society suggests that this group merits the "Forerunner" label. These are the young men and women who are most vocal in their disaffection with the "system," most concerned with social change and most willing (in contrast to their career-minded peers) to make a personal commitment to projects of the type considered here.

Fortune stated that the "forerunners" had the "attitude toward college and careers" which "will become more prevalent in the years ahead."°
The survey for *Youth and the Establishment*, as well as that done in

Table 123

CURRENT ISSUES—FORTUNE POLL**

Which, if any, of the presidential candidates comes close to your own point of view?

	No college	Practical college	Forerunner college
Nixon	31%	38%	27%
Humphrey	23	24	17
Wallace	25	9	3
None of these	15	25	50

What do you think is the most important problem facing this country today?

Vietnam war	48	37	27
Racial problems and civil rights	27	31	32
Crime and lawlessness	14	12	4
Politics (the election, leaders, etc.)	9	10	11
Lack of understanding	6	7	13
General unrest in the nation	5	11	17
Breakdown in morals, respect	5	7	6

° "What They Believe," an article based on a survey by Daniel Yankelovich, Inc., *Fortune,* January 1969, p. 70.
°° Ibid., pp. 70, 71.

1969 for the CBS program, *Generations Apart,* the data from which is included in the above-mentioned study, apparently uses the same categories and presumably the same sample and plotting techniques that were employed in the *Fortune* Yankelovich survey. The category, "practical college," is changed to "career-minded," but "forerunner" remains the same. More important, although the title indicates that this later study is also on "youth," non-students are not included this time. Nonetheless, this report, together with the *Fortune* survey, provides three years of data presumably on very similar samples of students, categorized in the same way by the same polling group, and, in several cases, the same questions were asked all three years. Where this occurred, data for all three years were recorded in the same table.

This and other data, though perhaps too current and spotty to show real "trends" among youth, has been more plentiful in the last few years and should be of value for comparisons with adults, and between different categories of youth.

The 1970 poll asking a different question and giving different choices, but on similar topics and using a similar student sampling (allowing

Table 124

ISSUES OF PARTICULAR CONCERN TO COLLEGE STUDENTS*

	Total	Career-minded	Forerunner
Bringing peace to Vietnam	77%	74%	83%
Fighting poverty	72	67	81
Combating racism	68	64	74
Reducing pollution	68	64	75
Reducing hard drug addiction	53	52	55
Controlling population	50	45	59
Combating crime	44	45	43
Reforming our political institutions	36	25	53
Extending the vote to the 18 year olds	34	33	36
Bringing peace to the Middle East	34	29	41
Curbing inflation	34	34	33
Changing the social system	34	25	51
Limiting the arms race	31	24	44
Legalizing marijuana	27	18	44
Helping the third world	17	10	28
Winning women's rights	14	8	25
Not sure	10	13	4

* *Youth and the Establishment,* p. 24.

292

limitless choices, which makes the percentages incompatible with the other two polls), is given in Table 124.

In answer to a quite different question ("What's wrong with America?"), a Gallup poll of college students (broken down by political views) in December 1970 showed the first two topics similarly lined up. The topics below them are not as closely related to those given in Table 123. The "general unrest in the nation" is somewhat close to "domestic unrest and/or strikes"; and "lack of communication/generation gap" might cover part of the *Fortune* topic, "lack of understanding." Table 124 above is also different and the choices are different, but the 1970 choices and their comparative rankings should be interesting for comparison with a similar sample in 1968 and the poll taken by Gallup in 1970:

Table 125

WHAT'S WRONG WITH AMERICA?*
College Students

| | | Student political views | |
	All students	Total Left	Total Right
Vietnam war	19%	20%	15%
Racial problems	15	14	14
Apathy/uninvolvement	14	13	15
Economic situation/inflation, unemployment, poverty	13	13	9
Polarities/inability to get together	13	20	8
Misplaced values	11	13	10
Domestic unrest/strikes	11	8	17
Youth unrest	10	5	14
Present administration	9	13	8
Air, water, environmental pollution	8	9	8
Lack of communication/generation gap	6	6	6
The system	6	10	2
All others	27	28	21
Don't know	2	1	3

Despite the difference in the question, comparison of polls on these questions might be between the rankings of similar topics. If so, such a comparison seems to show Vietnam and racial issues in the top three

* *Gallup Opinion Index,* No. 68, February 1971, p. 43.

public issues (as distinct from all issues, including those closer to home)* among students from 1968 through 1970. Poverty and unemployment crept into the top four in 1970, but pollution is fourth on the second table, and tenth on the last. In the 1968 poll, more non-students than students and more practical students than forerunners chose Vietnam as the most important problem. In 1970 the "concern" ranking had the forerunners higher than the practical students. In the following 1968 table, the forerunners had the highest percentage who

Table 126

CURRENT ISSUES—FORTUNE POLL**

(Emphasis by underlining added)

	No College	Practical College	Forerunner College
Do you agree with those who have called ours a "sick" society?***			
Yes	44%	32%	50%
Comments in support of this view (some made more than one):			
Too much extremism	34	35	28
Loss of human concern	27	31	34
High crime rate	25	27	15
Defiant, rebellious youth	24	17	11
Hypocrisy in politics	9	17	10
Breakdown of democracy	7	10	12
Fear of social or economic change	1	4	9

In view of the developments since we entered the fighting in Vietnam, do you think the U.S. made a mistake in sending troops to fight there?

Yes	46	51	67
No	42	39	27
Don't know	12	10	6

* For a comparison with college students' interpretation of the ranking of complaints of demonstrators covering both "personal" and public issues in 1969 see Table 105 (42 percent rated "not enough to say in running of college" as a prime "gripe," while 11 percent rated "the Vietnam war" fourth in the list).

** Yankelovich Survey for *Fortune*, January 1969.

*** Polls indicate the general (adult) public refusals to agree that ours is a "sick" society.

Table 126 (continued)

Would you describe yourself as a "hawk" or a "dove?"

Hawk	47	37	20
Dove	37	45	69
Don't know	16	18	11

Aside from the particular issues of the Vietnam war, which of these values do you believe are always worth fighting for?

	No College	Practical College			Forerunner College		
	1968	1968	1969*	1970*	1968	1969	1970
Protecting our national interest	73%	65%	51%	37%	40%	25%	20%
Containing the Communists	68	59	55	41	28	31	17
Counteracting aggression	65	75	64	60	50	47	35
Fighting for our honor	64	44	33	21	20	15	12
Maintaining our position of power in the world	54	46	33	20	22	17	11
Protecting allies	53	51	43	32	37	33	20
Keeping a commitment	30	24	17	14	14	12	14

thought it a "mistake" to have sent troops to Vietnam (about 15 percent higher than adults—see Figure 271) and the highest "dove" rating:

Seventeen magazine's late 1970 poll of students and non-students asked another question that might be considered to be about "fighting for something." It indicated that 90 percent of the boys and 70 percent of the girls in the 18-to-22-year-old bracket feel there is something they would "risk their life for." Fifty-one percent of the boys and 32 of the girls listed loved ones, family and friends as the "something"; 30 percent of the boys, but only 12 of the girls, gave country and United States. Because of the starkness of the question—"would you risk your life?"—combined with a greater range of choices given by *Seventeen,* compared to the broader question with more limited political choices listed in Table 126, it is hard to compare these polls. But "risking one's life for the United States" did not rank first.

On the other hand, the morality issue is apparently not total: 67 percent of all youth (15 to 21 years old) interviewed for the *Life* Harris poll mentioned earlier, said they would work for a "company that handles defense contracts."

* The 1969 and 1970 breakdown under this question comes from *Youth and the Establishment,* pp. 63 and 64.

Table 126A

FORTUNE POLL*

	No College	Practical College	Forerunner College
Which of the following statements express your own values and point of view?			
We should set our own house in order before we police the rest of the world	91%	83%	86%
There are worse things to fear politically than the threat of communism	47	64	82
Do you feel that draft resistance is justified under any circumstances?			
Yes	17	36	67
No	79	61	31
Do you feel that civil disobedience is justified under any circumstances?			
No	77	61	28
Yes	18	32	66
Do you feel that the action of the police at the Chicago Democratic Convention was justified?			
Yes	49	39	21
No	26	40	60
Both sides were at fault	6	13	12
No opinion	19	8	7
Do you feel this country is doing too much, enough, or too little for black people?			
Too much	20	15	7
Enough	45	47	22
Too little	35	38	71
Reasons given (some gave more than one):			
Blacks do not yet have equal opportunity	54	41	40
Blacks' living standard is still too low	36	14	16
There is still too much prejudice against blacks	31	34	38
Would you welcome more emphasis in this country on combating poverty?			
Yes	73	78	87

The following data from the same type of student samples for 1969 and 1970, on entirely different issues, nonetheless may indicate the temper of the two types of students for those two time periods.

* Yankelovich survey, *Fortune,* January 1969.

Table 127

CRITICISM OF AMERICAN SOCIETY*

	Total		Career-minded		Forerunner	
	1969	1970	1969	1970	1969	1970
Our foreign policy is based on our own narrow economic and power interests:						
Strongly agree	31%	48%	26%	42%	37%	56%
Partially agree	53	40	55	43	50	38
Strongly disagree	16	12	19	15	13	6
The whole social system ought to be replaced by an entirely new one; the existing structures are too rotten for repair:						
Strongly agree	7	8	4	5	10	12
Partially agree	28	34	26	29	30	42
Strongly disagree	65	58	70	66	60	46
Computers and other advanced technology are creating an inhuman and impersonal world:						
Strongly agree	18	20	15	17	21	26
Partially agree	46	46	43	46	49	48
Strongly disagree	36	34	42	37	30	26
Severe economic recession and depression are inevitable with our type of economy:	**					
Strongly agree		34		35		33
Partially agree		46		45		46
Strongly disagree		20		20		21
Economic well-being in this country is unjustly and unfairly distributed:						
Strongly agree	33	41	25	33	42	55
Partially agree	50	48	52	52	49	41
Strongly disagree	17	11	23	15	9	4
Basically, we are a racist nation:						
Strongly agree	38	53	32	47	45	63
Partially agree	40	36	45	40	35	29
Strongly disagree	22	11	23	13	20	8
Today's American society is characterized by "injustice, insensitivity, lack of candor and inhumanity":						
Strongly agree	15	26	9	22	21	35
Partially agree	50	49	49	49	53	47
Strongly disagree	35	25	42	29	26	18

* *Youth and the Establishment*, pp. 59 and 60.
** Not asked in 1969.

Table 127 (continued)

The American system of representative democracy can respond effectively to the needs of the people:

Strongly agree	27	23	34	29	20	13
Partially agree	60	55	57	55	62	54
Strongly disagree	13	22	9	16	18	33

Table 128

ATTITUDES TOWARD INSTITUTIONS*

(Should they be changed, reformed or eliminated)

	Total		Career-minded		Forerunner	
	1969	1970	1969	1970	1969	1970
Big Business						
No substantial change	10%	8%	12%	10%	8%	4%
Moderate change	52	42	64	50	40	28
Fundamental reform	35	45	23	37	45	58
Done away with	3	5	1	3	7	10
The Military						
No substantial change	10	5	13	6	6	4
Moderate change	29	23	34	28	23	14
Fundamental reform	50	56	45	57	56	56
Done away with	11	16	8	9	15	26
The Universities						
No substantial change	11	5	16	7	7	2
Moderate change	57	52	58	54	53	48
Fundamental reform	32	42	26	38	40	50
Done away with	—	1	—	1	—	1
Trade Unions						
No substantial change	14	7	18	7	9	6
Moderate change	43	45	39	45	48	44
Fundamental reform	32	40	28	40	34	40
Done away with	11	8	13	8	9	10
The Political Parties						
No substantial change	9	7	13	7	5	7
Moderate change	33	26	37	31	29	18
Fundamental reform	49	50	43	50	55	49
Done away with	9	17	7	12	11	26
The Mass Media						
No substantial change	18	19	23	22	12	14
Moderate change	46	45	49	44	43	48
Fundamental reform	33	34	25	33	41	35
Done away with	3	2	3	1	2	3

* *Youth and the Establishment*, pp. 53-56.

Table 128 (continued)

Congress
No substantial change	°	17	21	11
Moderate change		45	47	42
Fundamental reform		35	32	42
Done away with		3	1	5

FBI
No substantial change	°	40	50	27
Moderate change		29	29	28
Fundamental reform		19	16	22
Done away with		12	5	23

Supreme Court
No substantial change	°	27	28	25
Moderate change		40	41	40
Fundamental reform		30	29	31
Done away with		3	2	4

The Lower Courts
No substantial change	°	14	17	9
Moderate change		44	47	37
Fundamental reform		39	34	48
Done away with		3	2	6

The Penal System
No substantial change	°	5	5	3
Moderate change		26	29	19
Fundamental reform		62	59	68
Done away with		7	5	10

The High School
No substantial change	°	8	10	3
Moderate change		42	46	36
Fundamental reform		49	44	59
Done away with		1	—	2

The Constitution
No substantial change	°	47	51	40
Moderate change		37	35	42
Fundamental reform		14	14	14
Done away with		2	—	4

The last two tables show a degree of radicalism which, if deeply felt, could be disturbing to the average citizen, and which sets the tone for much of the specific data solicited in 1970. About two-thirds of the "forerunners" subscribe to the premise that "current laws do not protect the rights" of American Indians, drug addicts and six categories of radicals and dissenters (a majority of the career-minded agree on the first two). A majority of the "forerunners" "definitely believe" that seven categories of dissenters, radicals and drug

° Not asked in 1969.

addicts "cannot be assured of a fair trial" (a majority of the career-minded feel that way in regard to Black Panthers, radicals, and hippies).* Furthermore, the degree of radical thinking in the two-year samples apparently increased from 1969 to 1970.

Despite the obvious similarity of some high school students' views to their parents', discussed earlier, most youngsters have the normal youthful impatience with the pace of events. It is striking that in the first question in Table 126 on whether this is a sick society, a greater percentage of both non-students and "forerunners" thought so than did "practical" college students. But one must keep in mind that in 1968 the non-students and "forerunners" often had quite different reasons for considering it "sick." In the case of the non-students, part of this feeling apparently came from their apprehension about "defiant and rebellious youth." Fifty-six percent of this group preferred non-liberal candidates in 1968 (Nixon—31; Wallace—25); only a quarter were pro-Humphrey. Although only a third of the "practical" college students subscribed to the idea that this was a sick society, 47 percent of them preferred non-liberal candidates: thirty-eight percent chose Nixon and 9 Wallace; only about half that many (24) selected Humphrey. On this political issue, "practical" college students gave a rather strong "no opinion" response (25 percent), although not so strong as among the "forerunners" (50 percent). Nevertheless, in 1968 the 47 percent (Nixon and Wallace) of this 58 percent of college students ("practical" students), added to the 56 percent of that large majority of youth who were not students, constituted a formidable bloc of opinion among youth still bucking the apparent tide of opinion of much of the media, and of the vast majority of college instructors, particularly those at the "better" schools and in the social sciences.** This support for conservatives and conservatism apparently dwindle rapidly. By the spring of 1970 only 26 percent of students were calling themselves conservatives (see Table 99). Only 7 percent of the 18-to-20 year olds (students and non-students) and 14 of the 21-to-29 year olds were for Wallace in October 1971. But the latter figure had been down to 5 percent in July 1970 and had bounced back to 17 percent in May 1971—18-to-20 year olds were not polled before 1971 (see Table 43).

* Ibid., pp. 65 and 66.
** The "practical" students' political choices look somewhat more like the non-students' than the "forerunners."

Other questions in Table 128 such as "putting our own house in order" obviously could mean quite different things to different groups of youth; but if and insofar as the opinions of the "practical-minded" or "career-minded" students had shifted toward those of the "fore-runners" in 1969 and 1970, as shown in polls of presumably the same samples of students, some of the attitudes of forerunners could be thought to have been prophetic (in the short run) in 1968. According to this 1970 study, as well as other data, some evidence indicates that on several issues, and primarily among college students, this may have been the case. But there were other basic issues where this was not so clear.

Although the time between 1969 and 1970 (or for that matter between 1968 and 1970) may be too brief to substantiate even the simplest conclusions, one could nevertheless argue that, based on the increase or decrease in the percentage of negative or positive answers to the questions, these surveys showed evidence of a trend. On the other hand, there are some responses in these surveys that indicate that on some of these issues there was really a fluctuation in opinion from 1968 through 1970, rather than a trend. Particularly in some basic areas, such as feelings of identity with family and other groups, we get an equal or higher reading for all students in 1970 than we received in 1968 (including "forerunners," who apparently identified much more strongly with the middle class and their nationality in 1970 than in 1968); most 1969 readings on this question are considerably higher than they were in either 1968 or 1970. In other comparisons, the perturbation in 1969 was down from either 1968 or 1970. Perhaps the data in all student (and perhaps even youth) polls were affected because we were getting readings from two "crisis" years (1968—Democratic convention riot and presidential campaign; and 1970—Cambodia, Kent State, students' "strike"; and one "non-crisis" year, 1969). Much would depend on exactly when in each year the polls were conducted.

Another factor in judging changes in student opinions may be that of the parents' influence on them. If we accept the data that show that students identify strongly with their parents, we should probably not rule out the chance that, at least in "non-crisis" years, this will have some effect on students' opinions. If their parents' attitudes, including their political attitudes, do not fluctuate wildly (and they apparently are not doing so now) and the students maintain their identity with

301

their parents, as even most of the "forerunners" do, adult influence on students in "non-crisis" years may still be significant—at least as significant as the students' influence on their parents' opinions. In searching for trends on a chart like the following one, much seems to depend for certain topics on whether we compare 1968 with 1969, 1969 with 1970, or 1968 with 1970. It may even change the "indicator" group. For example, it is interesting to note that on the issue of identification with the family, the non-student attitude in 1968 serves as an indicator for all students in 1969, particularly the "practical" college ones. Even in 1970 more of both types of students identified with their family, according to this data, than in 1968, but when compared with 1969, less did.

The widest spread among the different categories of youth occurs in the identity with students. Less than one in four non-students (at least in 1968) identified with them, but almost three out of four students did.

Table 129

IDENTIFICATION—FORTUNE POLL*

With which of the following groups, if any, do you feel a sense of solidarity and identification?

	No college	Practical college			Forerunner college		
	1968	1968	1969	1970	1968	1969	1970
Your family	82%	78%	80%	84%	65%	75%	72%
The middle class	65	68	80	68	35	60	50
People of your race	61	46	67	48	28	48	35
People of your generation	60	65	85	75	68	81	76
People of your nationality	54	45	60	44	26	48	39
People of your religion	49	46	52	41	32	37	25
Students	23	75	88	94	72	87	91
The new left	3	5	6	7	19	23	26
The old left	2	3	5	2	8	11	5

* Yankelovich survey for *Fortune*, January 1969, p. 71. The 1969 and 1970 data are added for comparison from *Youth and the Establishment*, p. 73.

In another poll on youth the following somewhat related question showed the following:

Table 130

AGREEMENT WITH PARENTS*

Do you agree with your parents' values and ideals?

Yes—73%

This poll was taken of all youth 15 to 21. When asked to choose, from a list of well-known people, those whom they most and least admired, the results were as follows:

HEROES	NON-HEROES
Robert F. Kennedy	Fidel Castro
Bill Cosby	Eldridge Cleaver
Neil Armstrong	George Wallace
John Wayne	Ho Chi Minh

Other choices given, in non-ranked order, included: Vice President Agnew, Joe Namath, Mayor John Lindsay, Elliot Gould, John Lennon, Senator Edmund Muskie, Mark Rudd, General Westmoreland, Bob Dylan, President Nixon, Vince Lombardi, and John Gardner.

Table 131

ADMIRATION AND DISLIKE—FORTUNE POLL**

Which, if any, of these men do you admire?

	No college	Practical college	Forerunner college
Edward Kennedy	58%	50%	56%
Richard Nixon	30	29	19
George Wallace	30	17	7
Lyndon Johnson	26	24	11
Hubert Humphrey	25	16	16
Eugene McCarthy	24	45	65
Mayor Richard Daley	15	15	9
Stokely Carmichael	5	7	20
John Kenneth Galbraith	3	17	34
Allen Ginsberg	2	5	22
Paul Goodman	2	4	13
Che Guevara	1	6	20
Herbert Marcuse	1	2	9

* Louis Harris Poll, *Life*, January 8, 1971, p. 23.
** Yankelovich survey for *Fortune*, January 1969, pp. 71 and 72.

Table 132A

FOR PRESIDENT IN 1972?*

Whom would you like to see elected President in 1972?

Kennedy	20.9%
Nixon	19.0
McCarthy	12.7
Muskie	8.6
Wallace	7.8
Humphrey	6.1
Julian Bond	3.6
McGovern	3.0
Agnew	2.5
Reagan	2.1
Rockefeller	1.9
Howard Hughes	.6
Birch Bayh	.2
No opinion	2.6

Table 132B

HIGHLY FAVORABLE AND FAVORABLE RATINGS AMONG COLLEGE STUDENTS—DECEMBER 1970**

Lindsay	81%
McCarthy	79
Muskie	78
McGovern	76
Kennedy	75
Rockefeller	63
Humphrey	60
Nixon	49
Reagan	48
Agnew	36
Wallace	16

In their responses to these questions, in 1968 the "practical" students often looked more like the non-college youths than do the "forerunners"; but perhaps the most interesting single item in the foregoing tables was the overwhelming *lack* of identity with students on the part of the non-students in that same year. The general lack of identity with activists was also apparent, and the lack of identity with students who were destructive seems to have been almost universal with youth as a whole in 1970.

* *Seventeen*, February 1971, p. 119. The questions in this poll were asked of all youth between 14 and 22.
** *Gallup Opinion Index*, No. 68, February 1971, p. 21.

The *Seventeen* poll showed indications of a lack of sympathy with *disorderly* students on the part of all youth, including high school and college students, college-bound students and recent college graduates:[*]

College administrators in the handling of campus disturb- ances have	Total Youth	Total Boys	Boys 14–17	Boys 18–22	Total Girls	Girls 14–17	Girls 18–22
not been strict enough	43%	44%	44%	45%	42%	45%	39%
handled them about right	28	26	31	22	29	31	28
been too repressive	29	30	25	33	29	24	33
Should police or National Guard be called during a demonstration where damage or violence occurs							
Yes	95	93	93	94	95	97	94
No	5	7	7	6	5	3	6

The Purdue Opinion Panel showed even more hostility among tenth-, eleventh-, and twelfth-grade students toward disorderly college students:[**]

Law officers, like state or local police, should be called to the campus when college students cause disturbances.	Definitely Agree	Probably Agree	Definitely Disagree	Probably Disagree
All students	52%	23%	11%	10%
College-bound students	51	24	11	10

The lack of identity of the non-students with students does not at all mean that the person who did not attend college is mindlessly under the influence of adults. (In fact see Table 95 and the discussion before it, and the discussion after Table 142, for the possible similarities between all youth [15-21] and college students [mostly 18-22] in choices of political parties.) In Table 29 note that in 1968 the majority of non-students (60 percent—a smaller majority compared to even greater ones of 65 and 68 for "practical" and "forerunner" students, but still a clear majority) said they felt "a sense of solidarity and identification" with persons of their "generation," yet only 23 percent felt this way about students (compared to 75 and 72 percent in 1968, 88 and 87 percent in 1969, and 94 and 91 percent in 1970 for the two student categories). Clearly—at least according to the *Fortune* poll of late

[*] *Seventeen*, February 1971, p. 127.
[**] Purdue Opinion Panel, *Report of Poll No. 90*, January 1971, pp. 23a and 24a.

1968—this vast majority of youth did not feel that students spoke for them.*

According to the following 1968 table, many of the students' and non-students' responses indicated that they had the normal feelings of independence and impatience with their parents, as well as those feelings shared among all youth that differ from what they assume their parents' feelings on the same subjects to be. It is the intensity of these feelings among various categories of "youth" that differ; normally, the non-students were on one end of the continuum and the "fore-runners" on the other. On the "faith in the democratic process" ques-tion, however, the non-students are closer to the "forerunners." This response may be hard to evaluate, however, because like the "sick society" question, it could reflect some "right-wing" sentiment against excessive permissiveness as well as disillusioned "Radical Leftism."

Table 133
YOUTHS' AND PARENTS' ATTITUDES—FORTUNE POLL**
Are the following attitudes more applicable to you or your parents?

	No college	Practical college	Forerunner college
Likely to compromise with things you don't like			
Parents	44%	45%	56%
Self	20	20	16
Respectful of people in positions of authority			
Parents	41	42	56
Self	16	8	4
Likely to accept things as they are			
Parents	40	44	52
Self	31	26	24
Fearful of financial insecurity			
Parents	39	40	47
Self	33	28	18
Have faith in the democratic process			
Parents	38	30	50
Self	11	18	13

* Note also the wide spread between the numbers of high school Radical Leftists in 1970 (13 to 16 percent) and people of the same persuasion among the "forerunners" (38 percent), based on answers to virtually identical questions (see Table 96 and Youth and the Establishment, p. 36).

** Yankelovich survey for Fortune, January 1969, p. 179.

Table 133 (continued)

Tolerant of other people's views			
Parents	31	20	15
Self	43	57	60
Honest with oneself			
Parents	25	19	14
Self	24	26	39
Interested in other people			
Parents	24	16	11
Self	37	49	43
Interested in money			
Parents	23	28	48
Self	37	23	12
Likely to do something about what you believe to be right			
Parents	22	13	8
Self	33	36	50
Open to the world			
Parents	16	8	7
Self	55	54	66
Interested in beauty			
Parents	15	9	9
Self	40	42	43
Optimistic about the future			
Parents	14	17	23
Self	63	49	42
Self-centered			
Parents	14	9	17
Self	36	53	43
Concerned with what is happening to the country			
Parents	14	12	9
Self	36	35	45

In the area of some more basic questions, however, there is a striking difference of opinion between non-students and students. The feelings of non-students here are closer to their parents'; those of the "practical" college students lie in the center. But on some very important questions of self-discipline—"Which of these restraints, imposed by society and its institutions, can you accept easily? Requirement that you be married before you live with someone" and "The power and authority of the 'boss' in a work situation"—the "practical" students were closer to the "forerunners" than to the non-students in 1968.

Unfortunately, we have no figures on this question for non-students in 1969 and 1970. The polls of those two years seem to indicate that the work attitudes of the "forerunners" might have been prophetic for college students of 1970 because of the decreased numbers of college students who can "easily accept" the "power and authority of the 'boss' in a work situation." In 1968 the "forerunners" registered 52 percent who could, and by 1969 the "career-minded" had decreased to 50 percent. Whether all students will eventually drop to the 1970 figure for the "forerunners"— only 29 percent can "easily" accept this situation—and whether or not this trend should be discouraged (or at least not encouraged) can lead to some interesting speculation. On other issues—for example, staying away from marijuana and harder drugs, abiding by unpopular laws and even conforming in matters of dress—the opinion of both categories of students fluctuated over the three years, and the "practical" college students seemed not to follow the "forerunners'" earlier opinions. In fact, in two out of five cases, the "practical" college students could have been considered the prophetic group; that is, the "forerunners'" opinion in 1970 veered more toward the "practical" college opinion of 1969. (In another case—abiding by unpopular laws—the decrease of the positive response of the "forerunners" bottomed out at 12 percent in 1969 and stayed there in 1970, and the "practical" college students' response increased from 17 to 21 percent).

When the subject of careers was discussed with the young in 1969, their responses were more similar than the criteria—which supposedly led to the definition of the groups as "practical-minded" and "forerunners"—might imply. All three categories of youth rated the "challenge of the job" higher than the "money earned." All groups ranked "prestige and status of job" *last*. All categories put "opportunity to make a meaningful contribution" *above* "ability to express yourself," "importance of the job" and "prestige and status of the job." This seems to caution against reading more than may be warranted into the criterion of the "forerunners" and "career-minded" students given in the *Fortune* poll and in *Youth and the Establishment*.

The most pronounced difference was in their attitudes toward salary and the influence of their family on their decision to take a position— but, of course, there were differences of degree on all issues. On the matter of salary and family influence in 1968, "practical" students were closer to the non-students. The non-college group normally includes the largest number of young persons from low-income families, so this may be the reason for their citing the money interest. Among the

Table 134

ACCEPTANCE OF RESTRAINTS—FORTUNE POLL*

Which of these restraints, imposed by society and its institutions, can you accept easily?

	No college	Practical college			Forerunner college		
	1968	1968	1969	1970	1968	1969	1970
The prohibition against marijuana	77%	69%	59%	59%	37%	35%	30%
The prohibition against other drugs	85	83	82	90	63	63	84
The power and authority of the "boss" in a work situation	74	60	56	50	52	40	29
Requirement that you be married before you live with someone	69	50			36		
Conforming in matters of clothing and personal grooming	65	45	39	44	28	24	28
Outward respectability for the sake of career advancement	54	39			17		
Having little decision-making power in the first few years of a job	48	38			23		
Abiding by laws you don't agree with	43	35	17	21	21	12	12
Showing respect for people you may not, in fact, respect	33	25			17		
Pressures to close one's eyes to dishonest behavior	9	3			2		

"practical" college students, a third were from blue-collar families, and possibly some of the same incentive may be at work here. On the matter of the importance of the job, the non-students were closer to the "forerunners."

Some answers are interesting in respect to which groups have changed, and occasionally (considering other data, such as the growing disapproval of adults of so many things for which the "forerunners'" approval continued to grow) what unexpected directions these changes

* Ibid., p. 180. The 1969 and 1970 data are from *Youth and the Establishment*, pp. 51–52.

took. For example, "family" influence has increased among the "fore-runners" and decreased among "practical" college students; the importance of the ability to express themselves has decreased drastically among "practical" college students and only slightly among "fore-runners."

Table 135

INFLUENCE ON CAREER—FORTUNE POLL*

Which of these items will have a very great influence on your choice of career?

	No College	Practical College		Forerunner College	
	1968	1968	1970	1968	1970
Own family	62%	48%	46%	25%	32%
Challenge of the job	61	77	64	74	63
Money that can be earned	57	58	46	21	19
Opportunity to make a meaningful contribution	55	71	68	80	82
Stimulation of the job	52	70		77	
Ability to express yourself	50	63	48	75	71
Importance of the job	42	55		46	
Prestige or status of the job	34	33		13	

The Harris poll of all 15 to 21 year olds—students and non-students—in late 1970 also seemed to show a lack of interest in some of the more selfish career-related factors:**

"What factors are most important in choosing a job?"

1. Enjoyable work
2. Pride in the job
3. Pleasant working conditions
4. Creative satisfaction

"Least important factors":

1. Short hours
2. Recognition by society
3. Achieving status

A 1970 report by the Gilbert Youth Survey on the life styles most appealing to youth between the ages of 14 and 25 breaks down people by age, sex, education, status (student, non-student) and so forth. This report seems to show some "traditional" attitudes as far as the type of life style youngsters find appealing.

* Ibid., p. 181; the 1970 figures are from *Youth and the Establishment*, p. 39.
** Louis Harris Poll, *Life*, January 8, 1971, p. 24.

Table 136*

Females

Life style found to be most appealing:	Total	Age				Education					
		Under 17	17–18	19–21	22–24	Out of School—Not High School Graduate	In High School	Out of School—High School Graduate	Out of School—Some College	In College	College Graduate
1 Executive or professional, living with own family in good area	26%	29%	27%	21%	26%	22%	30%	16%	21%	35%	31%
2 Single girl with good job, living well in own apartment in major city	14	19	19	10	8	12	22	7	7	15	11
3 Free of obligations, living where and with whom you please	10	12	11	12	5	4	10	9	12	13	6
4 Working to solve social problems, unconcerned about material things	7	6	8	6	7	9	6	5	6	10	15
5 Average housewife with children, time for family and outside interests	42	32	34	50	53	53	31	63	54	26	37

* Finance-Related Attitudes of Youth—1970, A Report on a Nationwide Survey of Today's Young Americans between the ages of 14 and 25 (Gilbert Youth Survey), Institute of Life Insurance, Division of Statistics and Research: New York, 1970.

Table 137*

Females Life style found to be most appealing:	Total	Race		Financial Background					Father's Education			
		White	Nonwhite	Prosperous	Above Average	Average	Below Average	Poor	Some High School	High School Graduate	Some College	College Graduate
1 Executive or professional, living with own family in good area	26%	26%	27%	34%	28%	23%	32%	37%	26%	25%	24%	30%
2 Single girl with good job, living well in own apartment in major city	14	12	29	7	15	15	13	7	14	15	17	11
3 Free of obligations, living where and with whom you please	10	10	7	12	11	9	9	13	7	7	8	20
4 Working to solve social problems, unconcerned about material things	7	7	5	9	6	7	6	7	7	5	12	9
5 Average housewife with children, time for family and outside interests	42	44	31	35	40	45	37	40	46	46	38	28

* Ibid.

Table 138*

Males		Age				Education					
Life style found to be most appealing:	Total	Under 17	17–18	19–21	22–24	Out of School— Not High School Graduate	In High School	Out of School— High School Graduate	Out of School— Some College	In College	College Graduate
1 Executive or professional, living with own family in good area	30%	30%	28%	32%	31%	13%	30%	25%	42%	35%	25%
2 Bachelor with good job, living well in own apartment in major city	26	28	33	24	17	40	32	23	13	21	8
3 Free of obligations, living where and with whom you please	15	14	14	16	16	18	14	14	17	15	17
4 Working to solve social problems, unconcerned about material things	9	6	6	12	11	3	5	8	10	16	21
5 Average family man, nine-to-five job, time for family and outside interests	20	22	18	16	23	26	19	29	18	12	25

* Ibid.

313

Table 139*

Males	Total	Race		Financial Background					Father's Education			
		White	Nonwhite	Prosperous	Above Average	Average	Below Average	Poor	Some High School	High School Graduate	Some College	College Graduate
Life style found to be most appealing:												
1 Executive or professional, living with own family in good area	30%	29%	40%	28%	31%	31%	28%	10%	35%	29%	30%	25%
2 Bachelor with good job, living well in own apartment in major city	26	25	28	23	27	26	22	26	23	26	24	30
3 Free of obligations, living where and with whom you please	15	16	6	23	15	13	19	18	9	14	19	20
4 Working to solve social problems, unconcerned about material things	9	9	6	15	10	8	6	3	8	6	9	18
5 Average family man, nine-to-five job, time for family and outside interests	20	20	20	10	16	23	21	37	23	24	18	6

* Ibid.

This data from the Gilbert Survey, based on a 3,000 subject sample, seems to indicate that life style 4 ("Working to solve social problems, unconcerned about material things") attracts fewer across all categories of youth than "hippie" life style 3 ("Free of obligations living where and with whom you please"), and only a fraction of those who prefer the "squarest" life styles 1 ("Executive or professional living with own family in good area") and 5 ("Average family man or housewife, 9-to-5 job, children, outside interests"). Those in college or graduated from it show a heavier preference for life style 4, but still not nearly so strong a preference as for life style 1, 2 or 5. College graduates show the heaviest preference for life style 4 (15 percent of women and 21 percent of men), but in their case, too, both 1 and 5 are more appealing (particularly among women). College students show about 10 percent of girls and 16 percent of boys finding life style 4 the "most appealing." It seems clear, however, that college students and graduates differ significantly from other "youth" on the attractiveness of life style 4. It is also apparent that the affluence and educational level of the parents of male youth affects the probability of their choosing life style 4.

There appears to be some question, however, about how to interpret the relationship between this poll and the poll in Table 140 regarding attitudes of college students.

The questions on these surveys should, one feels, have had some relationship. One poll talks of commitments to certain efforts for a considerable time, the other talks of most appealing life styles. Presumably one of these life styles should be identified with the upper brackets of the commitment priorities, but probably without a strong sense of permanency in that life style. Yet in the preceding survey of all youth there is nothing like a 50 percent choice of such a life style among college students (which seems to be indicated by this table).*

The preceding data show a difference between types of youth. Furthermore, generally speaking, in any given year the "forerunners" differ with most students and non-students, as well as with adults. They

* When college students in the survey which produced Table 140 were asked the probability of their "devoting six months of their lives to working on social issues or problems," 36 percent (career-minded 27, forerunners 47) gave an 80 to 100 percent probability, and 13 percent for both categories gave a 60 to 70 percent probability. (Ibid, p. 40.) We have no breakdown for the probability the college students choosing life style number 4 in the preceding survey of all youth assign to their "devoting" themselves to it for any length of time, so we cannot make a comparison with these percentages.

Table 140

COMMITMENT ISSUES

(Issues to which young people will be willing to make a personal commitment such as devoting a year or two of their lives.)[*]

	Total	Career-minded	Forerunner
Fighting poverty	48%	43%	58%
Reducing pollution	34	33	37
Combating racism	33	26	34
Bringing peace to Vietnam	28	28	29
Reducing hard drug addiction	25	25	25
Controlling population	23	19	30
Reforming the political institutions	18	10	30
Changing the social system	17	10	29
Combating crime	15	15	15
Extending the vote to 18 year olds	10	10	9
Legalizing marijuana	9	6	16
Curbing inflation	8	6	10
Limiting the arms race	8	5	12
Bringing peace to the Middle East	9	7	14
Helping the third world	7	5	11
Winning women's rights	4	3	7
None	10	13	6
Not sure	33	35	29

are generally "left" of everyone[**]; in 1968 they were, in most cases, further left of the "practical-minded" students than the "practical" students were of the non-students. To the extent and on the issues that the students as a whole went left in 1969 and 1970, the 1968 and 1969 "forerunners" may be said to be "prophetic" for 1969 and 1970. As indicated earlier, the 1969 and 1970 samples in *Youth and the Establishment* deviated from the 1968 data for the *Fortune* poll. In the two later surveys no non-students were polled, so, strictly speaking, these two later surveys are not on "youth" but on students. Furthermore, the last survey conducted in 1970 also included adults. The 1970 sample was made up of 872 college students and 408 "business executives and other

[*] *Youth and the Establishment*, p. 27.
[**] Although internal evidence in the 1968 Yankelovich-*Fortune* data suggests that some could be considered "Right-wingers," as does even some later evidence in *Youth and the Establishment*, p. 36.

	Conservative		Middle Group		Radical Left	
	1969	1970	1969	1970	1969	1970
Career-minded	21%	13%	71%	74%	8%	13%
Forerunners	10	4	69	58	21	38

(See Table 96 for the choices of statements which lead to these classifications.)

Establishment leaders." (The choice of the latter group was "heavily weighted toward the larger corporations," and the higher management of these corporations: "the main target would be corporate leadership supplemented by other groups and persons. . . ."*)

As we have seen, the data gathered for *Youth and the Establishment* contains much interesting material on the two categories of students; but, unfortunately, all questions were not identical to those reported in the 1968 *Fortune* survey. The comparisons the study does make between 1969 and 1970 do, in many cases, seem to show an increase in what might be called "radicalism" in both the "forerunners" and the "career-minded" students during that period; and the evidence of this study, as well as some other data mentioned earlier, might have led some to contend that—at least on some issues—the "forerunners" seemed to be just that. For example, regarding the quetsion of whether the United States made a mistake in sending combat forces to Vietnam, the "forerunners" were not only forerunners for the attitude of youth, but for that of the nation as a whole.** But as we have seen earlier, as wars drag on (particularly "inconclusively") the direction of the degree of support for wars has normally been downward throughout the last quarter of the century, so what the "forerunners" did (no doubt unknowingly) was to take a position that was somewhat ahead of the public—although the latter was already headed in that direction.

The same is true about the "ecology" movement. This coincides with what has been a largely unheralded attitude of probably a majority of Americans since President Theodore Roosevelt. College activists may get more media coverage when they become involved, but that does not mean they are any better "forerunners" of the trend of the public mood on this issue than are longtime ecologists such as Conservative Senator James Buckley, the Audubon Society, the National Rifle Association, the National Wildlife Federation, and thousands of rod and gun clubs and citizens' associations. Of course, everyone welcomes the increased publicity for such a cause, but there may be some drawbacks; for example, the students' often simplistic "solutions" and their radical political outlook and personal behavior may "turn off" many

* Ibid., pp. 15 and 16.
** As of July 1971 the general population had not yet reached the level of 67 percent opposition to the war (see Figure 27) reached by the "forerunners" in 1968. On the other hand, fewer "forerunners" than non-students or even "practical" students considered it the "most important" problem facing the nation in 1968—see Table 123.

effective and experienced conservationists. Such phenomena, however, may make it difficult for commentators to identify the genuine pace-setting attitude. The army of traditional ecologists, contributing their money and time in the cause of conservation, may be dull and "non-newsworthy" compared to young, radical activists, but the "average man" might well ask if movements without majority support are more likely to turn into fads. Therefore, is not the opinion of the group capable of providing the momentum for true "trends" just as significant, if not more so, than that of any young "activist" group?

Another problem is that even in *Youth and the Establishment,* which, together with the Yankelovich survey for *Fortune* in 1968, on some topics, generally reflects a continuing study concentrating on students, and only the short time span between 1968 and 1970 is compared, some data, as we have seen, occasionally break the "trend." Further, we do not know what significance for the future lies in this data. Where a trend does seem to appear, from this data as well as others, it is far from a universal phenomenon, covering all subject areas. I am prone to be cautious in such analysis, particularly when dealing with young dissidents of either the Left or the Right. Historically, student groups touted as avant-garde have not always been prophetic, at least in the short run, even for campus attitudes. The vocal left-wing students who supported Henry A. Wallace for President in 1948 may have been considered—or even have considered themselves—"fore-runners." But they were hardly the "wave of the future" on the college scene in the 1950s. The hard-working, much more reserved G.I. Bill students, on the other hand, might have given a foretaste of the middle-of-the-road, "Silent Fifties." Nor were the "silent" student pace-setters for the "Silent Fifties" the precursors of the 1960s. In fact, the very same students, particularly the radical ones of the late 1940s, seemed to have altered their behavioral patterns at least when they graduated from college and reached their late twenties and early thirties. Further, as we have seen, some of the larger youth surveys between 1968 and 1970 apparently showed some deviations from some of these "trends."

3. ADULT EVALUATION OF THE ROLE OF "YOUTH" IN OUR SOCIETY

Youth's new role in society has perhaps been examined more closely by more people, and been defined by more important men in recent years than ever before in modern history. Some of what these persons and groups have discussed about this matter seems to conform to a rough general pattern. In this respect, one thrust of the Task Force rec-

318

ommendations in *Youth and the Establishment* is perhaps more interesting than the poll data on students and adults. The apparent aim was
to find ways to get students, particularly the "forerunners," and Establishment leaders to collaborate, initially during a week of "dialogue,"
on defining (in one case, the students' primary job) and finding ways
of solving (in the same case, the Establishment leaders' primary job)
some of the country's great problems.* Further, according to the report, "major emphasis would be on the 'forerunner' student group,
with secondary emphasis on the more 'career-minded' majority of college students," and this was one of the criteria used in "screening
candidate projects" to be undertaken by youth and influential members of the Establishment.** This would be a privileged and potentially
influential position for these Left-leaning young people—about whom
the average citizen might have some qualms. The subjects which these
college students (and/or new graduates) and Establishment leaders
were expected to be able to get together on—the study found that
despite their overwhelming rejection of, and "anger or impatience
toward student rebellion," there was much less "student backlash
among business leaders as a group than the general public"—
were poverty, racism, pollution, overpopulation, and drug addiction.
"Both groups" were said to "see the need of *reforming our political
institutions to get the job done*" (italics mine). In addition, the Task
Force apparently felt that the greater likelihood of the "forerunners"
making themselves available for this high-level conference group was
a reason for using them.***

This has been a far-from-unique approach recently. Similar ideas
have been discussed in other quarters, but availability (and even
"concern") is a somewhat questionable criterion—even a minor one
—for competence in dealing with complex issues. Among the other
pitfalls of placing the "forerunners"—a specific minority of students
—is the danger that in this "conference" environment the group may
progress from being only "forerunners" of the students to "forerunners"
of all society.

---

* In a suggested week of "dialogue" on eliminating poverty, for example:
"Individual projects would be planned to give young people primary roles
in diagnosis and problem identification and adult members primary roles
in problem solution." (*Youth and the Establishment*, pp. 17–18.)
Such efforts were looked on as the beginning of a long term "ongoing process"
(p. 89).
** *Youth and the Establishment*, p. 16.
*** See Table 6; ibid., pp. 28 (finding 3), 34, 38 and 39 (findings 5, 11, and 12).

Indeed, this study states: "We believe these young people [that is, the forerunners] will *not* change their basic outlook once they are out of college."* This may be true on some issues, but to the extent that this implies that their resistance to change will apply to "basic outlook" across the board, and that it will persist long after they leave college, this group could be somewhat atypical of college students. On issues where students as a whole were asked about their feelings in later life, they usually tended to feel they would have changing interests in some very basic areas. Further, this and other data indicate that not only do young persons (including college students) change their attitudes on some issues as they grow older, but that they may expect to (some perhaps under duress) in the basic areas. In a poll taken by a Johns Hopkins team in late 1970 of almost 8,000 freshmen and juniors of four-year colleges (but not including predominantly Negro schools or "specialized institutions"), 87 percent listed "family life" and 64 percent picked "their careers" as what "would be. . . most important to them in ten years." The Johns Hopkins study group claimed that this student group represented the life styles of about three-fourths of all students** A summary for all youth on the issues of current and future life styles, gathered in response to a different question on the same subject (life styles) for *Finance-Related Attitudes of·Youth 1970* (p. 14), is given in Table 140A.

We are, of course, aware that there has been a slow liberalizing trend in the nation over the decades. Liberals of one era may appear more conservative in subsequent decades, although their political outlook may have changed little. Nevertheless, behavioral attitudes and political views seem to change with age and additional responsibilities —particularly among the radical young, including those who are college students.***

We are also told "we must broaden our frame of reference from

* Ibid., p. 82.
** *Philadelphia Inquirer,* February 12, 1971, p. 20.
*** See Appendix, "The Changing Attitudes of a College Class," and Seymour Martin Lipset and Everett Carll Ladd, "The College Generations—from the 1930s to the 1960s," *The Public Interest,* No. 25 (Fall 1971). It seems logical to expect people to abandon some of their extreme ideas as they become older and are thrust into a position of responsibility; for example, a father of a teen-age girl is less likely to hold the same opinions on free love that he did as a late adolescent. In the political area, Lipset and Ladd point out, for example, that college student communists are likely not to be communists long. In the 1930s and 1940s, when 750,000 people belonged to the Communist party, the "turnover rate some years was 90 percent and most people had joined *and* left the party by the age of 23."

Table 140A*

LIFE STYLE THE RESPONDENT FINDS:

Five life styles:	Most Appealing			Least Appealing			What the Respondent Expects to Be 15 Years from Now		
	Total	Male	Female	Total	Male	Female	Total	Male	Female
1. Executive or professional, living with own family in good area	28%	30%	26%	9%	11%	7%	31%	34%	27%
2. Single person with good job, living well in own apartment in major city	20	26	14	17	16	19	8	10	6
3. Free of obligations, living where and with whom you please	13	15	10	35	28	42	8	10	5
4. Working to solve social problems, unconcerned about material things	8	9	7	20	21	19	8	9	7
5. Average family person (routine job if man, housewife if woman), time for outside interests	30	20	42	18	24	12	43	35	52

Note: Occasionally, table percentages may not add up to 100 percent due to rounding, or where multiple responses to questions are involved.

* Gilbert Youth Survey, Institute of Life Insurance, op. cit.

321

'forerunner' college students to include those of similar outlook who have already graduated from college or dropped out or never attended college."* This makes the concept even more confusing; this statement does not describe a valid "broadening" process. The difficulty here is that we may be working backward; that is, we may find the "outlook" then we "include" people based on their "similar outlook," not necessarily their qualifications, let alone a broadening (opposing?) outlook.

John D. Rockefeller, 3rd voiced an increasingly heard thesis in 1970 and early 1971: "The main responsibility for a movement toward reconciliation and joint action now rests with the Establishment. Young people have been involved and committed for some time. It is our turn now."** Mr. Rockerfeller stated that "we're not doing as effective a job as we could" to meet our problems and "we have young people who are. . . our leaders of tomorrow" who want "to have a part in decision making." Mr. Rockefeller stated that his "conclusion was based in part on a recent study of youth and the Establishment," and he was a member of the Task Force which produced *Youth and Establishment.***

If we mean largely forerunner types, and if this line of reasoning is widely accepted, it could be disquieting. First of all, how does one know that these "future leaders" will think the same in later life, when they are ready to lead, as they now think in college? In fact, there is some doubt that colleges are the best environment for reaching conclusions on hard, practical matters.**** Is not the "decoupled" nature of our campuses intentional? Are they not of necessity—particularly the non-physical science departments—places for the contemplative life: "Ideas for ideas' own sake," regardless of whether they are feasible? In fact, have they not attracted such people (and rightly so) as instructors?† But in recent years could one discuss at

* *Youth and the Establishment,* p. 82.
** *New York Times,* December 6, 1970, p. 65.
*** *Youth and the Establishment,* p. 10.
**** Referring to a study of our universities by a panel of academicians, financed by the Ford Foundation, the *New York Times* of March 9, 1971 (p. 45) reported:

 Both students and faculty members, the report said, live in an isolated community that bears little resemblance to the real world. It doubted whether education could be made more relevant to students and society simply by developing new curriculums because, it said, too few students and faculty members have enough experience outside the education system to know what is relevant.

 † "Perhaps the central element of the image of the college professor is his concern for ideas as such. His supposed 'absent-mindedness' and his reputed im-

colleges even the problems of the campuses, particularly if the definitions of the problems—to say nothing of their solutions—ran counter to the ideologies of the activist students and the militant, young instructors who inspired and abetted them? In fact, since many real problems on the campuses are of little interest to doctrinaire dissidents, they may (contrary to what some seem to think) have less chance of getting on the "agenda" during periods of great activism.

Without being an alarmist, one can have grave reservations about the wisdom of encouraging this minority of "ultra-liberal" young people to speak for "youth." Is it that clear why some "think that it is right" for older people to be "pushed to a re-think, both personally and institutionally"* by a process which emphasizes *this* particular group (if that is what we are being asked to do)?

I stress this point because an emphasis on the opinions of the Left-Wing element of "youth," at least as of late 1970 and early 1971, was surprisingly widespread in some circles. To some extent it was inherent in the approach of many persons in the universities, some in industry, government, and the clergy, and even some in the military services. Perhaps the most disquieting thing about such Left-leaning youth is the likelihood of finding among them many with the traits of the demonstrators and the Radical Left—their political philosophy, their reliance on drugs, their seeming lack of self-discipline.

As noted earlier, all youth, students and non-students alike, rate most "selfish" career aspects of their professions below the more "selfless" aspects. (It should be pointed out that most non-student youth are already in the career world; this is a "meaningful" decision for them, but for most students it is a "theory" that has yet to be tested.) It is possible that such students as the "forerunners" might care least about careers, but they apparently also care least about other things which are important to the public, and even to "youth." A critic could argue that these groups—"Radical Leftists," "demonstrators" and probably the "forerunners"—are unlikely groups to be

---

practicality reflect the notion that he is a man of thought rather than action . . . In other words, those whose concern is largely with the application of practical skills are, in our sample, highly unlikely to consider becoming professors." Ian D. Currie, Henry C. Finney, Travis Hirsch, and Hana C. Selvin, "Images of the Professor and Interest in the Academic Profession," *Sociology of Education*, Fall, 1966.

* Speech by John D. Rockefeller, 3rd., in the *New York Times*, December 6, 1970, p. 65.

heeded in the real worlds of politics, social welfare, business and and government. It could even be the case on campus.

For instance, the average citizen may ask, how seriously should anyone making long-range plans for an established institution take advice from a group of mostly late adolescents, among whom in late 1970 almost three out of five "strongly agree" that "our foreign policy is based on our own narrow economic and power interests"; one in three "strongly agrees" that "severe economic recession and depression are inevitable with our type of economy"; an increasing number feel (12 percent agree "strongly," 42 percent "partially") that "the whole social system ought to be replaced by an entirely new one; the existing structures are too rotten to repair"; and one in three "strongly disagree" (and only 13 percent "strongly agree") that American democracy can "respond effectively to the needs of the people"? What does one do with the advice of a group of youngsters in which better than one in four wants to "do away with the political parties," more than one in four wants to "do away with the military," and almost one in four wants to "do away with the FBI"? Furthermore, more than four in five of this group feel that the Black Panthers "cannot be assured of a fair trial"; seven to eight out of ten think this also is true for radicals and hippies; about three out of five feel the same is true for college protesters, conscientious objectors and drug addicts; 35 percent "strongly" agree that "today's American society is characterized by injustice, insensitivity, lack of candor and inhumanity," and only 18 percent "strongly disagree" (47 percent "partially agree"). Yet these are opinions of the "forerunners."*

The average citizen may well ask, how does one use the advice of persons with such outlooks, and why should their advice be more important than that of the majority—or for that matter, of any other minorities? That such ideas might have gained ground among students in colleges (and possibly even all youth) might have been reason for rejoicing or worrying (depending on one's point of view).

* See Tables 127 and 128, and *Youth and the Establishment,* pp. 59, 60 and 65.
In December 1970, 43 percent of the college students (49 percent of the freshmen, but only 23 of the graduate students) said change in America in the next 25 years would come through revolution—49 percent said through peaceful means and 8 had no opinion. Also, 44 percent agreed that "violence is sometimes justified to bring change in American society," 54 percent said not so, and 2 percent had no opinion. Compare this to the opinion of the general public on the issue if violence is sometimes justified for this cause: No—81 percent; yes—14; "don't know"—5. (*Gallup Opinion Index* No. 68, February 1971, pp. 40 and 41.)

But as grounds for bowing to the "inevitable" (and perhaps even easing up on the normal "braking" processes in our society which tend to restrain such radicalism) or contemplating great changes in our behavioral patterns or institutions, it is not likely to be a very persuasive argument for the average citizen.

How do we answer the query of the man in the street: What are the credentials of this minority? The "forerunners" are mostly social science majors (in the 1969 *Fortune* poll, 80 percent were in the "arts and humanities"), and fewer than in any other category come from "blue-collar" families (only one in four). This is also true of the 1969 and 1970 demonstrators. As we saw earlier, the majority of the best students going from high school to college, and the vast majority of all high school students, do not fit the activist mold. Many may be "converted" to activist ideas on campus (perhaps temporarily) but even so, they are still a minority of a minority (17 to 24 year olds) while in this mood.* The activist's value is said to be his ability to spot, from his critical (hostile?) position, the flaws in our society.** But one wonders whether the less-hostile, "career-minded" and non-student youngsters are not also sufficiently critical to spot our real flaws. Might it not be that using the young activist for this task is like asking a paranoid to look for plots: He will find plots—some real, plus dozens of imaginary ones—and may demand from a non-negotiable position that *all* "plots" be stamped out.

Of course, by early 1971 there were already some signs that could be taken to be the beginning of a cooling-off period and—barring some new upheaval—a swing back to normal on the campuses. By the fall of 1971 it was freely stated by many campus administrators, as well as students, that the students had "changed." Since the majority of students, and the overwhelming majority of youth, had never subscribed to the more extreme objectives and tactics of the activists, what may be happening is that the activists themselves may be changing. Or the students who were non-participators may be refusing to have their learning disrupted. But the reasons for the "swing back" ap-

* In 1970, 7 percent of "'forerunners" were said to be activists, 65 percent were "in sympathy with most of the activists' objectives, but not with all of their tactics," only 3 percent were in "total disagreement with the activists," and 11 percent "not emotionally involved one way or the other." The figures for career-minded students were 4, 46, 9, and 19 percent respectively. *Youth and the Establishment,* p. 70.
** Schwab, op. cit., p. 34.

parently span the spectrum from being shocked by violence on the campuses to fear for their own safety, to fear of disciplinary action, to disillusionment, to wanting to get their money's worth out of their education. The recession has made part-time jobs more sought after and important, keeping many students busy outside class. But overall, the general impression appears to be that the youngsters are tired of being harangued about the fate of the world, and are reverting to the natural role of students—caring about their education and their future. They apparently are acting more as individuals again, the work clothes "uniform" giving way somewhat to dresses, and students are beginning to discuss issues again, rather than acquiescing in the activists' mass meetings complete with chants and cheerleaders. They have little to complain of anymore in their private world on campus (although their parents might—dormitory rules have "all but evaporated" and birth-control information and contraceptives are distributed at quite a few college dispensaries. There is overwhelming *adult* opposition to such practices; see Figures 3 and 4 and the text preceding and following them). But one wonders if, in the near future, full credit courses on "the history of the student movement in the U.S." will not become a waste of time.

Demonstrations are said to be becoming passé on campuses, and administrators and "observers" have generally concluded that the youngsters have decided to work within the system. Reports are that things seem to have calmed down in high schools as well as on campuses.* If, as is implied by these statements, the students wish to work within the system at the level of influence young people usually have, and in the normal manner of increasing influence with increasing knowledge and experience, and if this estimate is true, then they have begun to revert to the direction of the non-activist students and the non-students.** Nor is changing the system from within, according to

* "Turn from Campus Violence," *U.S. News and World Report*, October 25, 1971, pp. 40–43. "Youth Rebellion of Sixties Waning," *New York Times*, October 24, 1971, Sec. 1, p. 1.

> Undoubtedly the changes in the attitudes of students on campuses during this year finds its parallel in the local schools. Also . . . there is evidence that discipline has been tightened in public schools, just as it has been in colleges and universities.

("The Third Annual Survey of the Public's Attitudes towards the Public Schools, 1971," by George Gallup, *United Teacher Magazine*, November 21, 1971, p. M-1.)

** It may be of interest to note in passing that students may not be good judges of what is likely to happen on campuses. Better than two out of three in the latter part of 1970 are said to have believed student radicalism would "continue to grow." *Youth and the Establishment*, p. 76.

the rules, feared or frowned upon in this country; on the contrary, it is encouraged. Everyone, according to his ability and energy, should have this chance. The built-in brakes in our system are real, and though often frustrating, usually are necessary and seldom totally and indefinitely stultifying. And, most of all, working within the system, within the rules, is an educational experience essential in developing into responsible adults, spouses, and parents. What is more important, the vast majority of youth has apparently always been willing to work toward these goals within the existing system.

To the extent that some aspects of the life style propounded by the "forerunner" types may now have been adopted by some non-student youth, the "forerunner" label may be apropos. The "reversal" on the campuses, therefore, may be seen as a "forerunner" trend which will come later among non-students who, by definition, must lag behind the "pace-setters." Another way to look at this, however, is that in 1968, 1969 and 1970, "forerunners" for the current "trend" were the "practical-minded" students or non-students, or even the adults. This could mean that predictions based primarily (and certainly solely) on tangents to the sine wave of "fashionable" youthful opinion are likely to turn out, at least in the short run (5–15 years), to be less reliable than we might expect. In any event, the traditional, flexible "system" in this country, though far from perfect, is a tried-and-true method of handling and incorporating most of the good aspects of all elements in our society in an orderly and productive manner. Furthermore, it is a highly complex and sophisticated system, where less human dignity and freedom is sacrificed for affluence and security than under any other system yet devised for a great nation.

It is of interest to note that after this section of the manuscript was written, more recent 1971 surveys of college students by Daniel Yankelovich, Inc., the group responsible for the poll data in *Youth and the Establishment*, are said to show what apparently could be called a reversal of many of the "trends" in campus thinking—a forthcoming book by Daniel Yankelovich should contain this material. The polls show the students still in disagreement with much in the "Establishment," but the reversal apparently is often in the very areas of radicalism which were one of the hallmarks of the "forerunners" (those who thought the country was racist, inhuman, unjust, purely selfish in foreign policy). Further, they tended to show the least number who believed in the viability of, or wanted to work within, the "system"; more of them believed in radical approaches. According to this new perturba-

327

tion, radical thinking apparently no longer is so appealing, and an increased number of students are willing to work within the system and the "Establishment." In this sense at least, the "forerunners" of 1968, 1969 and 1970 (whose numbers Yankelovich surveys show have decreased slightly each year from 1968 to 1971) apparently were not "forerunners" for the campuses; the "practical" college students, and perhaps even more so, the non-students might be thought to have played such a role on these issues.

This later Yankelovich, Inc., data also introduced a unique and significant distinction into its categories; it separated the opinion of business leaders into those with children in college and those without. The results are said to show a smaller amount of sympathy with dissident students and their opinions among the men who are not parents of students.*

4. A NEW "ELITIST" APPROACH?

As we have seen, at least in 1968, most non-student youth did not identify with students; in fact, there may be a greater gap between the attitudes of the ultra-liberal students and those of other youth than between most youth and adults.** Radical students could certainly not prove that they lived in an environment better suited to produce genuine, practical social awareness than the youth who live and work in society. Some upper-middle-class students who lean toward radicalism, including perhaps a significant number of the somewhat disturbed youngsters, may be more guilt-ridden; but this does not mean they really "care" more than the next person about their fellow men, nor that they are better equipped emotionally to suggest realistic cures for complex social problems. On the contrary, such people are normally more likely to be less well-equipped in this way, and any prudent man must hesitate to endorse their judgment on the evidence at hand.***

That the opinions of the more radical college students (or perhaps any college students) should be recommended for consideration by "busi-

* From a lecture given by Daniel Yankelovich at a Hudson Institute seminar, "Changing Values," held at the Harvard Club, New York, November 3, 1971.
** See Seymour Martin Lipset and Earl Raab, "The Non-Generation Gap," *Commentary*, 50 (August 1970): 35–39, for a discussion of this and other vertical "gaps" in society.
*** See the article from the *New York Times Magazine* by Lowell, cited earlier, for his description of the problems facing competent Negro students, on and off campus, largely because of the misguided efforts of such people.

ness executives and other Establishment leaders," and that they pre- ferably should be allowed to "have a part in decision-making," would be extremely hard to explain to the average citizen. Further, parti- cularly from his point of view, it is probably ironic: Millions of non- college youths (and adults with a lifetime of experience in society) work in the plants and government bureaus of these "executives" and "leaders," and while many are adequately represented by powerful unions on issues of working conditions and salaries, the overwhelming majority have never even had a plant superintendent or supervisor let them "have a part in decision-making" or solicited their ideas on politics, social problems, or corporate responsibility. Yet according to some adult recommendations, men "at the top" presumably should lend an ear to young, inexperienced, but more radical, "pampered" college students. Again, an average citizen need not be an alarmist to point out that carried very far, this could lead to attempted high- level "social engineering" at its worst, influenced by a group that the country has rejected.* Furthermore—and perhaps most important— by emphasizing this special group of college students, we may tend to "disenfranchise" the vast majority of our youth, which by all criteria, is more likely to include more energetic and practical, solution-oriented people, more people who are likely to be better adjusted emotionally and to have more self-discipline, and perhaps more, people with in- telligence, ability, and common sense. What gives one pause is that such ideas apparently were not confined to "a bunch of kooks." Only a minority, but still a surprising number of influential Americans, ap- parently bet on what is quite likely to be the wrong horse. This is not a "youth problem"; like so many other issues mentioned earlier, this situa- tion was largely generated by adults to "solve" a "youth problem."**

Of course, that the policy of paying what seems to be dispropor-

* It is interesting to note in passing that these "forerunners," "demonstrators," and "radical-left" youngsters' attitudes never coincide with those of youthful leaders, judged by standard, "square" leadership criteria. (See the data in *Survey of High School Achievers* [Northfield, Ill.: Merit Publishing Co., 1970]. See also Purdue's study on leadership in high schools, Purdue Opinion Panel, *Report of Poll No. 83*, May 1968.) But we should not dwell on this point because the criteria of leadership ability used in these studies is not necessarily the same in all cases as similar criteria for leadership in later life.

** If carried too far, this phenomenon might have in it the seeds of a self- fulfilling prophecy. If the people who have the power to make certain other people influential do so, then these newly influential people will begin to influence policy-making and hiring practices. These people will therefore have been prophetic; they are the new leaders, policies are what they said they would be,

tionate attention to these more radical students was being supported by intelligent men of good will in responsible positions is in itself evidence that there has been no conscious "plot" to create an influential "left-leaning, intellectual elite" at the expense of the rest of youth. Nor can such men have had anything but the good of the nation at heart. One can see, however, how it could be difficult for them to fend off criticism. The small but still perhaps significant number of at least partial adherents to the "youth cult" thesis, among men of some influence in our society, and—despite their vast rejection of student disorders (see Table 6) and their "anger or impatience" with rebels (*Youth and the Establishment*, p. 34)—the apparent greater sympathy for college students in 1970 among business leaders "as a group" than among the public as a whole, plus the remarks such as those of John D. Rockefeller, 3rd, as reported in the *New York Times*, do not help matters. The report, *Youth and the Eastablishment*, clearly states on page 89 that a "new alliance" (between youth and the Establishment) "can be forged that keeps faith with the best traditions and ideals of the nation." Yet, other statements in this report do not necessarily allay fears of the danger of some possible inadvertent ill-effects of excess concern for the feelings of students on the Left. On page 84, we find the following rather accurate description of our society's decision-making process:

Social science has made us familiar with the process of cultural diffusion. Change is often initiated by small extremist groups. The mass of the public react initially by rejecting the new ideas, and then begin to consider them with tempered selectivity. The proposals of the extremist groups become, in effect, one vast *smorgasbord* from which people of more moderate temperament pick and choose those ideas that fit in with their own traditional life styles.

On page 85, however, we learn that such processes were apparently thought to cause grave hardships on some youngsters whom the Task Force obviously felt were important:

It is possible that one part of the present generation of college students will be sacrificed. That is to say, the disparity between the outlook and values of

and they may even convince other "leaders" that the whole country thinks as they do. (Of course, we are aware some of this happens today, but it is not always necessarily good, and if this should occur with a disproportionate number of such people of the Left, it could, in my judgment, be bad.)

forerunner students and the ability of our institutions to respond to their needs may be so great that many of these young people may become totally embittered or alienated or anarchistic or hopeless in their outlook.

It was felt some would "embrace traditional values with a vengeance and turn angrily against their old selves," some would gradually adapt and be assimilated. "But some would be lost souls." Therefore, a change in our traditional process of selecting changes apparently was felt to be in order:

In the light of these considerations, the Task Force regards it as essential to the future well-being of our society *that the process of assimilating the new values to the old ones not be left wholly to the accidents of circumstance.* (Italics mine.)

Without the energies and passion for change of the young, it is unlikely that those in the Establishment who have learned to *accommodate themselves to the existing structures of the society will realize the full magnitude of the changes we must make in the years ahead.* (Italics mine.)

The group concluded, therefore, that:

Somehow we must make it feasible to bring together concerned Establishment leaders with those young people who would rather at this stage in their lives make a contribution to the community rather than pursue a private career.

Nor was this a short-term process. On page 89 we read:

But we are clear that any individual project must not be treated as a short-range, stand-alone effort, but more as a point of entry, *an opening wedge, into an ongoing process.* While it is important to start now, it is equally important to recognize the long-term fundamental character of the effort. There is a pressing need *to find new methods for bringing about basic institutional change in society.* Youth/Establishment collaboration can be a powerful force for accomplishing this larger objective, but it must move forward one step at a time. (Italics added.)

One wonders if people voicing such opinions, including this Task Force, appreciate the somewhat disturbing inferences that could be drawn from these statements. They might cause the general public to

331

begin to think about the situation in a way such as that voiced by Eric Hoffer:

[the people] can hear the swish of leather as saddles are heaved on their backs. The intellectuals and the young, booted and spurred, feel themselves born to ride us.°

Implicit in all such thinking, which attempts to bring left-wing youth "into the picture," seems to be the assumption that we are missing great opportunities through our current system, or, worse yet, that we are in or are headed for immense and perhaps even unique difficulties. While the vast majority of our "Establishment leaders" remained unruffled, from the point of view of the man in the street, some may have looked as though they were beginning to feel the "system," as now constituted, may be inadequate. These are, at least, highly debatable points, particularly if one considers the possible costs of accepting the recommendations on how to seize the "great opportunities" offered by the Left, secular humanists. In fact, it can be argued that in those instances in which the system has been found "wanting," it has been (at least partially) because of the very type of people these "Establishment leaders" felt they should listen to.

5. THE YOUNG WORKERS AND THE NEW LIFE STYLE

This is not "alarmist." Nor is it "backlash." The public has already lost much because of policies proposed by "ultra-liberal" academics and "intellectuals." Many of the universities that average Americans support directly and indirectly with their taxes, and which have been so vital to the society as a whole and to the upward mobility of their own children, recently became a source of trouble, and now many feel their public primary and secondary schools are deteriorating. This directly affects that majority of youth, including (or perhaps even particularly) those who do not go to college. Here, *avant-garde* "elitists," within and without the educational system, and largely with no evidence of the academic value of their "reforms," advocated changed curriculums, pushed the introduction of lavish new programs into the primary and secondary schools in many areas, eliminated discipline

---

° Eric Hoffer, "Whose Country Is America?" *New York Times Magazine*, November 22, 1970. This discussion of this phenomenon also mentions "a certain rapport between the rich and the would-be revolutionaries."

to a significant degree, and, thus inadvertantly, may have helped cause many schools to abdicate their responsibilities to provide a basic education. Schools in our greatest cities graduate alarming numbers of persons who lack the basic skills in arithmetic and are only semi-literate, not only because those who used to "flunk out" are now promoted, but also, one fears, because of less effective teaching processes and bad school environment.* In recent years, "new" approaches have led to less emphasis on difficult factual learning and drill, and more and more stress on discussion and even "encounter-group" approaches, on some vague theory of teaching children "how to think and make decisions" rather than giving them factual information. The effect on students is highly questionable, particularly in the social sciences, but one fears from some of the evidence, perhaps in the physical sciences as well. At the same time, the new programs have reduced the ordered existence in the schools. Some children are trying to learn in almost chaotic conditions in the classrooms (particularly the "new," big, "open" ones), and in and near our larger cities, sometimes in lawless and dangerous environments. This situation has a bad effect on all groups, but is perhaps most regrettable among the underprivileged. School children, white and non-white, cannot remain where their performance and behavior is gauged by some vague, unmeasurable criteria; they simply *must* learn to read and write well, they *must* learn basic mathematics and grammar, they *need* the basics of history. They *must* get these tools if the only proven road for "upward mobility" in this society, or any other, is to be open to them.

Such apparently is not the case. As a result, the situation in many large corporations has changed markedly in recent years. Some simply put many people they hire, both white and Negro, back in school for a year, in "training programs," to absorb much of what they should have learned in high school. It is no small job to instill in them the self-discipline, value systems, and training that normally came from the home and/or years in primary and secondary schools, and that equip the person for meticulous, complicated tasks. But apparently more progress is often made in one year in one of these "corporate schools" (with those willing to learn) than in several years of normal schooling. The "motivation" is the desire to earn a better living—not a disgraceful motive itself for high school youngsters. In our service industry-oriented society, these "academic" requirements become more

* See the discussion following Table 14 and on the last pages of Chapter I.

necessary than ever. Service industry in this technological era does not only mean laundries: It also means highly complex communications and transportation systems, sophisticated computerized data-gathering and -processing systems, and other complicated and vast business and governmental operations. Ditch-digging and even assembly-line jobs are proportionately decreasing, and installation and maintenance workers are becoming a larger segment of the work force. Needed today are "trouble shooters" on our vast systems and even our private transportation units, good blueprint readers and innovators for installation, skilled, meticulous craftsmen for building and maintaining the needed plant and equipment. Today it is not only more important to know how to read, it is more important to have the "work ethic," to be a "self-starter" and to be highly responsible, as well as to have the self-discipline for meticulous, complicated work. There are increasing signs that the young are often let down in being prepared by the schools for these disciplines, as well as those needed for college.*

This is not a simple yearning for the good old days, which often look "good" in hindsight only because we conveniently forget the bad. Nor is it a prediction of imminent catastrophe. Current productivity is high, and though the rate of increase has declined in recent years (which is supposed to be normal going into a recession, a decline in the rate of production and a lag in layoffs) the predictions are that it has bottomed out and it should now begin to rise. Most youngsters today could "make it" in a post-industrial society, but "most" may not be enough for the highly technical, service industry-oriented society of the future. We will need many such people simply because the momentum built up in the 1950s and 1960s will inevitably carry us into an era of technological dependency. What is more, our prosperity depends to a large degree on a constantly rising rate of *increase* in productivity.

To repeat, in the immediate future there may not be enough young people of this type to go around. This may be true partly because the huge numbers entering college take so many of the more intelligent youth out of the potential work force,** and partly because the self-discipline and skills needed for these increasingly technical jobs may

---

* These talents are not necessarily different; Schwab's description of the gaps in student capability in basic thought processes outlined earlier (see the discussion just prior to and following Table 122) are also deadly in the non-academic world.
** See the section on "Construction Workers Unions."

not be so easily acquired in school anymore. Even if this trend changes (as some imply is now occurring), and the "work ethic" is re-introduced into our schools, there could be a gap in the output of industrious and meticulous workers. The problem is not just simply the expansion of the economy and the resulting expansion of demand. During the 1970 recession, when demand fell off, telephone service still did not return to normal in some areas.* Automobile maintenance apparently did not improve during 1970 to the degree that the fall-off of sales might have led one to expect (though "hanging on to the car for another year" might have increased repair requirements). On the other hand, perhaps here again imaginative, technically skilled "trouble-shooters" and dependable, careful, talented maintenance workers may be getting relatively scarce. Even reading and understanding the increasingly technical repair manuals for this new equipment may be too much for many young people coming out of our schools today.

There is much anecdotal information, but little extensive definitive data to support the fear that the new "life style," apparently accepted by many of our schools, "intellectuals," members of the media and public personalities, is already affecting our technology. Despite the training programs mentioned earlier, it is seldom more than one year, and normally no more than a few weeks or even days, before new, young workers are placed in a spot where their productivity must be real and, in many cases, measurable. This can make difficulties for the unprepared youth. Non-productivity, and particularly counter-productivity, are quickly apparent here. This does not mean that the non-productive minority must immediately pay for their lack of ability—or even that they will pay in a short period of time—but it does mean that it will be quickly obvious to them that they cannot "measure up." It takes a neat degree of rationalization to tell oneself an automobile engine is running when it is not, or that the problem was so difficult that the "system" couldn't handle it, if an older worker has it running and out of the shop in thirty minutes. It is even more difficult for a young man to convince himself he is good at his job when he puts a half-dozen circuits out of operation while trying to repair one, has the quality-control man turn down his work time and again, or sees older people working at night balancing his cash drawer against his tape.

---

* It was reported on a 6:30 p.m. telecast on the subject on Channel 2, January 24, 1971, that the New York Telephone Company blamed its problems on, among other things, a "shortage of skilled personnel."

Certainly it cannot be good for young people to be disillusioned this way. As we have seen, it is usual for them to be enthusiastic and perhaps overestimate their capability; but today they are told that they are *not* overestimating their qualities. They are told they are brighter, more sensitive, competent and "better" than the adults, and have so much to offer the world. Of course, though these compliments are thrown indirectly at the schools as well, in many ways the schools do less for the students in the areas cited above than before. The result is that many young persons who buy this "bill of goods" find life difficult on the "outside." Instead of being able to make their great "contributions" to the rather dull, "hypocritical" older people, they find that they can contribute very little. More and more of them are almost totally dependent on these older people, not only to do their work for them, but to undo their mistakes.

Of course, the majority of children, who were better trained at home and school, still do have something to contribute, and know that young peoples' mistakes are part of the learning process. The minority who cannot "measure up" either assume a supercilious attitude and rationalize that they are too good for lower (that is, difficult), "dead-end" positions, or they experience a painful "period of adjustment" during which they are worth little and must change their outlook.

The "new" life style of college youth of the past few years could have an even greater effect on the production plants than that of the "decoupled" minority of young workers. If we have badly designed equipment, the "mean time to failure" will go down and more repair skills will be required. If bad design is added to sloppy production methods, the repair requirements will soar even higher. But we need this equipment and we need the people who can build and maintain it. We may have enough of those people today, but we have the people probably *despite* the "new" life style, not *because* of it. The glorifying and rationalization of this new life style may at least delay some young peoples' coping with the real world for a longer period. This could be bad for all concerned; in some cases, this life style is already being accepted by adults in decision-making positions.

Those in government, industry, and other private institutions who hire such people into new help-type "programs" may continue to make employment for these ill-trained, somewhat impractical, "superior" persons. Children's centers; supplemental, lay and even religious educational efforts; neighborhood and even larger VISTA-type programs (to which so much money is allocated) can be marvelous undertakings with the right people working in them. But they can also be havens for those young people decoupled from society. Here again, it is hard to measure productivity (or if such measures exist, it is hard to get them recognized or applied); and it is a wonderful place for self-righteousness. One has a suspicion that, insofar as this type of "decoupled" person is employed, the entire program suffers. Later efforts by VISTA (and the Peace Corps) to attract more practical people who can "add another resource to the communities" they join, seem to bear this out.

6. INDICATORS OF YOUTHFUL OPINION, POLITICAL STRENGTH AND AWARENESS

Until now, we have not had the continuing way of measuring youthful opinion that we have had with adults—the vote. Even checking the voting pattern of the 21-to-24-year-olds is not very productive. Only 51 percent of persons from 21 to 24 years old voted in 1968.* Further, in opinion polls this age group is usually included in a larger category of 21-to-29-year-olds, so it is difficult to check their particular stated attitudes against how they vote. Among the 21-to-29-year-olds as a whole, only 55 percent of them voted in 1968. And, in states in which the 18-to-20-year-olds could vote, only 33 percent exercised this right. This low vote may be due partly to the difficulties involved in first registrations. Some of this is because of residency requirements. Census data shows that 91 percent of the young adults between 18 and 24 lived with their families. This does not appear to indicate a high degree of individual mobility in this age group; and, for voting purposes, college students maintain their original residency rights, so they can be considered to be living at home (which is probably the grounds on which this finding was based). The voting among college-trained 21-to-24-year-olds was lower in the 1964 presidential election (despite their vast rejection of Barry Goldwater) than 45-year-olds with a grade-school education.** (If there were a low vote among students—mostly 21-year-olds—in college, it may have been because they more often required absentee ballots.)

There are 35 million 15-to-24-year-olds in the country, and there has been an 11 million increase in the size of the group since 1960. This

* U.S. Census figure as reported in the *Philadelphia Bulletin*, February 4, 1971, p. 1.

** Associated Press article by Dick Barnes, Washington, September 26, 1968.

figure is deceiving, however, because 1960 (as 1950) had an abnormally low number of people in this age bracket (depression birth-rates were very low); so the huge increase means this age group is just nearing the normal percentage of youth in the total population. As Table 141 shows, however, the number of 15-to-24-year-olds is still *lower* than it has been for most of the twentieth century. Furthermore, with the falling birth-rate in the 1960s, the "top out" of the 1950s' babies will be passed for this age category in the next ten years. In other words, it will not surpass the 1900–1940 "normal" percent of the population for that category by a significant amount in the foreseeable future. As this 1950s baby peak passes into the 25-to-49-year-old group, the proportion of youth compared to the rest of the population will drop sharply.

Table 141

TOTAL POPULATION AND PERSONS 15 TO 24*
YEARS OLD: 1900 TO 1970

(Numbers in thousands)

Year	Total Population	15 to 24 years old	
		Number	Percent
1970	204,265	35,441	17.35%
1960	180,007	24,020	13.34
1950	151,718	22,099	14.57
1940	131,669	23,922	18.17
1930	122,775	22,422	18.26
1920	105,711	18,708	17.70
1910	91,972	18,121	19.70
1900	75,995	14,891	19.60

We have seen that, during high school, young people think much like their parents do on many issues. As far as increasing or decreasing preference for major political parties is concerned, high school youngsters follow the trend of their parents. But they also tend to have a higher percentage who do not prefer either major party. In 1968, their choice of the Democratic party was closer to their parents' choice than was their preference for the Republican party. But both major party

* *Historical Statistics of the United States, Colonial Times to 1957* (a statistical abstract supplement), and *Statistical Abstract of the United States 1971*, both prepared by the Bureau of Census, U.S. Department of Commerce.

preferences were lower than their parents'. The number of high school students who chose either a third party or had no opinion was considerably higher than that of their parents. Younger persons generally tend to be more "liberal" than older persons. We know about the youth support for Eugene McCarthy in 1968. What is less known is that youth (although supporting him less than Liberal candidates) also gave greater support to George Wallace than did adults: While basically being more "liberal"-oriented, young people are more likely to go to extremes—in either direction—than adults. A 1970 Gallup poll found "that among college radicals of both the Left and Right, there is an apparent appeal in extremism for its own sake, among other factors." When asked to rate as favorable or unfavorable certain specified organizations, "a significant proportion" of those students who considered themselves to be Far Left politically, gave a highly favorable rating to the John Birch Society and the KKK; and "a sizeable percentage" of those who considered themselves to be Far Right gave a highly favorable rating to the SDS, the Weathermen and the Black Panthers. Moreover, the percentages of highly favorable ratings in these cases were almost always strikingly greater than those given by the vast majority of students politically in the center.[*]

Some data that came to light during the 1968 presidential election campaign offered some surprises: The 18-to-24-year-olds were as strongly, and possibly even more strongly, in favor of George Wallace than any other age group. Thirty percent "admired" him; of the "practical" college students, 17 percent felt the same. Compared to this, only 13 percent of the adults voted for him.

Furthermore, young white voters across the country showed the highest percentage voting for Wallace. In fact, the Wallace vote was inversely related to the age level: 21-to-24-year-olds registered the highest vote for him (17 percent) and it decreased to its lowest level for voters 50 and over (11 percent).[**] This higher percentage of youth voting for Wallace held in every category of the young: White, *nonsouthern* youth showed the same preference (in fact, non-southern voting showed the same pattern for all age groups as the national sample)[***]; more college-educated 21-to-29-year-olds voted for Wallace

[*] *Gallup Opinion Index*, No. 68, February 1971, pp. 12–19.
[**] Seymour Martin Lipset and Earl Raab, *The Politics of Unreason: Right-Wing Extremism in America, 1790–1970* (New York: Harper and Row, 1970), p. 382.
[***] Ibid., p. 386.

than did the college-educated in any other age group; and young people who were high school graduates followed the same pattern. The discrepancy between voting among people of the same age group with different educations, however, was largest between college- and high school-educated 21-to-29-year-olds. Twice as many high school-educated in this age group voted for Wallace as did the college-educated.

Table 142

EDUCATION, AGE AND WALLACE VOTE*

	Age Groups		
	21–29	30–49	Over 50
	Grammar School		
Percentage Wallace vote	+	29%	15%
Number		(41)	(137)
	High School		
Percentage Wallace vote	20%	14%	9%
Number	(79)	(236)	(103)
	College		
Percentage Wallace vote	10%	9%	8%
Number	(59)	(156)	(99)

+ Too few cases.

Only 39 percent of the 21-to-29-year-olds considered themselves Democrats in 1970, compared to 48 in 1965 and 44 for the overall population in 1970. The number of Republicans held steady, 22 percent, but the number of Independents rose from 30 to 39 percent between 1965 and 1970. The figures for the overall population in 1970 were 29 percent Republican and 27 Independent.** In December 1970, among young people between 15 and 21, 35 percent said they would vote Democratic, 18 Republican, 4 would vote for Wallace, 40 were undecided or had other choices, and 3 would "refuse to vote."*** These youngsters are close to college students. In June of 1970, college students showed 18 percent Republican, 30 Democrat, and 52 Independent. On this issue the students (mostly 18-to-22-year-olds) may reflect "a changing local or national environment" as well as change on

* Ibid., p. 393.
** *Gallup Opinion Index*, Reports No. 1, June 1965, and No. 62, August 1970, p. 3.
*** Louis Harris, *Life* Survey, op. cit., p. 24.

campus; see Table 95 and the discussion before it. As of October 1971, 7 percent of the 18-to-21-year-olds and 14 percent of the 21-to-29-year-olds said they would like to see Wallace win in 1972.*

In the off-year election of 1970, the 21-to-29-year-olds showed the least knowledge of any age group (or perhaps interest in) their congressional representatives. In fact, even though over three-fourths of these people were high school graduates (and among the 21-to-24-year-olds, 52 percent of the men and 40 of the women had completed some college), the number of 21-to-29-year-olds who knew who their local congressman was, even during the election campaign, much closer to the grade school-educated, and manual-occupation categories of the population than any others (see Table 49).

One possible significance of this data could be that the 21-to-29-year-olds as a whole, though quite interested in domestic and international affairs, may not be as disturbed by them as some may think. This may at least in part account for the high degree of "happiness" in the 21-to-29-age group today** (only 5 percent say they really are not happy), and the 90 percent of the 15-to-21-year-olds who said their life had been happy so far, and the 93 percent who said they expected it to be as happy or even happier in the future.*** Another point of view on youthful voting is that the young simply don't believe in the system anymore, so they do not vote or become interested in normal politics. As we have seen, this is indicated by a small minority of young persons, particularly among radical students, who say they think that society's problems cannot be solved by our normal political parties or even by our system. But the lack of interest and failure to vote in this age group is not a recent phenomenon; as we stated earlier, they did not turn out in 1964 against Goldwater either.

The idea that young people in this generally happy, exciting period of life are more caught up in things other than politics, international affairs or deep social problems, may be a valid one. They will voice

* See Table 43.
** In general, how happy would you say you are:

	Very	Fairly	Not Happy
1969 (National)	43%	48%	6%
1969 (21–29)	55	39	5
1947 (National)	38	57	4
1947 (21–29)	23	N/R	N/R

See Table 52 and the discussion following it.
*** Louis Harris, *Life* poll, 1971.

interest and concern, but these things are relative. Only 11 percent of the college student activists considered the Vietnam war more important than scholastic issues in 1969.* Most of these admittedly happy young people under 25 years of age are, quite possibly (and quite naturally and necessarily), involved in the much more exciting, and to them personally (and probably to their role in society) important, business of school, career, courtship, marriage, and the first child. It may take much prodding from older people to get many more of these youth to take time from attending to these essential activities to become more interested and spend more time in politics, to say nothing about more radical activities.

7. A CRITICAL DECISION POINT AND ITS SIGNIFICANCE TO SOCIETY

Despite the evidence in many areas that would seem to indicate caution in any drastic assessment of youth and its role in society, one gets the feeling that in the past few years, some of us may have brought ourselves to, and some few may have actually passed, an important decision point, not only on this role but on our society. There are, as always, many points of view on this issue, but two are paramount. A blunt description, from a "man in the street" point of view, of the attitude of the more radical of those who have pushed some of the more "in" changes might roughly be described as follows:

1) The period in which we live is one of great, almost inevitable change in all areas, and in the past few years, in a direction that is basically good and to which we must accommodate ourselves.

2) This trend must, in many cases, not only be tolerated but encouraged.

3) Values must be re-examined in the light of these new ideas with a readiness to jettison parts of our traditional system.

4) Opposition to change (often, if not usually, represented by the majority) is traditional and can generally be looked on as simply another part of the problem to be overcome, seldom as part of the solution. Under this premise, the traditional support of a number of the young, particularly college students, for extensive (according to some opinion, even extreme) changes, currently to the Left, is not only in order and good, presumably because it really is going in the "correct" direction, but now is something for which we must prepare. Only the

* *Gallup Opinion* Index, No. 48, June 1969, p. 8.

degree to which we should encourage and assist the youthful movement toward the Left varies among those who hold these beliefs.*

On the other hand, a sympathetic, but seldom articulated characterization of another point of view (which perhaps would be subscribed to by a majority of all employment and income categories of the population), holds that since ours is a sensitive societal structure, stemming from, among other things, a basic value system, changing this value system can have many grave effects on our society. Hasty, perhaps ill-considered changes have often proved to be counterproductive, sometimes in the very areas they were meant to improve, oftentimes in other vital areas that were not taken into account, but nevertheless were highly sensitive to the change. Those who are sympathetic to this viewpoint are likely to ask for the credentials of those who encourage any program, which goes against their own judgment, particularly a domestic program; they are quite likely to risk not achieving the benefits of programs pushed by those whom they consider to be unreliable (and they may occasionally miss substantial benefits this way), rather than risk the losses which implementation of the program might entail. This caution tends to make the activities of radical youth and their mentors unconvincing to the general public.** It also makes the public sympathetic to people with better "credentials" (which at times makes the public vulnerable, particularly to "charismatic" political leaders). Yet those who hold this view also are likely to include many who believe that this country is constantly changing and, though slowly, still at a rate greater than any orderly, stable country in history. Furthermore, they generally approve of the traditional trend of this change, toward ever greater freedom, human dignity, justice and prosperity for every citizen, in an orderly society. Objections to some recent suggestions, therefore, are likely not to be to the *rate* of change demanded by young radicals and their mentors, but to the apparent direction of the change. Even the slowest change in certain directions can be undesirable, yet considerable change in others is welcome.

The moderate public is normally likely to feel that we should direct our programs more toward the great majority of youth rather than toward the radical few. To the extent that the majority of young per-

* They may not have the same respect for the many youths with right-wing (Wallacite, for example) tendencies, who also want changes.

** This does not mean that if such New Left people, along with others with satisfactory credentials back a program, the majority will inevitably reject it because of the presence of radicals: witness the support for civil rights programs.

sons are abandoned by the adult population (as many moderate adults feel they largely were on the campuses, to some extent in the government and industry, and even to a degree in the military services, the high schools, and churches), they become quite concerned. They feel we should *really* have been worrying about "turning off" the majority of youth. Persons from this group might feel that if we abandon those youth who are more likely to subscribe to our value systems, we *are* hypocrites and do not have the courage of our convictions. Furthermore, they may feel that this vast majority of young people, who are their own children, are just too good to be left to radicals, Left or Right. They cannot understand why we must be afraid to tell them it is no sin to be happy and not "involved" (except in their work) when one is young, particularly if one is a student. These people may also tend to feel that, because of their relative lack of perspective, youngsters are more prone to see things in a crisis-charged atmosphere than are most adults. Furthermore, they seem to feel that worries come soon enough, and that (particularly in the case of college students) these youngsters will never have as good a chance again to be studious and contemplative—two functions these people may feel help to improve judgment when, in later life, "involvement" is paramount. That such traditional guidance by loving, concerned adults in the families was not being reinforced, and in many cases, was being undermined by non-family adults in the many official establishments which deal with our young people, as well as the many ad hoc "youth" groups which sprang up, was a source of worry for parents. This process of alienation from their parents, and in many cases (particularly on the college campuses) attempts at what amounted to extreme pressure tactics in attacks on value systems and political beliefs (by people preaching far-from-profound substitute "systems"), was bound to be confusing and, in some cases, quite disturbing to young persons.

Behind all this lies the curious, but absolutely vital, instinct about morale. This is an area where the opinion of the majority must be assessed as *it* reflects morale. It is also an area where some "intellectuals" refuse to be disturbed (and perhaps are even elated) by certain types of "bad news." If a "decoupled" ultra-liberal "intellectual" feels the country is too ethnocentric, or even chauvinistic or bellicose, a reduction of morale (particularly among young "squares") may appear good, or at least not alarming, to him. This may not be true, however, for the man in the street. He may feel that if this "square" majority of youth begins to feel abandoned, and its morale drops, this group may be up for grabs by anybody who wants to use it, Left *or* Right. Also, he knows the spin-off effects of a drop in morale, which can be disastrous for this democratic form of government and free society, both of which, despite everything, he values.

Recent events may prove that the "Middle American" adults and the non-activist, less vocal youngsters were the real prophetic groups. By and large they rejected the New Left and "youth cult" ideas. As indicated earlier, according to some observers, students seem to be beginning to act more like their parents feel students should ("they are reading books again"). If this occurs, the "action" may shift from the campus, and the "life style" portrayed in the media may no longer so largely originate there. If this image of "youth" changes, the pressure of the "peer groups" on youngsters to adopt "life styles," which are anything but admired by their parents, should be reduced. Even if these signs indicate a "swing back," the question remains, however, whether the after-effects of the objectionable life style will persist among our young college instructors, high school teachers, and other young professional and non-professional workers, to the extent that the economy and our children will be further adversely affected.

CHAPTER III

AN EXAMINATION OF NEGRO AND WHITE ATTITUDES

by Doris Yokelson

A. *Introduction*

The following chapter is an examination of some of the attitudes and opinions of Negroes as a group and in relation to the population as a whole. This work began as part of an overall effort to cut through stereotypes of many groups of the American population, after we discovered through our research that people's opinions often ran horizontally, across groups, rather than vertically, within tight groups. For workable material, I began to look at groups as they were normally broken down and reported by the large survey organizations—by race, age, education, occupation, income, etc. The first group I took up—race—grew into this long chapter; and time unfortunately did not permit me to make in-depth studies of the other groups.

It was not with pleasure that I set apart a particular group for examination. No one group or individual carries with it a set of fixed, immutable feelings, even toward one thing. Further, I believe that our democratic society, to be viable, must consist of the amalgamation of the expressions of its many individuals, whose feelings and needs are important to society as a whole. Setting apart one group represents a potential danger to this. But lately we have been increasingly confronted with the opinions of men who, either in the spirit of research or in public speeches and appearances, have presented themselves as knowledgeable of the feelings of entire blocs of people. In many ways, these men may touch upon the deep frustrations and aspirations of neglected and mistreated men and women. Certainly, impassioned, compassionate arguments are not to be underrated. But these arguments need to be based on reason and knowledge or they could be used as instruments for the forces of demagoguery rather than for the forces of democracy.

I would, therefore, like to offer the information gathered in this chapter as a tool for helping to understand the feelings of blacks and whites about themselves and toward each other. It will, of course, never be possible to present a complete and fixed picture, and this is not presumed here. However, opinion polls reveal certain data when they are observed over the years and studied comparatively. There are, of course, various drawbacks inherent in polling and reporting. For this reason I have relied only on the proven and prestigious survey organizations whose survey techniques have been carefully developed to a high degree of accuracy in measurable results. The correctness of the results could also be determined when the same or similar results occurred again and again in the polls. The data was carefully examined before comparisons were attempted. This report does not draw overall conclusions from that data.

Again, this is not the complete picture. It is a collection of public opinion material which, as I collected it, slowly revealed a more hopeful, human, and homogeneous picture of feelings of blacks and whites in our society than we were aware of in these turbulent years.

Although Gallup polls are considered to be among the most reliable, a word of caution must be given here in the use of nonwhite responses: The size of the respondent sample of nonwhites in the normal Gallup opinion polls is very small, and, for this reason, is sometimes unreported by Gallup. For example, the average size of the sample of a Gallup poll is approximately 1,500 persons, carefully chosen so as to represent an accurate cross-section of the population. From this number, the correctly relative size of nonwhite respondents, 21 years and over, is 130. Moreover, until the 18 year olds received the vote in the middle of 1971, Gallup did not poll the 18-to-21-year bracket. Since the average age of Negroes is 21,* Gallup polls before the middle of 1971 would also not be giving the opinion of a sizeable percentage of young Negroes. However, Gallup has taken such an extensive number of polls

* According to 1969 census data. The average age of whites is 29.

347

on related and similar issues, and has done so for so many years, that cumulative responses may be observed. In some years, sharp differences were noted that indicated changes had occurred; in other cases, the majority for or against an issue was clear. Also, some polls compared very well with those taken on similar questions by other organizations; other polls indicated a clear trend continuing over an extended period of time; some polls combined a number of these characteristics. This should be kept in mind when examining the Gallup polls that follow; where a special poll has been taken it will be noted. In some cases, the poll questions were specifically asked of Negroes and whites.

Throughout, please keep in mind that since the middle of 1971 the Gallup polls contain the opinions of 18 to 21 year olds.

B. *White and Negro Racial Attitudes*

In general, the attitude of the American population toward racial matters has become more liberal in the past decade. Nationwide polls show trends in this direction on numerous questions.* A 1970 Gallup poll that dealt with laws about racial intermarriage showed a significant change—a "dramatic change," wrote Gallup—in the feelings of the populace within the previous five years toward laws prohibiting marriage between whites and Negroes.

Table 143

INTERRACIAL MARRIAGES**

"Some states have laws making it a crime for a white person and a Negro to marry. Do you approve or disapprove of such laws?"

| | Nationwide | | Southern Whites | |
	1965	1970	1965	1970
Approve	48%	35%	72%	56%
Disapprove	46	56	24	38
No opinion	6	9	4	6

* Since this chapter was written, the fourth in a series of National Opinion Research Center surveys covering nearly 30 years on white attitudes toward Negroes in American society has been reported. The findings show that "in that time the trend has been distinctly and strongly toward increasing approval of integration. For the most part the trend has not been slowed by the racial turmoil of the past eight years." (Andrew M. Greeley and Paul B. Sheatsley, "Attitudes toward Racial Integration," *Scientific American*, 225 [December 1971]: 13–19.)

** Gallup polls as reported in the *New York Times*, September 10, 1970, p. 22. The 1970 poll was conducted July 31 to August 2.

348

As could be expected, the greatest approval of laws prohibiting racial intermarriage came from southern whites; but also the most striking change in attitude occurred among this group within this short time period: a 16-percentage point drop in approval and an increase of 14 percent in disapproval, considerably higher than the change nation-wide.

The feelings toward school integration also changed in the last decade, during which time southern white parents showed a remarkable shift in attitude.

Table 144

SCHOOL INTEGRATION*

"Any objection to sending your children to a school where there are a few Negroes, half are Negroes, or more than half are Negroes?"

	Northern White Parents Objecting					Southern White Parents Objecting				
	1963	1965	1966	1969	1970	1963	1965	1966	1969	1970
Where a few are Negroes	10%	7%	6%	6%	6%	61%	37%	24%	21%	16%
Where half are Negroes	33	28	32	28	24	78	68	49	46	43
Where more than half are Negroes	53	52	60	56	51	86	78	62	54	69

It is interesting that northern white opinion did not vary significantly during the 1960s, the objection levels remaining about the same throughout the decade, sometimes rising, sometimes falling within the level. There is even an intriguing statistic from July 1954, the time of the Supreme Court decision on segregation in public schools, when only 45 percent of northern whites objected to sending their children to a school where more than half of the children were Negroes. Compare this to 58 percent in 1959, 52 in 1965, 60 in 1966 and 51 in 1970.** Could this objection have congealed in the 1960s because of the great immigration of southern Negroes to northern cities during the 1950s? Almost one and one-half million Negroes moved North from 1950 to

* Gallup polls in the *Gallup Political Index*, No. 12, May 1966, p. 16; the *Gallup Opinion Index*, No. 51, September 1969, pp. 5, 6, 7; the *Gallup Opinion Index*, No. 59, May 1970, p. 5.

** However, I have not been able to find any correlation with this low 1954 figure in numerous other polls on race relations I have looked at. All other opinions on racial questions show a clear, gradually liberalizing trend from the 1940s through the 1960s.

1960; and between the years 1945 and 1965 the population of Negroes in urban areas more than doubled.*

Nearly 70 percent of the people would now vote for a Negro for president, a 31-point increase over 1958:**

Table 145

VOTE FOR A NEGRO?***

"If your party nominated a generally well-qualified man for President and he happened to be a Negro, would you vote for him?"

	Yes	No	No Opinion
1958	38%	53%	9%
1963	47	45	8
1965	59	34	7
1967	54	40	6
1969	67	23	10
1971	69	23	8

The busing of Negro and white schoolchildren from one school district to another was overwhelmingly opposed by the general population in Gallup polls taken in 1970 and 1971. However, it is apparent that other issues are involved in the matter of busing, such as sending the children away from their neighborhood into poorer and perhaps more dangerous sections; making them go to other than the neighborhood schools without free choice; the desire not to have little children do so much traveling and leave the parental neighborhood; and other disruptions of neighborhood arrangements. It is interesting to note that in 1970, nonwhites also clearly opposed the cross-busing—we can assume for the same basically parental reasons—and, in the two polls taken in the summer and fall of 1971, the majority of nonwhites still opposed busing.

In 1970, an almost eight-to-one ratio was maintained in all other categories of persons asked. At that time, in their respective categories,

* Gary Marx, "Black Protest," *California Monthly*, November 1966, p. 13.

** Compare this with some other interesting figures: Would vote for a Jew—46 percent in 1937; 62 in 1958; 77 in 1963; 86 in 1969; Would vote for a Catholic—64 percent in 1937; 68 in 1958; 84 in 1963; 88 in 1969; Would vote for a woman—31 percent in 1936; 52 in 1958; 57 in 1967; 54 in 1969. *Gallup Opinion Index*, No. 46, April 1969, pp. 3, 4, 7.

*** *Gallup Opinion Index*, No. 46, April 1969, p. 6, and No. 77, November 1971, pp. 11–14.

Table 146

BUSING*

	March 1970	August 1971	October 1971
		National	
Favor	14%	19%	17%
Oppose	81	73	77
No Opinion	5	8	6
		Nonwhites	
Favor	37	43	45
Oppose	48	46	47
No Opinion	15	11	8
		Whites	
Favor	11	16	14
Oppose	85	76	80
No Opinion	4	8	6

the college-educated, the most affluent and those in the professional and business world were most opposed to busing. The overall picture changed in August 1971, when opposition to busing was reduced in all groups except one, with great variations in changes within the categories. The highest income group changed the most (15 percent); cities under one million, the least (1 percent). In October 1971, opposition increased slightly in all groups, possibly because of problems that had arisen after the school year had begun. (See Table 13 for the actual figures.)

It is important to realize that although there has been a general tendency of liberalization of attitudes toward racial issues—and this liberalizing trend can also be noted in other domestic issues, such as Medicare, social security, welfare and poverty assistance, and aid to education, all of which are clearly favored by the general American populace—whites as a whole appear to feel that they are asked to accept changes in the racial balance too quickly. It is difficult to know how much of this opinion may be due to a persistent racism or to feelings about the places and circumstances in which racial changes are taking place, in which other things are at stake: the quality of education, the safety of streets, the tranquillity of surroundings, the value

* *Gallup Opinion Index*, No. 58, April 1970, p. 9; No. 75, September 1971, pp. 19 and 20; No. 77, November 1971, pp. 23 and 24.

of houses, the security of a job, which are also cherished by Negroes. These values are also naturally desired by most American Negroes and they would like to integrate more quickly into that society which provides the best of it for them. It should be evident that whites feel racial integration is being pushed too fast when they do not claim to be even aware that Negroes are being discriminated against, as we shall see later.

When the public is asked if racial integration in the United States is being pushed too fast or not, they respond by a solid five to two that it is. In fact, the feeling that it is being pushed too fast increased from the beginning to the end of 1968, and again when the question was asked differently, from 1969 to 1970.

Table 147

SPEED OF INTEGRATION*

"Do you think the Johnson administration is pushing integration too fast, or not fast enough?"

	Too Fast	Not Fast Enough	About Right	No Opinion
April 1968	39%	25%	21%	15%
June 1968	45	20	22	13

"Do you think the administration is pushing integration too fast, or not fast enough?"

May 1968	45%	20%	22%	13%
October 1968	54	17	21	8

"Do you think the racial integration of schools in the U.S. is going too fast, or not fast enough?"

July 1969	44%	22%	25%	9%
March 1970	48	17	21	14

The breakdown of opinions according to categories yields some interesting sidelights to the question of racial integration of the schools. There were significant variations in many of the categories, the most overwhelming one, of course, being between whites and nonwhites, nonwhites being the only group in all categories that did not think integration in the schools was proceeding too quickly. But even here,

* Compiled from Gallup polls in the *Gallup Opinion Index*, No. 37, July 1968, p. 15; *Gallup Opinion Index*, No. 39, October 1968, p. 30; *Gallup Opinion Index*, No. 58, April 1970, p. 7.

an unexpected 15 and 35 percent of the nonwhites felt it was moving too fast or about right.

Table 148

RACIAL INTEGRATION OF SCHOOLS*

"What is your opinion—do you think the racial integration of schools in the United States is going too fast or not fast enough?"

	March 1970			
	Too Fast	*Not Fast Enough*	*About Right*	*No Opinion*
National	48%	17%	21%	14%
Sex				
Men	54	15	19	12
Women	43	18	23	16
Race				
White	52	13	20	15
Nonwhite	15	42	35	8
Education				
College	41	27	19	13
High school	52	14	21	13
Grade school	47	12	24	17
Occupation				
Professional and Business	47	20	19	14
White-collar	49	18	23	10
Farmers	41	9	23	27
Manual	48	17	24	11
Age				
21–29 years	39	27	23	11
30–49 years	46	19	23	12
50 and over	53	11	19	17
Religion				
Protestant	53	14	20	13
Catholic	40	21	24	15
Jewish	x	x	x	x
Politics				
Republican	54	13	21	12
Democrat	46	18	24	12
Independent	47	18	19	16
Region				
East	40	21	25	14
Midwest	42	18	22	18
South	63	9	16	12
West	47	19	22	12

* *Gallup Opinion Index,* No. 58, April 1970, p. 7.

Table 148 (continued)

Income

$15,000 and over	46	20	21	13
10,000–14,999	53	16	21	10
7,000– 9,999	48	19	23	10
5,000– 6,999	48	12	24	16
3,000– 4,999	45	18	17	20
Under $3,000	46	14	22	18

Community Size

1,000,000 and over	34	24	30	12
500,000–999,999	47	15	23	15
50,000–499,999	52	21	17	10
2,500– 49,999	55	8	21	16
Under 2,500, Rural	51	14	18	17

A recent Gallup referendum survey showed the following results on a national and regional basis:

Table 149

INTEGRATION*

a. Racial integration *should* be speeded up.
—or—
b. Racial integration *should not* be speeded up.

	National Results Total	East	Regional Results Midwest	South	West
Should	38%	45%	35%	29%	43%
Should not	62	55	65	71	57

In an interesting series of questions put by the Gallup poll to a sample of whites only, in May 1968, about whether there was discrimination against Negroes or not, it was shown that an overwhelming majority of whites did not think that Negroes were actually discriminated against (see Table 150).

In a poll taken by Roper Research in 1970 in Louisville, Kentucky, which I describe in detail later in this report, only one fourth of the whites in Louisville thought that a white person would have a better chance of getting a job for which an equally qualified Negro and white were competing, than a Negro; 14 percent even thought a Negro would have a better chance.**

* *Gallup Opinion Index*, No. 65, November 1970, p. 25.
** Of the Negroes, 72 percent thought a white person would be preferred. See pp. 446–448 for a further discussion on job discrimination. The Roper Research

Table 150

IS THERE DISCRIMINATION AGAINST NEGROES?*

National Sample of Whites Only, Gallup Poll

May 1968

"Who do you think is more to blame for the present conditions in which Negroes find themselves—white people or Negroes themselves?"

White people	24%
Negroes	54
No opinion	22

"Do you think most businesses in your area discriminate against Negroes in their hiring practices or not?"

Yes	21%
No	65
No opinion	14

"Do you think most labor unions in your area discriminate against Negroes in their membership practices, or not?"

Yes	19%
No	50
No opinion	31

"In your opinion, how well do you think Negroes are being treated in this community—the same as whites, not very well, or badly?"

The same as whites	70%
Not very well	17
Badly	3
No opinion	10

One reason for these responses may be that a person may not think there is discrimination in his *own* area and community, as the questions asked. It must be "somewhere else." The reasons for this attitude are undoubtedly legion and very complex, with mixtures ranging from a purely pragmatic assessment, for better or worse, of what is actually perceived on one hand to apathy and extreme nonreaction to reality on the other.

---

poll taken in Louisville, Kentucky, was reported in Jean Heinig, "A Tale of Two Cities," *The Public Pulse*, April 1970. It was sponsored by the Louisville *Courier-Journal* and was conducted in the beginning of 1970. The survey was based on a 96-question questionnaire given to 508 whites and 506 Negroes living in and on the outskirts of Louisville.

* *Gallup Opinion Index*, No. 37, July 1968, pp. 19–22.

There is an overabundance of examples of white discrimination for pragmatic reasons. There are, however, indications that some middle-class Negroes are also discriminating against the penetration of lower-class Negroes (and whites) into their areas. An example might be that of home-owning blacks in the area of New Cassel, in the town of North Hempstead, Long Island, who refused to allow prefabricated ranch homes for low-income blacks to be built and subsidized by the Federal government throughout their community. The reasons cited sounded identical to those usually given by home-owning whites: "People who rent don't keep up their houses"; "We want these funds spent in a proper manner"; "My husband and I worked hard for 12 years to keep up our home and are not sure that families moving in under these circumstances will help the community."*

When whites only were asked about neighborhood racial integration in terms of class, they responded as follows:

Table 151

NEIGHBORHOOD RACIAL INTEGRATION BY CLASS**

"If a Negro family of the same income and education moved next door to you, would you mind it a lot, a little, or not at all?"

Whites Only

Mind a lot	19%
Mind a little	25
Not at all mind	49
Already a Negro next door	4

It seems a well-nigh impossible task to sift out from each other the bases for the discrimination, as to whether they are racial, class, social, economic or because of little-heard arguments that are important to the populace but are not carried by the media. Some of these latter in various areas of American public opinion have been thoroughly covered in the section of this book on "Unexplored Popular Perceptions and Issues." Busing is an example of an issue of this sort, in which the racial discrimination aspect seems to become secondary to a multitude of

---

* *New York Times,* July 24, 1970, p. 33.

** Angus Campbell and Howard Schuman, *Racial Attitudes in Fifteen American Cities* (Ann Arbor: Institute for Social Research, University of Michigan, July 1969), p. 33.

parent-child feelings. In the following question, racial discrimination might be a host to numerous discriminatory feelings; it is difficult to tell. A good part of "didn't like the people; undesirable people" might well be considered to be so.

Table 152

NEIGHBORHOOD ATTITUDES*

Sample of Metropolitan Area Householders, 1965 and 1966

"Let's imagine that Mr. and Mrs. Smith were looking for a new home. They found a place they liked but they decided not to take it because they didn't like the neighborhood. What do you think they didn't like about the neighborhood?"

Dirty; not well kept up; crowded	47%
Didn't like the people; undesirable people	28
Too many children	21
Undesirable minority groups	16
Noisy, heavy traffic	10

A series of Gallup polls on the reaction to the integration of the neighborhood, covering four years, showed a sharp upturn between 1963 and 1965 in those who would remain if one or a lot of Negroes moved in, and then a leveling off from 1965 to 1967, showing no trend. A majority said they would stay if "a Negro moved in," but not if "a lot" of Negroes did.

Table 153

NEIGHBORHOOD INTEGRATION**

Reaction to the Integration of the Neighborhood

National Sample

	Would stay if "a" Negro moved in next door	Would stay if a lot of Negroes moved into the neighborhood
1963	55%	22%
1965	65	31
1966	66	30
1967	65	29

* John B. Lansing and Gary Hendricks, *Automobile Ownership and Residential Density* (Ann Arbor: University of Michigan Survey Research Center, 1967).
** Gallup polls.

This is quite a different question from whether "you would mind or not" if a Negro moved next door, which was the question asked in Table 151. Undoubtedly a much greater percentage would "mind it" than think they would actually move if a Negro family moved next door. The difference in question invalidates whatever comparisons could have been made between these two questions in order to determine what role class might have played.*

Notably, in various surveys, whites consistently show an overwhelmingly greater preference for segregated neighborhoods than do Negroes. Despite the feelings by most whites that Negroes are not actually being discriminated against, as shown in the series of polls above, whites very clearly recognized racial discrimination in one poll on housing:

Table 154

RACIAL DISCRIMINATION IN HOUSING**

"Do you think in (Central City) many, some, or only a few Negroes miss out on good housing because white owners won't rent or sell to them?"

	Whites
Many	38%
Some	30
Only a few	22
None	4
Don't know	7

In a survey of the Castlemont section of Oakland, California, a blue-collar neighborhood which had been integrated and in which both whites and blacks seemed to feel that integration was working well, almost half of the whites preferred a segregated neighborhood and half said it did not matter one way or the other.

* See the work of Milton Rokeach pertaining to cultural differences between the rich and poor and between Negroes and whites. An article by Dr. Rokeach and Seymour Parker reported findings that "lend support to the idea that considerable value differences *do* distinguish the rich from the poor, but not Negroes from whites. For the most part, differences found between the latter disappeared when socioeconomic position is controlled." ("Values as Social Indicators of Poverty and Race Relations in America," *The Annals*, 388 [March 1970]: 97.)

** Campbell and Schuman, op. cit., p. 30. However, in the Roger-Louisville poll, mentioned earlier, 81 percent of the whites in Louisville felt that the government "is doing enough" to help Negroes get better housing, jobs and education; 70 percent of the Negroes disagreed with this.

Table 155

NEIGHBORHOOD INTEGRATION—CASTLEMONT*

"On the whole, how is it having both whites and Negroes living in the same block (neighborhood)? Does it work out very well, fairly well, or are there problems?"

	White	Black
Very well	29%	70%
Fairly well	50	24
There are problems	15	2

	White	Black
Prefer all one race	45%	1%
Prefer mixed	3	45
Doesn't matter	49	54

The Roper survey taken in Louisville, Kentucky in 1970 showed that three-fourths of the Negroes there preferred neighborhoods "evenly divided by race," but that almost two-thirds of the whites would like them all white and another fifth wanted them "mostly white." This was so despite the fact that "complete racial separatism was rejected strongly by both races."**

How do Negroes perceive white attitudes toward them? In the two questions below, asked of Negroes in fifteen American cities in 1969, those queried quite clearly differentiated when answering between "disliking Negroes" and "wanting to keep them down." Although most Negroes questioned thought that many whites disliked them, only a little more than a fourth felt that most whites wanted to keep them down; most thought that whites did not care one way or another. Moreover, very few thought that *almost all* whites disliked them; and although nearly half felt that many whites did, almost as many thought that only a few whites disliked Negroes. One could read the response to the phrase "most whites don't care one way or another" as a response to a feeling that whites are apathetic toward their problems; or it might be seen as a feeling that "whites and Negroes have basically the same kind of problems and whites don't see them as different."

* William L. Nicholls II, Esther S. Hochstim and Sheila Babbie, *The Castlemont Survey, A Handbook of Survey Tables* (Berkeley: Survey Research Center, University of California, June 1966), pp. 179 and 187.

** Heinig, op. cit., p. 4.

Table 156

NEGRO PERCEPTIONS OF WHITE ATTITUDES*

"Do you think only a few white people in (city) dislike Negroes, many dislike Negroes or almost all white people dislike Negroes?

	Negroes		
	Men	Women	Total
Few white people dislike Negroes	38%	37%	38%
Many dislike Negroes	44	46	45
Almost all dislike Negroes	13	11	12
Don't know	5	6	5

"On the whole, do you think most white people in (city) want to see Negroes get a better break, or do they want to keep Negroes down, or don't they care one way or the other?"

	Negroes		
	Men	Women	Total
Most whites want to see Negroes get a better break	30%	28%	29%
Most whites want to keep Negroes down	28	26	27
Most whites don't care	34	34	34
Don't know	8	12	10

In the Roper poll mentioned earlier, Louisville's Negroes were surprisingly much more optimistic about the improvement of white attitudes toward them than were whites.

Table 157

WILL WHITE ATTITUDES TOWARD NEGROES IMPROVE?**

"Will white attitudes toward Negroes improve or get worse in the next five years?"

	Negroes	Whites
Improve	51%	34%
Get worse	11	33

Something of the underlying white attitudes toward Negroes and of the whites' own basic sense of values was revealed in the following Gallup poll asked of whites only in 1965 on how they felt Negroes could attain their goals:

* Campbell and Schuman, op. cit., p. 25.
** Heinig, op. cit., p. 4.

Table 158

HOW NEGROES CAN ATTAIN GOALS*

"Negroes are interested in getting better jobs and gaining respect in their communities. What advice would you give them as a race to achieve these goals?"

Whites Only
September 1965

Get more education	44%
Work harder, try harder, don't expect something for nothing	19
Improve themselves, be good law-abiding citizens, earn respect	15
Be less aggressive, more cooperative, take it slower	14
Stop riots, demonstrations, civil rights activities	12
Cultivate self-respect	3
Work together, become united	2
All other	5

(Note: Table adds to more than 100 percent because some people gave more than one answer.)

But if the Negroes living in Louisville, Kentucky are not atypical of Negroes across the nation, then the greatest number of Negroes did not seem to disagree with whites with the means of getting ahead. Some might attribute these means to apathy and resignation; but they were clearly within the basic value system and were not meant to disrupt society, but to conform to it and take advantage of it.

Table 159

THE FAVORED WAY TO NEGRO PROGRESS**

1970 Roper Poll—Louisville, Kentucky

	Negro	White
"Get more education"	79%	78%
"Go to church and keep out of trouble"	59	52
"Stop quarreling among themselves and unite"	57	41
Greater militancy and aggressiveness	3	—
Mass demonstrations, boycotts and other public protests	6	—

A small minority of Negroes—6 percent—said they would be ready to participate in riots and revolution.

* *Gallup Political Index*, No. 4, September 1965, p. 16.
** Heinig, op. cit., p. 4.

In another part of the article describing this Roper poll, the discussion centered around questions referring to the civil rights movement as a means of achieving gains for Negroes. Whether it was directly related to their attitudes toward the civil rights movement or not, the article does not make clear, but here 27 percent of Louisville's Negroes said they had been active in civil rights causes (although only 18 percent reported that they were members of any civil rights organization, and this was most often the National Association for the Advancement of Colored People [NAACP]), and 22 percent said "They would be willing to engage in such activities as boycotts, marches, sit-ins or picketing stores."*

> Nearly all oppose violence; the approach favored by most Negroes is "nonviolent protest" (61 percent). Whites prefer even less militant behavior; 52 percent think blacks should "negotiate" their grievances. Whites tend to think past demonstrations have been harmful to the movement; blacks think they've helped, but are less sure of their value in the future. . . .

> Most whites agreed with the statement that "before Negroes are given equal rights, they have to show they deserve them." Most Negroes did not see the issue that way. Blacks and whites also differed on this statement: "Negroes will never get equal rights until they have the power to demand it." Most Negroes accepted this premise; whites sharply disagreed with this evocation of black power.

Comparable responses were given in a national survey of Negroes conducted by the Gallup organization for *Newsweek* (June 30, 1969). In response to a series of questions on violence, Negroes answered the following:

	Yes	No
Would you join a riot?	11%	68%
Should Negroes arm themselves?	25	59
Can Negroes win rights without violence?	63	21
Will there be more riots in the future?	64	9
Are riots justified?	31	48

Little basic change in Negro attitudes toward the use of violence to achieve gains could be noted in a late 1971 Harris survey reported in the *New York Post*, September 2, 1971, pp. 5 and 19. A cross-section of blacks across the nation was asked the following question:

* Ibid., pp. 2, 4.

"Different black leaders have different ideas on what it's going to take for blacks to finally achieve equality in this country. Which one of these statements comes closest to your own point of view?"

	1971	1970
Only revolution and a readiness to use violence will ever get blacks real equality.	11%	9%
Blacks should continue to push peacefully for equality, using violence only when nothing else works.	59	59
Until blacks give up violence altogether and rely on peaceful means of pressing their demands, they will not achieve real equality.	22	25
Not sure.	8	7

According to the Harris survey, the biggest rises in the percentages of blacks who were willing to use revolution and violence took place among "those under 30 (up from 12 to 18 percent) . . . in professional and managerial jobs (up from 7 to 10 percent)" and those "with incomes between $7,000 and $10,000 (up from 12 to 19 percent)."

One response of the majority (56 percent) of Louisville's whites was that the civil rights movement in Louisville was Communist-influenced. This response was not shared by Louisville's Negroes, of whom only 15 percent thought it was. In 1965, five years earlier, a similar feeling had been revealed among whites nationwide. In a Gallup poll conducted in November of that year, 51 percent of whites thought that Communists had been "a lot" involved in the demonstrations over civil rights. In light of the changes since 1965, perhaps this view no longer holds nationwide.

Table 160

COMMUNIST INVOLVEMENT IN CIVIL RIGHTS DEMONSTRATIONS*

"To what extent, if any, have the Communists been involved in the demonstrations over civil rights?"

	A Lot	Some	Minor	Not at all	Don't Know
National	48%	27%	10%	6%	9%
White	51	27	9	4	9

In Louisville, apparently, the races differed in their stress on the means of getting ahead: Negroes emphasized gaining political and economic power; whites advocated that Negroes advance through in-

* *Gallup Political Index*, No. 6, November 1965, p. 17.

dividual hard work, not "protests and demonstrations." Negroes clearly see that political and economic gains will advance their progress and position in life, but most whites either do not see a problem or think Negroes are pushing too fast.

In a poll on Negro feelings toward the Black Panthers, taken among 494 Negroes in New York, San Francisco, Detroit, Baltimore, and Birmingham in early March 1970 by the Opinion Research Corporation, the Black Panthers were shown to be a little more than half as well-known to blacks as the NAACP:

Table 161
NEGRO FEELINGS TOWARD BLACK PANTHERS

Know the Organization Very Well or a Fair Amount:

NAACP	73%
SCLC	62
Urban League	53
CORE	41
Black Panthers	39
SNCC	32

Very Favorable or Somewhat Favorable Toward:

NAACP	83%
SCLC	44
Urban League	66
CORE	52
SNCC	44
Black Panthers	37

The Black Panthers were most favorably thought of by Negro men under 30 years of age. Although the Black Panthers evoked the least favorable overall response, 70 percent thought the Black Panthers were an inspiration to young blacks. This may be reflected in the responses to another question in the same survey:

Table 162
NEGRO FEELINGS TOWARD BLACK PANTHERS

Which Organization Is Most Helpful to the Black Cause?

	Past 2 Years	Next 2 Years
NAACP	36%	32%
SCLC	26	22
Black Panthers	17	21
Urban League	9	9
CORE	5	3
SNCC	1	4

The results of this survey are surprisingly conservative, particularly since the survey was taken in the major cities, mainly in the non-South.

In a nationwide poll conducted by Gallup in July 1970, rating various "controversial" American organizations, nonwhites rated the NAACP "highly favorable" over the Black Panthers by seven to one. Moreover, the "highly favorable" rating of the NAACP increased by 10 percent from December 1965 to July 1970.

Table 163

HOW DO YOU RATE THE FOLLOWING ORGANIZATIONS?*

	Nonwhite			
	Highly Favorable		Highly Unfavorable	
	July 1970	December 1965	July 1970	December 1965
NAACP	76%	66%	1%	6%
Black Panthers	18		39	

The latest national survey of Negroes on this issue was taken by Louis Harris in the summer of 1971. A question similar to the one asked in 1971 had been asked by Harris in 1970, and the results of the polls of the two years are compared below:

Table 164

BLACK VIEWS ON BLACK PANTHERS

"Do you feel the Black Panthers represent your views or not?"

	1971	1970
Panthers represent my views	28%	25%
Do not represent my views	49	53
Not sure	23	22

Although the change nationwide was not significant, among specific groups in these surveys, the percentages of blacks who felt that the Black Panthers represented their views increased in the South from 21 to 25 percent, in smaller urban areas from 21 to 31 percent, and under age 30 from 33 to 40 percent.**

It should be pointed out that there have been indications of a rapidly growing unhappiness of Negroes with the institutions of American society. A Harris survey of August 1971 showed sharp increases be-

* *Gallup Opinion Index*, No. 62, August 1970, pp. 14, 17.
** Harris Survey, *New York Post*, September 2, 1971, pp. 5, 19.

tween 1970 and 1971 in Negro dissatisfaction with the fairness of American institutions and organizations in dealing with them on racial grounds.* But it is difficult to assess the meaning of these findings. One startling indicator of the direction some of this disaffection might be taking, or its effect, might be considered to be found in a recent Gallup poll in which most nonwhites agreed that "the South is a more livable place for blacks than any other place in the nation."

"James Meredith, the first Negro to enter the University of Mississippi, recently said that 'on a person-to-person, day-to-day basis, the South is a more livable place for blacks than any other place in the nation.' Do you agree or disagree?" **

| | Mid-July 1971 | | |
	Agree	Disagree	No Opinion
National	49%	30%	21%
Race			
White	49	30	21
Nonwhite	48	30	22

Surely some basic causes must have moved blacks today to prefer to live in the South. Either that or the South has changed enough so that Negroes are less apprehensive about living and working there. Or perhaps both are true. Or perhaps, by comparison, the South now holds less apprehension for them than the North.

Another consideration that makes it difficult to assess the degree and kind of Negro disaffection toward society today is that blacks are not the only Americans who are becoming increasingly dissatisfied with American institutions. Numerous polls and articles have shown that whites and the population as a whole are becoming more and more unhappy with the performance of the institutions of our present-day society. Again, this unhappiness appears to be an aggregation of feelings, both from left and right, that these institutions are either oppressive or lax. All sides feel that they are not being heard—perhaps even most of all today, the so-called forgotten Americans, Americans of all ages, educational backgrounds and vocations who seem to have the impression that they are carrying today's

* Harris survey, *New York Post*, August 31, 1971, p. 4.
** *Gallup Opinion Index*, No. 74, August 1971, p. 27.

problems without recourse to the institutions which normally should represent their point of view. This includes government, religion, courts, trade, and education. These Americans are anxious about the breakdown of the fabric of our society. Others feel that our institutions are outmoded, inadequate and, in some cases, oppressive, and are in need of great changes or replacements.*

Until recently, the preference for how they wished to be named remained unchanged among most Negroes. In two polls, the Louisville study in 1970 and a survey taken by Gallup for *Newsweek* (June 30, 1969), Negroes far and away preferred to be called "Negroes." Next preferred, though by considerably fewer, was "colored" (although in the Gallup poll this term was also least liked). For those who are interested in the actual breakdown, the preference polls are included here. (The Roper-Louisville poll asked whites as well, and there are striking variations between Negro and white responses):

Table 165

WHAT DO NEGROES PREFER TO BE CALLED?

Gallup Poll, *Newsweek*, June 30, 1969

	Negroes	
	Like Most	Like Least
Negro	38%	11%
Colored people	20	31
Blacks	19	25
Afro-American	10	11
Don't care	6	6
Not sure	7	16

Roper–Louisville poll, April 1970:

	Negroes	Whites
Negro	51%	27%
Colored	11	16
Black	8	25
Afro-American	8	6
Other	4	3
No difference	16	14
No opinion	3	8

* See Albert H. Cantril and Charles W. Roll, Jr., *Hopes and Fears of the American People* (New York: Universe Books, 1971); Jean. Heinig, "Is America Off the Track?", *The Roper Report*, No. 1, July, 1971; Harris survey, *New York Post*, October 25, 1971. For the results of the Harris survey, see Table 61.

It is interesting to note that in the Roper poll three times as many whites as Negroes seemed to feel that it was better to use the term "black." It was pointed out in the article on the Louisville study that the term "black" was formerly considered to be the most derogatory of all, and this may have been one reason why it was not appealing to Negroes.* In the Louisville study, "black" was not even preferred by Negro youth. But in the Gallup poll, the sharpest difference in preference was shown between younger and older Negroes—at least in the North: Among northern Negroes in their twenties, "black" was chosen either ahead of, or equal to, "Negro." Also in the same poll, the higher-income Negroes preferred "black" more often than those of lower income; southerners were less likely to name "black"; and the term "Afro-American" was not liked at any level, remaining in the 5 to 10 percentile.

The Louisville study also showed that in Louisville both races strongly rejected complete racial separation, and that a far greater percentage of Negroes preferred integration in all its aspects than whites. This included the integration of neighborhoods, housing, jobs, and social contacts, including even intermarriage. Negroes approved or "wouldn't care" if there were social intermingling of the races; 44 percent of the whites disapproved of partying together. Thirty-three percent of the Negroes and 86 percent of whites opposed intermarriage. In Louisville whites most against social contacts between races were those from the lower economic levels. Those who were college-educated did not mind getting together socially but were opposed to dating and intermarriage.

The Louisville survey brought out a clear difference between black and white concerns in the areas of their feelings about themselves— many more Negroes than whites felt depressed, lonely and blue:**

"I often feel quite lonely"—45 percent Negroes; 24 whites.

"Sometimes I can't help wondering whether anything is worthwhile anymore"—55 percent Negroes; 23 whites.

"A person nowadays has to live pretty much for today and let tomorrow take care of itself"—67 percent Negroes; 44 whites.

A similar series of questions was asked by the National Opinion Research Center in November, 1963.***

* Heinig, op. cit., p. 4.
** Heinig, op. cit., p. 2.
*** Reported in *Public Opinion Quarterly*, 33 (Spring 1969): 151.

"I'm going to read several statements, and I'd like to know whether you agree or disagree with each one."

	National Total	Negroes
Agree:		
You sometimes can't help wondering whether anything is worthwhile anymore	30%	55%
Most people in government are not really interested in the problems of the average man	31	56
Nowadays a person has to live pretty much for today and let tomorrow take care of itself	48	61
If you try hard enough, you can usually get what you want	82	90

"Here are a few statements that describe people. Please tell me whether each statement is true for you or not true for you."

True:		
When problems come up, I'm generally able to find out how to solve them.	94	89
I worry a lot.	42	43
I tend to go to pieces in a crisis.	14	24

"We are interested in the way people are feeling these days. During the past few weeks, did you ever feel:"

Pleased about having accomplished something.	68	62
Particularly excited or interested in something.	52	58
Proud because someone complimented you.	54	55
Depressed or very unhappy.	36	54
So restless couldn't sit in a chair.	45	53
Things were going your way.	57	52
Lonely or remote from other people.	28	45
Bored.	32	42
Upset because someone criticized you.	17	23
On top of the world.	25	17

Two Louis Harris surveys, one taken in August 1966, the other in April 1968, asked the same questions in both polls pertaining to these feelings. The 1966 survey also gives the figures for low-income whites, and it is interesting to see that at that time low-income whites registered higher to much higher percentages than Negroes on every question. Unfortunately their response is not reported in 1968.

"I want to read off to you a number of things that some people have told us that they have felt. From time to time do you tend to feel that:"

	August 15, 1966			April 15, 1968	
	National Total	Negroes	Low-income whites	National Total	Negroes
The rich get richer, the poor get poorer	48%	49%	68%	52%	57%
What I personally think doesn't count very much	39%	40%	60%	48%	61%
Other people get lucky breaks	19%	35%	37%	—	—
People running the country don't really care what happens to people like me	28%	32%	50%	39%	52%
Few people understand how it is to live like I live	18%	32%	36%	25%	66%
Almost nobody understands the problems facing me	17%	30%	40%	22%	52%
Important things in the world don't affect my life	18%	12%	26%	25%	45%
I feel left out of things	—	—	—	14%	43%

In each question the feeling of "alienation" increased from 1966 to 1968 among the population as a whole, but Negroes showed a very sharp increase in these feelings during the two years.*

In a Gallup poll taken in September 1969, in which Americans were asked to rate their lives, the responses were the following:**

"In general, do you find life exciting, pretty routine, or dull?"

	Exciting	Routine	Dull	No Opinion
National	47%	43%	8%	2%
White	49	43	7	1
Nonwhite	29	45	19	7

The Louisville survey also disclosed clear differences between black and white feelings about their living conditions: housing, crime, and neighborhood improvement. Although Louisville's whites most frequently answered "nothing" in response to the question, what are the "real problems" in their neighborhoods, Negroes had a plethora of real

* Survey reported in Public Opinion Quarterly, 33 (Spring 1969): 152.
** Gallup Opinion Index, No. 52, October 1969, p. 25.

problems. In conducting the interview, the interviewers did not mention race until the interview was half over. This particular question was asked before this time, and responses were later compared as to black and white. Apparently the living problems were not a direct result of living in a poor neighborhood: "Almost without exception, every neighborhood problem on the list is less troubling to *lower* economic level whites than to *upper* level Negroes."*

Table 166

A REAL PROBLEM IN THIS NEIGHBORHOOD

Roper Poll—Louisville, 1970

	Negroes	Whites
Supply of good housing	43%	3%
Juvenile delinquency	41	14
Crime	39	12
Upkeep of houses and yards	35	13
Street cleaning and repairs	30	18
Street lighting	26	23
Child day care for working mothers	23	10
Public transportation	21	21
Unemployment	19	2
Concern of public officials	16	10
Police treatment	11	2
Schools and education	10	6
Garbage collection	10	6
None or don't know	7	28

And crime:

Table 167

A REAL PROBLEM IN THIS NEIGHBORHOOD—CRIME

Roper Poll—Louisville, 1970

	Negroes	Whites
Breaking into houses	59%	48%
Drunkenness	54	21
Gambling	52	3
Drug use among youths	38	14
Purse snatchings	36	13
Prostitution	33	4
Knifings and shootings	32	4
Muggings	17	4
Loan sharking	6	2
None or don't know	14	34

* Heinig, op. cit., p. 1.

Again, each crime was more troubling to upper-level Negroes than poor whites. This was brought out again in the recent report on crime published by a Task Force of the President's Commission on Violence. The panel found that "urban blacks are arrested eight to twenty times more often than whites for homicide, rape, aggravated assault and robbery."* Moreover, in 90 percent of the serious crimes —homicide, rape and aggravated assault—the victims are of the same race as the offenders. Of this percentage, 60 to 66 percent are carried out by Negroes against Negroes and 24 to 30 percent by whites against whites. The report supported the data of the Louisville poll that a higher crime rate was primarily sustained by blacks against blacks.**

Table 168
CRIME AND ITS VICTIMS, BY RACE, 1970***

Race of Offender and Victim	Criminal Homicide	Aggravated Assault	Forcible Rape	Armed Robbery
Both same race	90%	90%	90%	51%
Black versus black	66	66	60	38
White versus white	24	24	30	13
Black versus white	6	8	10	47
White versus black	4	2	—	2

Source: Victim-offender survey made by Task Force on Individual Crimes of Violence, an agency of the National Commission on the Causes and Prevention of Violence, 1969–70.

C. Attitudes of Negroes Toward Their Own Lives

I have been dwelling on racial attitudes, in social and political aspects of life, of the general American public, Negro and white. Let us now look at certain feelings of Negroes toward their own lives, their work, their families. I shall deal with a series of questions asked by Gallup involving Negro satisfaction with family income, housing, their job, and education.

A series of Gallup opinion polls examining Negro and white satisfaction and dissatisfaction with their family income from 1949 to

* New York Times, September 8, 1970, p. 1. A long article discussing the results of this report, "Black Crime: The Lawless Image," by Fred P. Graham, appeared in Harper's Magazine, September 1970.

** "For the population as a whole," the report said, "persons 18 to 24 commit almost four times as many violent crimes as do persons over 25." New York Times, September 8, 1970, p. 1.

*** New York Times, September 8, 1970, p. 32.

1971 reveals a much greater dissatisfaction than satisfaction among Negroes throughout most of this time—almost the reverse of the feeling among whites. The gap between Negro satisfaction and dissatisfaction closed considerably in 1966—the year after it was widest—when there was only a 4 percent difference. Satisfaction with family income rose slowly until 1966, except for the great perturbation around 1965 at the height of the racial turbulence. After 1966, satisfaction slowly began to decline.

Figure 37

NEGRO AND WHITE SATISFACTION AND DISSATISFACTION
WITH FAMILY INCOME*

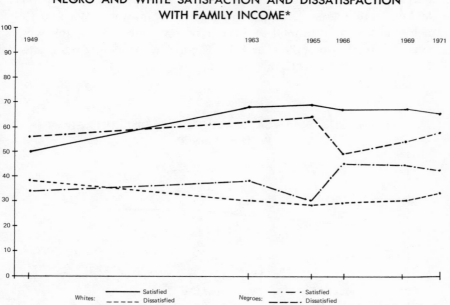

Whites: ——— Satisfied — — — Dissatisfied   Negroes: — · — · Satisfied — — — · Dissatisfied

Closely similar results were reported in an Opinion Research Corporation poll done for CBS in June 1968:**

"I would like to ask you if you are satisfied or dissatisfied with some things in your life. For example, would you say you are satisfied or dissatisfied with your family income?"

* Compiled from data in the *Gallup Political Index,* No. 4, September 1965, p. 21; the *Gallup Political Index,* No. 18, November–December 1966, pp. 14 and 18; the *Gallup Opinion Index,* No. 47, May 1969, p. 10; and the *Gallup Opinion Index,* No. 76, October 1971, pp. 11 and 12.
** As published in Hazel Erskine, "The Polls: Negro Finances," *Public Opinion Quarterly,* 33 (Summer 1969): 275.

	Whites	*Nonwhites*
Satisfied	67%	43%[a]
Dissatisfied	30	50
No opinion	3	7

[a] Negroes

A slightly different picture emerges for Negro satisfaction and dissatisfaction with their housing. Again, whites have been very much more satisfied with their housing than blacks and far more satisfied than dissatisfied. In 1949, 32 percent of Negroes were dissatisfied—only 4 percent more than whites—compared to 66 in 1965, 48 in 1969 and 46 in 1971. Again, the peak of dissatisfaction was in 1965, at the height of the racial turmoil, and the trend reversed itself the following year. From 1966 to September 1971, Negroes were slightly more satisfied than dissatisfied with their housing.

Figure 38

NEGRO AND WHITE SATISFACTION AND DISSATISFACTION WITH HOUSING*

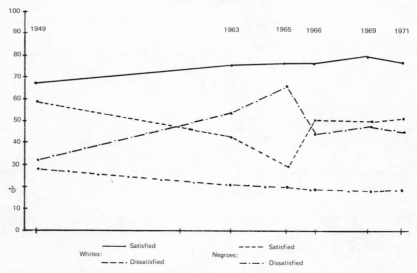

* Compiled from information in Gallup polls in the *Gallup Political Index*, No. 4, September 1965, p. 21; *Gallup Political Index*, No. 18, November–December 1966, pp. 14 and 16; the *Gallup Opinion Index*, No. 47, May 1969, p. 12; and the *Gallup Opinion Index*, No. 76, October 1971, pp. 10 and 11.

Over the years from 1949 to 1971 Gallup opinion polls show that most Negroes have been satisfied with their work—though, again, much less satisfied than whites—and in the period 1965-69, very highly satisfied in comparison with the earlier years. There was a sharp downturn of satisfaction from 1969 to 1971 (13 percent).

Figure 39

NEGRO AND WHITE SATISFACTION AND DISSATISFACTION
WITH WORK THEY DO*

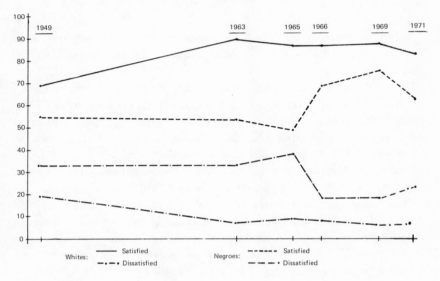

The Roper-Louisville poll, mentioned earlier, lent support to these responses: In 1970, 68 percent of whites and 61 percent blacks in the city of Louisville thought their present jobs were "about right." Only 18 percent of Negroes said "discrimination" was the reason they were held back in their jobs; 23 percent blamed "lack of training"; 16 percent "lack of experience." When asked what kind of job they would like to have if nothing stood in the way, twice as many blacks as whites did not know.**

* Compiled from information in Gallup polls in the *Gallup Opinion Index*, No. 47, May 1969, p. 7; the *Gallup Political Index*, No. 4, September 1965, p. 20; the *Gallup Political Index*, No. 18, November–December, 1966, pp. 14 and 15; and the *Gallup Opinion Index*, No. 76, October 1971, pp. 14 and 15.
** Heinig, op. cit., p. 2.

An Opinion Research Report in early 1970, "Equal Opportunity: Its Time Has Come," showed a striking switchover in the last decade in Negro responses toward job discrimination. The poll takers asked:

When companies turn down Negroes for jobs, do you think it is more because of:

	Negroes naming		Whites naming	
	1956	1969	1956	1969
Management prejudice	61%	35%	19%	11%
Negroes unqualified	9	39	50	75

A sharp increase is also revealed here in the white attitude that Negroes are not being discriminated against, but are unqualified for certain jobs.

How much of the white feeling that some Negroes are "unqualified" is a cover for deeper feelings of prejudice cannot be known; and how much of the lack of training and experience is due originally and presently to keeping Negroes back because of their race also cannot be determined. Today, job training and training program opportunities are open to Negroes in numerous skilled occupations. The reasons why some of these programs may not be working satisfactorily may be legion: Some may be because of racial prejudice; but others may be attributed to other complex issues playing a greater role than the racial problem. (See the section of Chapter 1 on "Underexplored Popular Perceptions and Issues" for a view of some of these issues.)

Today, most Negroes themselves apparently feel that their jobs are satisfying, and that with training and experience, they would now have better access to job opportunities. This is borne out by the slow, but steady gain in tolerance by whites and blacks in living and working together. The sharp drop in job satisfaction within the past two years may or may not be the beginning of a new trend—it may be a perturbation. It might conceivably be part of the general increased unhappiness of Negroes and all Americans, described earlier in this chapter, with American institutions and with the economic recession of the past two years. Note that in every area covered in these Gallup polls—family income, housing, work and education—the satisfaction of whites dropped in the last two years.

A series of polls taken by the Opinion Research Corporation in 1944, 1951 and 1956 showed a steady decline in white racial discrimination in every aspect of employment: on equal jobs; on working next to Negroes; on having Negro supervisors; and on having integrated departments in a factory. Three Louis Harris surveys also showed a clear reduction between August and October 1963 and October 1965 in the percentage of whites who objected to working next to a Negro on the job.* In the Opinion Research polls, the greatest jump toward tolerance was shown to have occurred between 1944 and 1951. Here again, the authors of the article reporting these polls indicated that racial prejudice alone did not seem to be the reason for management's reluctance to hire Negroes.

In view of the growing acceptance of working with Negroes that developed in the mid-1950s and the passage of Equal Opportunity legislation in the early 1960s, other factors appear to be responsible for the supervisor's lack of enthusiasm to implement training programs for Negroes.

Our studies further indicate that this reluctance may be a reflection of (a) their reaction to the educational and cultural gap between the average white worker and his black counterpart, and (b) their continuing emotional commitment to the tradition of individualism, which favors self-help over corporate philanthropy. More likely, perhaps, it reflects a conflict in values inherent in their own supervisory situations.

Yet, the unemployment rate for Negroes throughout the nation is twice the white race. The Louisville poll showed that in Louisville in 1970, 14 percent of Negroes interviewed were out of a job and 3 percent of whites; 38 percent of blacks and 15 percent of whites were employed as unskilled laborers; twice as many whites as Negroes were in white-collar jobs; and a very tiny percentage of Negroes were in executive positions.

In response to the Gallup poll question, "On the whole, would you say you are satisfied or dissatisfied with your children's education?" both blacks and whites became more satisfied with it from 1963–1965

---

* Joseph R. Goeke and Caroline S. Weymar, "Barriers to Hiring the Blacks," *Harvard Business Review*, 49 (September-October 1969): 144–152, and Hazel Erskine, "The Polls: Negro Employment," *Public Opinion Quarterly*, 33 (Spring 1968): 138. Another in-depth public opinion study, conducted in 1970, revealed similar findings in other areas of integration—integration in transportation, restaurants, schools and socially. See Andrew M. Greeley and Paul B. Sheatsley, "Attitudes Toward Racial Integration," *Scientific American*, 225 (December 1971): 13–19.

to 1966 and then less satisfied in the period 1966–1969. The 1966 figures are puzzling, for they show a 20-percent increase from the previous year of the number of Negroes satisfied, a corresponding dip of 22 percent in Negro dissatisfaction, and a small drop in white dissatisfaction from the previous year, all of which were considerably reversed from 1966 to 1969. In general, Negroes were much more satisfied with their children's education in 1969 than they were in 1963–1965: A slightly greater percentage of Negroes were dissatisfied than satisfied in 1965, but in 1969 the figures were reversed and the percentage of those satisfied was 20 percent higher than those who were dissatisfied.° In 1971, blacks felt a little more satisfied than they had in 1969, but whites continued their drop in satisfaction.

Figure 40

NEGRO AND WHITE SATISFACTION AND DISSATISFACTION WITH EDUCATION OF THEIR CHILDREN**

"ON THE WHOLE, WOULD YOU SAY YOU ARE SATISFIED OR DISSATISFIED WITH (YOUR) CHILDREN'S EDUCATION?"

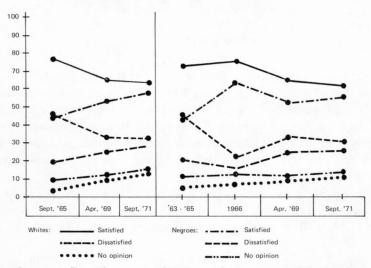

° In the Louisville study, examined earlier, only 10 percent of the blacks named schools as a neighborhood problem; Negroes in Louisville considered their local schools comparable to those in other parts of the city.

°° Compiled from information in Gallup polls in the *Gallup Political Index*, No. 4, September 1965, p. 20; *Gallup Political Index*, No. 18. November–December 1966, pp. 14 and 17; *Gallup Opinion Index*, No. 47, May 1969, p. 7; and the *Gallup Opinion Index*, No. 76, October 1971, pp. 16 and 17.

In summary, it appears from the trends that we have examined in the Gallup opinion polls and from various other polls, that since the middle of the last decade, Negroes have become in general more satisfied with their economic condition. The following figure gives an over-all picture of these trends, according to Gallup polls, beginning with the area of most satisfaction—work—and descending to that of least satisfaction—family income.

Figure 41

TREND OF NEGRO VIEWS SINCE 1949*

% Satisfied With . . .

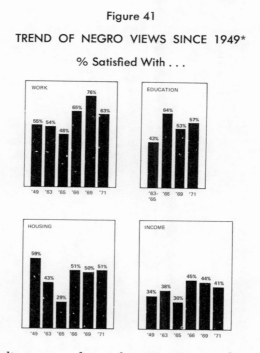

In their feelings toward racial integration, evidence shows that Negroes on the whole strongly favor racial integration, not black separatism. There are indications that feelings of segregation among Negroes are strongest among the very young and, in some issues connected with segregation, among the young college graduates. It is interesting to note in Table 169 that fewer older college graduates are for segregation than any other category, including Negroes as a whole. This "conservatism" compares well with the "con-

* Views on satisfaction with education were not available for 1949 and 1963. There was a combined figure for 1963–1965.

Table 169

NEGROES FAVORING SEPARATIST RESPONSE TO EACH QUESTION*

	Total	Men	Women	Age 16–19 Total	Age 20–39 College Graduate	Age 40–69 College Graduate
Believe stores in "a Negro neighborhood should be owned and run by Negroes"	18%	21%	15%	22%	30%	13%
Prefer to live in all Negro or mostly Negro neighborhood	13	14	12	N/A†	N/A	N/A
Believe school with mostly Negro children should have mostly Negro teachers	10	13	7	16	20	3
Agree that "Negroes should have nothing to do with whites if they can help it"	9	11	8	14	0	4
Believe whites should be discouraged from taking part in civil rights organizations	8	9	6	15	10	5
Agree that "there should be a separate black nation here"	6	7	4	10	4	0

† N/A—No answer given

* Campbell and Schuman, op. cit., pp. 16 and 19.

380

servatism" registered by all college-educated, both white and black, on numerous issues in nationwide polls.*

Has support for black separatism increased among Negroes within the last half decade? According to evidence gathered by a prestigious survey organization, it has not.**

Although the doctrine of black separatism has been increasingly voiced by some members of the black community, it still has only minority support; and there has been little change in black attitudes toward desegregation over the four-year period. For example, in 1964 some 72 percent of the blacks questioned said they were in favor of desegregation (with only 6 percent favoring strict segregation) and four years later 75 percent were favoring desegregation (with only 3 percent for strict segregation).

None of this is to say that Negroes do not have differing opinions from a majority of whites on numerous social and political issues. Their needs are pressing and real, and improvement of their conditions is one of the urgent problems of our time. Negroes have traditionally and overwhelmingly voted Democratic, the party of the workingman, the poor and the ethnic minorities. On most foreign policy, political, and domestic issues today, Negroes have been voting the way of the Democratic liberal, except in those issues that directly affect their children and the school—such as legalization of marijuana, busing, and discipline in the school—in which they not only strongly line up with the majority of the population, but in some cases, such as discipline in the school, favor stricter action than the majority.***

D. *Negro Feelings about their Economic and Financial Status.*

The following is a series of polls illustrative of Negro responses to their economic and financial status with white responses as a comparison. Some of them deal with what you might call "comfort" status and whether it has improved over the past years. Here again, we see

* See the chapter, "Unexplored Popular Perceptions and Issues," passim.
** From an article in the *Newsletter* of the University of Michigan Institute of Social Research, carrying some of the findings gathered during the 1964 and 1968 election studies by Angus Campbell and other analysts at the University of Michigan Survey Research Center.
*** See the Chapter, "Some Underexplored Popular Perceptions and Issues," Table 16.

that, as of 1965 to 1967, Negroes, by a large percentage, considered that their standard of living and comfort in life had improved over the past. Despite this, the great disparity of level of earnings between whites and Negroes is clearly shown: In a Roper poll in 1967 practically all Negroes are bunched in the lower half of the income levels ($5,000–9,000 and below) and most whites in the upper half ($5,000–9,999 and above).* In January 1938, a Roper poll for *Fortune* showed that about 65 percent of Negro respondents felt that a family of four could live on less than $25 a week; 71 percent of the whites said it needed $25 to $40 per week and over. An interesting Gallup poll from May 1937 found that southern Negroes felt that a family of four needed half the amount of weekly income that southern whites said was needed to live decently ($25 and $12).

By 1967, a Roper poll for the *Saturday Evening Post*, asking the same question that was asked in 1938, showed that the average response as to income needed by a family per week was, whites: $127.12; Negroes: $98.25. As of late 1970, a national sample of nonfarm population reported in a Gallup poll that they thought a typical family of four needed a minimum of $126 per week to live—$96 per week more than in 1937, $54 per week more than in 1957.**

Table 170
NEGRO AND WHITE ECONOMIC STATUS***

Gallup
In your opinion, what is the smallest amount of income a family of four (husband, wife and two children) needs a week to live decently?
1937: May 24

	By Week	By Year
National average (median)	$30[a]	$1,560
South:		
Whites	25[a]	1,300
Negroes	12[a]	624

[a] A similarly worded question in a January 13, 1952 Gallup release showed identical amounts.

* The Negro median family income as a percent of white increased in the years 1965–68 from 54 to 60 percent and in 1969 and 1970 to 61 percent. The Negro median family income in 1968 was $5,359; the white, $8,936. Source: U.S. Department of Commerce, Bureau of the Census.

** Presumably the difference between the Roper and Gallup figures may be accounted for by the difference in the wording of the question: Roper asked, "How much money do you need?"; Gallup asked for a minimum figure.

*** Hazel Erskine, "The Polls: Negro Finances," *Public Opinion Quarterly*, 33 (Summer 1969): 273–276.

Table 170 (continued)

Roper for *Fortune*

How much money per week do you think the average family of four needs to live on around here, including necessities and a few inexpensive pleasures?

1938: January

	Total National	Negroes	Economic Status	
			Prosperous	Poor
Over $40 per week	22.3%	10.3%	30.2%	13.2%
$25–$40	49.0	25.0	45.5	53.9
Under $25	21.6	59.2	14.9	25.6
Don't know	7.1	5.5	9.4	7.3

Roper for *Saturday Evening Post*[b]

1967: December

	Race		Economic Status	
	Whites	Negroes	Upper	Lower
$200 and over/week	12%	7%	35%	5%
$150–199	24	14	23	14
$120–149	24	15	10	15
$101–119	12	6	5	12
$90–100	13	20	7	21
$60–89	8	24	7	18
Under $60	3	9	—	12
Don't know	6	5	14	5
Median	$127.12	$98.25	$172.06	$99.54

[b] Columns in this table are not rounded out to 100 percent and may total from 99 to 102 percent.

Roper for *Saturday Evening Post*

When it comes to living within your income, do you find it quite easy, not too difficult, fairly difficult, or almost impossible to live within your income?

1967: December

	Race		Economic Status	
			$15,000 or over	Under $5,000
	Whites	Negroes		
Quite easy	28%	18%	40%	14%
Not too difficult	35	26	36	28
Fairly difficult	29	37	19	39
Almost impossible	7	18	5	18
Don't know, no answer	1	1	—	2

Table 170 (continued)

Roper for *Saturday Evening Post*
Finally, into which of these general groups did your total family income fall this past year—before taxes, that is?
1967: December

	Race	
	Whites	*Negroes*
$15,000 and over	11%	1%
$10,000–$14,999	17	4
$5,000–$ 9,999	39	26
$2,500–$ 4,999	13	26
Under $2,500	7	27
Don't know, refused	14	16

Gallup for *Look*
All things considered, would you say your family's standard of living is generally improving from year to year, or not? That is, are you able to live better as time goes on?
1965: February

	Race		Economic Status	
	Whites	*Negroes*	*Upper*	*Lower*
Improving	81%	68%	94%	60%
Not improving	16	26	5	36
Don't know	3	6	1	4

Roper for *Saturday Evening Post*
Would you say that you live about as comfortably as your parents did when they were your age, or that your life is less comfortable than theirs, or that your life is more comfortable than theirs when they were your age?
1967: December

	Race		Economic Status	
	Whites	*Negroes*	*Upper*	*Lower*
More	78%	65%	77%	66%
Less	4	6	2	11
Same	17	21	21	16
Don't know	1	9	2	7

Harris for *Newsweek*
As far as your pay goes, do you feel you are better off today than you were three years ago, worse off, or about the same as you were then?
1966: Summer

	National Total		Non-South		South	
	1963	*1966*	*1963*	*1966*	*1963*	*1966*
Negroes only:						
Better	54%	55%	55%	55%	54%	55%
Worse	13	9	15	11	12	7
Same	28	29	25	28	29	30

CHAPTER IV

CONCLUSION

A. Some Important Factors in the Current Milieu

The foregoing analysis, though very far from being exhaustive, does seem to indicate that, with some exceptions, our society is progressing and changing at a normal rate. These changes are occurring because of the tugs and pushes of many forces and groups. Like the ocean tides or the planets in the solar system, the combined groups of forces, while largely counteracting one another, nonetheless do tend to shape and direct our society. The forces at work within society are not new in most cases; if anything, the only new thing in the past decade may have been the unusual attention paid to some of these forces. This, of course, is important; fashionable attitudes tend, over a long enough period, to have some effect on people's reasoning and priorities. If one force is given the lion's share of attention it may have effects out of proportion to its real size. This could occur either from the effects of a miscalculation based on a straight-line projection of the depth and strength of one or more forces, or because of a reaction to this miscalculation. But reaching conclusions based on fads in itself is far from unique in history, and, over the long run, has also been part of the normal trends in our society.

We have seen such phenomena influence policy decisions over the years in this country. Fads were also behind much accepted "wisdom" in our intellectual and governmental communities when considering foreign and defense issues. For example, in the 1930s, despite much evidence to the contrary, guilt feelings about the Versailles Treaty and the "perfidy" of our former allies, among other things, caused many "sophisticated" people to look on Nazism as merely a silly, over-publicized rationalization for the normal adjustment back to the pre-war balance in Europe. In the late 1940s, despite the total lack of evidence to support the assumption, it was the vogue among many intellectuals and even media people, some of them rather influential, to consider Mao Tse-tung's party to be a group of "agrarian reformers" rather than true Communists. In the mid-1960s there was a widely accepted assumption, again without any evidence to support it, that the Soviet nuclear arms buildup was an attempt only to bring their stockpile up to parity with the U.S.; it was thought acceptable for them to reach "parity" with the United States, when they would, of course, stop. Our strategic nuclear arms buildup was actually restricted, partly because of this anti-arms race assumption. The Soviets had never said they would stop at parity (and, of course, in strategic missiles they did not) but the "fad wisdom" was not to be questioned.

We have had several such policy shifts which could not be completely explained by sound or sometimes even logical techniques for the solution of problems in the main area of concern. Generally, however, these changes, as in the above examples, were in foreign and military policy in which, in the non-crisis, day-to-day activity of the nation, the short-range effects were not very obvious.

In the area of domestic policies and approaches to domestic issues there have, of course, been significant changes that have had more quickly felt effects on the everyday life of the average citizen, particularly in this century. Many of these, however, were brought on by the new demands after the heavy industrialization of the United States and were clearly apropos: labor and anti-trust laws, housing and sanitary regulations. Others, particularly in recent decades, however, were less easily traceable to a logic connected to a demonstrable solution of a particular problem. Some changes in our educational system, for example, might fit this description: the idea that pupils should no longer be treated as people to be informed but primarily to be communicated with; that lecturing should no longer be looked upon as teaching, but "inquiry learning" at almost all stages should (see the discussion on this issue in the pages following Table 94).

This "fad"-approach to policy is in itself not necessarily bad, and all changes have had a touch of this in them (including the very

386

apropos laws mentioned above). But, if in the face of a pure (irresponsible?) fad-approach on important issues, the balancing forces are muted enough, our society—that very sensitive "planetary system"—might begin to gyrate unevenly and it might either become somewhat unstuck, or potentially dangerous forces might be applied to hold it together.

One gets the feeling that in some instances in the past decade, domestic, as well as foreign and military, policy recommendations began to shift even more in the direction of the "fad"-approach, and a disproportionate number of ideas might have originated from the less reliable sources. Here again, certain ideas and premises were pushed by people for reasons that might not have had much to do with the direct effect of adopting these premises and the policies to which they led. We have tried to highlight some of the parallel, if sometimes less emphasized, factors which also bear on these issues.

As discussed earlier, the second half of the past decade has seen a swing back in the direction of believing that solutions would come from the Left, and lately from the young. One sometimes wonders if turning to these "adults of the future" might not have come from the constant desire to look into and be one step ahead of the future. Furthermore, this is a comfortable position to hold in mid-twentieth century America, when we care so much about and have such pride in our youth. But, according to the fad, not all youth qualify. Those to whom we were generally told to look comprise a particular section of our youth, many of them rather obstreperous. This emphasis on "swinging" youth looks a little (but not too much) like the 1920s.

The interesting thing is that some *avant-garde* adults apparently think that, by turning in the direction of these Left-wing youth, they are striking a blow against those "mossbacks" who are against change, or who even want to "turn back the clock." The argument could be made that they themselves might sometimes be backing ideas that would *really* turn the clock back. As mentioned earlier, they, and the youth they support, sound quite a bit like the intellectual, elitist revolutionaries of 1848 (who were largely made up of writers, students and professors), and one is prompted to point out that this line of reasoning prevailed in an era *before* the Industrial Revolution. This comparison, one feels, is more appropriate than the comparison with the "roaring" twenties. In mid-nineteenth century Europe, intellectuals (with the possible exception of workers in the new, industrial cities of

387

England and, in some cases, France) were one of the few "organized" groups in the cities, besides the privileged classes, who could make common cause.

Since the Industrial Revolution, however, the people in areas affected by it have no longer needed such an elitist, "vanguard-of-the-revolution" leadership. The people started their own organizations, with their own organizers; no longer were they just ignorant "mobs" in cities, with nothing in common but the fact that they lived together. Education became available, then mandatory, in the lower grades.* Also, bad as their lot still was, they had begun to raise themselves above the level of abject poverty and brute existence. They were reaching the level from which they as a group could "take off."** Many could now read and write; in many cities large groups had much in common: they were all weavers, miners, ironworkers, and so forth. They had unions and an approach to achieving better living by selective and professional pressures on the places that had the power to enact immediate change for their benefit—the industrial companies. This process, of course, also had many shortcomings but, because the people handling the pressure tactics now were professionals, and of the people, the baby was much less likely to be thrown out with the bathwater. Much could be accomplished within the system. As early as the 1840s in Britain, it was the revolutionary content of Chartism that had the effect of alienating it from the trade unions.***

This is not to say that leaders springing from the people and legitimate, even elected, officials of labor unions have never had or caused severe problems. For example, there has been corruption in American unions. Furthermore, disastrous general strikes have at times hit Europe and led to chaotic conditions; but even then, normally some framework remained, so that total anarchy (apparently recommended [knowingly or unknowingly] by a number of recent elitist revolutionaries) did not occur. In Western Europe of the 1960s, the intellectuals were apparently deluding themselves when they thought they could again truly lead the masses. The worst thing that happened to the

* René Albrecht-Carrié, *Europe Since 1815* (New York: Harper and Brothers, 1962), p. 29.
** Real wages in England and France by 1830 were already 60 percent higher than they were in 1780. See C. W. Crawley, *War and Peace in the Age of Upheaval*, The New Cambridge Modern History (Cambridge: Cambridge University Press, 1965), 4: 59.
*** Albrecht-Carrié, op cit., p. 28.

French students' "May Revolution of 1968," from the revolutionaries' point of view, was that they were reinforced by a general strike by the unions. Though many observers did not seem to realize it at the time, the revolution was over the minute the alliance with the unions came about.*

By the early twentieth century, the increased knowledge, common outlook and organizational ability of modern workers, along with their very numbers and concentration, made them an important political force. Since the Industrial Revolution, in the democracies, the real power has gone to the people, through formal and (particularly in the United States) ever more representative political parties, with a subsequent loss of power by all traditional elitist groups.

Many of these factors had long more or less applied to the independent-minded Americans; they had a strong belief in the two-party democratic system, even before the Industrial Revolution really took place in the United States. Afterward, they were strongly reinforced and supported by an increasing number of literate people, a larger suffrage, expanding enterprise, and a unique form of independent unionism. It was separated from politics to a degree experienced just about nowhere else in the world (somewhat like the almost uniquely American separation of church and state). Furthermore, native-born from the lower education and economic levels and illiterate immigrants, from coolies to Russian peasants, have found that opportunity for upward mobility for them and/or their children is real under this system.

In this century, this country has not been fertile ground for vanguard elitists. The time-tested, yet flexible forces at work for progress in this country have led to great accomplishments in improving the personal and material conditions of the people. This all has been achieved without a loss of the freedom and human dignity so important to the average citizen; therefore, he traditionally opposes extremists who appear to threaten the system.

1. A RETURN TO THE OLD CITY STRUCTURE?

But, at the present time (besides the impersonal existence in sections of commercial cities), perhaps we can no longer emphasize the point of the homogeneity of industrial groups of people in our cities quite as

* See Sanche de Gramont, "The French Worker Wants to Join the Affluent Society Not Wreck it," *New York Times Magazine,* June 16, 1968, p. 62. Most of the workers, young and old, had little in common with the student sons of the rich and told them so in no uncertain terms.

strongly as we could two or three decades ago. The change in the cities is occurring for many reasons, including the smaller percentages of the labor force in production work and the tendency for craft- or even company-wide unions in now predominant service industries not to contain large numbers of people. Many such workers are not unionized at all; in addition, some may have trouble unionizing in the old way in the face of opposition by militants who do not trust the "masses" and their union elections, any more than they trust them in political elections. This phenomenon, and also partly the growing number of people on welfare, and the sizeable percentage of the eight million college students (about five million of them full-time) and several hundreds of thousands of instructors, who are disassociated from many of the workings of society and live in the metropolitan areas, are causing our cities to change. As in pre-Industrial Revolution Europe, large masses of people in an increasing number of our cities again often have little in common except the fact that they happen to live together.

One might be tempted to argue that today the new vanguard-type might have a better opportunity to lead a city mob than he has had since before the Industrial Revolution. One must quickly note, however, that this may be too simplistic a conclusion; for although in the Europe of the 1840s, also, he could only mobilize a minority, he could count on the neutrality, or even the tacit acquiescence, of many more of the masses who felt they had no loyalty to the privileged oligarchy who ruled them, had no other spokesman, were illiterate and in desperate need, and therefore would risk the dangers of giving power to the radical intellectuals. This is no longer true in Europe, let alone here. Today, even among the neediest, there are other responsible, effective and popular spokesmen and organizations to turn to (see Tables 161, 162, and 163 for data on the overwhelming choice of the NAACP among Negroes), and there is still a high rate of literacy in our cities. Most important, the voting franchise is very broad in this country. Further, there is no lack of talent for full-time elective positions among all groups, if the system is not unduly hampered by special interest forces.

The lessening of influence in the past few years on learning the fundamentals in our schools, and the effort to make social reform and "relevant" (and sometimes, one fears, somewhat doctrinaire) current events-type teaching predominant, however, may inadvertently have weakened the universal educational bulwark against the vanguard

390

types. It may have made college students and some others more vulnerable to efforts to convince Negroes and the lower-economic level segments of our society that groups like the NAACP are "Uncle Tom" organizations; that the traditional helping organizations and the government itself do not have the peoples' interest at heart; that all unions and corporations are racist and fascist; that progress (no matter how great) is an illusion; that elections are snares and frauds. All this tends to undermine the balancing forces in our cities which, among other things, make them so sociologically and politically different from cities ripe for "intellectual" elitist-led revolts.

Furthermore, unstructured, participatory democracy (the apparent preferred process of many recent "intellectual" elitists) may be potentially more disruptive than it appears at first glance. Without a truly democratic set of rules and professional organizers from the traditional, responsible organizations, the probability of getting rigorous, intelligent, talented leaders (with the possible exception of some ideologues or even ideological fanatics) is slim. Competent moderates are in great demand in industry, government and education, and are usually so overworked that they have great difficulty finding time to serve on community committees. With the exception of some retired people (who in recent years often could no longer meet the sheer physical demands of serving on community groups, particularly in the quasi-violent, strenuous way many have recently operated), mediocre people are more likely to have plenty of time, and ideologues from the right and left are bound to turn out to "help the people," or "look out for their rights." Jobs with the establishment are often not important to the Left-wingers anyhow, and though the Right-winger's "hang-up" with work keeps his numbers down, some Right-wing fanatics always seem to be able to find time for these committees. In this unstructured type of activity, common in the past few years, such groups can create more problems than many good people could ever clear up, even on the off-chance that the ideologues and fanatics would submit to somebody's review. These groups are likely to jump into any issue, from the electoral college to ecology, from anti-poverty programs to the anti-ballistic missile—and take "right off"; some because they do not know how difficult it is; others because they "know" what is right, so they don't have to worry about the "details." What is more important, their extremist statements and activities are usually considered "newsworthy," so they are likely to get the coverage. And even if emotional, often simplistic, "solutions" are challenged, a battle of hyperbolic rhetoric is likely to ensue, generating much heat and little light. Then the fact often seemed to be forgotten that the battle may really be between a reasonable majority and a usually tiny, often ill-informed, extremist group, or even between two tiny, ill-informed extremist groups, to the exclusion of the large middle majority.

2. VOICES FROM THE PAST

Insofar as this whole new, primarily Leftist life-style has a tendency to foster this process, the recent emphasis on the desires of today's Left-wing youngsters and their proponents is again significant. But even this emphasis is, in itself, not without some recent precedent. In 1948, as mentioned earlier, a group of similar young Left-wingers, primarily college students, and a phalanx of adults of like views, were saying things somewhat similar to those of the last few years. They vocally and energetically backed Henry Wallace in his third-party bid for the presidency. There was, however, a difference in the coverage they received. Then there were no hungry TV networks desperately trying to keep 100 million TV sets supplied with "newsworthy" events. Newspapers and radio just did not seem to be in that much need of "action." One has the feeling that if TV had been there in 1948, many vocal, young, Left-wing Henry Wallacites might have been on it, and they probably would have learned the name of that heady game quickly. They also may have had some sympathetic commentators and might have ended up by getting enormous amounts of attention, perhaps even being called pace-setters. But we had no TV; those adults who took up their cause as coming from the prophetic generation did not get the coverage either—and apparently little was lost. As indicated earlier in this study, it turned out that, at least in the short run, this segment of youth was not even prophetic about the universities, let alone the country. Interestingly then, too, the almost ignored, great majority of serious, plugging, uninvolved but scholastically competent students (including the G.I. Bill veterans) were the real precursors of the climate of the campuses in the 1950s.

This, of course, should have been no surprise for any historian who believes in the cyclical theory of events, particularly among the young. And the same theory could, and perhaps should, be applied today. But, again, for many reasons it would be somewhat imprudent to say, "it's just the same old cycle." First (partly for the reasons mentioned above), nothing is ever *exactly* the same. It is quite possible to believe this, however, without losing sight of the fact that we cannot ignore the almost ever-present analogies of history. Second, those who really see certain youth and others of similar outlook as precursors and as the inevitable recipients of the reins of power, and with their disproportionate literary and TV coverage, may have "converted" some powerful men in and out of government who (as indicated earlier) may have taken actions which could be hard to undo. But, should even this be cause for concern? The acceptance of the new life-style may have been accelerated, but we have experienced this and even the effect of the affluent young on our national life-style before, without disastrous results. The automobile and the young, primarily those under thirty, probably set the pace for the Roaring Twenties. Basic values held up and the Depression snuffed out the affluence and much of this life-style, or perhaps simply accelerated an inevitable swing back. As indicated earlier, some see such a swing occurring now, particularly among the students.

The traditional, extreme left-leaning elements in the society also "came into their own" to some degree in the 1930s, particularly in academia and in some unions, and opposition to them mounted as their perceived objectives and tactics became more extreme, as it did recently. There were differences from the 1920s in the recent experience, however, and some think there were some changes that tend to slow the "return of the pendulum." Furthermore, one could argue that today the *period* of the pendulum is of extra importance. Feelings of *ancien régime* morale are only tolerable when there is no dynamic force ready to step into the vacuum. This is not the day of Calvin Coolidge, some argue: there is a powerful, dynamic competitor to the democratic system abroad in the world and if we falter in our faith in our system, it could bode ill for many small nations and eventually our own.* Be that as it may, a drop in morale is seldom good for the system (even

* See Seymour Martin Lipset, "The Socialism of Insanity," *New York Times Magazine,* January 3, 1971, p. 6, for a discussion of the anti-Zionist, anti-Israel sentiment among the extreme Left. The 1970 non-support of the premise that "containing communism" was worth fighting for by college students, particularly the "forerunners" (see Table 126), probably also indicates this. But we cannot be sure, because there was no question about containing fascism. The greater number who felt that fighting to defend someone "against aggression" might have meant that they felt that "containing communism" did not refer to defending people against communist aggression; or it may have meant they felt we should fight to defend specific people against any kind of aggression or most people against aggressions other than communist aggression.

the economic sector), and sustained erosion of belief in our democratic processes and prolonged, unjustified pessimism can be very bad.

Domestically, too, things could be different than in the 1920s and 1930s. Because of the heed that has been paid to this particular "Left" segment of society by some men in "opinion-making," government, education, and now apparently, the church and industry, it could have a disproportionate influence on domestic issues. For example, in the face of overwhelming opposition by all age groups of adults (see Table 9) and still heavy opposition among high school students (see Table 88), the drive to legalize marijuana nevertheless goes forward, largely propelled by and for the latter group. This is no small issue, particularly when one considers marijuana's appeal to the young and the traditional concerns for and by the young in such matters. The spectacular rise in the use of drugs in places where de facto immunity from prosecution for possession just about exists today—such as in some slums, at rock concerts and on so many college campuses (see the section on drugs in the chapter on youth, and Tables 115, 116, and 117)—seems to justify the overwhelming majority's opposition to legalization of marijuana. This is particularly true when one sees that on campuses *all* the users of the "harder" hallucinogens had used marijuana. Similarly, pornography of almost all types flourishes in the face of overwhelming public opposition. To the average person, it probably also appears that the 2 percent of the people who believe our courts are too harsh on criminals (see Figure 19) have driven courts to be more and more lenient with perpetrators, and the 98 percent who oppose this view have had less and less success in maintaining the effectiveness of the courts in "keeping criminals off the streets." Even the President seems to have had trouble reversing this trend.

In addition to these and the other issues mentioned earlier, there have been some other largely unheralded possible and actual important changes related to these unusual sociological factors of the last few years, the consequences of some of which could be as grave, or more so, than those of the more fashionable problems. For example, the specter of one such change (this one of gargantuan proportions) began to seem capable of rising, when one considered the increasing implications that the Democratic party—that great American coalition of the working class, "ethnic" groups, small business, labor unions, classical liberal journalists, and, increasingly since the 1930s, classical liberal intellectuals—was beginning to show signs that it could break up.

This is a low probability issue, but in our basically two-party system even this remote possibility could outweigh many other considerations which draw so much attention today (it has been over a hundred years since a major party has disappeared). In recent years a great portion of the rank and file of the party apparently thought they had detected a swing of the ultra-liberals, as well as some Democratic public personalities, well to the Left on many national and international issues. This swing seemed to have made some of the traditional, classical liberals uncomfortable, and, according to many in the rank and file, to have drawn other liberals too far Left. In addition, some feel that certain members of some ethnic groups, in certain key areas, are in conflict with other ethnic, social, and economic groups.* The argument of many of the moderate Democratic majority is that they have held their liberal values while the minority has abandoned them for heavy-handed radicalism.

The polls show that this is hardly a universal principle that can be applied to all issues. On many basic issues, the majority and many of the minority are still close, but on others there is wide divergence. A number of Democrats also argue, and apparently from a not completely groundless position, that active members of this "radical minority" have control of the party structure in many areas, and have tried to move the party to the Left to such a degree that the platforms of some committees and candidates begin to impinge on the American value system. The feeling of this large group of "traditional" Democrats of being disenfranchised and alienated from those who control the party tends to erode the party as an organization and (to the degree that it is) as a social force, particularly in and on the fringes of large cities.

There still is no reason to feel the cyclical historian is not correct: The pendulum will swing back. To the extent that the normal braking forces on the leftward swing have been and are muted or ignored, however, the period of the pendulum could be lengthened with unknown effects in the short run, and even the long run. Even the length of exist-

* Speaking of what are primarily Democratic groups in New York City, Nathan Glazer and Daniel P. Moynihan say of the late 1960s: an "elite Protestant group . . . and better-off Jews determined that the Negroes and Puerto Ricans were deserving and in need, and on those grounds, further determined that these needs should be met by concessions of various kinds from the Italians and Irish (or generally speaking from the Catholic players [sic]) and the worse-off Jews. The Catholics resisted and were promptly further judged to be opposed to helping the deserving and the needy." (Nathan Glazer and Daniel P. Moynihan, *Beyond the Melting Pot* [2nd. ed.; Cambridge, Mass: M.I.T. Press, 1970], p. lxiii.)

ence and publicity the "radical movement" has already enjoyed may have had a significant impact on policy decisions in important areas of our society (some outlined earlier), perhaps directly because of its real strength, but perhaps also as a result of reaction to possible exaggerated impressions of that strength.

B. *The Work Force*

It is difficult to decide whether or not the change in milieu of the young and the schools could have significantly adverse effects on our society, and particularly on our vastly expanding, highly technologically-oriented service industries. The effect of the new technology on the nation's life-style has been imaginatively covered by many writers,* so I will not go into it here except to repeat the previous caveat: the process is circular, and the life-style could also affect technology, particularly its rate of advance and its implementation. This is not to say that, if morale holds up, drastic effects such as a downturn, or even a significant leveling-off, of technological development need occur. But since all projections discussed to date are based on an ever-rising rate of increase in the development and use of technology, any change (even a slight one) in the capability to do so would change the projections.

Before it gets turned around, the effects of this new life-style might indirectly have an erosive effect on our prosperity and, therefore, our ability to finance real progress through technology. From 1968, at least through 1970, there was a *decrease* in the "spendable average weekly earnings" (in 1957–1959 dollars) of a "production or non-supervisory" worker with three dependents, "on private, non-agricultural payrolls," from $78.61 in 1968 to $77.57 in 1970.** Actually, his "take-home" pay was not $77.57, because state income taxes (and their increases), Social Security (and its increase), and union dues (and their increases) have not as yet been deducted from this sum; only Federal taxes have been deducted from his gross. This subject may be one of the most important factors for the future, but predicting economic trends (to say nothing of public reaction to economic developments)

* See Herman Kahn and Anthony J. Wiener, *The Year 2000* (New York: Macmillan Company, 1967), Chap. 11, "Comments on Science and Technology," pp. 66–117, passim.
** *Monthly Labor Review*, Vol. 94, No. 1 (January 1971): 101, U.S. Department of Labor, Bureau of Labor Statistics.

is an extremely complex area to enter. Insofar as the new life-style and its adherents might have even a minor, adverse effect on the rate of growth of productivity, however, and thus perhaps add to the inflationary spiral or force a decline of living standards, it must be of particular concern to everyone in this country.

Overall productivity is measured in such a gross fashion, and measures of productivity are so arbitrary or hard to come by in our vastly expanded service industries, federal, state and local governmental departments, education, and so forth, that the possible specific effect of this life-style on the "output per man hour" is hard to measure. As indicated earlier, the rate of increase in productivity declined as the followers of the new life-style increased. But this is likely to be mere coincidence, because the sharpest decline (1968–1969) can be explained by the generally accepted economic phenomenon of the lag in lay-offs catching up with the actual drop in orders (production). And, as indicated earlier, predictions are for an increase in productivity as production goes up, due originally in part to a lag in hiring. But, for what it is worth, our overall rate of growth in productivity stayed the same in 1969 and 1970—2.5 percent, low for a large industrial nation in the free world.

The work areas, however, are where the new life-style could have quite adverse effects above and beyond those mentioned earlier in discussing working youth (see the section on "The Young Workers and the New Life Style," Chapter 2). On every job, there are (or were) unwritten, or sometimes even contractual, norms of both quantitative and qualitative productivity. Most workers are (or were) not too disturbed by a shirker or two. (They might not have liked "company men" who raised the norm by their work rate, but they also knew a "lazy" guy when they saw him.) He used to "catch hell" from the foreman, cause embarrassment for the shop steward, lose the respect of fellow-workers (on gangs or crews, such a man got the reputation of not being able to "hold up his end"), and if he were from a family who were all in the trade, he might suffer the worst of all censures—his family might be a little ashamed of him. On dangerous or piece-work jobs,* this man was an anathema.

---

* This is work where a man and his helper(s) are paid by their output (such as loggers), but here it also means any kind of job in which more money is made by "hustlers," including transportation jobs in which over-the-road and turn-around time means more pay per month, etc.

Some compulsive workers will continue if everyone else is sleeping on the job, but they are few and far between. When workers begin to feel they are chumps if they work harder than other men around them for the same pay, the productivity quickly "seeks its own level." And there are signs that the old norms may be beginning to change. Corporations cannot seem to handle some things as well as they used to. Workers often no longer lose their jobs for unexcused absenteeism; on the contrary, in some auto plants they were actually given green stamps as a reward if they did show up. Absenteeism "is so high before and after weekends and holidays that quality falls sharply as men are shifted to unfamiliar jobs"* (as many as 10 percent of the production-line workers may be absent at such times).** Absenteeism means decreased productivity; even on the most humdrum production-line job, there are tricks to the trade. A replacement on a non-piece-work job gets the same salary but cannot produce as much; on a piece-work job, he only gets paid for what he produces, but he is likely to do poorer work. Such conditions, along with new problems including violence in some plants (plant guards are working with management "to try to stop the flow of guns, knives and narcotics" into at least some auto plants), may also contribute to early retirement of experienced personnel.***

New approaches often triggered by studies by "experts" brought into the plants, "young turk" (and even not-so-young) union leaders, and guilt-ridden employers dealing with minority groups, can do much more than fail to foster better work habits. They can undermine the work ethic. Work is important and honorable, and performing any job well *is* "helping to build America." The new approach of some experts is more "realistic." Telling a worker something else, however, is not only incorrect, it can have ill effects. Further, efficient work at the lower levels makes possible a system with better jobs further up the ladder, and in this country a man usually has some opportunity to, and will, change jobs when he feels he can better himself. (The current recession, of course, has reduced this opportunity.) The danger, however, may lie in the possibility that those fostering the new "realistic" approach will fail to realize that degrading a man's job degrades his self-respect. Overlooking the fact that a man did not show up for work

* Jerry M. Flint, "Auto Industry Struggling to Stop Lag in Productivity," *New York Times,* August 8, 1970, p. 10.
** "The Assembly Line," by William Serrin, *Atlantic Monthly* 228 (October 1971): 66.
*** "Violence in the Factories," *Newsweek,* 29 June 1970, pp. 66 and 67.

on a "dead-end," "dehumanizing" job does not help him. It reinforces the feeling that the job is unimportant and he is unimportant. Furthermore, gripes about a job come easy, and the more personal inner feeling (perhaps of such things as skill and/or manliness connected with any job) may be almost impossible for the average worker to describe, largely because he frowns on such "sentimentality."* He feels the boss and others know and appreciate these unmentioned aspects of the job. When he becomes convinced they don't, effects can be far-reaching.**

A very important area in which something similar to this apparently has happened is in our schools. Teachers in some areas learned that they would not be censured for not enforcing discipline in schools, and those who enforced discipline sometimes found themselves in trouble, facing an irate parent and/or lawyer, and embarrassing a school administrator who did not back them up against parents or lawyers. Teachers in those areas quickly got the message—with very bad results. The same thing seemed to happen in places where teachers had to have the consent of many hard-to-convince parents to make children repeat a grade, and where no one was penalized for passing on dullards. Now in many areas everyone passes—sometimes with disastrous results.

Overall, even though some workers are dissatisfied with their jobs and environment for perhaps some complex reasons, a large majority are still satisfied with their income and the overwhelming majority with their employment (see Tables 53-57). One feels instinctively, however, that if we tamper with this work force and its traditional rules and bargaining structure in even a somewhat cavalier fashion (and some "limousine liberal intellectuals" seem to be aching to) the effects could be even more far-reaching than their tampering with our schools.

---

* Miners were notoriously hard to get out of the mines once they went down to the dark, back-breaking, dangerous work. This is still true of many jobs which from the outside seem to have no attraction. (Of course, no worker wants avoidable dirt, discomfort or excessive physical exertion.) Yet the mines, the railroads, line gangs, steel mills, and parts of any plant (usually those where the dirty, hard jobs are located) are a "man's world" with all that this means. Very few workers can or will articulate what this highly important sociological and economic factor means to them, their families, and their communities.

** In effect, downgrading a Negro father's job in this way, making him feel his work means little or nothing to the big picture, downgrades *him* and can foster bad conditions both in the plant and in his home and community. Negroes contribute heavily to the absenteeism in auto plants. For a description of some new and old attitudes and conditions in auto plants (which now have about a 35 percent Negro work force), see Serrin, op. cit.

C. *The Leaders*

For reasons which are probably still not clear to the public, even though so much has been written on it in the past few years, a number of leaders of industry and government, a similar number of clerics and a much larger number of educators in academia have not (from the public's point of view) held up their end of the "dialogue" over the value of a system which (with all its faults) is looked on by the man in the street as far superior to others, and which has given "us" (and "them") so much.* The fact that more of these influential men were not solidly and obviously in the forefront of the defense of our way of life did nothing to help the average man weather the attacks on the system. That a small number of leaders of industry and government were apparently "converted" by what to him must have sounded like claptrap of the New Left, must have made the average man (when he was aware of it) feel very much alone on the barricades. The mass defection of so many instructors in academia, though probably less traumatic, did not help matters either. The statements of "crazy," pampered, upper-middle-class students could be explained; but (to the average man) extreme statements by adults on campus, and by at least one man of great stature in academia,** were something else. Further, when some non-family adults in the colleges, secondary and sometimes religious educational systems began to propound simplistic, doctrinaire ideas, and thus reinforce alienation from parents and their value systems, and sometimes even make true academic achievement secondary to doctrinaire, naïve "social engineering," a ripple of disturbance became evident through all economic, religious, and ethnic groups in the country.

As far as the average citizen is concerned, the attitudes of the minority of "defecting" leaders of big business and government could not have been based on a careful consideration of the fundamental philosophy, structure, and achievements of this system of ours, as he sees them. And from his point of view, these attitudes certainly could not

* As a leadership group, the labor leaders of this country often seem to have been much more united, outspoken and articulate in defense of the traditional values than industrialists. But even some union leaders, perhaps largely younger "radicals," have recently begun to pick up some New Left-type attitudes.

** Kingman Brewster, Jr., president of Yale University, said he was "skeptical of the ability of black revolutionaries to achieve a fair trial anywhere in the United States." (*New York Times,* April 25, 1970.)

have been based on a careful consideration of the "recommendations" and logic of the New (or even Old) Left. The apparent lack of faith in the system of some leaders, and the failure of others to stand up and defend our way of life, are said by some to stem from more personal causes.

Perhaps some industrialists should feel guilty, maybe they are not being entirely fair to their employees or the public as a whole. The entire fault for expensive, yet shoddy products, cannot always lie with the workers. Some of the blame should be laid at the door of the industrialists for the bad engineering and alleged "planned obsolescence" of very expensive and essential products (like automobiles), the non-durable plastic parts of so many items, their apparent shorter mean time to failure, the lack of inventory of spare parts, the apparent standard prices for similar products. Yet if this is the source of their guilt feelings, it often seems to manifest itself in other areas in addition to (or even instead of) correcting these things. It sometimes reveals itself in ways which may be far less likely to be productive, and might even be counterproductive. Instead of just concentrating on building a better product for the money, their efforts also often show signs of attempts at social endeavors. Apparently the efficient production of durable goods at a decent price to attract buyers in a free market, and thus continue the raising of standards of living and the level of employment in a free job market (at both of which they have some expertise), is not looked on by some of these people as an adequate (or perhaps even very honorable) contribution to our democratic society. They seem to feel that they should share their gains, not only with their consumers or workers (usually amply represented by unions), who helped them make those gains, but with society. This is not unusual and is quite commendable; what is important, the sharing is no longer just recommended in the traditional areas—libraries, parks, and museums. Now they seem to feel called upon to back programs which tend to tamper with the lives of people in ways in which their expertise is less likely to qualify them to make judgments. Some will allow their young executives to spend part time "helping" solve the problems of schools and minority "ghettos." These are highly sensitive areas which can be some of the worst places to inject what might more than occasionally be well-meaning but guilt-ridden, high-paid, second-generation, upper-middle-class, junior (and sometimes even not-so-junior) industrial executives to "solve" things. They are often likely to be out of their element and to some extent at the mercy of unscrupulous or naive activists, and often less-than-expert "experts."

Of less, but still considerable impact on the communities in which their plants are located, may be the side effects (as well as direct effects) when they leave the normal channels of arranging working conditions for their employees. Effects on consumers can be similar. If the consumer feels that he is being exploited by some industrialists who (while apparently doing little to alleviate his plight—which the industrialists have the power to do) begin to use the profits made from him to tamper with the lives of the underprivileged and his own children, in "social programs," the effects could be far reaching.

The "social consciousness" of some wealthy industrial and governmental leaders is even said to stem from pressures from family situations triggered by their alienated offspring. This is no doubt too simple an explanation, for one can find support for their positions in the media (not all of it written by men under similar pressures) and elsewhere, which probably also influences them. Whatever the reason, a surprising minority of business executives seemed to accept the Left-liberal approach to some degree.

Nor were such attitudes restricted to the business world. Aside from the primary and secondary education areas, perhaps one of the most disturbing places where such activity became evident was among the clergy. In the late 1960s a surprising number of these people, who used to be quite influential among their laymen, began to feel a different perspective was needed, and lectured their parishioners to this effect. The same held true for some lay religion teachers. Up until late 1970, this often meant injecting a good deal of sociology, sometimes, some feared, almost verging on secular humanism, into religious teaching and sermons, often, it seemed to many, at the expense of the fundamentals of a deeper, broader, all-loving religious, *spiritual* humanist thought. Parents were told this was deemed necessary, among other reasons, because adults—though they professed these "old-style" principles—were quite hypocritical. Further, unless they dropped the outmoded, heavily spiritual approach to religion, youth would fall away from the church. The fundamentals of religion, therefore, were often said to have little attraction for youth, to the great displeasure of many parents in the congregation who were themselves not "fire and brimstone" types. Nevertheless, "youthful" defections apparently were

402

greater in some of the more "liberal" churches* and a few short months later, the "sociology" types had begun to fade, and the "new" young "Jesus people" hit the headlines, preaching the values of spiritualism and the unchanging relevancy of the gospels and the fundamentals of Christianity.

Secular and religious leaders should be leery of the sine wave curve of *au courant* "youthful" opinion. If they get too caught up in it at one point in time, they may be less likely to be right about the future slope of the median line of the real direction of society (or perhaps even of "youth") than the man who watches the total population and takes heed of the "history" of opinion among all groups of the society.

A similar blow to the average man's morale came when a number of elected government officials appeared to bend an ear to some less-than-brilliant (or even very logical) demands of the Left, which flew in the face of the (not completely illogical) opinions of most of the country.** This must truly have appeared as a crisis in leadership, for this group represented the backbone of the system the "average guy" was trying to defend. Further, they were the ones who had the power to fix things—they could clean house in those government agencies, they could get the attention of the media, they could act as a conduit for the opinions of the "little man." When many of them came out on the "other side," it must have been the unkindest cut of all.***

In any event, what apparently was happening was somewhat unsettling to the thoughtful average citizen (nor has this completely disappeared). A disturbing number of the normal "leaders" in our society were apparently responding to an unpopular Left-wing minority. Furthermore, these leaders even began to implement policy changes (some hard to undo) based on "new and lasting" changes in society.

Whatever the reason, the apparent lack of faith in the system on the part of a disturbing number of industrial, governmental, and academic leaders and clerics, points to a possible crises in morale of

* See Tables 2 and 3 and the text following them for the situation among 21 to 29 year olds.

** Even the Republican President established his 1970 Commission on Campus Unrest, mentioned earlier. It was run at taxpayers' expense to discover what was upsetting a fraction of a few percent of the population which resided in the enviable milieu of the universities, at a time when the "unrest" of four out of five of the population as a whole over the bad behavior of those dissidents on campuses was evident, yet never examined by a government commission.

*** The reduction in confidence in this leadership between 1966 and 1971, indicated by Table 61, may, in part, reflect this feeling. Of course, the recession and other factors also greatly affect this level of confidence.

403

some significance among these people, which may be the most serious symptom of all. Further, the very lack of faith in the system among lay leaders may stem from a malaise which "elitism" may tend to accentuate—inadequate "bluing."*

The qualified, upwardly mobile, newly successful citizens (direct descendents of, or even themselves lately "blue-collar" workers) are apparently some of the greatest defenders of the system among the upper-middle class. The constant infusion of this new blood from the "working classes," selected through the traditional proving ground of industry and the educational system, may be what is largely responsible for the viability of this unique American system. In this respect, the "dropouts" from the second generation wealthy should perhaps not be mourned excessively, for they serve a purpose—they make more room for the new blood from the working classes.

Assuming this "bluing" process is not hampered excessively by the enforcement of artificial "elitist" parameters in universities, industry and government, even the recent apparent low morale among some of our leaders has a built-in cure in our system. The more bad blood, the more transfusions of new blood, and the patient continues to thrive. The fact that some academicians, government, and business leaders apparently may even have been talked into tampering with our important academic and other "filter systems" for the "bluing" process, however, indicates the degree to which some of our leadership was faltering.

D. *The Majority Opposition*

It is difficult to describe what has been occurring in this country over the past decade, let alone why it was (and is) happening. It is even difficult to describe what put the average American "in the doghouse" with some of our "elite." It is much more difficult to evaluate where we stand at any given moment, but a capsulized version of just the "polarization" process, from the point of view of the average American, might be as follows.

* A term, to my knowledge, first coined by Peter and Brigitte Berger in an article on p. L-23 of the *New York Times*, February 15, 1971, and used (in apposition to Professor Reich's term "greening" of America) to mean the infusion of qualified people with blue-collar backgrounds into our leadership positions. They pointed out that "greening" (dropping out) of upper-middle-class youth would simply mean more "bluing," that is, young people from blue-collar families would fill the slots.

Efforts in the 1960s to solve some of our outstanding problems did not bear fruit quickly enough for some, so that by the late 1960s a significant amount of the effort was spent blaming people for the problems. This is perhaps normal when would-be reformers experience the frustrations of trying actually to implement changes in any society. The failure of the Left to effect an immediate shutdown of military operations in Vietnam, of course, probably helped to magnify our "defects" for them. Yet the reaction of some seems to have been excessive, for many reforms were carried out. More civil rights and social legislation was passed in the mid- and late 1960s than in the first few years of the decade, and, as we have seen, attitudes toward integration and equal opportunity for Negroes became more and more favorable. In fact, some government actions (such as cross-busing of school children for exact racial balance for large diversified communities), and much non-government action, initiated in the rush to "stamp out injustice" and help the under-privileged, seem to have been somewhat ill-advised, both from the point of view of the amount of benefit that could be expected to accrue to the main objective, and the bad side effects. Yet even these programs were initiated. However, as opposition became evident to the more extreme, often very expensive and obviously questionable practices (including those propounded by "reformers" on our campuses), the "lines were drawn" and these questionable "programs" were often mis-takenly lumped in with the more desirable, logical, and productive reforms. Extreme, potentially disastrous plans for new work and man-agement patterns (let people come to work whenever they wish, let young radicals determine responsibility and activities of industry) were sometimes lumped with efforts to improve working conditions along with productivity in plants and dependability of products; reverse discrimination (where because of their color—white—job applicants or prospective students were discriminated against in favor of another group of applicants because these were black) was often categorized with equal opportunity efforts. Potentially harmful programs for large segments of our population were often confused with efforts to help the needy. "Educational" programs which might do grave damage to our school system were (and still are) often included with efforts to improve reading skills. Naive schemes of unilateral disarma-ment and pacifism in the face of violent, predatory forces were often categorized with efforts to alleviate the suffering from wars while im-proving the chances of survival for weaker victims. Conversely, those

405

opposing the wilder schemes were often condemned (right along with the minority who might fit that mold) as "anti-youth," "puritanical," "anti-education," "bigots," "warmongers," "racists," and, of course, ignorant, and far from intelligent.

The Right (with some questionable positions of its own) responded with terms like "anti-American," and even "Comsymp" and "revolutionary" (of course, also often too liberally applied), but with much less volume and coverage. In between, on many pressing domestic issues, sat the majority of citizens in every occupation, education and income category, with too few prominent moderates "defending our system" against the Left to the satisfaction of the "middle American." Soon some thought he was on the Far Right and/or didn't represent the majority.

It took a long time to sort out the facts from the caricature too widely held among the "intellectual elite" (and it is not yet complete), but meanwhile, up 'til at least 1970, attacks on the "opponents of reform" were often directed against the mass of the Amercan public. Majority opposition was too often seen as part of the problem to be overcome, by-passed, rather than as contributing to the parameters within which the problems might be solved. But this great cross-section of America makes up "the bone and sinew" of the nation; if its members falter, the republic could be in trouble. To date, of course, they have not faltered; this admittedly imperfect but not totally reprehensible group has shown most of its traditional stamina, and its values and beliefs have remained essentially intact. There have, however, been inroads into the "system," many made over the obvious opposition of the majority, which could have lasting, less-than-desirable effects in the educational system, government, industry, and perhaps even organized religion.

The American public apparently remains resilient, however, and, barring some stupendous bad luck or colossal blunders, its morale will probably remain high enough so that it can repair whatever damage has been done to the system. As (and if) the great majority once more begins to have its old influence on decision-making, the effects of decisions on domestic issues are, on balance, probably less likely to be damaging to the society. If this "re-enfranchising" of the majority is delayed, one may be more reluctant to make such statements. There seem to be some signs, however, that we may soon begin to "see the light at the end of the tunnel" and, to the extent this is true, some optimism may soon be in order. Despite (or perhaps because of) his growing disillusion with much of the leadership today (see Table 61), the average man is still far more likely to support close adherence to this admittedly flawed, but proven system of ours. Its flexibility yet stability and freedom, and its splendid record compared to that of any system in any large country in the world, will make it hard to sell him substitute processes suggested by the left or right. Barring divine revelation to the contrary, from the point of view of the pragmatic, average American this can only be good, but to the "average man," shoring up the dike must occasionally have seemed a rather thankless job over the last few years.

THE CHANGING ATTITUDES OF A COLLEGE CLASS

by

Doris Yokelson

A. *Introduction*

This appendix is an examination of some of the attitudes and values of one segment of the population—the college graduates of 1961. This group is drawn from a survey made of them in 1968, seven years after they were graduated from college. With this survey as a base, I also look back to surveys made in the years when they were in high school to see how the high school youth of that time—including this group—felt about themselves and about certain issues. I also touch upon some survey material that was available from 1961, when this group was the senior class in college. In the latter part of this appendix, I compare the feelings of high school students over the last decade and a half toward particular issues, beginning with the years when the 1961 college graduates were in high school.

Though no broad generalizations about the significance of the be-havior of the present and future generations of college students can be made by studying this one group, it is worthwhile to take a look at the changes in attitudes that took place in this group over a span of more than a decade that encompassed their going to high school and college and into careers, marriage and family.

The 1961 generation of college graduates we are studying here is considered to have been quiescent, uninvolved, and conservative. By comparison with the recent generation of college graduates, this would certainly appear to be true. Yet who could have predicted that in a few short years the campuses would become centers of political, social, and moral turmoil? Or who could also have predicted that from this turmoil a generation of far less issue-oriented college students would begin to emerge?

Do the beliefs and activities of young people while in college make a profound change in their basic attitudes and values? Can the behavior of one college student body be an indicator of the behavior of the next one?* Neither of these seems to be supported by evidence. This appendix is a description of what did happen to the attitudes of one college class over a period of time.

* For a recent study comparing the liberal-conservative orientations of college generations over the last few decades, see Seymour Martin Lipset and Everett Carl Ladd, Jr., "College Generations—from the 1930s to the 1960s," *The Public Interest*, No. 25 (Fall 1971): 99–113. The authors found that "variations in political orientation among college generations over the last half century *follow an essentially linear and age-related progression*" (their italics). Measured by presidential choice, each succeeding generation of college graduates was more liberal than the one before while, at the same time, there was a steady increase of conservatism or moderation according to the increase in age of the graduate.

The basic findings of the authors of this article lend support to the material presented in this chapter. The authors write:

> If past American experience is any guide, . . . it is likely that as a cohort those who experienced the radical and activist campus politics of the late 1960s will not continue in the distinctive frame of mind which they now show. Colleges are encapsulated communities. . . . After graduation, . . . most . . . reenter the highly differentiated larger society and take part in middle-class life in job, family and community. The intellectual legacies of the college years are by no means all lost, but the intense pressure of the encapsulated community which make for the distinctive and wildly fluctuating character of student political opinion are for most removed as abruptly as they had been introduced.

The authors mention, for example, that "there is little indication in our four sets of data that exposure to the radical-liberal politics which prevailed at many universities in the 1930s left its mark on the student body as a whole so that they held distinctive liberal-left orientation in succeeding years." Earlier in their article, Lipset and Ladd brought up the point that among the three-quarter of a million people who belonged to the Communist party during the late 1930s and early 1940s, the annual turnover rate sometimes reached 90 percent and that most had joined *and* left the party by the time they were 23 years of age.

Because they find that college generations have been getting successively and gradually more liberal over the past decades, Lipset and Ladd do point out that "even if the 1960s generation becomes more moderate, it, like earlier ones, is still likely to end up at a point further to the 'left' than its predecessors, and to the 'right' of its successors." The authors note that two factors—the increased number and the cultural alienation of college students of the past five years—are new and might possibly lend support to a more permanent increase in radicalism. But they doubt that these two factors would have a lasting influence on most of those who had become more radical while they were in college.

B. *The 1961 College Class*

The charts and the descriptive material of the 1961 college class, based on a survey done in 1968, are taken from the book, *Recent Alumni and Higher Education,* by Joe L. Spaeth and Andrew M. Greeley, prepared for the Carnegie Commission on Higher Education.* This material is used as the basis for this chapter and is used liberally throughout. The data for the earlier period—the high school years —is drawn from the extensive survey material in *Reports of Poll, The Purdue Opinion Panel* of the Measurement and Research Center at Purdue University.** The Roper Public Opinion Research Center at Williams College is the source of the data on the Gallup poll of May-June 1961.

The majority of the 1961 college class were graduated from high school in 1957. They were in the tenth grade from September 1954 to June 1955; eleventh grade from September 1955 to June 1956; and twelfth grade from September 1956 to June 1957. The material for these years was taken from the obtainable *Purdue Opinion Panel, Reports of Polls* on high school students across the nation. At the time these polls were taken, there was no breakdown of the opinions of college-bound students, who would have closely approximated our group. Had I had more time to do so, it might have been possible to compute the percentage of each opinion as to mother's education and level of family income—two strong indicators of who goes to college —within the class years. But, for the scope of this chapter, opinions by high school year will have to suffice. This material will be compared with that on some of the attitudes held by the 1961 college graduates in 1968 to see what changes took place as the group went to college and then into careers. Comparisions between this high school and alumni material are not easily made. First, only certain questions were available and, of course, in many cases they did not correlate between the years. Second, the opinions of exactly those students in the grades we wanted who planned to go to college could not be broken out. Third, at least 13 percent of these alumni did not go straight from high school to college, and 18 percent of the 1961 class had dropped out and returned at some later time. Fourth, the data on the alumni might be to some degree questionable because of the method of survey; that is, sending out questionnaires and using the answers of those who responded—though the analysts conducting the survey have stated that the responses which they reported were weighted to take into account discrepancies in the original sampling design and that the sample of respondents returning all questionnaires was only minimally biased by nonresponse. But despite these short-comings, a useful picture of trends in attitudes may emerge or some startling perturbation observed. We are also able to corroborate some trends emerging from this material with other sources.

1. *Characteristics of the June 1961 College Graduates as of 1968—From the Carnegie Commission Study:* °

Sample	Based on a sample of 40,000 graduates of 135 accredited or large colleges and universities. Data were collected in 1961, 1962, 1963, 1964, and 1968.°° The 1968 survey was commissioned by the Carnegie Commission and is based on a 30 percent subsample of respondents who had returned all four previous questionnaires. Of the 6,005 persons drawn, 4,868 returned completed questionnaires—a response rate of 81 percent. Fifty-eight percent of the respondents were male and 42 percent were female.
Marriage Status	One-fourth of all graduates were married as seniors; two-thirds of the married had children. In 1964, three years later, two-thirds were married and two-thirds of the married had children. In 1968, over 80 percent were married and 80 percent of these were married. The average number of children per family in 1968 was two, the oldest child averaging between three and four years of age. Nearly one-fourth had met their spouses at their own college and over one-fifth were married to people who had not attended college at all.
Family Background	One-third of their mothers and 40 percent of their fathers had gone to college. About one-half of their fathers were professionals, proprietors, managers or officials. One-third of the alumni came from families with incomes of at least $10,000 a year (in pre-1960 dollars). By 1968, three-fourths of the alumni were making as much as their parents; 11 percent of the parents and 9 percent of the alumni were making at least $20,000 a year.

° Abstracted from Spaeth and Greeley, op. cit., pp. 3–5.
°° The 1961–1964 surveys were mainly concerned with careers and career plans. Some of the data from the 1964 survey—on political preference—as it was reported by Spaeth and Greeley, appears in this chapter.

411

<table>
<tr><td>College
History</td><td>When they graduated in June 1961, 30 percent were 23 or older; 6 percent were 30 or older; 13 percent did not go straight from high school to college—the median delay was about three years. Eighteen percent of this class dropped out and came back; they left college for a term or more.</td></tr>
</table>

College History — When they graduated in June 1961, 30 percent were 23 or older; 6 percent were 30 or older; 13 percent did not go straight from high school to college—the median delay was about three years. Eighteen percent of this class dropped out and came back; they left college for a term or more.

Number Going to Graduate School — Thirty-five percent enrolled in graduate school during the year after college. This percentage remained about the same during the next two years. By 1968, 17 percent were enrolled in graduate school. Three-fifths had attended graduate school for some period; nearly half had attended for one year or more; one-fifth had attended for at least three years.

Higher degrees — One-third had some kind of higher degree: Twenty-one percent held a master's, 10 percent a professional and 4 percent a doctoral degree. One-sixth said they planned to earn a doctorate; over two-thirds said they intended to earn some kind of advanced degree.

Plans for Children to Attend College — Ninety-three percent of the alumni expected all their boys to attend college and 86 percent expected all their girls to attend. Nearly all wanted some of their children to attend. Sixty percent had done something financially for this—savings accounts, insurance, investments or trust funds. Ninety-nine percent said they would make some contribution to financing their children's education; nearly half said they would contribute at least three-fourths of a child's expenses. The average parent thought the cost of keeping a child in school for a year would be about $3,000.

This is a brief picture of the 1961 graduates as of 1968. At first glance, a third of the alumni having enrolled in graduate school seemed inordinately high, but this has been found not to be out of line. Although the breakdown of the percentages of alumni according to college type and major are not given, we do know that the 1968 sample was weighted to represent the proper distribution of types of colleges attended and we hopefully assume that the course representatation was similarly weighted. It is obvious from this and various other studies we have examined that the attitudes of persons in different fields differ considerably and are fairly consistent according to field.*

* Seymour Martin Lipset and Everett Carl Ladd, Jr., "And What Professors Think," *Psychology Today*, 4 (November 1970): 49; Ian D. Currie, et al., "Images of the Professor and Interest in the Academic Profession," *Sociology of Education*,

C. Social and Political Attitudes of the 1961 College Graduates from 1955 to 1968

1. POLITICAL ORIENTATION

How liberal or conservative were these college alumni of the early 1960s? How did their social and political attitudes change as a group from high school to post-college and then as parents and emerging leaders of our society? Were their basic attitudes toward their colleges and studies and the role of students very different from the basic attitudes of college students today?

The 1961 college graduates grew up in a time when fewer high school students than in 1970 were planning to go to college and almost twice as many were thinking of working after they got out of high school. In the 1950s, World War II was not long over. Among those who had preceded these high school students in college were large numbers of veterans of the war who were highly motivated and goal-oriented; money was scarcer than now; young persons were still considered to help in bringing in the family income; fear of war and the premonition of another war were strong. As seen in Table 171 below, by 1955, 37 percent of high school students planned to go to college as compared to 50 percent in 1970. In this table—as in all other tables in this study—the high school grade the 1961 graduates were in at the time is outlined by a block: Thus, in Table 171, in March 1955 they were in the tenth grade. It is interesting to note in this table that the percentage of high school students planning to go to college in March 1955 decreased slightly from the tenth grade to the twelfth; and in June 1970 this percentage increased slightly from the tenth to the twelfth grade. One would assume this percentage would increase, because those with lower grades and those who are disinterested in school, would be the ones to drop out between the tenth and twelfth grades: Figures in March 1964 show that the drop-out rate from grades ten to twelve was 30 percent.* Nearly twice as many students planned to go to work in March 1955 than in June 1970 and considerably fewer were thinking of going into military service in June 1970.

In political party preference and voting choice, the high school

Fall 1966, available in reprint from the Survey Research Center, University of California; Rodney Stark, "On the Incompatibility of Science and Religion," *Journal for the Scientific Study of Religion,* Fall 1963, also available as a reprint from the Survey Research Center, University of California.

* Purdue Opinion Panel, *Report of Poll No. 70,* March 1964, p. 7.

Table 171

HIGH SCHOOL STUDENTS BY FUTURE PLANS—MARCH 1955 AND JUNE 1970

March 1955*

After high school, what do you plan to do? (boys answer as though you would not be drafted immediately).	Total Sample	Grade			Grade Achievement			Vocabulary score			Income		
		10	11	12	Poor	Average	Good	Low	Middle	High	Low	Middle	Upper
Go to work	23%	21%	22%	27%	31%	28%	14%	29%	25%	13%	32%	25%	14%
Go to college	37	38	37	36	17	28	57	25	35	57	20	36	55
Take special training other than college	12	12	12	13	9	13	11	12	13	11	11	13	11
Enlist in military service	12	12	14	10	21	14	5	14	12	8	15	12	9
Girls: get married and be a housewife	7	7	7	8	7	8	7	8	8	5	11	7	6
Other plans or don't know	9	10	8	6	15	9	6	12	7	6	11	7	5

June 1970**

Which one of the following do you plan to do after finishing high school? (Mark only one).	Total Sample	Grade			Course Grades					Mother's Education		
		10	11	12	Very Low	Below Average	Average	Above Average	Excellent	Grade	High School	College
Go to college	50%	46%	50%	52%	7%	24%	38%	72%	73%	32%	54%	71%
Take special training other than college	15	15	16	15	12	23	20	10	3	20	14	8
Go to work	12	11	11	15	33	21	15	7	4	21	9	4
Enter military service	8	9	8	7	33	13	9	3	9	8	8	6
Other plans or don't know	15	19	15	10	14	21	18	9	12	18	14	12

* Purdue Opinion Panel, Report of Poll No. 41, p. 2a.
** Purdue Opinion Panel, Report of Poll No. 89, p. 1a.

students of the middle 1950s tended to follow the choices of their parents. In November 1956, when the alumni were in the twelfth grade, 58 percent of the twelfth graders said they would vote for the same party as their parents. During this high point of President Eisenhower's popularity, the twelfth graders were even more enthusiastic supporters of Eisenhower than their parents were. Interestingly, the tenth and eleventh graders gave considerably less support to Eisenhower than the twelfth graders and were even less pro-Eisenhower than their parents. In the three questions below, the twelfth graders showed themselves more Republican-minded than either of the two earlier grades, though less inclined to vote for the same party as their parents.*

Table 172

HIGH SCHOOL PARTY PREFERENCE**

10th, 11th and 12th Grades

November 1956	Total Sample	10th	11th	12th	(1961 college class—graduating high school June 1957)
"Which political party do you think has the most to offer the country?"					
Republican	41%	40%	39%	45%	
Democratic	36	38	38	31	
Some other party	1	1	0	0	
Undecided	20	20	20	20	
"If you could vote in the November elections, do you think you would vote for the same party as your parents?"					
Yes	60%	60%	62%	58%	
No	19	20	18	20	
Undecided	20	18	20	21	

* I was not able to isolate the party preferences of those twelfth graders who specifically intended going to college. These students would, of course, have more closely correlated with our 1961 college graduates. In this November 1956 poll, the students were not asked what they planned to do after high school and there was also no breakdown of answers by post-high school plans or by course grades. A previous Purdue opinion poll, May 1956, showed that those whose mothers had attended college and those whose families had a higher income (two strong indicators of those who intended going to college) were very much more pro-Eisenhower than other students.

** Purdue Opinion Panel, *Report of Poll No. 47*, p. 1a.

415

Table 172 (continued)

"If you could vote in the coming election for whom would you vote?"

Eisenhower and Nixon	53	50	49	62
Stevenson and Kefauver	36	39	40	28
Some other candidate	1	1	1	1
Undecided	9	9	9	8

The following figure shows the comparision between the election choices of the twelfth graders and the 30-to-49-year-old group which includes their parents at the end of 1956. Though the pattern of their choice is similar to the 30-to-49-year-old age group in this year, the students were more in favor of Eisenhower than the 30 to 49 year olds.

Figure 42

ELECTION CHOICE—1956*

12th Graders and the 30–49 Year Olds

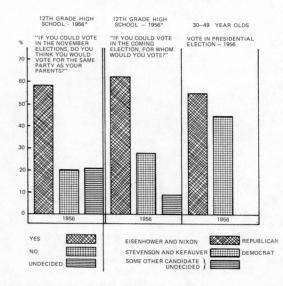

* Compiled from Purdue Opinion Panel, *Report of Poll No. 47*, November 1956 and election results.

In 1970 there was also a similarity in the party preference pattern of adults and high school students. In this year both groups preferred the Democratic party over the Republican. The figure below compares the party preference in 1970 of all adults and all high school students. The choice of the 30 to 49 year olds—the group which would include the parents of the high school students—was not given, but their responses are usually close to the center on most issues. The twelfth graders, who were polled here, are seen to be slightly more liberal than the other grades, a finding that holds for them on most issues in recent years. The college-bound in this poll are a little more conservative than the total sample; in recent polls, the responses of the college-bound have held close to those of the total sample. In the past, when the 1961 college class was in high school, and a greater percentage of those going to college were recruited from the higher-income and better-educated families, the college-bound were likely to have been more conservative as a group than they are today.

In the polls below, the adult choice of parties was limited to the two major ones, whereas the high school students had a choice among these two and the American Independent party. Noteworthy in the student opinion is the very high percentage of "undecided." It is possible to conjecture that this, in addition to the "no difference" response, may be the form the independent vote took among the high school students: They are not yet aware of the performance of the two major political parties and, in addition, the nationwide trend is to an increased Independent vote. In the figure below, the adult Independent vote can no doubt be found in the high percentage of those who said there was "no difference" between the parties. Following this figure is a breakdown of the high school students' preference by grade levels and by college-bound.

In 1961, while the alumni were seniors in college, they continued to prefer the Republican choice of candidate over the Democratic. In a Gallup poll taken in May-June 1961 of college students in 78 colleges across the nation,* 53 percent of the college seniors would have preferred Nixon over Kennedy if they had voted in 1960. Moreover, their voting pattern was similar to the way they reported their parents had

* The data from this poll was provided by the Roper Public Opinion Research Center at Williams College, Williamstown, Massachusetts. The entire Gallup survey was called "Attitudes of Young Adults," and polled youth from the ages of 14 through 22, including juniors and seniors from 78 colleges, sophomores and seniors in high school and nonschool working youth.

Figure 43

PARTY PREFERENCE—ADULTS AND HIGH SCHOOL STUDENTS

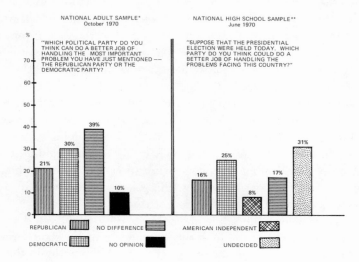

NATIONAL ADULT SAMPLE*
October 1970

NATIONAL HIGH SCHOOL SAMPLE**
June 1970

Table 173

PARTY PREFERENCE***

June 1970—10th, 11th & 12th Grade High School

"Suppose that the presidential election were held today. Which party do you think could do a better job of handling the problems facing this country?"	Total Sample	10th	11th	12th	College-bound
The Republican Party	16%	18%	15%	14%	19%
The Democratic Party	25	23	25	26	23
The American Independent Party	8	8	7	7	6
No difference between parties	17	15	18	18	19
Undecided	31	32	30	30	29

* *Gallup Opinion Index*, No. 64, October 1970, p. 3.
** Purdue Opinion Panel, *Report of Poll No. 89*, June 1970, p. 21a.
*** Purdue Opinion Panel, *Report of Poll No. 89*, June 1970, p. 21a.

418

voted. When the college seniors were asked, "How did your parents vote in the last presidential election—for Kennedy or for Nixon?" their responses were: 45 percent Nixon, 34 percent Kennedy, and 9 percent "parents split vote—one for Kennedy, one for Nixon." In contrast to this, the vote of the 30 to 40 year olds (the group which would include their parents) in the 1960 presidential election was 54 percent Kennedy and 46 percent Nixon. The high school students in the Gallup poll taken in May-June 1961 would have overwhelmingly chosen Kennedy over Nixon, again similar to what they reported their parents had chosen in the 1960 election. As you recall, when the alumni were in high school in 1956, both the high school students and the 30 to 49 year olds preferred Eisenhower.

In the figure below, the 1960 candidate preference of the college seniors polled in 1961 is compared with how they reported their parents had voted and the actual 1960 presidential vote of the 30 to 49 year olds.

Figure 44

ELECTION CHOICE—1960

**1961 College Seniors, Their Parents
(As Reported by the Seniors)
and the 30-49 Year Olds**

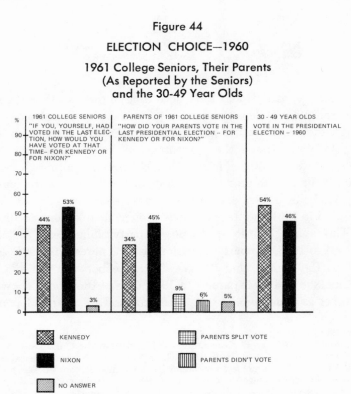

419

Figure 45

PARTY PREFERENCE AND VOTING CHOICE—1961 COLLEGE GRADUATES*

1956, 1961, 1964, 1968

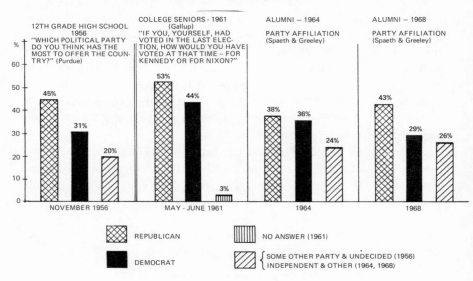

After college, in 1964 and 1968, according to the Spaeth and Greeley survey, the 1961 college graduates preferred the Republican Party, although they preferred it less than they thought their parents did. Figure 45 above shows the percentages of party preference of the twelfth graders in 1956 (which is given for reference, although the composition of the twelfth graders does not compare exactly with that of the college students and college alumni**), the election choice of the college seniors in 1961 and the party affiliation of these alumni in 1964 and 1968. The tables give the net change in party affiliation of the alumni from 1964 to 1968, the party affiliation of their parents in 1964, as described by the alumni, and the net difference between the alumni in 1964 and 1968 and their parents in 1964. One of the results shows that three times as many alumni considered themselves to be independents

* Compiled from information in Spaeth and Greeley, from the Purdue Opinion Panel, *Report of Poll No. 47*, November 1956, and from the Gallup survey, "Attitudes of Young Adults," May-June 1961. The Spaeth and Greeley material is copyright © 1970 by the Carnegie Foundation for the Advancement of Teaching.

** As noted before, however, according to other available evidence, the college-bound students were more inclined to be pro-Eisenhower than other high school students.

than they reported their parents to be. According to Figure 45 and tables below, this group was Republican in high school and college and after college. As alumni, they seemed to have moved away from the Democratic toward the independent party and to have increased in Republicanism. It is important to remember that 1964 was the year that Barry Goldwater ran for President, and it is consequently not a good year for looking at political trends. Even in this year, however the majority of the 1961 college graduates retained their Republican affiliation.

Table 174

PARTY AFFILIATION OF 1961 COLLEGE CLASS IN 1964 AND 1968 AND NET CHANGE FROM 1964 TO 1968*

Party Affiliation 1964		Party Affiliation 1968		Net Change 1964 to 1968
Republican	38%	Republican	43%	+5
Democratic	36	Democratic	29	−7
Independent	24	Independent	26	+2
Other	2	Other	2	0

Table 175

POLITICS OF PARENTS IN 1964**

(As Described by 1961 Alumni)

1964—Parent Party Affiliation

Republican	44%
Democratic	44
Independent	8
Other	3

Net Change in Party Affiliation Between the Parents in 1964 and the Alumni in 1964 and 1968

	Parents to Alumni 1964	Parents to Alumni 1968
Republican	− 6%	− 1%
Democratic	− 8	−15
Independent	+16	+18
Other	− 1	− 1

* From Spaeth and Greeley, op. cit., pp. 100–101. Copyright © 1970 by the Carnegie Foundation for the Advancement of Teaching. For another discussion by Spaeth and Greeley of the political attitudes of these alumni, see Andrew M. Greeley and Joe L. Spaeth, "Research Note. Political Change Among College Alumni," *Sociology of Education*, 43 (Winter 1970): 106–113.

** Spaeth and Greeley, op. cit., pp. 100–101. Copyright © 1970 by the Carnegie Foundation for the Advancement of Teaching.

The question arises as to whether the college experience makes students more liberal and whether this liberalism is permanently retained. I have already mentioned the work of Lipset and Ladd pertaining to this, in the first footnote of this appendix.

As far as political orientation was concerned, about half of the alumni considered themselves liberal—and quite a bit more liberal than they felt their parents were. When they were asked to describe their and their parents' political orientation they responded as follows:

Table 176
LIBERAL ORIENTATION OF ALUMNI AND THEIR PARENTS*
(According to Alumni)

		1961 Alumni	
Political orientation:	Parents	1964	1968
Liberal	40%	56%	52%

There was, however, a slight decrease of liberalism from 1964 to 1968. Also when political orientation and party preference were combined, the 1961 graduates were found, in that time period, to have increased in numbers of conservative Republicans and to have lost in numbers of liberal Democrats. According to the authors of the

Table 177
POLITICAL LEANINGS OF ALUMNI, 1964 AND 1968**

Political Leaning	1964	Rank	1968	Rank	Net Difference Between 1964–1968
Conservative Republican	18%	3	22%	1	+4%
Liberal Republican	20	2	21	2	+1
Conservative Democrat	13	4	12	5	−1
Liberal Democrat	23	1	18	3	−5
Conservative Independent	11	5	12	5	+1
Liberal Independent	13	4	14	4	+1
New Left	—		1	6	+1
Other	2	6	1	6	−1

* Ibid., pp. 100–101. Copyright © 1970 by the Carnegie Foundation for the Advancement of Teaching.
** Ibid., p. 102. Rank is our addition. Copyright © 1970 by the Carnegie Foundation for the Advancement of Teaching.

survey on the alumni, the Democratic party lost mainly to the Independents but also to the Republicans, who, in 1968, were able to retain most of those who were from a Republican background and were Republicans in 1964, to gain back more than a fifth from Republican backgrounds who had declared themselves Democrats in 1964, and to have pulled away a third of those who had considered themselves Independents in 1964. Since the number of Independents increased slightly from 1964 to 1968, a little more than a third of them must have come from the Democratic party during those four years.

In 1964, the highest percentage of 1961 college graduates considered themselves to be liberal Democrats; by 1968 this had changed to conservative Republican, with liberal Republican second and liberal Democrat third. However, the liberals of all parties still outnumbered the conservatives by 7 percent in 1968.

According to the criteria set up by Spaeth and Greeley—that approval of student and Negro protests would be a mark of "liberality" —the liberals of any party among the alumni showed themselves to be more in favor of these protests than conservatives of any party; that is, liberal Republicans favored these protests more than conservative Democrats and Independents. Moreover, both liberal and conservative Independents among these college alumni responded more favorably to student and Negro protests than their counterparts in the other two parties; that is, liberal Independents were more in sympathy with these protests than liberal Democrats or Republicans; conservative Independents approved of them more than conservative Democrats and Republicans. Thus, in the table below, if sympathy toward protests may be taken as a measure of liberalism, in the scale from Republican to Democrat to Independent, the Independent college alumni in 1968 were clearly more liberal as a group than either of the other two parties, and liberals of every party favored protests.*

* The quality of "liberalism" of the Independents among these college alumni in 1968 was in strong contrast to the orientation of Independents among the general populace in the 1968 presidential election. Independents nationwide in 1968 voted 31 percent Humphrey, 44 percent Nixon, 25 percent Wallace. The 25 percent independent vote for Wallace was almost twice as great as the national vote (13.6 percent). That the Independents nationwide were pulled away from the Democratic party was supported by the evidence in this study on college alumni. As an added note: Independents nationwide have favored the Republican candidate by large margins in every presidential election since 1952, with the exception of the Goldwater year of 1964, when they voted for Johnson.

Table 178

ATTITUDES ON STUDENTS AND NEGRO PROTESTS, BY POLITICAL LEANINGS*

(Percent Agree Strongly or Somewhat)

| | Political Leaning | | | | | | |
| | Republican | | Democratic | | Independent | | |
Attitude	Conserv-ative	Liberal	Conserv-ative	Liberal	Conserv-ative	Liberal	New Left
Student protests a healthy sign for America	30%	55%	36%	64%	43%	77%	97%
Negro protests will be healthy for America	33	58	44	73	50	78	97
n=	(1,638)	(1,595)	(899)	(1,292)	(914)	(1,031)	(89)

The Gallup poll of college seniors in May–June 1961 showed that although the seniors would have voted for the Republican candidate, Nixon, in 1960 (in contrast to the national vote which favored the Democrat, Kennedy), they preferred the liberal type of Republicanism. When asked by Gallup, "which wing of the Republican party do you agree with most," they slightly favored the liberal over the middle group. The right-wing group, represented by Senator Goldwater, was strongly rejected.

Table 179

REPUBLICAN ORIENTATION

College Seniors—1961**

"Which wing of the Republican Party do you agree with most— the right wing represented by Senator Goldwater, the middle group represented by former Vice President Nixon, or the liberal wing headed by Governor Rockefeller?"

	Right Wing— Goldwater	Middle Group— Nixon	Liberal Group— Rockefeller
College Seniors	9.1%	41.7%	43.4%

One noteworthy point Spaeth and Greeley made was that the income of the alumni had very little effect on changes in party affinities during the 1964-1968 period. As we can see in the table below, parties that

---

* Spaeth and Greeley, op. cit., p. 105. Copyright © 1970 by the Carnegie Foundation for the Advancement of Teaching.

** Gallup survey, "Attitudes of Young Adults," May–June, 1961.

we would normally think would hold people of higher or lower income, did not necessarily do so, and changes took place—or a party was able to retain its members—quite similarly across income lines. The fact that there was very little percentage difference in party changes among income groups may, in itself, however, represent a substantial shift in the outlook of some income groups which formerly might have differed more radically from each other.

Table 180

ALUMNI RETENTION OF PARTY AFFILIATION
BETWEEN 1964 AND 1968, BY PRESENT FAMILY INCOME*

| | *Party Affiliation* | | |
Present Family Income	*Republican*	*Democratic*	*Independent*
$15,000 and over	81%	66%	53%
$11,000–$14,000	84	66	54
$ 8,000–$10,000	79	68	50
Under $8,000	77	65	63

To sum up: Politically, the alumni were liberal and Republican in their orientation until seven years after graduation from college. This preference does not appear to have differed substantially when they were seniors in college in 1961, at which time they strongly preferred Nixon over Kennedy and slightly favored Rockefeller, as a liberal Republican, over Nixon as a representative of the middle group. The majority of the alumni—a little more than half—considered themselves to be liberals in 1964 and 1968; the Democrats lost members between 1964 and 1968, mainly to the Independents; and the Republicans gained. About a fourth of the alumni called themselves Independents, a preference which Spaeth and Greeley argued was in itself more "liberal" among these alumni.

That the alumni have basically a moderate, sober and liberal-hued attitude will be shown later in their feelings about social and political experiences and in how they regard the college curriculum. The alumni considered themselves substantially more liberal than their parents and remained more liberal seven years after graduation from college.

° Spaeth and Greeley, op. cit., p. 104. Copyright © 1970 by the Carnegie Foundation for the Advancement of Teaching. The percentages represent the percentage of 100 percent who retained the party affiliation during the period from 1964 to 1968.

Whether this was because they were college-educated and the college experience tends to make people liberal, or whether this was the political tide, is not clear. No more than 40 percent of their fathers and mothers had gone to college; thus, taking only the criterion of a college education, it would have appeared to have made the alumni more liberal than their parents. However, age certainly plays a role, as well as political climate.* According to the authors of the alumni survey, there is evidence to show that college makes orientation more liberal; however, there is also evidence in nationwide polls to indicate that on a number of domestic social and political issues, other than civil rights and civil liberties, college-educated people are more conservative than the less-educated.**

2. ATTITUDES TOWARD CURRENT DOMESTIC ISSUES

According to the 1968 survey, although a very small percentage of the 1961 college class had participated in a number of experiences that are today considered important to a segment of college students, a significantly higher percentage would have approved if their children were able to have these experiences. (As we have seen, about 90 percent of the alumni expected their children to go to college.) This does not include taking drugs: although 4 percent of the alumni said they had experimented with drugs, only 1 percent would have liked their

* One explanation for the greater liberalism of the college generation over their parents' may be the findings reported in the article by Lipset and Ladd in *The Public Interest*, No. 25, mentioned earlier. Their basic findings were that each generation of college graduates over the past fifty years was politically more liberal than the preceding one and that the conservatism of the graduates increased in proportion to increased age. This does not explain, however, whether college was the liberalizing catalyst or whether the percentage increase of "liberalism" with each generation of college graduates could have been accounted for by a generally increasing liberalism of the entire American population.

Lipset and Ladd also found that the radical-liberal orientation of college does not permanently remain with the overwhelming majority of students after graduation. (See the first footnote in this appendix.)

** See the chapter, "Some Underexplored Popular Perceptions and Issues," *passim*. In one study, published in 1968, analysts from the prestigious University of Michigan Survey Research Center concluded: ". . . on most questions involving social welfare, domestic expenditures, and transfers of wealth from more to less prosperous citizens, better-educated Americans have been clearly more conservative, or less liberal, than the educationally underprivileged. . . . College-educated Americans have been as much as three or more times as opposed as grade schoolers to such concepts as 'the welfare state,' 'socialized medicine,' and even Medicare and other less 'radical' programs." (John P. Robinson, Jerrold G. Rusk, Kendra B. Head, *Measures of Political Attitudes* [Ann Arbor: Institute for Social Research, The University of Michigan, 1968], p. 45.)

children to do so.* As for antiwar and civil rights demonstrations, less than 10 percent of the alumni had taken part in them, but 15 percent would have approved if their children were to participate in an antiwar demonstration and a third would not have minded if it were a civil rights demonstration. These figures seem low and bespeak a moderate stance toward activism, but compare well with the number of college students in June 1969—a year after this survey—who said they had demonstrated (28 percent).** However, the percentage of college demonstrators might well have increased over 1970 and 1971 as the antiwar and anticollege-administration campaigns mounted.

In the table below on "Alumni Attitudes Toward Certain Experiences," it seems necessary to separate the cause from the activity,

Table 181

ALUMNI ATTITUDES TOWARD CERTAIN EXPERIENCES***

Experiences	I have	I would approve if one of my children
Experimented with drugs	4%	1%
Participated in an antiwar protest	5	15
Participated in civil rights protest	9	30
Worked full time for a service organization such as the Peace Corps, VISTA, or the American Friends Service Committee	2	73
Volunteered to help others (a project to tutor underprivileged students, helping in a mental hospital, etc.)	43	91

* See the *Gallup Opinion Index*, No. 68, February 1971, p. 1 for the latest figures on drug use among college students. The subject of the use and approval of drugs has been carefully explored in Chapter 2 of this book, "Today's Youth." All adults nationwide are almost nine to one against the legalization of marijuana (*Gallup Opinion Index*, No. 65, November 1970, p. 25); yet according to the latest Gallup poll, taken in December 1970, 42 percent of the college students said they had tried marijuana, almost double the 22 percent in 1969 and eight times the 5 percent in 1967; and 14 percent said they had used LSD compared to 4 percent in 1969 and 1 percent in 1967. Furthermore, in mid-1970, a half of all college students thought the use of marijuana should be made legal. (*Gallup Opinion Index*, No. 60, June 1970, p. 22.)

** *Gallup Opinion Index*, No. 48, June 1969, p. 13.

*** Spaeth and Greeley, op. cit., p. 100. Copyright © 1970 by the Carnegie Foundation for the Advancement of Teaching.

particularly regarding how the alumni would have felt if one of their children were to have participated. It would be wrong to surmise from this information, for example, that only 15 percent of the alumni considered themselves "doves" as far as the Vietnam war was concerned, although only that percentage were in favor of having their chilren protest. Apparently, the alumni, as parents, would not have liked to have seen their children involved in the more militant, and possibly violent, aspects of activism, but were highly in favor of having them do service.

In May-June 1961, when the alumni were seniors in college, the

Table 182

MOST SERIOUS PROBLEMS FACING YOUNG PEOPLE TODAY

College Seniors—1961*

"Thinking about your own circle of friends, what are the most serious problems facing young people today?"

The future; indecision, lack of direction, lack of thought toward the future, big *decisions* (unspecified), finding themselves	31.2%
Threat of war, nuclear war; world instability	13.7
Job security, getting a job, lack of work	13.0
Money, money problems, getting money, extravagance, too much materialism	11.8
Marriage decisions	11.0
Getting through school (college), getting educated, grades	7.3
Failure to accept responsibility that comes with age, becoming mature	5.6
Temptations, morals, drinking, sex	5.5
Lack of love; getting enough dates, friends; getting a husband (wife)	4.1
Military obligation, being drafted	3.9
Religion, returning to God, retaining belief in God	1.8
Getting away on own; breaking parental hold	1.7
Getting along with parents, not being able to talk things over with parents	1.3
None, no big problems	.2
Miscellaneous	6.9
No answer, don't know	4.9

* Gallup survey, "Attitudes of Young Adults," May–June 1961.

most serious problem they thought facing them was in the broad area of "the future, making decisions and finding themselves." More than twice as many seniors mentioned this than any other category. Next was war and world instability, followed by jobs, money, marriage decisions and getting through college. The question in Table 182 was "open-ended"; that is, the students gave their own responses, which were later grouped under broad categories; they were not given a list to choose from.

The above question seemed to be more personalized in nature than the questions given below, which were asked of college students in 1969 and at the end of 1970. Despite this and the fact that in 1961, memories of the Korean war had faded and deep involvement in the Vietnam war was still to come, the 14 percent of seniors in 1961 who considered war the most serious problem compares well with the proportionate percentage interest of college students in 1969 and the end of 1970 toward the Vietnam war.

The questions below, and the choices given the respondent with which to answer them, deal basically with "externalized" problems; that is, "What do you think students in schools around the country are demonstrating about?" "What disturbs you about America?" It is interesting to note that both in 1961 and December 1970, "getting along with parents" and the "generation gap" were considered to be the least of all problems to college students.

Table 183

ALL COLLEGE STUDENTS
April–May 1969

"Why do you think students in many schools around the country are demonstrating—that is, what do you think is their biggest gripe?"*

Not enough say in running of college	42%
Current inadequacies of society	22
Adult and governmental authority	16
Vietnam war	11
Want to have their voices heard	7
Civil rights	6
They have no real gripe	8
Other responses	5

* *Gallup Opinion Index*, No. 48, June, 1969, p. 8. Table adds up to more than 100 percent due to multiple responses.

The alumni in the 1968 survey did not think students should have a say in the administration of a college. See Table 189.

Table 184

DECEMBER, 1970

"What disturbs you most about America today?"[*]

	Student Political Views		
	All Students	Total Left	Total Right
Vietnam war	19%	20%	15%
Racial problems	15	14	14
Apathy/uninvolvement	14	13	15
Economic situation/ inflation, unemployment, poverty	13	13	9
Polarities/inability to get together	13	20	8
Misplaced values	11	13	10
Domestic unrest/strikes	11	8	17
Youth unrest	10	5	14
Present administration	9	13	8
Air, water, environmental pollution	8	9	8
Lack of communication/ generation gap	6	6	6
The system	6	10	2
All others	27	28	21
Don't know	2	1	3

As alumni in 1968, the college class of 1961 showed selective and moderate attitudes toward Negro and college students' protests. According to the 1968 survey, two-thirds thought that "Negro militancy is needlessly dividing American society," yet more than a half felt that "in the long run" it "will be healthy for America." About an equal percentage—52 and 51 percent—felt that college protests were unhealthy and healthy for the country, respectively, and only a third could see white racism as the main cause of the Negro riots.[**]

[*] *Gallup Opinion Index*, No. 68, February 1971, p. 43.
[**] Spaeth and Greeley, op. cit., p. 104. See a Gallup poll taken at the end of 1970. In this poll both adults among the population and college students felt that the American system "is not responsive enough to public needs." However, 44 percent of the college students felt that violence is sometimes justified to bring about change, but only 14 percent of the adults thought so. (*The Gallup Opinion Index*, No. 68, February 1971, pp. 38–43.)

430

Table 185

ALUMNI ATTITUDES ON CURRENT ISSUES*

Statement	Agree Strongly or Somewhat
College students should get draft deferments	69%
Negro militancy is needlessly dividing American society into conflicting camps	67
Graduate students should get draft deferments	63
In the long run, current protests of Negroes in the cities will be healthy for America	56
This country would be better off if there were less protest and dissatisfaction coming from college campuses	52
The protests of college students are a healthy sign for America	51
College students should lose their draft deferments for participating in demonstrations against the draft	42
The main cause of Negro riots in the cities is white racism	36

The alumni reactions to protest were considered by the authors of the survey to have correlated highly enough to be called "support for militancy." An index of support for militancy was made up of agreement or disagreement with the previous items that were asked the alumni.**

1. The protests of college students are a healthy sign for America. (Agree)
2. This country would be better off if there were less protest and dissatisfaction coming from college campuses. (Disagree)
3. In the long run, current protests of Negroes in the cities will be healthy for America. (Agree)
4. The main cause of Negro riots in the cities is white racism. (Agree)
5. Negro militancy is needlessly dividing American society into conflicting camps. (Disagree)
6. College students should lose their draft deferments for participating in demonstrations against the draft. (Disagree)

* Spaeth and Greeley, op. cit, p. 104. Copyright © 1970 by the Carnegie Foundation for the Advancement of Teaching.
** Ibid., pp. 105–106. Copyright © 1970 by the Carnegie Foundation for the Advancement of Teaching.

According to the findings of the survey, the alumni who were from good quality and private colleges, had good grades, had spent a number of years in graduate school, were from upper-middle-class backgrounds and were younger, were most likely to have been in sympathy with the Negro and student protests. The authors state that this correlates rather well with what they know from other research—that the more intelligent, younger students from high-quality colleges are the ones who are likely to protest.*

Table 186

SUPPORT-FOR-MILITANCY INDEX BY TYPE OF COLLEGE ATTENDED**

Type of College Attended	Percent in highest Quartile
University (large public)	24%
University (private)	37
University (other)	28
Protestant (low quality)	18
Protestant (high quality)	34
State college	18
Catholic	28
Liberal arts college	34

Table 187

SUPPORT-FOR-MILITANCY INDEX BY AGE AND COLLEGE QUALITY***

Percent in Highest Quartile

College quality	Age 28 or younger	29–31	Over 31
High	44% (1,208)	35% (737)	28% (158)
Medium	30 (1,151)	23 (879)	21 (304)
Low	23 (1,368)	16 (1,097)	10 (661)

* Ibid. Copyright © 1970 by the Carnegie Foundation for the Advancement of Teaching. For another point of view on the nature and intelligence of activists, see the chapter, "Today's Youth."

** Ibid., p. 107. Copyright © 1970 by the Carnegie Foundation for the Advancement of Teaching.

*** Ibid., p. 109. Copyright © 1970 by the Carnegie Foundation for the Advancement of Teaching.

In this material, as well as in another large study recently done on college faculty members for the Carnegie Commission on Higher Education and released in part in an article by Seymour Martin Lipset and Everett Carll Ladd, Jr., the age of the respondent was shown to play a major role in whether he would support militancy.* In the table above, those under thirty were one and a half to two times more likely to support militancy than were those over thirty, regardless of the type of college attended. When type of college was introduced, those who were 28 or younger and had attended a "high"-quality college were four times more inclined to support militancy than those who were over 31 and had gone to a "low"-quality college. Lipset and Ladd reported a similar phenomenon among college faculty members: ". . . the differences associated with age were surprisingly large. In each discipline, as age increases, support for student activism decreases. It is almost too neat: We are accustomed to more vagaries in opinion distribution when the control variable is one so generally inclusive as age."

When analyzed by career field, the alumni who were in the humanities and social sciences gave the highest percentage of support for militancy, those in business and engineering, the lowest. This general conclusion also correlates well with the survey analysis by Lipset and

Table 188

SUPPORT-FOR-MILITANCY INDEX BY 1968 CAREER FIELD**

1968 Career Field	Percent in highest Quartile
Physical sciences	36%
Biological sciences	33
Social sciences	54
Humanities	62
Engineering	14
Medicine	33
Other health	11
Education	24
Business	15
Law	48
Other professions	35

* Lipset and Ladd, *Psychology Today*, 4 (November 1970): 106.
** Spaeth and Greeley, op. cit., p. 108. Copyright © 1970 by the Carnegie Foundation for the Advancement of Teaching.

Ladd on college professors: "The percentage of social scientists giving at least tentative endorsement to student activism is more than twice that of professors of business, more than three times that of professors of agriculture."*

Table 189

ALUMNI ATTITUDES TOWARD STUDENT INVOLVEMENT**

Statement		Favorable to antistudent position
The students are capable of regulating their own lives and the college should stay out of this area	(disagree)	66%
The college should take the responsibility to see that students do not break the law	(agree)	55
Students should have the right to protest against recruiters on campus if the students think the recruiters are helping to carry out immoral practices	(disagree)	47
The college should assume responsibility for a student's behavior just as parents do	(agree)	45
Rules governing student behavior should be made by the students	(disagree)	43
Students should make the rules governing their participation in off-campus political activity	(disagree)	34
Rules governing student behavior should be enforced by students	(disagree)	27
The college should not try to stop students from taking part in political activity	(disagree)	17
Students should have the right to participate in decisions on		
Faculty tenure	(disagree)	82
Admission standards	(disagree)	80
Tuition and fees	(disagree)	81
What is taught in specific courses	(disagree)	58
Organization of the curriculum	(disagree)	40

* Ibid., p. 50. For a further discussion of this work of Lipset and Ladd, see the chapter, "Today's Youth." See also an interesting study on the images of the professor and the characteristics of undergraduates considering college teaching as a profession which shows correlations between field of study and attitudes. (Ian D. Currie et al., "Images of the Professor and Interest in the Academic Profession," *Sociology of Education* 39 [Fall 1966], available in reprint from the Survey Research Center, University of California.)

** Spaeth and Greeley, op. cit., p. 77. Copyright © 1970 by the Carnegie Foundation for the Advancement of Teaching.

Thus, in the alumni study, if the respondent were young, had attended a "high"-quality private university and were in the field of humanities or social sciences, he would have been more likely to support militancy.

The alumni split their feelings about the ways students should be involved on the college campus. They did not think students should have a say in issues dealing with faculty and college administration, nor as to what is taught in specific courses; they did feel that students should be able to participate in organizing the curriculum, and to the extent that they are not breaking laws, in monitoring their own behavior and governing their participation in off-campus political activity. According to the findings of the survey, women more than men, younger alumni more than older, and graduates of "high"-quality colleges more than those from "low"-quality colleges were most inclined to support student involvement in college activity and in regulating their own behavior.

The student involvement items in the preceding table were combined into four indices: student politics; student control over rules; student power; and student freedom, and in the following tables were applied to the type of college attended and the career field.*

1. Student-politics index:
   a) The college should not try to stop students from taking part in political activity.
   b) Students should have the right to protest against recruiters on campus if the students think the recruiters are helping to carry out immoral practices.
   c) Students should make the rules governing their participation in off-campus political activity.
2. Student-control-over-rules index:
   a) Rules governing student behavior should be made by the students.
   b) Rules governing student behavior should be enforced by the students.
3. Student-power index:
   a) Students should have the right to participate in decisions on:
      1) Faculty tenure
      2) Organization of the curriculum
      3) What is taught in specific courses
      4) Tuition and fees

* Spaeth and Greeley, op. cit., p. 78. Copyright © 1970 by the Carnegie Foundation for the Advancement of Teaching.

4. Student-freedom index:
    a) The college should assume responsibility for a student's behavior just as parents do. (disagree)
    b) The students are capable of regulating their own lives and the college should stay out of this area. (agree)
    c) The college should take the responsibility to see that students do not break the law. (disagree)

Table 190

STUDENT-INVOLVEMENT INDICES

By Type of College Attended*
(Percent in Highest Quartile)

Type of college attended	Student-politics index	Rules index	Student-power index	Student-freedom index
University (large public)	28%	17%	23%	36%
University (private)	37	21	19	36
University (other)	27	13	21	35
Protestant (low quality)	21	13	11	17
Protestant (high quality)	35	25	20	33
State college	18	15	20	21
Catholic	28	14	22	23
Liberal arts college	33	21	18	32

Again, the "high"-quality public and private college alumni whose career fields were in social sciences and humanities would have been generally most likely to support student involvement. According to the table, the alumni in these two fields who were in sympathy with the students seemed particularly concerned about the students' right to take part in political activities and to regulate their own behavior.

In light of the belief by a number of analysts today that the student from a "high"-quality college is bound to be more intelligent and creative, some particular data which came out of the alumni survey was startling: "How much you read does not seem to be influenced by the quality of the college you attended."** This was based on answers given by the alumni concerning the frequency of their cultural and

* Ibid., p. 80. Copyright © 1970 by the Carnegie Foundation for the Advancement of Teaching.
** Ibid., p. 33.

Table 191

STUDENT-INVOLVEMENT INDICES BY 1968 CAREER FIELD*

(Percent in Highest Quartile)

1968 Career Field	Student-politics index	Rules index	Student-power index	Student-freedom index
Physical sciences	31%	15%	24%	40%
Biological sciences	40	13	28	33
Social sciences	53	17	35	51
Humanities	52	32	28	42
Engineering	20	12	16	33
Medicine	39	19	19	28
Other health	14	24	30	24
Education	26	20	22	21
Business	20	11	13	25
Law	36	15	18	42
Other professions	34	16	25	35

reading activities and the number of books they owned seven years after graduation. Two indices were then made up indicating these activities: a serious reading index (read—not necessarily finish—a nonfiction book and a work of serious fiction; read poetry; and number of books owned), and an interest-in-the-arts index (listen to classical or serious music; go to concerts, plays and museums or art galleries).** The survey showed that whether the alumni had gone to a "high"- or "low"-quality college had very little to do seven years later with the extent and frequency of their cultural activities, most especially their reading habits. This was particularly true of women, who registered much higher percentages of interest in the arts and reading than men regardless of college attended, and when they were from "low"-quality colleges were shown to have just as much interest in cultural activities and reading as men from "high"-quality colleges. Some of this could have been due to the fact that women may have more time than men, who are busily pursuing their careers directly after college, to listen to music and read serious books; on the other hand, women may be inclined to pursue arts and reading whether they have time or not. "Nevertheless, the major point in this table is that sex is a far stronger predictor of serious reading and interest in serious music than is col-

* Ibid. Copyright © 1970 by the Carnegie Foundation for the Advancement of Teaching.
** Ibid., pp. 26–27. Copyright © 1970 by the Carnegie Foundation for the Advancement of Teaching.

lege quality." And, "relatively little more has been achieved in modifying reading and interest in the arts by the best colleges in the country than has been done by the poorest colleges."

Table 192
CULTURAL ACTIVITIES BY SEX AND COLLEGE QUALITY*

College quality	Frequently listen to serious music		Frequently read serious fiction	
	Men	Women	Men	Women
High	40%	57%	27%	35%
	33	40	19	42
	35	43	22	37
	32	38	16	44
	19	32	16	29
	25	34	15	35
Low	16	37	12	29

Even more surprising is that the same held true for graduate school. Although the level of cultural activities increased with good grades and the *number* of years in graduate school, the *quality* of the graduate school had practically no effect on the reading behavior of the alumni in 1968.

Moreover, although there is a belief among some researchers and

Table 193
COEFFICIENTS OF ASSOCIATION BETWEEN INDICES OF CULTURAL ACTIVITIES AND BACKGROUND VARIABLES (GAMMA)**

Background variable	Interest-in-the-arts index	Serious-reading index
College quality	.14	.08
College size	-.01	-.02
Control (private)	.05	.05
College grades	.17	.21
Years in graduate school	.18	.20
Graduate school quality	.18	.09
Father's education	.13	.11
Sex (male)	-.27	-.30
Age	-.12	-.09
Present family income	.10	.07

* Ibid., pp. 31 and 32. Copyright © 1970 by the Carnegie Foundation for the Advancement of Teaching.

** Ibid., p. 27. Copyright © 1970 by the Carnegie Foundation for the Advancement of Teaching.

Table 194

PERCENT RESPONDING TO THE QUESTIONS:

"Which of the following do you think your college should have given you?" and "Whether or not you think you should have gotten each of these things, please rate the extent to which your college affected you in each of these ways."*

Item	I think my college should have	My college actually affected me	
		Greatly	Greatly or Somewhat
Developed my abilities to think and express myself	98%	41%	87%
Given me a broad knowledge of the arts and sciences	90	35	77
Expanded my tolerance for people and ideas	90	35	75
Helped me to learn how to make my own decisions	81	20	73
Helped me to formulate the values and goals of my life	80	20	64
Prepared me to get ahead in the world	70	18	66
Helped me to learn how to get along with others	69	23	68
Trained me for my present job	65	34	67
Helped me to learn ways of helping people	60	10	43
Helped me to form valuable and lasting friendships	54	25	57
Helped prepare me for marriage and family	39	7	30

analysts today that a segment of today's youth is particularly non-materialistic and noncareer-minded in outlook,** the 1961 college alumni, by overwhelming majorities, were shown to have wished that college would primarily have prepared them for understanding themselves and for cultural and social concerns rather than for practical, career training. They also expected college to be able to train them for

* Spaeth and Greeley, op. cit., p. 40. Copyright © 1970 by the Carnegie Foundation for the Advancement of Teaching.
** See especially the work of Daniel Yankelovich for *Fortune*, January 1969, and for John D. Rockefeller, 3rd. For one discussion of the "forerunner" theory according to Yankelovich, see the chapter, "Today's Youth." According to the Yankelovich *Fortune* survey, 58 percent of college students were categorized as "practical-minded"; that is, for them college was a practical matter, useful for earning money, having a more interesting career and gaining prestige in society. A majority of 54 percent of these were taking business, engineering or science

careers, but this concern was far behind their concern for personal, cultural, and social values. Seven years after graduation, the alumni reported that they would be most strongly in favor of colleges giving a broader general education in the arts and sciences, especially the fine arts, and that college had generally failed to provide this to the extent they thought it should have.

Table 195

WHAT ALUMNI WOULD HAVE DONE DIFFERENTLY*

"On looking back over the things we have done in the past, there are always some things that we wish we could have done differently. Please indicate whether you would like to have done each of the following more, the same, or less during college."

Item	Would like to have done more
Read books not related to specific courses	57%
Learn about poetry, art, or music	53
Learn about history, philosophy, or English	52
Learn about psychology or sociology	48
Study	46
Try to get to know the faculty	43
Participate in extracurricular activities (sports, drama, student government, etc.)	38
Learn about science or mathematics	37
Take course(s) in an area directly related to my present job	37
Participate in activities that were of service to others	36
Read books related to specific courses	35
Date	30
Worry about getting good grades	10

As college seniors in May–June 1961, looking back over their last few years in school, this group overwhelmingly felt that there were courses they wish they had taken. Again, these courses were strongly "non-career"—languages, literature, science, philosophy, and art.**

---

courses. The rest of the college students were classified as "forerunners"; that is, they chose the statement about college aims that said they were not really concerned with the practical benefits of college, which they took for granted, but for them college meant the opportunity to "change things rather than make out well within the existing system." Of this group, 80 percent were in the arts and humanities. The "practical-minded" were later called by Yankelovich, the "career-minded."

* Spaeth and Greeley, op. cit., p. 76. Copyright © 1970 by the Carnegie Foundation for the Advancement of Teaching.

** Gallup survey, "Attitudes of Young Adults," May-June 1961.

Table 196

ANY COURSES YOU WISH YOU HAD TAKEN?

College Seniors—1961

"As you look back over the last few years of school, are there any courses you wish you had taken which you did not take?"

	Yes	No	No Answer
College Seniors	83.8%	15.6%	.4%

Table 197

WHAT COURSES DO YOU WISH YOU HAD TAKEN?

College Seniors—1961

"As you look back over the last few years of school, are there any courses you wish you had taken which you did not take? If yes: what courses were they?"

Foreign Languages	16.7%
Literature, English, Creative Writing	16.1
Science	15.2
Philosophy	12.8
Art and Art History	11.6
History	11.4
Math	11.2
Psychology	9.6
Sociology and Anthropology	8.8
Political Science	7.0
Music and Music Appreciation	6.6
Business Courses	5.2
Economics	3.6
Public Speaking	3.3
Typing	2.8
Shorthand	1.8
Home Economics	1.8
Humanities*	1.6
Engineering	.6
Shop and Mechanical Courses	.3
Miscellaneous	7.6
No Answer	.2

* This seems to refer to the term "humanities" in its specific sense, that is, "the study of the Latin and Greek classics," whereas when Spaeth and Greeley use this term, it is apparently meant in its more general sense, "the study of literature, philosophy and art, etc. as distinguished from the social and physical sciences." Although Spaeth and Greeley reported the alumni's wish to have studied the humanities, the term itself was not included in their list of choices given to the alumni.

The question asked of the college seniors was "open-ended"—that is, respondents gave answers which were afterward categorized under general topics—as compared with the similar question above asked of the alumni, in which they had to pick from among specific choices. Apparently, the attitude of gaining a broader, "non-career"-oriented education was held by the alumni throughout the seven years after graduation from college and may have intensified among those alumni who were not in fields for which they had had specific career training in college.

The alumni in 1968, furthermore, thought that the college faculty and administration should have also had the goal of preparing the student with a well-rounded, broad, general education. Again, specific career training and gaining a high status in life were far down the list. In the table above and the one following, the discrepancy is clearly shown between what the alumni thought they should have gotten and what they thought the college actually gave them. They clearly felt that changes were needed.

Table 198

ALUMNI EVALUATION OF GOALS OF FACULTY AND ADMINISTRATION AT THEIR COLLEGES*

Aims, intentions, or goals of higher education	Absolute top importance		Absolute top or great importance	
	Should have been	*was*	*Should have been*	*was*
Produce a well-rounded student, that is, one whose physical, social, moral, intellectual, and aesthetic potentialities have all been cultivated	32%	14%	80%	50%
Assist students to develop objectivity about themselves and their beliefs and hence examine those beliefs critically	24	7	74	37
Produce a student who, whatever else may be done to him, has had his intellect cultivated to the maximum	22	6	60	32
Train students in methods of scholarship, and/or scientific research, and/or creative endeavor	20	9	70	42
Serve as a center for the dissemination of new ideas that will change the society, whether those ideas are in science, literature, the arts or politics	18	6	59	27

* Spaeth and Greeley, op. cit., pp. 42–43. Copyright © 1970 by the Carnegie Foundation for the Advancement of Teaching.

Table 198 (continued)

Develop the inner character of students so that they can make sound, correct moral choices	18	10	64	37
Produce a student who is able to perform his citizenship responsibilities effectively	16	6	67	37
Prepare students specifically for useful careers	16	14	57	54
Provide the student with skills, attitudes, contacts and experiences which maximize the likelihood of his occupying a high status in life and a position of leadership in society	12	5	46	30
Make sure the student is permanently affected (in mind and spirit) by the great ideas of the great minds of history	11	4	41	24
Make a good consumer of the student— a person who is elevated culturally, has good taste, and can make good consumer choices	5	2	31	19

To sum up the basic interest of the alumni in what college should give students and their attitudes toward career-training versus a humanistic education, Spaeth and Greeley wrote:

When asked what they would do differently, the alumni overwhelmingly choose courses and express interests in the arts and sciences, especially in the humanities, and most especially in the fine arts.

It is precisely those whose careers were such that little specific career preparation was possible in college who are the most likely to display such humanistic inclinations. Those such as engineers, educators, or businessmen, for whom rather specific undergraduate career training was possible, seem much less humanistic in their actions than do the others. Nonetheless, even this group shows reasonably strong humanistic orientations.*

3. SOME PERSONAL PERCEPTIONS OF HIGH SCHOOL STUDENTS IN 1956 AND 1970

Concerning their feelings about themselves as persons, and consequently their willingness to be independent individuals and make decisions on their own, the high-schoolers in May 1956 were more desirous of being natural than popular; generally did things because they wanted to, and not because they felt forced to conform; strongly

* Ibid., p. 94.

wanted to have other people's opinions in making decisions, although not in order to make their decisions acceptable to others; were not afraid to be "different" from the group, though the majority felt greatly upset if the group did not approve of them; thought that new ideas were good, though they generally did not feel that they themselves were the impetus for new ideas; and thought they had quite a bit of freedom. In the following table, the 1961 college graduates were in the eleventh grade at the time of the poll, and this is indicated, as in earlier tables, by a box.

Table 199

AN INDEX OF INDIVIDUALISM OR WILLINGNESS TO BE
"DIFFERENT" FROM THE GROUP—HIGH SCHOOL STUDENTS*

May 1956

		Sex			Grade	
	Total	Boys	Girls	10	11	12
I feel greatly upset if the group doesn't approve of me	50%	44%	55%	50%	51%	50%
There is nothing worse than being considered an "oddball" by other people	38	37	39	38	42	27
I try very hard to do everything that will please my friends	51	49	53	56	51	46
A person who is different is almost always immoral	6	8	5	7	7	4
More than anything, I want to be accepted as a member of the group that is most popular at school	26	29	23	28	25	28
I fear being different from my friends so much that I try to find ways to be like them	15	18	12	17	15	11
Sometimes I go along with the group and sometimes I don't	77	76	78	74	77	89
One should try to be popular and natural at the same time	77	73	81	76	76	76
Sometimes, when making an important decision, I like to hear other people's opinions	81	76	85	80	80	88
I like discussion but I don't like arguments	60	52	67	62	61	65

* Purdue Opinion Panel, *Report of Poll No. 44*, May 1956, pp. 16a, 18a, 20a. Here again there was no category of post-high school plans, so I was not able to get specifically the opinions of those who intended to go to college. See footnote preceding Table 172.

Table 199 (continued)

	Total	Sex Boys	Girls	Grade 10	11	12
Sometimes I feel that I have to go along with the group	39	39	38	38	38	38
Sometimes I will do something just to make people like me	29	31	27	29	28	35
It's more important to be your natural self, even if it doesn't make you popular	78	74	82	78	78	84
I think things out for myself and act on my own decisions	45	49	42	45	50	37
I don't care whether I'm popular or not	19	22	17	18	21	33
I don't care to have other people's opinions influence my decisions	15	17	13	15	17	14
My tastes are quite different from my friends'	18	20	16	18	18	16
I quite often disagree with the group's opinion	26	27	25	27	25	31
When I feel that people aren't interested in my company, I find others to associate with	56	56	57	56	56	55
I often suggest new activity for the gang to do	38	37	39	41	38	21
I am considered to be original at times	31	29	33	29	31	34
Occasionally, I suggest something new, rather than follow what the gang wants	43	42	43	42	42	49
Sometimes it is good to introduce new ideas	78	72	83	75	78	82
My freedom may be a little too limited	19	20	18	21	17	16
I don't think my freedom is too limited	63	59	67	60	67	59
I like to have other people's opinions before I make up my mind	59	56	62	59	59	60
I avoid dating people that my friends don't know	11	11	11	12	11	1(*sic*)
Before making any important decision I try to find out what is most acceptable to others	42	41	44	46	40	42
It's more important to be popular than to be your natural self	4	6	2	5	4	—
My life is pretty well planned for me	26	25	26	25	25	28

How might these feelings of the high school students in 1956 compare with those of students today? In January 1970, high schoolers were also asked some questions about how they felt about themselves, their friends and their parents:

Table 200

PERSONAL FEELINGS OF HIGH SCHOOL STUDENTS*

January 1970

		Sex		Grade		
	Total	Boys	Girls	10	11	12
Do you worry about what your best friends think about what you say and do and how you look?						
Always	23%	21%	25%	27%	24%	17%
Frequently	26	25	26	25	27	25
Sometimes	32	32	33	31	33	33
Seldom	11	12	10	10	9	16
Never	7	9	5	7	7	8
How much influence do you feel you have in family decisions that affect you?						
A great deal of influence	20	20	20	19	19	21
Considerable influence	29	28	31	28	29	32
Moderate influence	22	22	22	23	24	19
Some influence	16	15	16	17	14	15
Little or no influence	13	14	12	13	14	13
All in all, how strict are your parents (or guardians) with you?						
Extremely strict	4	4	3	4	4	3
Very strict	9	9	10	11	10	8
Moderately strict	49	49	49	51	49	47
Not very strict	27	27	27	25	27	28
Not strict at all	7	8	7	5	6	11

And again, in April 1970, high school students were asked comparable questions about their feelings toward friendships, parents, and values (see Table 201).

Exact comparisons between the years cannot be made because the questions were asked differently. The difficulty in comparing these two years is made even greater by the fact that the high school students in 1956 were being asked about their feelings toward their friends and their group and in 1970 they were asked about their feelings toward

* Purdue Opinion Panel, *Report of Poll No. 87*, January 1970, pp. 5a and 9a.

Table 201

THINGS HIGH SCHOOL STUDENTS WORRY ABOUT*

April 1970

| | Total | *Sex* | | *Grade* | | |
		Boys	Girls	10	11	12

In the past year, how much have you been bothered by [these items] . . . about which high school students worry?

Friendships (getting acquainted; awkwardness; keeping a conversation going; etc.)

	Total	Boys	Girls	10	11	12
Very much	12%	11%	12%	13%	11%	10%
Quite a bit	19	20	18	19	20	19
Some	23	23	24	25	22	23
A little	16	16	15	15	17	15
Not very much	28	28	27	25	27	31

Relationships with parents and other adults (having too many decisions made for me; being too easily led by them; getting into arguments; hurting their feelings; being different; being talked about or made fun of; etc.)

	Total	Boys	Girls	10	11	12
Very much	14	13	15	15	12	14
Quite a bit	16	15	18	17	16	16
Some	23	25	20	22	24	21
A little	16	15	17	15	17	16
Not very much	29	30	27	26	28	31

Values (wondering how to tell right from wrong; confused on some moral questions; doubting the value of worship and prayer; not living up to my ideal, etc.)

	Total	Boys	Girls	10	11	12
Very much	14	11	17	12	15	15
Quite a bit	17	16	18	17	16	18
Some	23	24	21	22	23	23
A little	17	18	16	18	17	15
Not very much	27	28	25	27	27	27

friends, family and other adults. In general, however, the high schoolers in 1956 seemed less disturbed about their own sense of personal worth, their independence and their ability to make decisions. Both groups, however, generally worried quite a bit about pleasing their friends, felt able to make decisions about themselves and did not think their

* Purdue Opinion Panel, *Report of Poll No. 88*, April 1970, pp. 15a and 19a.

freedom was too limited. The great majority of the 1956 high schoolers seemed quite willing to sacrifice conformity for the sake of being themselves and leading their lives as they wished—that is, perhaps as much as a high school student could be expected to do.

4. SOME FEELINGS OF HIGH SCHOOL STUDENTS TOWARD CHANGE
   AND DEMOCRATIC PRINCIPLES

The 1956 high school students were overwhelmingly for trying new ideas rather than always sticking to the old ways.

Table 202

WILLINGNESS TO TRY NEW IDEAS*

High School Students—May 1956

We should be willing to try new ideas rather than always sticking to the old ways of doing things	Total	Sex Boys	Girls	Grade 10	11	12
agree	91%	90%	92%	90%	92%	3 [sic]%
?; probably agree	5	5	5	5	5	8
?; probably disagree	1	1	1	1	1	7
disagree	1	2	1	1	1	16

Nor were they any more likely to want to force the continuation of the traditional American way of life than a high schooler in 1967 or 1971.

Table 203

RESISTANCE TO CHANGING THE AMERICAN WAY OF LIFE**

High School Students

The true American way of life is disappearing so fast that the government may have to force the people back into the old tradition.	Total	1956 Grade 10	11	12
agree	6%	8%	5%	4%
undecided; probably agree	12	15	11	1
undecided; probably disagree	20	24	17	18
disagree	60	53	64	66

* Purdue Opinion Panel, *Report of Poll No. 44*, May 1956, p. 14a.
** Ibid., p. 10a; Purdue Opinion Panel, *Report of Poll No. 81*, November 1967, p. 5a; and *Report of Poll No. 90*, January 1971, p. 7a.

448

Table 203 (continued)

We should firmly resist any attempts to change the American way of life.	1967 Total
agree	19%
undecided	13
disagree	67

We should firmly resist any attempts to change the American way of life.	1971 Total
definitely agree	12%
undecided; probably agree	12
undecided; probably disagree	19
definitely disagree	51

In the above table, the difference in the number of response alternatives makes comparison difficult. Moreover, the wording of the question asked in 1956 might have been so unpleasant that there was an extremely high negative reaction to it. Despite these drawbacks, a general band of overwhelming disagreement covering all three years may be seen. Also, the highly negative reaction in 1956 seems to be supported in another question involving belief in democratic principles; and it compares well with later years. In the following table on obedience and respect for authority, we again run across the problem of unequal numbers of responses and different wording of the questions. In the 1967 poll, the question is asked about children—a far different person from an adult citizen.

Table 204

OBEDIENCE AND RESPECT FOR AUTHORITY*

High School Students

Obedience and respect for people in authority are the most important rules for being a good citizen.

May 1956

	Total Sample	Grade 10	Grade 11	Grade 12
Agree	65%	66%	66%	64%
Undecided; probably agree	15	15	16	12
Undecided; probably disagree	6	5	5	11
Disagree	12	11	11	12

* Purdue Opinion Panel, *Report of Poll No. 44*, May 1956, p. 12a; *Report of Poll No. 72*, October 1964, p. 17a; *Report of Poll No. 81*, November 1967, p. 3a.

Table 204 (continued)

Obedience and a proper respect for authority should be the very first
requirements of a good citizen.

October 1964

	Total Sample	Grade		
		10	11	12
Agree	69%	69%	69%	68%
Undecided; probably agree	14	13	13	15
Undecided; probably disagree	5	5	5	5
Disagree	9	8	9	9

Obedience and respect for authority are the most important virtues
that children should learn.

November 1967

	Total Sample	Grade		
		10	11	12
Agree	76%	78%	78%	71%
Undecided	9	9	8	10
Disagree	15	13	14	19

Another series of questions in this vein also shows the 1956 high
school students to have had a strong belief in democratic principles.
The same caveats mentioned above apply here as well.

Table 205

FAITH AND TRUST IN A LEADER*

High School Students

Strict and strong leaders who demand that we follow them unquestioningly
are not desirable in this country.

May 1956

	Total Sample	Grade		
		10	11	12
Agree	66%	66%	65%	63%
Undecided; probably agree	13	14	14	12
Undecided; probably disagree	9	8	10	8
Disagree	10	9	9	17

* Purdue Opinion Panel, *Report of Poll No. 44*, May 1956, p. 12a; *Report of Poll
No. 72*, October 1964, p. 17a; *Report of Poll No. 81*, November 1967, p. 3a.

Table 205 (continued)

Strict and forceful leaders who demand an unquestioning trust are not desirable in this country.

October 1964

	Total Sample	Grade		
		10	*11*	*12*
Agree	47%	49%	47%	45%
Undecided; probably agree	14	13	14	14
Undecided; probably disagree	13	12	14	13
Disagree	21	20	19	23

What this country needs most is a few strong, courageous, tireless leaders in whom the people can put their faith.

November 1967

	Total Sample	Grade		
		10	*11*	*12*
Agree	56%	59%	56%	54%
Undecided	14	14	14	15
Disagree	26	23	27	28

All the above tables and comparisons do not mean that the 1961 college graduates, as high school students in 1956, were necessarily any more or less democratic than their counterparts in other years. Other surveys and studies throughout the years up to the present time, both of high school students and of adults, show a grievous lack of knowledge of constitutional guarantees and principles. But the above polls give no evidence that the 1956 high school students were less democratic or individualistic than were students a decade later. They may show that there has been much less variation than expected among students throughout the years in their personal aims and in their desire for change within the democratic framework.

D. *Alumni Attitudes on Science and Technology*

In general, college-educated people have been more in favor of scientific progress than the rest of the population; however, very recently various other issues have begun to throw shadows on this usual optimism and scientific curiosity—issues such as pollution, invasion of privacy, high costs and pressing domestic problems, as well as possible increasing suspicion of technology itself among the better-educated who had formerly been among its strongest supporters. In 1968, however, the 1961 college graduates were much less worried about the effect of science and technology on the rate of world change and the power structure than the general populace was.

Table 206

ATTITUDES ON SCIENCE AND TECHNOLOGY FOR ALUMNI AND FOR THE GENERAL POPULATION*

Attitude	Alumni	General Population
Scientific research is causing the world to change too fast	26%	54%
Because the experts have so much power in our society, ordinary people don't have much of a say in things	38	72

An "antiexperts" index, made up of the above items and a third one—"It's not enough to be a college graduate these days, you have to graduate from a good college to get a job worth having"—was related to a number of background variables. Measured by the antiexperts index, those who went to "lower"-quality, smaller, and state colleges, who got lower grades, and were women, were more likely to be worried by science and technology. And alumni who were in the humanities and education had a greater objection to the power of the experts than those in other professional fields. It was found, however, according to the index, that there was very little difference in feeling toward science and technology between alumni from a "high"-quality or "low"-quality college: those who had gone to a "high"-quality college were only slightly less suspicious of science and technology.**

Little has been done on how widespread the recently verbalized suspicion of technology has become and whether this suspicion is gen-

* Spaeth and Greeley, op. cit., p 26. Copyright © 1970 by the Carnegie Foundation for the Advancement of Teaching.
** Ibid., pp. 33, 34. Copyright © 1970 by the Carnegie Foundation for the Advancement of Teaching.

Table 207

COEFFICIENTS OF ASSOCIATION BETWEEN ANTIEXPERTS INDEX AND BACKGROUND VARIABLES*

Background Variable	Gamma
College quality	—.09
College size	—.08
Control (private)	—.01
College grades	—.08
Years in graduate school	—.01
Father's education	—.08
Sex (male)	—.08

Table 208

ANTIEXPERTS INDEX BY TYPE OF COLLEGE ATTENDED**

Type of College Attended	Percent in Highest Quartile
University (large public)	18%
University (private)	17
University (other)	26
Protestant (low quality)	27
Protestant (high quality)	19
State	27
Catholic	23
Liberal arts	19

Table 209

ANTIEXPERTS INDEX BY 1968 CAREER FIELD***

1968 Career Field	Percent in Highest Quartile
Physical sciences	15%
Biological sciences	21
Social sciences	13
Humanities	30
Engineering	20
Medicine	14
Other health	22
Education	27
Business	18
Law	16
Other professions	22

erally confined to those in the humanities and education fields.* A small pilot study, concerning popular attitudes toward technology of 200 persons of different ages, social classes and races in the suburbs of Belmont, Cambridge and Maynard around Boston in 1970 showed that occupation and education made more of a difference in attitudes than any other variable, and that within the category of education, the level of information made the greatest impact. Those with a low level of information about technology were significantly more likely to feel that "technology has made life too complicated," and "it would be nice if we could return to nature," than respondents with a high level or moderate amount of information.**

E. *Summary*

In summary, this brief study of the changing attitudes of one college class from 1956 to 1968 showed that these young people tended to have been open-minded, willing to change and to support democratic principles while in high school in 1956 and to have had moderate, selective, humanistic, liberal-hued attitudes toward the college experience and toward activism when they were surveyed in 1968, seven years after their graduation from college. They remained Republican throughout the entire span from 1956 to 1968, and, as college seniors and alumni, preferred liberal Republicanism. The college experience did not seem to have permanently changed their basic political and social orientation (although it also apparently did not give them what they thought they should have had). Whether this will be the case with those presently in college cannot be inferred from this study—it remains to be seen whether the increased activism and new mores of the college campus will have a changing, lasting effect on the outlook of the new generation.

* Since this was written, a nationwide Louis Harris survey on public reaction to science and scientists has been released (February 17, 1972). Although overwhelming majorities agreed that science has benefited the United States and the world, and has made modern life much better, substantial majorities also agreed with the idea that scientific progress has been made without enough thought to the human side of life. However, the vast majority (78 percent to 9) felt that scientific discoveries had done more good than harm. Pollution was overwhelmingly chosen as the biggest problem science has created for them personally.

** Irene Taviss, "A Survey of Popular Attitudes Toward Technology," Harvard University Program on Technology and Society, Cambridge, Mass., 1970, p. 6. This paper was prepared for delivery at the American Association for the Advancement of Science meetings, Chicago, December 28. 1970.